Bioinformatics: A Catalyst of Modern Life Science

Bioinformatics: A Catalyst of Modern Life Science

Edited by **Gretchen Kenney**

New York

Published by Callisto Reference,
106 Park Avenue, Suite 200,
New York, NY 10016, USA
www.callistoreference.com

Bioinformatics: A Catalyst of Modern Life Science
Edited by Gretchen Kenney

© 2015 Callisto Reference

International Standard Book Number: 978-1-63239-096-7 (Hardback)

Printed in the United States of America.

Contents

Preface

Bioinformatics has been described as a catalyst of modern life science in this book. It is a collection of numerous research works on bioinformatics and related disciplines including high-performance computing, data analysis, networking and molecular modeling. The book discusses various bioinformatics fundamentals and applications which makes it a comprehensive account of information for both students and experts.

The information contained in this book is the result of intensive hard work done by researchers in this field. All due efforts have been made to make this book serve as a complete guiding source for students and researchers. The topics in this book have been comprehensively explained to help readers understand the growing trends in the field.

I would like to thank the entire group of writers who made sincere efforts in this book and my family who supported me in my efforts of working on this book. I take this opportunity to thank all those who have been a guiding force throughout my life.

Editor

Analysis of Biological Networks

Investigation on Nuclear Transport of *Trypanosoma brucei*: An *in silico* Approach

Mohd Fakharul Zaman Raja Yahya,
Umi Marshida Abdul Hamid and Farida Zuraina Mohd Yusof

Additional information is available at the end of the chapter

1. Introduction

1.1. Trypanosomiasis

A group of animal and human diseases caused by parasitic protozoan trypanosomes is called trypanosomiases. The final decade of the 20th century witnessed a frightening revival in sleeping sickness (human African trypanosomiasis) in sub-Saharan Africa. Meanwhile, Chagas' disease (American trypanosomiasis) remains one of the most widespread infectious diseases in South and Central America. Arthropod vectors are responsible for the spread of African and American trypanosomiases, and disease restraint through insect control programs is an attainable target. However, the existing drugs for both illnesses are far from ideal. The trypanosomes are some of the earliest diverging members of the Eukaryotae and share several biochemical oddities that have inspired research into discovery of new drug targets. Nevertheless, discrepancies in mode of interactions between trypanosome species and their hosts have spoiled efforts to design drugs effective against both species. Heightened awareness of these neglected diseases might result in progress towards control through increased financial support for drug development and vector eradication [1].

Trypanosome is a group of unicellular parasitic flagellate protozoa which mostly infects the vertebrate genera. A number of trypanosome species cause important veterinary diseases, but only two cause significant human diseases. In sub-Saharan Africa, *Trypanosoma brucei* causes sleeping sickness or human African trypanosomiasis whilst in America, *Trypanosoma cruzi* causes Chagas' disease (Figure 1) [2]. Meanwhile, the life cycle of these parasitic protozoa engage insect vectors and mammalian hosts (Figure 2) [1]. All trypanosomes require more than one obligatory host to complete their life cycle and are transmitted via vectors. Most of the species are transmitted by blood-feeding invertebrates, however there

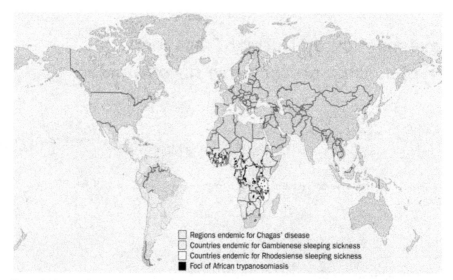

Figure 1. Geographic distribution of *Trypanosoma brucei* and *Trypanosoma cruzi*, showing endemic countries harboring these diseases [2].

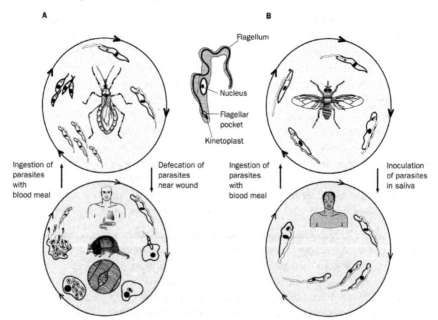

Figure 2. Life cycles of (A) *Trypanosoma cruzi* and (B) *Trypanosoma brucei*. Upper cycles represent different stages that take place in the insect vectors. Lower cycles represent different stages in man and other mammalian hosts [1].

are distinct mechanisms among the varying species. In the invertebrate hosts they are generally found in the intestines as opposed to the bloodstream or any other intracellular environment in the mammalian host. As trypanosomes develop through their life cycle, they undergo a series of morphological changes [3] as is typical of trypanosomatids.

The life cycle often consists of the trypomastigote form in the vertebrate host and the trypomastigote or promastigote form in the gut of the invertebrate host. Intracellular lifecycle stages are normally found in the amastigote form. The trypomastigote morphology is unique to species in the genus Trypanosoma.

The genome organization of *T. brucei* is splitted into nuclear and mitochondrial genomes. The nuclear genome of *T. brucei* is made up of three classes of chromosomes according to their size on pulsed-field gel electrophoresis, large chromosomes (1 to 6 megabase pairs), intermediate chromosomes (200 to 500 kilobase pairs) and mini chromosomes (50 to 100 kilobase pairs) [4]. The large chromosomes contain most genes, while the small chromosomes tend to carry genes involved in antigenic variation, including the variant surface glycoprotein (VSG) genes. Meanwhile, the mitochondrial genome of the Trypanosoma, as well as of other kinetoplastids, known as the kinetoplast, is characterized by a highly complex series of catenated circles and minicircles and requires a cohort of proteins for organisation during cell division. The genome of *T. brucei* has been completely sequenced and is now available online [5].

1.2. Nuclear transport

Nuclear transport of proteins and ribonucleic acids (RNAs) between the nucleus and cytoplasm is a key mechanism in eukaryotic cells [6]. The transport between the nucleus and cytoplasm involves primarily three classes of macromolecules: substrates, adaptors, and receptors. The transport complex is formed when the substrates bind to an import or an export receptor. Some transport substrates require one or more adaptors to mediate formation of a transport complex. Once assembled, these transport complexes are transferred in one direction across the nuclear envelope via aqueous channels that are part of the nuclear pore complexes (NPCs). Following dissociation of the transport complex, both adaptors and receptors are recycled through the NPC to allow another round of transport to occur. Directionality of either import or export therefore depends on the formation of receptor-substrate complex on one side of the nuclear envelope and the dissociation of the complex on the other. The Ran GTPase is vital in producing this asymmetry. Modulation of nuclear transport generally involves specific inhibition of the formation of a transport complex, however, more global forms of regulation also occur [7]. The general concept of import and export process is shown in Figure 3 [8].

1.3. *In silico* approach

In silico study is defined as an analysis which is performed using computer or via computer simulation. It involves the strategy of managing, mining, integrating, and interpreting

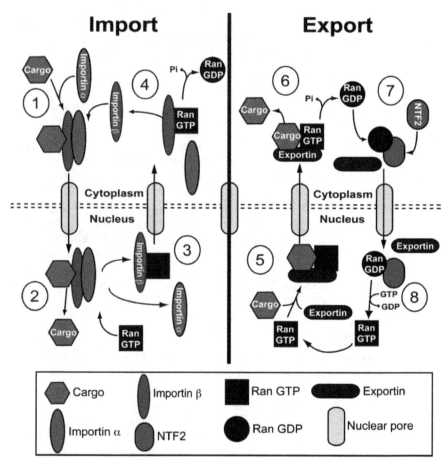

Key:

GTP   Guanine triphosphate
GDP   Guanine diphosphate
NTF2   Nuclear transport factor 2
RCC1   Regulator of chromosome condensation 1

Figure 3. For import of molecules, cytoplasmic cargo is identified by Importin *a*, which then binds to Importin b (1). This ternary complex translocates through the nuclear membrane and into the nucleus. Once there, RanGTP binds to Importin b and causes a dissociation of the complex, which releases cargo to the nucleus (2). Import receptors are then recycled back to the nucleus (3) through binding of RanGTP and export to the cytosol. RanGTP is then hydrolyzed to the GDP-bound state and causes the release of the import receptors (4) and the cycle starts over again. Export of cargo undergoes a similar mechanism. Exported molecules will bind to the export receptor with RanGTP and exit the nucleus (5). Next RanGTP is hydrolyzed to cause release of cargo into the cytoplasm (6). NTF2 specifically identifies RanGDP and returns it to the nucleus (7) for RCC1 to then exchange it to RanGTP (8) [8].

information from biological data at the genomic, metabalomic, proteomic, phylogenetic, cellular, or whole organism levels. The bioinformatics instruments and skills become crucial for *in silico* research as genome sequencing projects have resulted in an exponential growth in protein and nucleic acid sequence databases. Interaction among genes that gives rise to multiprotein functionality generates more data and complexity. *In silico* approach in medicine is not only reducing the need for expensive lab work and clinical trials but also is possible to speed the rate of drug discovery. In 2010, for example, researchers found potential inhibitors to an enzyme associated with cancer activity *in silico* using the protein docking algorithm EADock [9]. About 50 % of the molecules were later shown to be active inhibitors *in vitro* [9]. A unique advantage of the *in silico* approach is its worldwide accessibility. In some cases, having internet access or even just a computer is sufficient enough. Laboratory experiments either *in vivo* or *in vitro* both require more materials. In protein sequence analysis, *in silico* approach gives highly reproducible results in many cases or even exactly the same results because it only relies on comparison of the query sequence to a database of previously annotated sequences. However, in sophisticated analysis such as development of the 3-D structure of proteins from their primary sequences, discrepancies in results are to be expected due to the manual optimization which must consider several crucial steps such as template selection, target-template alignment, model construction and model evaluation.

1.4. Problem statements

Considering the importance of nuclear shuttling in many cellular processes, proteins responsible for the nuclear transport are vital for parasite survival. The presence of nuclear transport machinery was highlighted in the eukaryotic parasites such as *Plasmodium falciparum, Toxoplasma gondii* and *Cryptosporidium parvum*. However, the nuclear transport in *T. brucei* has not been established. Nuclear shuttling is one of the overlooked aspects of drug design and delivery. Exploitation of macromolecules movement across the nuclear envelope promises to be an exciting area of drug development. Furthermore, the divergence between host and parasite systems is always exploited as a strategy in drug development. Therefore, the exploitation of peculiarities of *T. brucei* nuclear transport machinery as compared to its host might be a promising strategy for the control of trypanosomiasis, which remains to be further investigated.

1.5. Objectives

This study is carried out to investigate the nuclear transport constituents of *T. brucei* by determining the functional characteristics of the parasite proteins. This includes functional protein domain, post translational modification sites and protein-protein interaction. The parasite proteins identified to exhibit the relevant functional protein domains, post translational modification sites and protein-protein interaction, are predicted as the true components for nuclear transport mechanism. This study also aims to evaluate the unique characteristics of proteins responsible for nuclear transport machinery between the parasites and human by determining the degree of protein sequence similarity. The information on the sequence level divergence between *T. brucei* proteins and their human counterparts may provide an insight into drug target discovery.

2. Materials and methods

Our *in silico* analyses were carried out using the public databases and web based programs (Table 1). The programs were employed to identify and annotate the parasite proteins involved in the nuclear transport mechanism. The identified parasite proteins were then compared with the human counterparts.

Analysis	Programme name	URL and Reference where available
Protein sequence retrieval	National Centre for Biotechnology Information (NCBI)	www.ncbi.nlm.nih.gov/
	Universal Protein Knowledgebase/SwissProt (UniProtKB/ SwissProt)	http://www.uniprot.org/
	TriTrypDB	http:// tritrypdb.org/ tritrypdb/
Clustering of protein sequences	BLASTClust	www.vardb.org/vardb/analysis/blastclust.html
Identification of protein domains	Conserved Domain Database (CDD)	http://www.ncbi.nlm.nih.gov/cdd/
	Simple Modular Architecture Research Tool (SMART)	http://smart.embl-heidelberg.de/
	InterPro	http://www.ebi.ac.uk/interpro/
Identification of post translational modification sites	PROSITE	http://prosite.expasy.org/
Sequence similarity search	BLASTp (NCBI)	http://blast.ncbi.nlm.nih.gov/

Table 1. Databases and web-based programs used in the analysis of nuclear transport of *T. brucei*.

We utilized a personal computer equipped with AMD Turion 64x2 dual-core processor, memory size of 32 gigabytes and NVIDIA graphics card to perform the analyses. Our *in silico* work is summarized in Figure 4.

The nuclear transport refers to a process of entry and exit of large molecules from the cell nucleus. To identify *T. brucei* proteins of nuclear transport, the protein sequences of other various eukaryotic organisms were retrieved in FASTA format from National Centre for Biotechnology Information (NCBI) server and Universal Protein Knowledgebase/SwissProt (UniProtKB/ SwissProt) database based on biological processes and protein name search. The number of hits obtained for the query was recorded after manual inspection. The retrieved protein sequences were clustered into groups with more than 30% similarity using

BLASTClust [10] to reduce non-redundant protein sequences. The non-redundant data set was subjected to BLASTp [11] analyses against an integrated genomic and functional genomic database for eukaryotic pathogens of the family Trypanosomatidae, TriTrypDB. The analysis was using cutoff point with E-value of less than 1e-06 and score of more than 100. Hits that pointed to the same location or overlapped location were removed manually. The identified protein sequences then were then retrieved from the TriTrypDB.

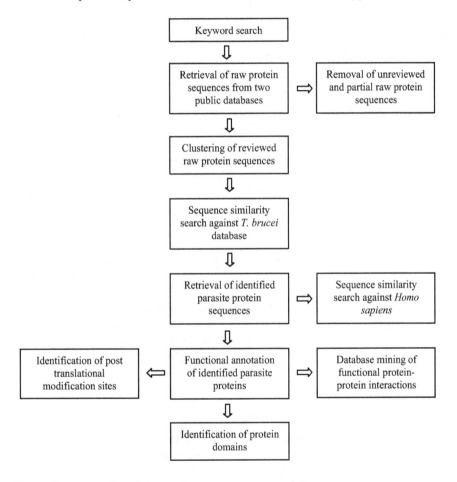

Figure 4. *In silico* analysis workflow.

A portion of protein that can evolve, function, and exist independently is called protein domain. It is a compact three dimensional structure, stable and distribution of polar and non-polar side chains contribute to its folding process. To determine the functional protein domains, all identified protein sequences of *T. brucei* from TriTrypDB were subjected to functional annotation which makes use of Conserved Domain Database (CDD) [12], Simple Modular Architecture Research Tool (SMART) [13] and InterPro [14] programs. The protein sequences were submitted in FASTA format as queries.

Posttranslational modification (PTM) is the chemical modification of a protein after its translation. It is one of the later steps in protein biosynthesis, and thus gene expression, for many proteins. In this part of study, in relation to regulatory aspects of nuclear transport mechanism, we focused on potential glycosylation and phosphorylation sites. To analyze the post translational modification sites, all protein sequences of *T. brucei* from TriTrypDB were subjected to PROSITE [15] programme. The proteins sequences were submitted in FASTA format as queries.

Protein–protein interactions occur when two or more proteins bind together, often to carry out their biological function. Proteins might interact for a long time to form part of a protein complex, a protein may be carrying another protein, or a protein may interact briefly with another protein just to modify it. To analyze the participation of parasite proteins in protein-protein interactions, all protein sequences of *T. brucei* from TriTrypDB were subjected to mining of STRING 8.2 database [16]. The STRING 8.2 database integrates information from numerous sources, including experimental repositories, computational prediction methods and public text collections. The proteins sequences were submitted in FASTA format as queries. All information on protein-protein interaction were recorded and evaluated accordingly.

The degree of similarity between amino acids occupying a particular position in the protein sequence can be interpreted as a rough measure of how conserved a particular region or sequence motif is. To compare the parasite proteins with human homologues, all protein sequences of *T. brucei* from TriTrypDB were subjected to BLASTp analysis against *Homo sapiens* proteins. The proteins sequences were submitted in FASTA format as queries. The criteria such as cutoff point with E-value of less than 1e-06 and score of more than 100 were used.

3. Results and discussions

3.1. Parasite proteins involved in the nuclear transport machinery

Table 2 shows a summary of protein sequences used in this *in silico* analysis. A total of 904 and 642 protein sequences were retrieved in FASTA format from NCBI server and UniProt/SwissProt database respectively. A total of 18 protein sequences with less than 100 amino acid residues were excluded from the study as they were considered not completely functional [17]. Hence, 1528 protein sequences were used for protein sequence clustering. The 30% identity and above at the amino acid level is considered sufficient to imply functional relatedness [17]. Therefore, protein clustering with more than 30% similarity on the retrieved protein sequences produced a non-redundant data set of 248 protein sequences.

Protein sequences	Total
Raw protein sequences retrieved from NCBI and UniProtKB	1546
Raw protein sequences subjected to BLASTClust programme	1548
Non redundant protein sequences resulting from BLASTClust analysis	248
Query sequences for BLASTp analysis against TritrypDB database	248

Table 2. Summary of protein sequences retrieved in *in silico* analysis.

The BLASTp analyses against TriTrypDB using cut off point with E-value of less than 1e-06 and score of more than 100 for the whole 248 query protein sequences resulted in 34 hits of parasite proteins. However our approach failed to identify a Ran GTPase-activating protein (RanGAP) protein in this parasite. In reference [18] also reported that sequence similarity searches have been unable to identify a RanGAP protein in any protozoan. Keyword searches among annotated proteins in the *T. gondii* genome database identified one candidate which was shown to have strong similarity to Ran-binding protein 1 (RanBP1) based on sequence analysis. Perhaps the RanGAP function in apicomplexans is performed by a single protein with multiple cellular responsibilities (i.e., a fusion of Ran binding protein 1 and RanGAP). It is also possible that a completely unique parasite protein possesses the RanGAP function.

Table 3 shows the identified and characterized parasite proteins involved in the nuclear transport machinery. The functional annotation based on protein domains, showed that, out of 34, only 22 parasite protein sequences were predicted with high confidence level to be involved in the nuclear transport mechanism with the presence of relevant protein domains. This includes guanine triphosphate (GTP)-binding domain, Nucleoporin (NUP) C terminal domain, Armadillo repeat, Importin B N-terminal domain, regulator of chromosome condensation 1 (RCC1) repeat and Exportin domain (Table 4). All these protein domains were experimentally verified to regulate the nuclear transport mechanism in eukaryotes. There were seven *T. brucei* proteins that exhibited functional features of the Importin receptor. This finding is consensus with the number of Importin receptors in another eukaryotic pathogen, *Toxoplasma gondii* [8]. In addition, our results of other nuclear transport constituents in *T. brucei* such as RCC1, Ran, nuclear transport factor 2 (NTF2), cell apoptosis susceptibility (CAS), Exportin and Ran binding proteins were also in agreement with reference [18].

The nuclear and cytoplasmic compartments are divided by the nuclear envelope in eukaryotes. By using this compartmentalization and controlling the movement of molecules between the nucleus and the cytosol, cells are able to regulate numerous cellular mechanisms such as transcription and translation. Proteins with molecular size lower than 40 kDa are able to passively diffuse through the nuclear pore complex (NPC), whereas larger proteins require active transport through the assistance of Karyopherins, specific transport receptors that shuttle between the nucleus and cytosol. Karyopherins which are able to distinguish between the diverse proteome to target specific cargo molecules for transport, can be subdivided into those that transport molecules into the nucleus (Importins) and those that transport molecules out of the nucleus (Exportins). It has been reported that more than 2000 proteins are shuttled between the nucleus and the cytoplasm in yeast [19]. From our result, with the identification of Karyopherin and Nucleoporin proteins in *T. brucei*, we expect that the parasite employs the typical components for the nuclear transport machinery.

Subject sequences	E-value	Score	Functional protein domains
Tb927.3.1120	1.70E-72	718	Ran GTPase, GTP-binding domain
Tb09.211.4360	5.50E-33	348	Karyopherin Importin Beta, Armadillo repeat
Tb11.01.5940	9.30E-149	1391	Exportin-1 C terminal, Importin Beta N terminal domain
Tb11.02.0870	3.20E-16	187	Ran binding domain
Tb927.2.2240	2.40E-15	190	Exportin-like protein
Tb927.6.2640	9.10E-83	815	Karyopherin Importin Beta, Armadillo repeat
Tb927.6.4740	1.10E-75	748	CAS/CSE domain, Importin Beta N terminal domain
Tb927.7.1190	6.90E-20	172	RCC1 repeat
Tb11.03.0140	5.80E-09	107	NUP C terminal domain
Tb927.10.8170	2.10E-28	315	NUP C terminal domain
Tb927.8.3370	2.50E-48	281	Ran-binding protein Mog1p
Tb11.01.7010	8.20E-42	464	Armadillo repeat, Karyopherin Importin Beta
Tb11.02.1720	2.60E-26	276	Armadillo-like helical
Tb11.01.8030	1.70E-18	218	HEAT repeat, Armadillo repeat, Importin Beta N terminal domain
Tb11.01.7200	7.10E-07	137	Nsp1-like
Tb927.7.6320	1.20E-11	136	RCC1 repeat
Tb927.3.4600	3.70E-08	149	Armadillo-like helical
Tb09.160.2360	1.40E-36	379	WD40 repeat
Tb927.6.3870	8.50E-14	164	RNA recognition motif
Tb927.7.5760	1.30E-08	115	Nuclear transport factor 2 domain
Tb10.70.4720	4.60E-77	761	Importin Beta N terminal domain, Karyopherin domain
Tb927.8.4280	2.90E-08	112	Nuclear transport factor 2 domain

Key:

GTP	Guanine triphosphate
CAS	Cell apoptosis susceptibility
CSE	Chromosome seggregation
RCC1	Regulator of chromosome condensation 1
NUP	Nucleoporin
HEAT	Huntingtin, elongation factor 3 (EF3), protein phosphatase 2A (PP2A), and the yeast PI3-kinase TOR1
WD	Trp-Asp (W-D) dipeptide
RNA	Ribonucleic acid

Table 3. Identified and characterized *T. brucei* proteins of nuclear transport. Protein domain identification involved CDD, SMART, InterPro and PROSITE programs.

Protein domain	Accession	Description
Ran GTPase	SM00176	Ran is involved in the active transport of proteins through nuclear pores.
Ran binding domain	PDOC50196	This domain binds RanGTP and increases the rate of RanGAP1-induced GTP hydrolysis.
Armadillo	IPR000225	The Armadillo (Arm) repeat is an approximately 40 amino acid long tandemly repeated sequence motif first identified in the *Drosophila melanogaster* segment polarity gene armadillo involved in signal transduction through wingless. Animal Arm-repeat proteins function in various processes, including intracellular signalling and cytoskeletal regulation, and include such proteins as beta-catenin, the junctional plaque protein plakoglobin, the adenomatous polyposis coli (APC), tumour suppressor protein, and the nuclear transport factor importin-alpha, amongst others
Importin beta	IPR001494	Members of the Importin-beta (Karyopherin-beta) family can bind and transport cargo by themselves, or can form heterodimers with importin-alpha. As part of a heterodimer, Importin-beta mediates interactions with the pore complex, while Importin-alpha acts as an adaptor protein to bind the nuclear localisation signal (NLS) on the cargo through the classical NLS import of proteins.
HEAT	IPR000357	Arrays of Huntingtin, elongation factor 3 (EF3), protein phosphatase 2A (PP2A), and the yeast PI3-kinase TOR1 (HEAT) repeats consists of 3 to 36 units forming a rod-like helical structure and appear to function as protein-protein interaction surfaces. It has been noted that many HEAT repeat-containing proteins are involved in intracellular transport processes.
Exportin 1-like protein	pfam08389	The sequences featured in this family are similar to a region close to the N-terminus of yeast exportin 1 (Xpo1, Crm1). This region is found just C-terminal to an importin-beta N-terminal domain (pfam03810) in many members of this family. Exportin 1 is a nuclear export receptor that interacts with leucine-rich nuclear export signal (NES) sequences, and Ran-GTP, and is involved in translocation of proteins out of the nucleus.

Protein domain	Accession	Description
CAS/CSE	IPR005043	In the nucleus, cell apoptosis susceptibility (CAS) acts as a nuclear transport factor in the importin pathway. The Importin pathway mediates the nuclear transport of several proteins that are necessary for mitosis and further progression. CAS is therefore thought to affect the cell cycle through its effect on the nuclear transport of these proteins
WD40	IPR001680	WD-repeat proteins are a large family found in all eukaryotes and are implicated in a variety of functions ranging from signal transduction and transcription regulation to cell cycle control and apoptosis. Repeated WD40 motifs act as a site for protein-protein interaction, and proteins containing WD40 repeats are known to serve as platforms for the assembly of protein complexes or mediators of transient interplay among other proteins.
RCC1	PDOC00544	The regulator of chromosome condensation (RCC1) is a eukaryotic protein which binds to chromatin and interacts with ran, a nuclear GTP-binding protein (see <PDOC00859>), to promote the loss of bound GDP and the uptake of fresh GTP, thus acting as a guanine-nucleotide dissociation stimulator (GDS)
NUP C-terminal	PDOC51434	Communication between the nucleus and cytoplams of an eukaryotic cell is mediated by the nuclear pore complexes (NPCs), which act as selective molecular gateways. Through these gateways, ribonucleic acids (RNAs) and proteins are exported into the nucleus. Each NPC consists of ~30 distinct proteins termed Nucleoporins, each present in at least eight copies, reflecting the octagonal symmetry of the complex.
NSP 1	IPR007758	The NSP1-like protein appears to be an essential component of the nuclear pore complex, for example preribosome nuclear export requires the Nup82p-Nup159p-Nsp1p complex.
NTF 2	IPR002075	Nuclear transport factor 2 (NTF2) is a homodimer which stimulates efficient nuclear import of a cargo protein. NTF2 binds to both RanGDP and FxFG repeat-containing Nucleoporins.

Table 4. Summary of protein domains

3.2. Regulatory aspect of the parasite nuclear transport

Table 5 shows the presence of phosphorylation and glycosylation sites in the parasite proteins. The phosphorylation sites were found to be present in all parasite proteins. It was predicted that the parasite proteins could be phosphorylated at Serine, Threonine and Tyrosine amino residues. However, the O-glycosylation sites were not present in three parasite proteins, namely Tb11.02.0870, Tb927.8.3370 and Tb927.7.5760.

Subject sequences	Phosphorylation site	Glycosylation site
Tb927.3.1120	+	+
Tb09.211.4360	+	+
Tb11.01.5940	+	+
Tb11.02.0870	+	-
Tb927.2.2240	+	+
Tb927.6.2640	+	+
Tb927.6.4740	+	+
Tb927.7.1190	+	+
Tb11.03.0140	+	+
Tb927.10.8170	+	+
Tb927.8.3370	+	-
Tb11.01.7010	+	+
Tb11.02.1720	+	+
Tb11.01.8030	+	+
Tb11.01.7200	+	+
Tb927.7.6320	+	+
Tb927.3.4600	+	+
Tb09.160.2360	+	+
Tb927.6.3870	+	+
Tb927.7.5760	+	-
Tb10.70.4720	+	+
Tb09.211.2550	+	+
Tb927.8.4280	+	+

Key:

(+) indicates presence
(-) indicates absence

Table 5. Phosphorylation and O-glycosylation sites in the *T. brucei* proteins. Identification of these functional sites involved ScanProsite programme.

Most of the parasite proteins were predicted to be involved in O-linked glycosylation. In eukaryotes, the O-linked glycosylation takes place in the Golgi apparatus. It also occurs in archaea and bacteria. Phosphorylation was reported to be crucial in the regulation of protein-protein interactions of the NADPH oxidase in the phagocytic cells [20]. The phosporylation-based signaling in *T. brucei* has been reported by reference [21]. Thus we believe that the phosphorylation could also regulate the nuclear transport components of *T. brucei* to participate in various functional interactions. Meanwhile, it was suggested that O-linked glycosylation may be analogous to protein phosphorylation. According to [22], phosphorylation by proline-directed kinases share the same sites with those potentially O-glycosylated by O-linked N-acetylglucosamine transferase (OGT). From this it is possible that O-glycosylation and phosphorylation may compete for sites of modification. Therefore, it is a strong likelihood that the nuclear transport of *T. brucei* could be regulated by both phosphorylation and O-glycosylation.

Apart from acting simply as an architectural structure which facilitates nuclear transport, the NPC may also play a more dynamic role in regulating transport. The specificity of import and export may be influenced by recognition of different substrates and alteration of the Nucleoporin expression. This would allow different interaction between the NPC and Karyopherins and modulate the nuclear import and export. However, the most common impact on nucleocytoplasmic movement stems comes from the post translational modifications of the cargo proteins themselves [23]. The post translational modification of NPC was reported by [24]. Post-translational modification of NUPs by ubiquitylation and phosphorylation can affect NUP turnover and pore disassembly, respectively. Our study identified four parasite proteins containing the Nucleoporin-related domain. We anticipate that the assembly and disassembly of the parasite Nucleoporin proteins might also be modulated by phosphorylation.

The NPC becomes an ideal target for inhibition of nuclear import or export. One of the most common features of Nucleoporins is the presence of conserved FG or FXFG repeats that bind to the Importin family members [25]. The monoclonal antibodies such as mAb414 and RL2 can interrupt translocation through the NPC by blocking the FG and FXFG epitopes of the Nucleoporins. Consequently, several Nucleoporin proteins were identified by their reactivity against the anti-FG antibodies. Most of these FG repeat proteins exist as the cytoplasmic fibrils or projections on the nuclear side of the NPC. The monoclonal antibodies prevent cargo from associating with the edge of an NPC so it cannot cross the membrane [26]. Thus, there is a possibility that the pathogenesis of *T. brucei* could be controlled by inhibiting its Nucleoporin proteins.

3.3. Participation of parasite proteins in functional interaction network

Figure 5 illustrates the protein interaction data obtained from STRING 8.2 database. The mining of protein interaction data which is useful in contextual annotation of protein function showed that, out of 22 parasite homologues, only nine parasite proteins were interacting with each other. Out of the seven identified *T. brucei* Importins, only two namely Tb927.6.2640 and Tb10.70.4720 were found to be involved in that protein interaction network. This database mining approach indicated that *T. brucei* nuclear transport is typical of eukaryotic organisms. Importins initially recruit cargo at low RanGTP concentrations in the cytoplasm and release cargo at high RanGTP levels in the nucleus. Importin–RanGTP complexes return afterwards to the cytoplasm, where the Ran-bound GTP is finally hydrolysed and Ran dissociates from the receptor. The Importin can then bind and import another cargo molecule, while nuclear transport factor 2 (NTF2) recycles RanGDP back to nucleus. The cargo binding to exportins is controlled in a reverse manner compared to Importins; they recruit cargo at high RanGTP levels in the nucleus and release cargo at low RanGTP concentrations in the cytoplasm.

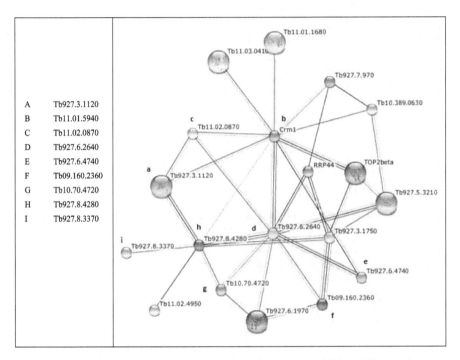

A	Tb927.3.1120
B	Tb11.01.5940
C	Tb11.02.0870
D	Tb927.6.2640
E	Tb927.6.4740
F	Tb09.160.2360
G	Tb10.70.4720
H	Tb927.8.4280
I	Tb927.8.3370

Figure 5. Protein functional interaction network in the nuclear transport of *T. brucei*. This protein interaction data was obtained from STRING 8.2 database. The letters (a-i) indicate the parasite proteins involved in the nuclear transport.

Table 5 shows evaluation of the obtained protein interaction data of the parasite nuclear transport. There were 13 functional interactions between parasite proteins identified from the mining of STRING 8.2 database. The score values of functional interactions range from 0.45 to 0.976. The Importin alpha (Tb927.6.2640) was found to be the most interactive parasite proteins by participating in six functional interactions. Based on the relevant protein domains and previous reports, four out of 13 functional interactions were considered with high confidence level. It should be emphasized that our approach only considered the protein interaction data derived from experiments, gene fusion and text mining. To our knowledge, this is the first report of functional protein interactions in the nuclear transport of the eukaryotic parasites. Whether other eukaryotic parasites share the common protein interaction network for the nuclear transport machinery remains to be elucidated.

Subject sequence	Interacting partner	Source	Score	Confidence level	Reference
Tb927.3.1120	Tb11.01.5940	Experiment	0.45	High	Lounsbury and Macara (1997)
Tb927.3.1120	Tb11.02.0870	Experiment,Text mining	0.512	Moderate	None
Tb927.3.1120	Tb927.8.4280	Experiment	0.534	High	Fried and Kutay (2003)
Tb11.01.5940	Tb11.02.0870	Experiment,Text mining	0.88	High	Lounsbury and Macara (1997)
Tb11.01.5940	Tb927.6.2640	Experiment,Text mining,Co-expression	0.812	Moderate	None
Tb11.01.5940	Tb927.6.4740	Text mining,Co-expression	0.46	Moderate	None
Tb11.02.0870	Tb927.6.2640	Experiment,Text mining	0.453	Moderate	None
Tb927.6.2640	Tb927.6.4740	Experiment,Text mining,Co-expression	0.976	Moderate	None
Tb927.6.2640	Tb09.160.2360	Experiment,Text mining	0.647	Moderate	None
Tb927.6.2640	Tb10.70.4720	Experiment,Text mining	0.769	High	Fried and Kutay (2003)
Tb927.6.2640	Tb927.8.4280	Experiment,Text mining	0.641	Moderate	None
Tb10.70.4720	Tb927.8.4280	Experiment,Text mining	0.535	Moderate	None
Tb927.8.4280	Tb927.8.3370	Experiment	0.502	Moderate	None

Table 6. Evaluation on protein interaction data obtained from STRING 8.2 database. The evaluation was based on the identified protein domains.

To gain an insight into nuclear transport, understanding on interactions between transport receptors and proteins of the nuclear pore complex (NPC) is essential. According to [27], the fluorescence resonance energy transfer (FRET) can be employed between enhanced cyan and yellow fluorescent proteins (ECFP, EYFP) in living cells in order to explain the transport of receptor through the NPC. A FRET assay has been used to analyze a panel of yeast strains expressing functional receptor--ECFP and nucleoporin-EYFP fusions. Based on this approach, points of contact in the NPC for the related Importin Pse1/Kap121 and Exportin Msn5 were successfully characterized. That study proved the advantage of FRET in mapping dynamic protein interactions in a genetic system. In addition, both Importin and Exportin have overlapping pathways through the NPC. However, our database mining approach did not reveal any functional interaction between Nucleoporin and Karyopherin proteins of *T. brucei*.

3.4. Sequence similarity between parasite proteins and their human counterparts

Table 6 shows the degree of protein sequence similarity between parasite and human proteins. The similarity search for the sequence was carried out with the help of BLASTp tool. All the parasite proteins of nuclear transport machinery were found to have their counterparts in human. The degree of sequence similarity between parasite proteins and human counterparts range from 19% to 72%. The resulting score values range from 49.3 to 558. Meanwhile, all the identified human proteins contain the same protein domains involved in the nuclear transport.

Subject sequence	Human counterparts	Score	E-value	Sequence similarity (%)
Tb927.3.1120	NP_006316.1	313	1.00E-109	72%
Tb09.211.4360	NP_694858.1	221	6.00E-62	25%
Tb11.01.5940	NP_003391.1	558	0	33%
Tb11.02.0870	AAA85838.1	79.3	5.00E-20	40%
Tb927.2.2240	AAH20569.1	79.3	2.00E-16	29%
Tb927.6.2640	NP_036448.1	360	4.00E-119	42%
Tb927.6.4740	AAC50367.1	368	9.00E-113	29%
Tb927.7.1190	AAI42947.1	453	2.00E-27	27%
Tb11.03.0140	AAH45620.2	258	2.00E-09	38%
Tb927.10.8170	NP_705618.1	134	1.00E-33	28%
Tb927.8.3370	AAF36156.1	70.9	2.00E-17	27%
Tb11.01.7010	NP_002262.3	207	2.00E-56	23%
Tb11.02.1720	NP_006382.1	156	9.00E-28	24%
Tb11.01.8030	NP_002262.3	101	3.00E-23	21%
Tb11.01.7200	CAA41411.1	59.7	4.00E-10	19%
Tb927.7.6320	NP_001041659.1	146	4.00E-17	28%
Tb927.3.4600	NP_006381.2	65.9	2.00E-12	20%
Tb09.160.2360	NP_003601.1	142	2.00E-39	30%
Tb927.6.3870	NP_001073956.2	75.5	8.00E-18	31%
Tb927.7.5760	NP_037380.1	49.3	6.00E-11	26%
Tb10.70.4720	NP_002256.2	277	2.00E-81	28%
Tb927.8.4280	NP_005787.1	73.6	1.00E-19	31%

Table 7. Comparison of the identified parasite proteins with human counterparts at protein sequence level. This comparison involved BLASTp programme.

A study reported by [28] showed that despite the high degree of similarity in the primary structure of human and *T. cruzi* ubiquitins, the three amino acid difference is sufficient to distinguish parasite versus host proteins. In this study, a simplified one step purification procedure to partially purify *T. cruzi* ubiquitin was performed. Following this preparation, ELISA and Western blots were carried out to show that chagasic sera recognise *T. cruzi* but not human or Leishmania ubiquitin indicating a species-specific response. Thus, it is probable that the *T. brucei* proteins could also be distinguished from human counterparts at primary sequence level by using the immunodetection method.

4. General discussions

4.1. Transport of cargoes

In RanGTPase system, Ran-binding protein 1 (RanBP1) which is cytoplasmic localized binds RanGTP and eases the RanGAP-dependent conversion of RanGTP to RanGDP [29]. This indicates that RanBP1 catalyses the cytoplasmic disassembly of RanGTP–transport receptor complexes. These complexes are kinetically so stable that RanGAP alone fails to trigger GTP hydrolysis [30-32]. RanBP2 [33] is a major constituent of the cytoplasmic filaments of NPCs and exhibits similar functions as RanBP1. It has four RanBP1 homology domains and forms a stable complex with sumoylated RanGAP [34,35], in order to dismantle the RanGTP–transport receptor complexes that exit the nucleus. Importin- and exportin-mediated transport cycles can accumulate cargoes against gradients of chemical activity, which is an energy-dependent process. The RanGTPase system hydrolyses one GTP molecule per transport cycle, and a number of evidences suggest that this contains the sole input of metabolic energy [36-39]. We have successfully identified all the required key components in the *T. brucei* nuclear transport. Whether their functionalities *in vivo* are consensus with the known ones still remains to be further investigated.

4.2. Relationship between signaling pathways and nuclear transport

Many aspects of cell physiology are greatly dependent on the signaling pathways. This includes members of the mitogen activated protein (MAP) kinase family as well as phosphatidyl inositol 3 (PI3) and adenosine monophosphate (AMP) kinases which are crucial in controlling the cell growth, proliferation, apoptosis and the response to stress. By activating the signaling pathway through multiple kinase cascades, various stressors are able to regulate the nuclear transport. For example, oxidative and heat stress activate both MAP kinase kinase (MEK)-extracellular signal regulated kinase 1/2 (ERK1/2) and PI3 kinase-Akt pathways [40]. Based on these observations and the fact that many of the transport components are modified post-translationally, it was sensible to investigate whether these modifications are regulated by stress. A study reported by [41] showed that oxidant treatment induced phosphorylation and/or GlcNAc modification of soluble transport factors and nucleoporins. Interestingly, changes in transport factor modifications are not limited to stress conditions, as modifying ERK or PI3 kinase activities in unstressed cells also affect the transport factors. This is exemplified by the regulation of RanBP3 through ERK1/2-ribosomal S6 kinase (RSK) signaling, a regulatory link which ultimately controls the Ran concentration gradient. Furthermore, phosphorylation of Nup50 which is dependent on ERK, reduces its association with importin-β1 and transportin *in vitro*, and ERK2 is responsible to the oxidant-induced collapse of the Ran gradient [42]. It remains unknown how much modulating individual transport factors contributes to the overall regulation of nuclear trafficking. However, it is noteworthy that the kinase inhibitor PD98059, which targets ERK1/2 and ERK5, significantly increases classical nuclear import, both under normal and stress conditions. Taken together, these results highlight a critical role of ERK activity in nuclear transport, with ERK kinases targeting both soluble factors and nucleoporins [41]. Thus, there is an urgent need to investigate the possible connection between upstream signaling apparatus with nuclear transport components in *T. brucei*.

4.3. *In silico* approach for drug target discovery

We have provided interpretation of heterologous data sets for nuclear transport system of *T. brucei* from various resources. With the availability of protein databases and computer-aided softwares, we are able to explain various functional interactions between identified parasite proteins and how these functional interactions give rise to functionality and behavior of the parasite nuclear transport. This would partially facilitate the exhausted effort to obtain system-level understanding of *T. brucei* pathogenesis. Our *in silico* approach has the potential to speed up the rate of drug target discovery while reducing the need for expensive lab work and clinical trials. The conventional approaches *in vivo* and *in vitro* have high tendencies to produce inefficient results when investigating complex large scale data such as proteins associated with nuclear shuttling of macromolecules across the nuclear envelope. Therefore, the systematic *in silico* approach from this study provides a tremendous opportunity of cost effective drug target discovery for the pharmaceutical industry.

4.4. Experimental validation of *in silico* data

Experimental techniques such as yeast two-hybrid assay and affinity purification combined with mass spectrometry are useful to investigate the possible protein-protein interaction. However, they have their limitations in detecting certain types of interactions. They also have technical problems to scale-up for high-throughput analysis. In conjunction with this, *in silico* approach may solve those problems in inferring the protein function. The scope of experimental data can be expanded to increase the confidence of certain interacting protein pairs with the availability of databases containing *in silico* data such as protein domain and 3D structure. The databases integrate information from various resources such as computational prediction methods and public text collections. Since *in silico* and experimental approaches are complementary to each other, the combination of these different approaches is very useful to obtain a more accurate picture of *T. brucei* nuclear transport.

4.5. Our further direction

In silico approach offers various advantages over *in vivo* and *in vitro* approaches such as non-use of animals, low costs, and reduced execution time. This approach allows identification of proteins of interest from a particular biological study. From a protein function standpoint, transfer of annotation from known proteins to a novel target is currently the only practical way to convert vast quantities of raw sequence data into meaningful information. Many bioinformatics tools now provide more sophisticated methods to transfer functional annotation, integrating sequence, family profile and structural search methodology. Thus, in addition to data mining for protein-protein interaction, further *in silico* approach should also consider structural alignment, molecular docking and pathway modeling in order to obtain a comprehensive and more reliable insight into protein-protein interaction of *T. brucei* nuclear transport.

5. Conclusion

The availability of protein databases and computer-aided softwares to identify probable components of cellular mechanisms has become a new trend in the present scientific era. We demonstrate here a computational analysis of nuclear transport in *T. brucei* as an initial step and proof of concept for further investigation. Our approach successfully identified 22 *T. brucei* proteins essential for nuclear transport. All those parasite proteins were found to contain relevant functional domains that drive the translocation of macromolecules in the parasite. The phosphorylation and O-glycosylation sites were also detected in all identified parasite proteins. This has given us an insight into the regulatory aspect of parasite nuclear transport. The database mining of protein interaction has shown that nine out of 22 parasite proteins possess relevant functional interactions for nuclear transport activities. However, more functional interactions from nuclear transport constituents of *T. brucei* are required to elucidate the exact mechanism. The homology between the parasite proteins and human counterparts was shown by BLASTp analyses. Whether there are structural differences between them remain unknown.

The nuclear transport in *T. brucei* has been characterized by using the *in silico* approach. The predicted functionalities and regulatory aspects of parasite nuclear transport constituents were in agreement with the previous reports. Moreover, the protein interaction data derived from the public database has made the participation of parasite proteins in the mechanism more convincing. Thus, we have laid a path for understanding the nuclear transport machinery in *T. brucei*. The development of drugs that target as well as alter nuclear import and export will undoubtedly become beneficial in controlling Trypanosomiasis in future. Drugs that have a direct effect on a single protein must be able to localize to the same site as the protein and interact with one or more of its domains. Alternatively, a drug that effectively blocks the target protein from reaching its proper organelle can also inhibit the protein's function.

Author details

Mohd Fakharul Zaman Raja Yahya* and Umi Marshida Abdul Hamid
School of Biology, Faculty of Applied Sciences, MARA University of Technology Shah Alam, Shah Alam Selangor, Malaysia

6. References

[1] Barrett M P, Burchmore R J and Stich A (2003). The trypanosomiases. Lancet 362 (9394): 1469–80.

[2] Miles M (2003). American trypanosomiasis (Chagas disease). GC Cook, A Zumla (Eds.), Manson's tropical disease (21st edn.), Elsevier Science, London, pp. 1325–1337.

[3] Hecker H and Bohringer S (1977). Morphometric analysis of the life cycle of *Trypanosoma brucei*. Ann. Soc. belge Med. trop., vol. 57 (4-5), pp. 465-470.

[4] Ogbadoyi E, Ersfeld K, Robinson D, Sherwin T, Gull K (2000). Architecture of the *Trypanosoma brucei* nucleus during interphase and mitosis. Chromosoma 108 (8): 501–13.

[5] Acosta-Serrano A, Vassella E, Liniger M, Renggli C K, Brun R, Roditi I and Englund P T. (2001). The surface coat of procyclic *Trypanosoma brucei*: Programmed expression and proteolytic cleavage of procyclin in the tsetse fly. PNAS, vol. 98(4), pp. 1513-1518, 2001.

[6] Gorlich D and Mattaj I W (1996). Nucleocytoplasmic transport. Science vol. 271 (5255), pp. 1513-1518.

[7] Mattaj I W and Englmeier L (1998). Nucleocytoplasmic transport: The Soluble Phase. Annual Review of Biochemistry, vol. 67, pp. 265-306.

[8] Fried, H., and Kutay, U. (2003). Nucleocytoplasmic transport:taking an inventory. Cell Mol Life Sci 60, 1659–1688.

[9] Röhrig U F, Awad L, Grosdidier A, Larrieu, P, Stroobant V, Colau D, Cerundolo V and Andrew J. G. (2010). Rational Design of Indoleamine 2,3-Dioxygenase Inhibitors. Journal of Medicinal Chemistry 53 (3): 1172–89.

[10] Hayes, C N (2008). varDB: a pathogen-specific sequence database of protein families involved in antigenic variation, Bioinformatics.

[11] Altschul S F, Gish W, Miller W, Myers E W, and Lipman D J. (1990). Basic local alignment search tool. J. Mol. Biol, vol. 215, pp. 403-410.

[12] Marchler-Bauer A, Anderson J B, Cherukuri P F, DeWeese-Scott C, Geer L Y, Gwadz M, He S, Hurwitz D I, Jackson J D, Ke Z, Lanczycki C J, Liebert C A, Liu, Lu C F, Marchler G H, Mullokandov M, Shoemaker B A, Simonyan V, Song J S, Thiessen P A, Yamashita R A, J. J. Yin, D. Zhang, and S. H. Bryant (2005). CDD: a Conserved Domain Database for protein classification. Nucleic Acid Research , vol. 33, pp. 192-196.

* Corresponding Author

[13] Letunic I, Doerks T and Bork P (2009). SMART 6: recent updates and new developments. Nucleic Acid Research. vol. 37, pp. 229-232.

[14] Hunter S, Apweiler R, Attwood T K, Bairoch A, Bateman A, Binns D, Bork P, Das U, Daugherty L, Duquenne L, Finn R D, Gough J, Haft D, Hulo N, Kahn D, Kelly E, Laugraud A, Letunic I, Lonsdale D, Lopez R, Madera M, Maslen J, McAnulla C, J. McDowall, Mistry J, Mitchell J A, Mulder N, Natale D, Orengo C, Quinn A F, Selengut J D, Sigrist C J, Thimma M, Thomas P D, Valentin F, Wilson D, Wu C H, and Yeats C (2009). InterPro: the integrative protein signature database. Nucleic Acids Research, vol. 37, pp. 211-215.

[15] Hulo N, Bairoch A, Bulliard V, Cerutti L, De Castro E, Langendijk-Genevaux D S, Pagni M, and Sigrist C J A (2006). The PROSITE database. Nucleic Acid Research, vol. 34, pp. 227-230.

[16] Jensen L J, Kuhn M, Stark M, Chaffron S, Creevey C, Muller J, Doerks T, Julien P, Roth A, Simonovic M, Bork P, and Von Mering C (2009). STRING 8--a global view on proteins and their functional interactions in 630 organisms. Nucleic Acid Research. Vol. 7 pp 412-416.

[17] Schmid M (1998). Novel approaches to the discovery of antimicrobial agents. Curr. Opin. Chem. Biol. vol. 2, pp. 529-534.

[18] Frankel M B and Knoll L J (2009). The Ins and Outs of Nuclear Trafficking: Unusual Aspects in Apicomplexan Parasites. DNA and Cell Biology vol. 28, pp. 277-284.

[19] Macara, I G (2001). Transport into and out of the nucleus. Microbiol Mol Biol Rev 65, 570–594.

[20] Babior B M (1999). NADPH oxidase: an update. Blood 93 (5): 1464–76.

[21] Nett I R E, D. Martin D M A, Miranda-Saavedra D, Lamont D, Barber J D, and Mahlert A (2009). The phosphoproteome of bloodstream form *Trypanosoma brucei*, causative agent of African sleeping sickness. Molecular & Cellular Proteomics, vol. 8 pp. 1527-1538.

[22] Miller, M. W., Caracciolo, M. R., Berlin, W. K., and Hanover, J. A. (1999). Phosphorylation and Glycosylation of Nucleoporins. Archives of Biochemistry and Biophysics, 367(1), 51-60.

[23] Gasiorowski, J. Z. and Dean, D. A. (2003). Mechanisms of nuclear transport and interventions. Advanced Drug Delivery Reviews, 55, 703-716.

[24] Schuldt, A. (2012). Post-translational modification: A monoubiquitylation pore anchor. Nature Reviews Molecular Cell Biology, 13, 66.

[25] Radu A, Blobel G and Moore M S (1995). Identification of a protein complex that is required for nuclear protein import and mediates docking of import substrate to distinct nucleoporins, Proc. Natl. Acad. Sci. USA 92: 1769– 1773.

[26] Gasiorowski, J. Z. and Dean, D. A. (2003). Mechanisms of nuclear transport and interventions. Advanced Drug Delivery Reviews, 55, 703-716.

[27] Damelin M, S. P. (2000). Mapping interactions between nuclear transport factors in living cells reveals pathways through the nuclear pore complex. Mol Cell., 5(1), 133-40.

[28] Télles S, Abate T and Slezynger T C (1999). *Trypanosoma cruzi* and human ubiquitin are immunologically distinct proteins despite only three amino acid difference in their primary sequence. FEMS Immunol Med Microbio, 24(2), 123-30.

[29] Bischoff F R, Krebber H, Smirnova E, Dong W H, and Ponstingl H. (1995). Coactivation of RanGTPase and inhibition of GTP dissociation by Ran GTP binding protein RanBP1. EMBO J, vol. 14, pp. 705-715.

[30] Bischoff F R and Görlich D. (1997). RanBP1 is crucial for the release of RanGTP from importin β -related nuclear transport factors. FEBS Lett, vol. 419, pp. 249-254.

[31] Floer M, Blobel G and M. Rexach M (1997). Disassembly of RanGTP–karyopherin β complex, an intermediate in nuclear protein import. J Biol Chem, vol. 272, pp. 19538-19546.

[32] Lounsbury K M and Macara I G (1997). Ran-binding protein 1 (RanBP1) forms a ternary complex with Ran and karyopherin β and reduces Ran GTPase-activating protein (RanGAP) inhibition by karyopherin β. J Biol Chem, vol. 272, pp. 551-555.

[33] Yokoyama N (1995). A giant nucleopore protein that binds Ran/TC4. Nature, vol. 376, pp. 184-188.

[34] Mahajan R, Delphin C, Guan T, Gerace L and Melchior F (1997). A small ubiquitin-related polypeptide involved in targeting RanGAP1 to nuclear pore complex protein RanBP2. Cell, vol. 88, pp. 97-107.

[35] Matunis M J, Coutavas E, and Blobel G (1996). A novel ubiquitin-like modification modulates the partitioning of the Ran-GTPase-activating protein RanGAP1 between the cytosol and the nuclear pore complex. J Cell Biol, vol. 135, pp. 1457-1470.

[36] Englmeier L, Olivo J C and Mattaj I W (1999). Receptor-mediated substrate translocation through the nuclear pore complex without nucleotide triphosphate hydrolysis. Curr Biol, vol. 9, pp. 30-41.

[37] Kose S, Imamoto N, Tachibana T, Shimamoto T, and Yoneda Y (1997). Ran-unassisted nuclear migration of a 97 kD component of nuclear pore- targeting complex. J Cell Biol, vol. 139, pp. 841-849.

[38] Ribbeck K, Kutay U, Paraskeva E and Görlich D (1999). The translocation of transportin–cargo complexes through nuclear pores is independent of both Ran and energy. Curr Biol, vol. 9, pp. 47-50.

[39] Weis K, Dingwall C, and Lamond A I (1996). Characterization of the nuclear protein import mechanism using Ran mutants with altered nucleotide binding specificities. EMBO J, vol. 15, pp. 7120-7128.

[40] Kodiha M, Banski P and Stochaj U (2009). Interplay between MEK and PI3 kinase signaling regulates the subcellular localization of protein kinases ERK1/2 and Akt upon oxidative stress. FEBS Lett, 583:1987-93.

[41] Kodiha, M., Crampton, N., Shrivastava, S., Umar, R., and Stochaj, U. (2010). Traffic control at the nuclear pore. Aging, 237-244.

[42] Czubryt M P, Austria J A and Pierce G N (2000). Hydrogen peroxide inhibition of nuclear protein import is mediated by the mitogen-activated protein kinase, ERK2. J Cell Biol, 148:7-16.

Chapter 2

Hierarchical Biological Pathway Data Integration and Mining

Shubhalaxmi Kher, Jianling Peng, Eve Syrkin Wurtele and Julie Dickerson

Additional information is available at the end of the chapter

1. Introduction

Biological pathway data is the key resource for biologists worldwide. Interestingly, most of these sources that generate, update, and analyze data are open source. One of the observations that motivated this research work is that, the repositories of data created by a variety of laboratories and research units worldwide represent same pathways with significant details. Generally, if the pathway data has resulted from experimentation, then it is expected that across different resources, under similar conditions, pathways would be exactly identical and biologists may pickup from any source. Interestingly, almost all of the biological data sources refer to data integration of some kind. It may involve rigorous integration mechanisms within the data source and the purpose of integration may change the perspective of looking at the integration.

These efforts in integration may be either local to the source or lack details associated with integration within a pathway, across pathways, or from various data sources etc. Further, the key attributes or design criteria may not be well documented and or may not be readily available to the biologist. In other words, the integration may be achieved as vertical integration (within the data source), or horizontal integration (across data sources). Since most of the extensively integrated data sources (plants or humans) like BioCyc-level-I, Reactome are human curated, it is hard to identify the integration done by the sources like; BioCyc. Also, on a similar note, it may not be apparent to find exactly when the data was integrated looking at a pathway.

Data in general refers to a collection of results, including the results of experience, observation, or experiment, or a set of premises and can be utilized at the maximum when made available to all in a common format. Different organizations and research laboratories around the world store the data in their own formats; this diversity of data sources is caused due to many factors including lack of coordination among the organizations and research laboratories. These intellectual gaps can be bridged by adopting new technology, mergers, acquisitions, and geographic coordination of collaborating groups [1].

For the open source biological databases, it is common for the biologists and researchers to refer to many databases in order to pursue inference or analysis; though it is one of the most challenging tasks. Biological pathway data integration is aimed to work with repositories of data from a variety of sources. As such, two or more databases may not provide identical information for a given pathway, but integrating these two databases may yield a richer resource for analysis. Additionally, the conditions under which data is collected, either by experimentation or by collecting evidence of the published material, in either case the supporting references play a crucial role and is of interest to the biologists in making the analysis more meaningful. At present there are over 200 biological pathway databases. However, very few of them are independently created. Some of these databases may be derived from different data sources. Unfortunately, the documentation often does not reveal details of the data collection, sources, and dates. Further, the research groups involved in analysis of the data usually selectively use data from a single data source. For example, for yeast studies, the Saccharomyces Genome Database (SGD) is the reference for most analyses [2].

In case of biological pathway data, rapid accumulation of genomic and proteomic data have made two major bioinformatics problems apparent.

- The lack of communication between different bioinformatics data resources; whether they are databases or individual analysis programs.
- Biological data are hierarchical and highly related yet are conventionally stored separately in individual database and in different formats.
- Additionally, they are governed more by how data is obtained rather than by what they mean.

Most commercially available bioinformatics systems perform functional analysis using a single data source; an approach that emphasizes pathway mapping and relationship inference based on the data acquired from multiple data sources. Each pathway modality in the data has its own specific representation issues which must be understood before attempting to integrate across modalities.

1.1. Overview

There has been a dramatic increase in the number of large scale comprehensive biological databases that provide useful resources to the community like; Biochemical Pathways (KEGG, AraCyc, and MapMan), Protein Interactions (biomolecular interaction network database), or systems like; Dragon Plant Biology Explorer and Pathway Miner for integrating associations in metabolic networks and ontologies [3-8]. Other databases such as Regulon DB, PlantCARE, PLACE, EDP:Eurokaryotic promoter database, Transcription Regulatory Regions Database, Athamap, and TRANSFAC store information related to transcriptional regulation[9-15].

The aim of molecular biology is to understand the regulation of protein synthesis and its reactions to external and internal signals. All the cells in an organism carry the same genomic data, yet their protein makeup can be drastically different; both temporally and spatially, due to regulation. Protein synthesis is regulated by many mechanisms at its different stages. These include mechanisms for controlling transcription initiation, RNA splicing, mRNA transport, translation initiation, post-translational modifications, and degradation of mRNA/protein. One of the main junctions at which regulation occurs is mRNA transcription. A major role in this machinery is played by proteins themselves that bind to regulatory regions along the DNA, greatly affecting the transcription of the genes they regulate [16]. Friedman introduces a new approach for analyzing gene expression patterns that uncovers properties of the transcriptional program by examining statistical properties of dependence and conditional independence in the data.

For protein interactions, it is intended to connect related proteins and link biological functions in the context of larger cellular processes [17]. The content of these data sources typically complements the experimentally determined protein interactions with the ones that are predicted from gene proximity, fusion, co-expressed data, as well as those determined by using phylogenetic profiling. Each pathway modality in the data has its own specific representation issues which must be understood before integration across modalities is attempted. At present, the bioinformatics database owner only develops private system to provide user with data query and analysis services; such as NCBI develops Entrez database query system which is used on GenBank. European Molecular Biology Laboratory (EMBL) develops Sequence Retrieval Systems. The EMBL Nucleotide Sequence Database maintained at the European Bioinformatics Institute (EBI), incorporates, organizes, and distributes nucleotide sequences from public sources [18]. The database is a part of an international collaboration with DDBJ (Japan) and GenBank (USA). Data are exchanged between the collaborating databases on a daily basis to achieve optimal synchrony. The key point is how to share the heterogeneous databases and make a common query platform for users [19].

Friedman [16] describes early microarray experiments that examined few samples and mainly focused on differential display across tissues or conditions of interest. Such experiments collect enormous amounts of data, which clearly reflects many aspects of the underlying biological processes. An important challenge is to develop methodologies that are both statistically sound and computationally tractable for analyzing such data sets and inferring biological interactions from them. Most of the analysis tools currently used are based on clustering algorithms. The clustering algorithms attempt to locate groups of genes that have similar expression patterns over a set of experiments. Such analysis has proven to be useful in discovering genes that are co-regulated and/or have similar function. A more ambitious goal for analysis is to reveal the structure of the transcriptional regulation process. This is clearly a hard problem. Not only the current data is extremely noisy, but, mRNA expression data alone only gives a partial picture that does not reflect key events such as; translation and protein (in) activation. Finally, the amount of samples, even in the largest experiments in the foreseeable future, does not provide enough information to construct a fully detailed model with high statistical significance.

Some conventional bioinformatics approaches identify hypothetical interactions between proteins based on their three dimensional structures or by applying text mining techniques. Emerging protein chip technologies are expected to permit the large scale measurement of protein expression levels. Corresponding structural data are stored in data source such as protein data bank and represent invaluable sources of understanding of protein structures, functions and interactions. Successful use of high throughput protein interaction determination techniques such as yeast two hybrids, affinity purification followed by mass spectrometry and phage display has shifted research focus from a single gene/protein to more coherent network perspectives. Large scale protein-protein interaction data and their complexes are currently available for a number of organisms and data are stored in several interaction data sources such as BIND [6], DIP [20], IntAct [21], GRID [22] and MINT [23] that is all equipped with basic bioinformatics tools for protein network analysis and visualization. INCLUSive is a web portal and service registry for microarray and regulatory sequence analysis [24]. This provides a comprehensive index for all data integration research projects.

The integration and management technique of heterogeneous sequence data from public sequence data source is widely used to manage diverse information and prediction. It is important for the biologists to investigate these heterogeneous sources and connect the public biological data source and retrieve sequences which are similar to sequences they have, and the results of their retrieval are used in homology research, functional analysis, and predication. However, there are few software packages available to deal with the sequence data in most biological laboratories and they are stored in file formats. File formats is another important issue for biological pathway data sources. XMl, SBML (systems biology markup language), KBML (KEGG), BSML (Bioinformatic Sequence Markup Language) based on XML, and a variety of versions of XML are used for representing the complex and hierarchical biological data. Each flat file from public biological database has different format. Recent tools which convert formats among standards are implemented in JAVA or Perl module. The constraints associated with biological pathway formats are the following;

- Conversion among different formats needs different parsers to extract the user interesting field.
- Formats can be modified anytime.
- Understand the range of field, its value is difficult, and data types in the same field in each format can be different.

From the discussions above, one of the major challenges of the modern bioinformatics research is therefore to store, process, and integrate biological data to understand the inner working of the cell defined by complex interaction networks. Additionally, the integration mechanisms may not register the important details like, copies of inputs files and time of integration along with the integrated output file.

In this chapter, issues related to biological pathway data integration system are discussed and a user friendly data integration algorithm across data sources for biological pathway, particularly, metabolic pathway as a case is presented. i.e. the data integration (BPDI) algorithm that integrates pathway information across data sources and also extracts the abstract information embedded within them are addressed. Today, a bioinformatics information system typically deals with large data sets reaching a total volume of about one terabyte [25]. Such a system serves many purposes;

- User can select the data sources and assign confidence to each selected data source
- It organizes existing data to facilitate complex queries
- It infers relationships based on the stored data and subsequently predicts missing attribute values and incoming information based on multidimensional data.
- Data marts (extension of data warehouse) support different query requests.

2. Data management and integration

The Pathway Resource List contains over 150 biological pathway databases and is growing [26]. Usually, first step for the user is to identify a subset of these data sources for integration. To consolidate all the knowledge for a particular organism, extract the pathways from each database need to be extracted and transformed into a standard data representation before integration. Representation of the pathway data in each data source poses another challenge as each pathway modality has its own specific representation issues which must be understood before attempting integration across modalities. For example, metabolic pathways, signal transduction pathways, protein-protein interaction, gene regulation etc.

Commonly employed styles of data integration may be implemented in different contexts and under requirements, in order to reuse the data across applications for research collaboration. Some of the data integration and management efforts are presented in [27-32]. Several major approaches have been proposed for data integration, which can be roughly classified into five groups [33-34] namely; data warehousing, federated databasing, service-oriented integration, semantic integration and wiki-based integration. Across all of these groups, to a significant extent, an increasingly important component of data integration is the community effort in developing a variety of biomedical ontologies to deal in a more specific manner with the technicality and globality of descriptors and identifiers of information that has to be shared and integrated across various resources. Variety of approaches for data integration is discussed below.

Data Warehousing

The data warehouse approach offers a "one-stop shop" solution to ease access and management of a large variety of biological data from different data sources. The user does not need to access many web sites for multiple data sources. Despite its advantages, the data warehouse approach has a major problem; it requires continuous and often human-guided updates to keep the data comprehensive of the evolution of data sources, resulting in high costs for maintenance. Many biological data sources change their data structures roughly twice a year.

Data integration with Federated Approach

Unlike data warehousing (with its focus on data translation), federated databasing focuses on query translation. The federated database fetches the data from the disparate data sources and then displays the fetched data for its user base. Queries in federated databases are executed within remote data sources and results displayed in federated databases are extracted remotely from the data sources. Due to this capability, federated databasing has two major advantages.

- Federated databases can be regarded as an on-demand approach to provide immediate access to up-to-date data deposited in multiple data sources.
- Compared with data warehousing, federated databasing does not replicate data in data sources; therefore, it presents relatively inexpensive costs for storage and curation. However, federated databasing still has to update its query translation to keep pace with data access methods at diverse remote data sources.

Service –Oriented Approach

A decentralized approach is also being developed, in which individual data sources agree to open their data via Web Services (WS). The service-oriented approach enables data integration from multiple heterogeneous data sources through computer interoperability. The service-oriented approach features data integration through computer-to-computer communication via Web API and up-to-date data retrieval from diverse data sources. Heterogeneous data integration requires that many data sources should become service providers by opening their data via WS and by standardizing data identities and nomenclature to ease data exchange and analysis.

Semantic Web

Most web pages in biological data sources are designed for human reading. RDF provides standard formats for data interchange and describes data as a simple statement, containing a set of triples: a subject, a predicate, and an object. Any two statements can be linked by an identical subject or object. OWL builds on RDF and Uniform Resource Identifier (URI) and describes data structure and meaning based on ontology, which enables automated data reasoning and inferences by computers. Application of semantic Web technologies is a significant advancement for bioinformatics, enabling automated data processing and reasoning. The semantic integration uses ontologies for data description and thus represents ontology-based integration. [27] reviews the current development of semantic network technologies and their applications to the integration of genomic and proteomic data. His work elaborates on applying a semantic network approach to modeling complex cell signaling pathways and simulating the cause-effect of molecular interactions in human macrophages. [31] Illustrates his approach by comparing federated approach versus warehousing versus semantic web using multiple sources.

Wiki-based Integration

A weakness common to all the above approaches is that the quantity of users' participations in the process is inadequate. With the increasing volume of biological data, data integration inevitably will require a large number of users' participations. A successful example that harnesses collective intelligence for data aggregation and knowledge collection is Wikipedia: an online encyclopedia that allows any user to create and edit content. It is infeasible to integrate such large amounts of data into a single point (such as a data warehouse). Data sources are developed for different purposes and fulfill different functions. Therefore, it is promising to establish an efficient way for data exchange among these distributed and heterogeneous data sources. However, a dozen of data sources are designed merely for data storage, but not for data exchange.

2.1. Survey of Pathway Databases and Integration Efforts

Table 1 below shows various data integration efforts and projects for biological pathways worldwide.

Biochemical pathways	Description
BRITE	Bio molecular Relations in Information Transmission and Expression
EcoCyc/MetaCyc	Encyclopaedia of E. coli genes and metabolism; Metabolic encyclopedia
EMP	Metabolic pathways
KEGG	Kyoto encyclopaedia of genes and genomes
Biochemical Pathways	Enzyme database and link to biochemical pathway map
Interactive Fly	Biochemical pathways in Drosophila
Metabolic Pathway	Metabolic pathways of biochemistry
Molecular interaction	Kohn molecular interaction maps
Malaria parasite	Malaria Parasite metabolic pathways
aMAZE	Protein function and biochemical pathways project at EBI
PathDB	Metabolic pathway information
UM-BBD	Microbial bio catalytic reactions and biodegradation pathways primarily for xenobiotic, chemical compounds
WIT	Function assignments to genes and the development of metabolic models
THCME Medical Biochemistry	Description of several metabolic and biochemical pathways
Signaling pathways	
Apoptosis	Pathways of apoptosis at KEGG
BBID	Database of images of biological pathways, macromolecular structures, gene families, and cellular relationships
BioCarta	Several signalling pathways
BIND	The bio molecular interaction network database

CSNDB	Cell signalling networks database
GeneNet	Information on gene networks, groups of co-ordinately working genes
GeNet	Information on functional organization of regulatory gene networks
SPAD	Signalling pathway database
STKE	Pathway information
TransPath	Pathways involved in the regulation of transcription factors
Protein-protein interactions	
Blue Print	Biological interaction database
CYGD	Protein-protein interaction map at Comprehensive Yeast Genome Database
CytoScape	Visualization and analysis of biological network
DIP	Database of interacting proteins
GenMAPP	Gene Map Annotator and Pathway Profiler
GRID	The General Repository for Interaction Datasets
Proteome Bio knowledge	Biological information about proteins comprise Incyte's Proteome Bio Knowledge Library
Protein Interaction Domains	Signal transduction
Reactome	A knowledgebase of biological processes
Yeast Interaction Pathway	PathCalling Yeast Interaction Database at Curagen

Table 1. Various Data integration Efforts

Other efforts towards designing new applications for data mining and integration at the K.U.Leuven Center for Computational Systems Biology include;

- aBandApart (2007): A software to mine MEDLINE abstracts to annotate human genome at the level of cytogenic bands.
- ReModiscovery (2006): An intuitive algorithm to correlate regulatory programs with regulators and corresponding motifs to a set of co-expressed genes
- LOOP (2007): A toll to analyze ArrayCGH loop designs. ArrayCGH is a microarray technology that can be used to detect aberrations in the ploidy of DNA segments in the genome of patients with congenital anomalies.
- SynTReN (2006): A generator of synthetic gene expression data for design and analysis of structure learning algorithms.
- BlockAligner (2005): Provides an API in R to query BioMart databases such as Ensemble.
- BlockSampler (2005): Finds conserved blocks in the upstream region of sets of orthologous genes.

- M@cBETH (2005) (a Microarray Classification Benchmarking Tool on a host server): Web service offers the microarray community a simple tool for making optimal two class predictions.
- TxTGate (2004): A literature index database designed towards the summarization and analysis of groups of genes based on text.
- Endeavour is a software application for the computational prioritization of test genes based on training genes using different information sources such as MEDLINE abstracts and LocusLink textual description, gene ontology, annotation, BIND protein interactions, and Transcription Factor Binding Sites (TFBS).
- TOUCAN2 (2004): A workbench for regulatory sequence analysis on metazoan genomes: Comparative genomics detection of significant transcription factor binding sites and detection of cis-regulatory modules in sets of coexpressed/ coregulated genes.
- INCLUSive (2003): A suit of algorithms and tools for the analysis of gene expression data and the directory of cis-regulatory sequence elements.
- Adaptive Quality-Based Clustering (AQBC) (2002): AQBC is a heuristic, iterative two-step algorithm to cluster gene expression data.
- MotifSampler (2001): Finds over represented motifs in the upstream region of a set of co-regulated genes.

2.2. Types of pathways

Biological networks are studied and modeled at different description levels establishing different pathway types, For example; metabolic pathways describe the conversion of metabolites by enzyme-catalyzed chemical reactions given by their stoichiometric equations, such as the main pathways of the energy household as Glycolysis or Pentose Phosphate pathway. Another pathway type is signal transduction pathways, also known as information metabolism, explaining how cells receive, process, and responds to information from the environment. A brief description about various types of pathways is given below.

A. Metabolic Pathways describe the network of enzyme-catalyzed reactions that release energy by breaking down nutrients (catabolism) and building up the essential compounds necessary for growth (anabolism). Experimentally determined metabolic pathways have established for a few model organisms, but most metabolic pathways databases contain pathway data that has been computationally inferred from the genomes annotations. Because most genome annotations are incomplete, metabolic pathway databases contain pathway holes which can only be addressed by experiment or computational inference. A good test of a reconstructed metabolic network is to ask if it can produce the set of essential compounds necessary for growth, given a known minimal nutrient set. To solve this problem, metabolism can be represented as a bipartite directed graph, where one set of nodes represents metabolites, the other set represents biochemical reactions with labeled edges used to indicate relationships between nodes (reaction X produces metabolite Y, or metabolite Y is-consumed-by reaction X.

B. Gene Regulatory Networks describe the network of transcription factors that bind regulatory regions of specific genes and activate or repress their transcription. Gene regulatory networks or transcription networks have been found to contain recurring biochemical wiring patterns, termed network motifs, which carry out key functions. How does one find the most significant recurring network motif in a given transcriptional network? To answer this question, transcription networks can be described as directed graphs, in which nodes are genes, and edges represent transcription interactions, where a transcription factor encoded by one gene modulates and transcription rate of the second gene.

C. Signaling Pathways describe biochemical reactions for information transmission and processing. Unlike metabolic pathways that catalyze small molecule reactions, signaling pathways involve the post translational modification of proteins leading to the downstream activation of transcriptional factors. They are often formed by cascades of activated/deactivated proteins or protein complexes. Such signal transduction cascades may be seen as molecular circuits which mediate the sensing and processing of stimuli. They detect, amplify and integrate diverse external signals to generate responses, such as changes in enzyme activity, gene expression, or ion channel activity. Integration of signaling pathways poses a greater challenge than with metabolic pathways because of diversity of representation schemes for signaling. Some Signaling databases like; PATIKA [35] and INHO [36] use compound graphs to represent signaling pathways, while other object oriented databases use inheritance to establish relationships between post translational modifications of proteins.

D. Protein-Protein Interaction: In proteomic analysis, target genes are used as bait in immuno-precipitation to identify potential binding patterns in cell lysate. The higher level databases such as; KEGG [3], TRANSPATH [37], ReactomeSTKE [38], and MetaCyc [39] networks of interacting proteins with definite cellular processes including metabolism, signal transduction and gene regulation. These resources typically represent biological information in the form of individual pathway diagrams summarizing experimental results collected during years of research on particular cellular functions. Currently, no single method is capable of predicting all possible protein interactions and such integrative resources as SPRING and predictome combine multiple theoretical approaches to increase prediction accuracy and coverage. A problem with these networks is the high number of false alarms.

E. Ontology Vocabulary Mapping: Ontology provides a formal written description of a specific set of concepts and their relationships in a particular domain. GO ontology has three categories molecular function, biological process and cellular composition. Integration of signaling pathways poses a greater challenge than with metabolic pathways because of the diversity of representation schemes for signaling.

2.3. Integration issues

Biological plant pathway data integration is a multi-step process. It includes integration of various types of pathways, interactions, and gene expression. On another level, it includes various species and different databases. A hierarchical pathway data integration scheme is presented in Figures 1 and 2 below.

Each database also defines supporting evidence codes specifically defined to consider criteria for selection, however may not be explicitly illustrated and that may not be similar across various sources. This heterogeneity in evidence codes and their representation needs consideration [40]. Since the evidence code may originate as a result of experimentation or as evidence from published text, integration of the plant pathway data across databases involves standardizing the evidence code prior to the integration. The first step is to integrate the evidence codes for a given pathway across database. Biological databases are results of experiments carried out with different conditions and controls, mostly open source, and employs a variety of formats [41]. Integrating such databases is a multi-step procedure and involves handling the complexities associated with heterogeneous data integration.

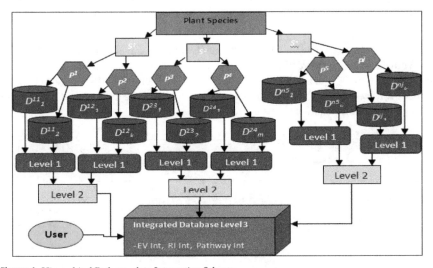

Figure 1. Hierarchical Pathway data Integration Scheme

A. Ontology Development

Since isolation of ontologies complicates data integration, so in order to use ontologies at their full potential, concepts, relations, and axioms must be shared when possible. Domain ontologies must also be anchored to an upper ontology in order to enable the sharing and reuse of knowledge.

B. Synonym Integration

While integrating information about a pathway from a database, entities require independent approach. One such entity is synonym. Each database lists a set of synonyms that need integration to configure a pool of synonyms without causing duplication. In the data integration platform developed the synonym integration has issues like avoiding duplication and accommodating number of synonyms associated with one entity. Some pathways may include two compounds with different names but having same empirical formula. In such cases integration is challenging as biologists may be further interested in reviewing the chemical structure along with the integrated output. However, almost all biological pathways are vertically extendable and can associate further details. The point here is to include all the salient features (from a biologist's standpoint) of the pathway. There is no thumb rule to define biologist's interests.

C. Evidence Codes and issues

For defining an evidence code with an entity, granularity is another variable. Depending on the database, EV may be either for an entity within a pathway such as a gene, a compound, reaction or enzyme or for the pathway itself. In other words, many databases use the same evidence code for an entire pathway and map that code to each interaction in the pathway. Others assign different EV codes to each interaction and sometimes to each compound or gene.

The Gene Ontology (GO) defines a set of thirteen EVs that assign evidence to gene function. BioCyc defines a class hierarchy structure of four basic EVs with subclasses. MetNetDB incorporates four EVs [42]. KEGG defines only one EV. Ideally, the EVs also reflect on the individual nodes within a specific pathway. Figure 2 depicts the data integration platform highlighting multiple data sources and integration based on user inputs.

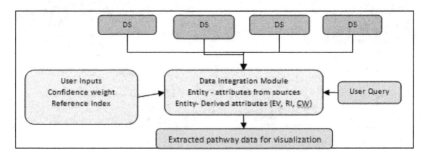

Figure 2. Data Integration Platform

1. Many databases use the same evidence code for an entire pathway and map that code to each interaction in the pathway. Others assign codes to each interaction and sometimes each compound or gene. In other words, the granularity to which we can assign an EV may be either an entity such as a gene, a compound, reaction or enzyme within or across the pathway itself. The Gene Ontology (GO) defines a set of thirteen EVs that assign evidence to gene function [43]. BioCyc defines a class hierarchy structure of four basic EVs with subclasses [17]. MetNetDB incorporates four EVs. KEGG defines only one EV. Ideally, the EVs also reflect on the individual nodes within a specific pathway.

2. Since pathway information cannot be assessed with any reliability, it is hard to assign a measure of the orrectness/authenticity to any one database. We propose assignment to be user selective to resolve the issue. To combine the information, a heuristic rule set computes the composite EVs for the integrated database. The unification can be done using any one EV code set as a key. Since each database follows their own standard, it is likely that EVs may not find a perfect match among the databases or that there may be more than one likely match. To handle these situations, two matching sets, a *perfect match* and a *likely match* are considered. The EVs to find a match for *IEP* and *ND* from GO in EV set above with those in BioCyc result in more than one likely match *{GO: IEP → BioCyc: EV1, BioCyc: EV2}.*

3. Integrated Evidence Code (EVint) for Perfect Matches: The EV codes encompass the quantitative information giving an insight into how the data was obtained. They define the conditions/ constraint associated with obtaining the data.

4. Computing the Reference Index (RIint)
   For biological databases, the pathway information is mostly inferred by the curators based on experimental, computational, literature or other evidence. The references associated with the database are mostly accounted as a measure of support for the data. We introduce a qualitative approach to associate the references supporting the pathway or organism (or compounds or reactions). The reference index *RIint* is computed using a heuristic:

   1. For *Rank = High,* Ignore *VF.*
   2. For Rank = Low, Use only VF.
   3. For all other combinations of *Rank* and *VF,* compute the average.

Citations may be a robust way of supporting the claim in a database. However, some journals are ranked over other journals and citations from those journals will be valued more than citations in other sources. To accommodate this, we associate ranks with the journals. The *Rank* specifies the order of importance of journal as designated by the user. Additionally, we classify citations based on both the journal *Rank* and the *value factor (VF).* Finally, based on the *Rank* and *VF,* the *Reference index (RI)* is computed.

3. Evidence codes integration algorithm

   Given: Set of *n* databases *{D1, D2, D3, D4,......, Dn},*
   (For illustration, only three data sources namely, Bio-Cyc, KEGG and MetNetDB are considered)
   User input: Confidence weight (CW)
   List: Evidence Codes (EVi) for the object/entity *(Ei)* among the databases *(Di),*
   for example; D1/E1 {EV1}, D2/E1 {EV2},....
   The steps below list the mapping process.

Step 1. For a given pathway/organism/entity,

   List: EV codes across the databases. (See Tables III(a) and III(b))

Assign: **Direct** = *1.0*; **Indirect** = *0.8*; **Computational** =*0.6*; **Hypothetical** = *0.5*.

Step 2. EV Unification (Rule Set –I)

BioCyc is a collection of 371 pathway/genome databases. Each pathway/genome database in the BioCyc collection describes the genome and metabolic pathways of a single organism. It considers a class hierarchy with four main classes. Since BioCyc and MetNetDB virtually use the same number of EV codes, the mapping is framed considering four major EV codes. KEGG uses only one EV for pathways namely *'manually entered from published materials'*. The EV code for KEGG to *Direct* is mapped using the rules like;

If Di = BioCyc/AraCyc/MetaCyc, and EV = EV-Exp, then Change EV = Direct

Unification of the EV codes for the databases is based on the expert knowledge. EV code mapping is done with respect to a reference data source and unified according to the set of rules above.

Step 3. Confidence Weight (*CWi*) Assignment

Researchers typically have databases that they treat as favored sources for different types of information. Since there is no precise rule for deciding which database is more correct and up to date, a user defined score, a *confidence weight (CW)* is applied. The EV mapping process is interactive and provides flexibility in choice for databases. Confidence is defined as,

> CWi = *{Very Strong, Strong, Moderate, Poor, Very Poor}*
> For example: *CW **KEGG**: Strong, CWBioCyc: Normal*

Step 4. EVint (Rule Set-II)

> Using heuristic rules, integrated EVcode is calculated.

Step 5. Decode *EVint* value

> The EV value from Step 4 is decoded using:
> $EVint = \Sigma\ (CWi^* \ EV)/|i| = x$

Step 6. Rank Index

> - Rank the journals in their order of importance.
> - Make an ordered list of journals assigning *Rank*.
> - Rank the conferences in order of their importance.
> - Make an ordered list of conferences.
> - *Assign:*
>> If the publication in not in the list, Then, *Rank = low*
>> Else, *Rank = as defined by the list*

Step 7. Value Factor *(VF)*

The *VF* measures support for the entity using the publication evidence. This is a quantitative index with a temporal function.

For t = current year, compute $VF(t) = |P(t\text{-}2)| / |P|$ where,

$|P(t\text{-}2)|$ = Number of publications in the last $(t\text{-}2)$ years for Di, and
$|P|$ = Total number of publications listed in Di.

Step 8. Reference Index $(RIint)$

- Compute RI for $\{D1,...Dn\}$ given by,
$$RIi\{t\} = f\{Rank, VF\}$$
- Compute $RIint$ for a pathway as;
$$RIint = max\{RIi\}$$

3.1. Integration models

Data integration aims to work with repositories of data from a variety of sources. As such, two databases may not provide identical information, and integrating these two databases may yield a richer resource for analysis. The conditions under which data is collected and the supporting references play a crucial role in making the analysis more meaningful. So far, the integration approaches have focused on different types of pathways. The same pathway can have different representations in different databases.

For example, a known pathway like Glycolysis is represented in different ways in KEGG and BioCyc as shown in Figure 3. A universal tool to integrate all types of pathways may not be a focus. Additionally, different databases employ various data representations that may not provide easy user access or user friendly. Figure 3(a) and 3(b) illustrate representational difference between two data sources for the same pathway. Various data integration models are defined below.

- *Syntactic Networks*: Syntactic networks adhere to the syntax of a set of words as given by the representation of the data and do not interpret the meaning associated. Syntactic heterogeneity is a result of differences in representation format of data.
- *Semantic Networks* (SN): Semantic heterogeneity is a result of differences in interpretation of the 'meaning' of data. Semantic models aim to achieve semantic interoperability, a dynamic computational capability to integrate and communicate both the explicit and implicit meanings of digital content without human intervention.
- Several features of SN make it particularly useful for integrating biological data include, ability to easily define an inheritance hierarchy between concepts in a network format, allow economic information storage and deductive reasoning, represent assertions and cause effect through abstract relationships, cluster related information for fast retrieval, and adapt to new information by dynamic modification of network structures [44]. An important feature of SN is the ease and speed to retrieve information concerning a particular concept. The use of semantic relationships ensures clustering together related concepts in a network. For example, protein synonyms, functional descriptions, coding sequences, interactions, experimental data or even relevant research articles can all be represented by semantic agents, each of which is directly linked to the corresponding protein agent.

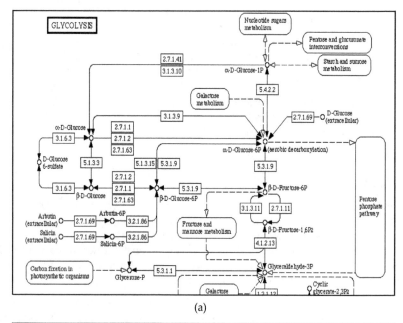

(a)

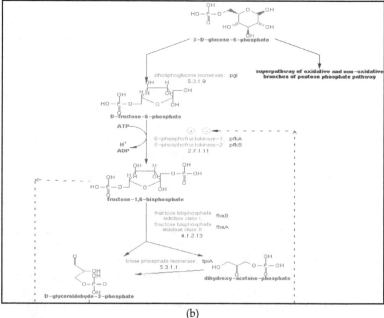

(b)

Figure 3. (a) Pathway from KEGG- Glycolysis (b) BioCyc- Glycolysis

Biological information can be retrieved effectively through simple relationship traversal starting from a query agent in the semantic network. Two approaches primarily in practice for SNs are;

1. memory-mapped data structure and
2. indexing flat files.

In the memory-mapped data structure approach, subsets of data from various sources are collected, normalized, and integrated in memory for quick access. While this approach performs actual data integration and addresses the problem of poor performance in the federated approach, it requires additional calls to traditional relational databases to integrate descriptive data. While data cleaning is being performed on some of the data sources, it is not being done across all sources or in the same place. This makes it difficult to quickly add new data sources. In the indexing flat files approach, flat text files are indexed and linked thus supporting fast query performance.

-   *Causal Models*: A causal model is an abstract model that uses cause and effect logic to describe the behaviour of a system. Ex: Expression Quantitative Trait Loci: (eQTLs) eQTL analysis is to study the relationship between genome and transcriptome. Gene expression QTLs that contain the gene encoding the mRNA are distinguished from other transacting eQTLs. eQTL mapping tries to find genomic variation to explain expression traits. One difference between eQTL mapping and traditional QTL mapping is that, traditional mapping study focuses on one or a few traits, while in most of eQTL studies, thousands of expression traits get analyzed and thousands of QTLs are declared.
-   *Context likelihood of relatedness* (CLR): It uses transcriptional profiles of an organism across a diverse set of conditions to systematically determine transcriptional regulatory interactions. *CLR* is an extension of the relevance network approach. (http://gardnerlab.bu.edu/software&tools.html). [34] Presented architecture for context-based information integration to solve semantic difference problem, defined some novel modeling primitives of translation ontology and propose an algorithm for translation.
-   *Bayes Networks (BN)*: Probabilistic graphical models that represent a set of variables and their probabilistic independencies. For example, a BN could represent the probabilistic relationships between diseases and symptoms. Given symptoms, the network can be used to compute the probabilities of the presence of various diseases. Bayes networks focus on score-based structure inference. Available heuristic search strategies include simulated annealing and greedy hill-climbing, paired with evaluation of a single random local move or all local moves at each step. [45] Bases his approach on the well-studied statistical tool of Bayesian networks [46]. These networks represent the dependence structure between multiple interacting quantities (e.g., expression levels of different genes). His approach, probabilistic in nature, is capable of handling noise and estimating the confidence in the different features of the network.
-   *Hidden Markov Models (HMM)*: HMM is a statistical model that assumes the system being modeled to be a Markov process with unknown parameters, and determines the

hidden parameters from the observable parameters. The extracted model parameters can then be used to perform further analysis, for example for pattern recognition applications. An HMM can be considered as the simplest dynamic Bayesian network. HMMs are being applied to the analysis of biological sequences, in particular DNA since 1998 [47].

3.2. Need to use open grid service architecture ogsa-dai for data access and integration

Apart from the ubiquitous call for more functionality, bioinformatics projects with commercial users/partners are very anxious about the security of their data. The issue is further complicated by the lack of coherent security models with the evolving WS-RF and WS-I specifications which OGSA-DAI now supports. This issue needs to be resolved if bioinformatics projects with commercial users/partners are not to be deterred from adopting the product despite its utility. In contrast to the diversity of its data resources, a limited range of operations on these resources is typically required. For instance, one operation is to create a study data set by aggregating data from iterative searches of remote data collections using the same taxonomy object (representing a species or other group) as the search parameter [48].

3.3. Handling the heterogeneity in data representation among databases

For biological plant pathways, various databases incorporate information about an entity/reaction/pathway to a level of detail and define their own data format. This includes information like number of fields, column label/tag, pathway name(s), etc. At the outset, common information across the tables may look limited and hard to extract mainly because of the tag or synonyms (other names) of pathway. Before proceeding for integration of a pathway across data sources following steps need to be carried out. For biological pathway integration, following needs to be considered.

- What is the aim of integration?
  To query autonomous and heterogeneous data sources through a common, uniform schema (TARGET SCHEMA).
- How will the integrated data be used?
  - Resolving various conflicts between source and target schema.
  - Offering a common interface to access integrated information.
  - Preserving the autonomy of participating systems.
  - Easily integrating data sources without major modification.
- Is it within a single data source or across sources?
- Does it support web based integration?
- Does it encompass the dynamic nature of the data?
- What are the data, source, user models, and assumptions underlying the design of integration system?

Specific data integration problems in the biological field include:

- Some biological data sources do not provide an expressive language
- Derived wrapper (operate in two modes)
  - Traditional wrapper
  - Virtual source that buffers the execution result of a local application
- Data Model Inconsistencies requires complex data transformation coding
- Data Schema Inconsistencies
- Schema matching: error-prone task
- Mapping info: systematically managed
- Domain Expert participation
- Along with the data schema consistencies there may be data level inconsistencies such as:
- Data conflict as each object has its own data type, and may be represented in different formats
- Different Query Capabilities affect the query optimization of data integration system
- Miscellaneous: Network environment, Security

File formats: For biological pathways, various data sources incorporate information about an entity/reaction/pathway to a level of detail and define their own data format. This includes information like number of fields, column label/tag, pathway name(s), etc. At the outset, common information across the tables may look limited and hard to extract mainly because of the tag or synonyms (other names) of pathway. One of the other important differences in the way these data sources are developed lies in the synonym representations. Some of the data sources limit the synonyms to 10 others may not result into may be over 40 synonyms. While we look at the data integration mechanism, if the names of the compounds do not match, then the search should be carried forward with the list of synonyms. In integrating different data bases this will take different search time. Also, since the field names (compound names) did not match, the search must unify the field names and generate a new list of synonyms.

Granularity of information: Different pathway databases may model pathway data with different levels of details. This primarily depends on the process definition. For example, one database might treat processes together as a single process, while another database might treat these as separate processes. Also, one database might include specific steps to be part of the process, while another database might not consider these steps. Additionally, the levels of details associated with a certain data base necessitate pathway data modeling with different levels of granularity. Different pathway data formats (e.g., SBML and BIND XML) have been used to represent data with different levels of details. A semantic net based approach to data integration is proposed in [49].

Heterogeneous formats: As the eXtensible Markup Language (XML) has become the lingua franca for representing different types of biological data, there has been a proliferation of semantically-overlapping XML formats that are used to represent diverse types of pathway data. Examples include the XML-derivatives KGML, SBML, CellML, PSI MI, BIND XML, and Genome Object Net XML. Efforts have been underway to translate between these formats (e.g., between PSI MI and BIND XML, and between Genome Object Net and SBML). However, the complexity of such a pair-wise translation approach increases dramatically with a growing number of different pathway data formats. To address this issue, a standard pathway data exchange format is needed. While the Resource Description framework (RDF) is an important first step towards the unification of XML formats in describing metadata (ontologies), it is not expressive enough to support formal knowledge representation [50]. To address this problem, more sophisticated XML-based ontological languages such as the Web Ontology Language (OWL) have been developed. An OWL-based pathway exchange standard, called BioPAX, has been released to the research community [51].

4. Biological Pathway Data Integration

An integration model may serve as a tool to the user for a specific type of pathway. An algorithm for integration is presented next.

Metabolic Pathways: Integrating pathways from different data sources for the same species extract similar structures in them as the first step; this step integrates vertically given pathway within a species across data sources. (Database is the variable) this includes sorting a graph $G\ (V,\ E)$ for common V's and E's in $G_i\ (V_i,\ E_i)$ and $G_j\ (V_j,\ E_j)$. In the discussion that follows, integrating pathway as the TCA cycle given by two data sources namely; *KEGG* $(D^{ij}{}_1)$ and BioCyc $(D^{ij}{}_2)$ for *E. coli K-12* is considered. For metabolic pathways the details associated with each graph include the nodes and edges as given below. For Protein-Protein interaction the nomenclature and associated fields for nodes and edges may change. However, it is possible to come up with a structure that can describe the Protein-Protein interactions or signal transduction pathways.

- *Node:* Biological Name, ID, Neighbor, Type, Context, Pathway, Data Source, PubList, SynList, empirical formula, Structure
- *Edge:* EdgeID, EdgeSource, EdgeDest, Reactiontype (Rev/ Irreversible), Data Source, Enzyme, Genes

Signal Transduction Pathways: The information contained in signal transduction pathways is not similar to the metabolic pathways. In signal transduction pathways, the interactions can be represented as a class hierarchy. Our aim is also to integrate a sample pathway like insulin from sources like KEGG, SPAD to see the performance of our algorithm. Interestingly, SPAD assigns evidence code to the edges (interactions) and KEGG assigns only one evidence code to the pathway (nodes and edges). The format of the table for integration is given above. Before integration information associated with every object (node) and edge (interactions) should be considered.

Before proceeding for integration of a pathway across data sources following steps need to be carried out.

Step 1

-    Check for the pathway name across the input pathways.

- If a synonym matches then, go to step 2 else, search for synonyms of pathway name.

Step 2

- Choose the integrated output table format as the reference (number of columns, column tag)
- Check for number of columns in the output table.
- Match each of the column names in the output table with each of the column names in the input data files,
  - if column names are same then continue, else see alternate tag for the column, and match them.
- Match order in the output table format with the inputs from different sources.
  - If the order matches, then continue, else reorder the columns as given in output table.
- Check for number of columns in the output table,
  - If the number of columns is not same, then append the table with new columns.

Step 3

- Apply EV and Integration algorithms

The notations used in our algorithm are presented next.

4.1. Notations

- $S = \{s^1, s^2, s^3, \ldots s^n\}$ is set of species.   (1)
- $P^{ij} = \{p^{i1}, p^{i2}, \ldots p^{ip}\}$ is a set of pathways within s^i (2)

Consider a tuple $(S^i, (P^{ij}, (D^{ij}_i)))$ (3)

Where, $D^{ij}_k = \{d^{ij}_1, d^{ij}_2, d^{ij}_3, \ldots d^{ij}_k\}$ is a set of 'k' data sources for (S^i, P^{ij}) (4)

- $s^1 = \{(s^1, p^{1j} (D^{1j}_k)\} = \{(s^1, p^{1j}, d^{1j}_1) (s^1, p^{1j}, d^{1j}_2), \ldots (s^1, p^{1j}, d^{1j}_k)\}$ for 'k' databases,

For example; s^1: E.coli; p^{1j}: TCA Cycle; d^{1j}_1= BioCyc, d^{1j}_2= KEGG.

Then, the tuple $(v^{11}_{1n}, e^{11}_{1m})$ gives (node, edge) in Biocyc for TCA cycle in E.coli, and the tuple $(v^{11}_{2p}, e^{11}_{2p})$ gives (node, edge) in KEGG for TCA cycle in E.coli

- $s^2 = \{(s^2, p^{2j} (D^{2j}_k)\} = \{(s^2, p^{2j}, d^{2j}_1), (s^2, p^{2j}, d^{2j}_2), \ldots, (s^2, p^{2j}, d^{2j}_r)\}$ for 'r' databases,

  For example; s^2: Arabidopsis; p^{2j}: TCA Cycle; d^{2j}_1= BioCyc, d^{2j}_2= AraCyc

  Then, the tuple $(v^{22}_{1p}, e^{22}_{1p})$ gives the (node, edge) in AraCyc for TCA cycle in Arabidopsis, and the tuple $(v^{22}_{2p}, e^{22}_{2p})$ gives the (node, edge) in KEGG for TCA cycle in Arabidopsis.

  Each pathway p^{ij} for a d^{ij}_k is given by a graph $G(V^{ij}_k, E^{ij}_k)$, where,

- $P^{ij}_k = G(V^{ij}_k, E^{ij}_k)$ represents Pathway 'j' from k^{th} datasourcesS for species i'…   .(5)

Where, $V^{ij}_k = \{v^{ij}_{k1}, v^{ij}_{k2}, \ldots v^{ij}_{kn}\}$ = set of nodes in d^{ij}_k.   (6)

$E^{ij}_k = \{e^{ij}_{k1}, e^{ij}_{k2}, \ldots e^{ij}_{km}\}$ = set of edges in d^{ij}_k.   (7)

- *SynList {pathway name} = SynList {P^{ij}}*

- ***SynList {entity name} = SynList {v^{1j}_{kn}}***
- ***EV^{ij}_k*** = {EV^{ij}_{k1}, ... EV^{ij}_{kh}} set of '*h*' EV Codes for {s^i, p^{ij}, d^{ij}_k }, for example;
  - EV^{1j}_1= {Set of EVcodes given by Biocyc for E.coli for TCA cycle}
  - EV^{1j}_2= {Set of EV codes given by KEGG for E.coli for TCA cycle}
  - EV^{2j}_3= {Set of EV codes given by AraCyc for Arabidopsis for TCA cycle}
  - EV^{2j}_2= {Set of EV codes given by KEGG for Arabidopsis for TCA cycle}
- ***RI^{ij}_k***: Reference index for a database d^{ij}_k
- ***RI^{ij}_{int}***: Reference index for the integrated pathway
- ***CW^{ij}_k***: Confidence weight for a database d^{ij}_k
- ***CW^{ij}_{int}***: Confidence weight of the integrated pathway p^{ij} within a species
- ***V^{ij}_{int}***: Integrated node table for a species S^i, for a pathway p^{ij}
- ***E^{ij}_{int}***: Integrated edge table for a species S^i, for a pathway p^{ij}
- (v^{1j}_{kn}, e^{ij}_{km}) = (node '*n*', edge '*m*') in d^{1j}_k of s^1 for p^{1j};
- ***ATT*** {(v^{1j}_{kn} ,(A)}= {v^{1j}_{kn}, (A_1, A_2, A_3, A_4, ...A_s)} = set of attributes of the node v^{1j}_{kn}
- ***ATT*** {(e^{ij}_{km}, (B)} ={(e^{ij}_{km}, (B_1, B_2, B_3, ... B_t)} = set of attributes of edge e^{ij}_{km}
- ***DATT*** {v^{1j}_{kn} ,(δA)} = set of derived attributes of the node v^{1j}_{kn} (EV_i, CW_i, RI_i)
- ***DATT*** {e^{1j}_{kn} ,(δB)}= set of derived attributes of the edge e^{1j}_{kn} (EV_i, CW_i, RI_i)
- $δV^{ij}_k$ = Set of derived node attributes for Integrated pathway {EV_{int}, CW_{int}, RI_{int}}
- $δE^{ij}_k$= Set of derived edge attributes for Integrated pathway {EV_{int}, CW_{int}, RI_{int}}
- ***V^{ij}_{int}*** = {Σ ***V^{ij}_k*** } for k= 1 to n
- ***E^{ij}_{int}***= {Σ ***E^{ij}_k***} for k= 1 to n
- ***P^{ij}_{int}*** = Integrated pathway from multiple DSs = {Σ ***P^{ij}_k*** } for k=1 to n

4.2. Biological Pathway Data Integration Algorithm

Following selections and inputs are defined by the user.

- User selected inputs: Species, Pathway, Data sources/database
- User inputs: Confidence assigned to each database
- User defined filters (**UDF**) for entities like substrate nodes, H_2O, CO_2 etc. for integrated pathway [P^{ij}_{int}= G (V_{int}, E_{int})],

Step 1.

> For each user selected pathway P^{ij} *for a species s^i*

List D^{ij} (d^{1j}_1,... d^{nj}_k),   ***(KEGG, BioCyc, MetNetDB etc)***

Step 2. **Define** rules to classify the interactions, for example;

- If the pathway is *signal transduction*, then use the *classifier (Table 1)*for interactions
- If the pathway is *metabolic*, then *reaction* is a general representation of the interaction
  Sort (d^{1j}_1,... d^{nj}_k) according to species (s^i,d^{ij}_1), (s^i,d^{ij}_1) etc.
  Generate a set of (nodes, edges) from all the input data sources {(V^{ij}, E^{ij})} = {(V^{ij}_1, E^{ij}_1), (V^{ij}_2, E^{ij}_2)..... (V^{ij}_s, E^{ij}_s)}

where, $V^{ij}_k = \{v^{ij}_{k1}, v^{ij}_{k2}, \ldots v^{ij}_{kt}\}$ and $E^{ij}_1 = \{e^{ij}_{k1}, e^{ij}_{k2}, \ldots e^{ij}_{ku}\}$

Step 3.

For $k = 1, \ldots, q$ ($d^{1j}_1, \ldots d^{1j}_k$),
  For $s = 1, \ldots, n$, and $q = 1, \ldots m$,
        List ATT *$\{(v^{1j}_{ks}, (A)\}$*
        List ATT *$\{(e^{ij}_{kq}, (B)\}$*
        Select *$v^{ij}_{k1} \in V^{ij}_k \subset d^{1j}_k$*
        For all *$p = 1$ to n*
        Check *for $v^{ij}_{k, 1} \in V^{ij}_p$* (node name match across data sources)
        If *YES*, then **Apply** *EV integration algorithm*
                Generate **DATT** *$\{v^{1j}_{kn}, (\delta A)\}$,* **DATT** *$\{e^{1j}_{kn}, (\delta B)\}$,*
      Else, *For $p = 1$ to n,*
                For $t = 1, z$
                Check if *$v^{ij}_{k1} \in$* **SynList** *$\{v^{ij}_{p,t}\}$* (node name(A) with Synlist(B))
                If YES, then Apply EV integration algorithm,
                Generate **DATT** *$\{v^{1j}_{kn}, (\delta A)\}$,* **DATT** *$\{e^{1j}_{kn}, (\delta B)\}$,*
    Else,
                Check if **SynList** *$\{v^{ij}_{k,1}\}$* has a match with *$v^{ij}_{p,t}$*
                If YES, then Apply EV integration Algorithm
    Else,
                Check if **SynList** *$\{v^{ij}_{k,1}\}$* has a match with **SynList** *$\{v^{ij}_{p,t}\}$*
                If $v^{ij}_{k,1} = v^{ij}_{p,l}$ is TRUE,
                Then,
                Include *$v^{ij}_{k, 1}$* with the matched node name *$v^{ij}_{k-1, p} \in V^{ij}_{k-1}$*
                Compute *$(\delta V^{ij}_k, \delta E^{ij}_k)$*

This is the node name for the integrated database for the species. **Level 1

        Generate SynListInt = *{* **SynList** *$(v^{ij}_{k, 1})$* U **Synlist** *$(v^{ij}_{p,l})$U…}* without duplication
        Associate DOI (date of integration)
        Generate *P^{ij}_{int}*

$P^{ij}_{int} = \{\Sigma\ P^{ij}_k\}$ *for $k=1$ to n* $= [\{\ V^{ij}_{int}, E^{ij}_{int}\} + \{\ \Sigma\ \delta V^{ij}_{kt}, \Sigma\ \delta E^{ij}_k\}$ *for $k=1$ to n* $]$ *at $t = t1$*

   $= \Sigma\ \{ATT\ [(v^{1j}_{kn}, (A)]\}, ATT\ [(e^{ij}_{km}, (B)]\} + \Sigma\ \{DATT\ \{v^{1j}_{kn}, (\delta A), DATT\ \{e^{1j}_{kn}, (\delta B)\}$*for*

all n, m $\{\delta V^{ij}_k\ \delta E^{ij}_k\}$

Step 4.

        Repeat *Step 2-3 for $e^{ij}_k \in E^{ij}_k$ in ($d^{ij}_1, \ldots d^{ij}_k$), for p^{ij}*
        Include information associated with the edge, as given by 'edges' such as reaction, enzyme, by products and substrates along with attributes like evidence, reference publications, context etc.
** Outputs E^{ij}_{int} table for s^i using ($d^{1j}_1, \ldots d^{1j}_k$), with EV^{ij}_{int}, CW^{ij}_{int} and RI^{ij}_{int}. **Level 1.** **

Step 5.

Generate integrated pathway by consolidating outputs $G(V^{ij}_{int}, E^{ij}_{int})$ for s^i

Step 6.

For $i = 1,...n$
Repeat steps 2- 4 to integrate P^{ij} for all species s^i
** This generates Table $(V^i_{int}, E^i_{int}) = \{(V^{ij}_{int}, E^{ij}_{int})$ U $(V^{ji}_{int}, E^{ji}_{int})U...\}$ for S^i, for all $i = 1, ..n)$, for a p^{ij}. Level 2***

Step 7.

For $(j = 1,....p)$
Integrate for all P^{ij}
This generates output table $(V_{int}, E_{int}) = (V^j_{int}, E^j_{int})$ U (V^k_{int}, E^k_{int}) U....for all $(j = 1,....p)$. Level 3*

Step 8.

Apply UDF (User defined filter)

5. Querying Integrated Pathway

Once the data integration is accomplished, extracting information from the integrated data will be of interest to the biologist. There are various mechanisms to extract information from the integrated database generated. Some of these are described below.

Granular computing with semantic network structure captures the abstraction and incompleteness associated with biological plant pathway data. It is inspired by the ways in which humans granulate information and reason with coarse grained information. The three basic concepts underlying the human cognition are granulation, organization, and causation. Granulation involves decomposition of whole into parts, organization involves integration of parts into whole, and causation involves associations of cause and effects. The fundamental issues with granular computing are granulation of the universe, description of granules, and relationships between granules. The basic ideas of crisp information granulation have appeared in related fields, such as interval analysis, quantization, rough set theory, Demster Shafer theory of belief functions, divide and conquer, cluster analysis, machine learning, data bases and many others. Granules may be induced as a result of 1) equivalence of attribute values, 2) similarity of attribute values, and define the granules 3) equality of attribute value. We use granules for defining the user queries associated with the integrated pathway. Based on user (biologist) choice, granules can be defined to view the integrated pathway. This provides flexibility to the biologist for using the information.

Previous approaches towards metabolic network reconstruction have used various algorithmic methods such as name-matching in IdentiCS [52] and using EC-codes in metaSHARK [53] to link metabolic information to genes. The AUtomatic Transfer by Orthology of Gene Reaction Associations for Pathway Heuristics (AUTOGRAPH) method

[54] uses manually curated metabolic networks, orthologue and their related reactions to compare predicted gene-reaction associations.

Arrendondo [55] Proposes to develop a process for the continuous improvement of the inference system used, which is applicable to any such data mining application. It involves the comparison of several classifiers like Support Vector Machines (SVMs), Human Expert generated Fuzzy, and Genetic Algorithm (GA) generated Fuzzy and Neural Networks using various different training data models. In his approach, all classifiers were trained and tested with four different data sets: three biological and a synthetically generated mixture data set. The obtained results showed a highly accurate prediction capability with the mixture data set providing some of the best and most reliable results.

6. Conclusion

Biological database integration is a challenging task as the databases are created all over the world and updated frequently. For biological data sources that may be derived from an earlier existing data source, it is also important to identify the evidence of the data source represented by the evidence code, to be included as a candidate for integration. In most data integration algorithms the user does not participate thus leading to an integrated data source with any effective utility towards analysis.

Large scale integration of pathway databases promises to help biologists gain insight into the deep biological context of a pathway. In this chapter, we presented algorithms that help user to select their choice of data sources and apply Evidence code algorithm to compute an integrated EV code and RI for the pathway data of interest. The ultimate goal is to generate a large-scale composite database containing the entire metabolic network for an organism. This qualitative approach includes aspects like user confidence scores for databases for mapping EV and generating RI for a given pathway. For the TCA pathway results show that generating such a mapping is helpful in visualizing the integrated database that highlights the common entities as well as the specifics of each database. As the database confidence weight selection is user specific, the integration yields different results for different users for the same database which will allow users to explore the effects of different hypotheses on the overall network. Once the integrated evidence code is generated, then data integration algorithm is applied to get the integrated pathway data. To best attempt integration of such data it is imperative to include user participation as user mostly identifies the associations and behavior of various compounds, reactions, genes in a given biological pathway leading to significant diagnosis.

Author details

Shubhalaxmi Kher
Electrical Engineering, Arkansas State University, USA

Jianling Peng
Samuel Roberts Noble Foundation, USA

Eve Syrkin Wurtele
Department of Genetics, Development and Cell Biology, Iowa State University, USA

Julie Dickerson
Electrical and Computer Engineering, Iowa State University, USA

7. References

[1] Akula, S.; Miriyala, R.; Thota, H.; Rao, A.; Gedela, S. Techniques for Integrating –omics Data, Bioinformation, Views and Challenges, 2009.

[2] Saccharomyces genome database. http://www.yeastgenome.org/

[3] KEGG: Kyoto Encyclopedia of Genes and Genomes. http://www.genome.jp/kegg/

[4] TAIR- AraCyc: http://www.arabidopsis.org/biocyc/

[5] Thimm, O; Blasing, O; Gibon, Y; Nagel, A; Meyer, S; Kruger, P; Selbig, J; Muller, L; Rhee, S; and Stitt, M. MAPMAN: a user driven tool to display genomics data sets onto diagrams of metabolic pathways and other biological processes, The Plant journal (2004) 37, pp 914-939. http://www.uky.edu/~aghunt00/PLS620/papers.htm/ Systems%20approaches%20copy/MAPMAN.pdf

[6] BIND: Biomolecular Interaction Network Database
http://metadatabase.org/wiki/BIND_-_Biomolecular_Interaction_Network_Database

[7] Bajic VB, Veronika M, Veladandi PS, Meka A, Heng MW, Rajaraman K, Pan H, Swarup S. Dragon Plant Biology Explorer. A text-mining tool for integrating associations between genetic and biochemical entities with genome annotation and biochemical terms list, Plant Physiol. 2005 Aug; 138(4):1914-25.

[8] Pandey R, Guru R K, Mount D W. Pathway Miner: extracting gene association networks from molecular pathways for predicting the biological significance of gene expression microarray data, Bioinformatics. 2004 Sep 1;20(13):2156-8. Epub 2004 May 14.

[9] RegulonDB database: Escheichia Coli k-12 transcriptional network.
http://regulondb.ccg.unam.mx/

[10] PlantCare a database. http://bioinformatics.psb.ugent.be/webtools/plantcare/html/

[11] PLACE: a database of Plant Cis-acting regulatory netowrk.
http://www.dna.affrc.go.jp/PLACE/

[12] EPD: Eukaryotic promoter database. http://epd.vital-it.ch/

[13] TRRD: transcription regulatory regions database
http://wwwmgs.bionet.nsc.ru/mgs/gnw/trrd/

[14] Athamap: http://www.athamap.de/

[15] TRANSFAC: http://www.gene-regulation.com/pub/databases.html/

[16] Friedman N, Linial, M; Nachman,I; and Pe'er, D. Using Bayesian Networks to Analyze Expression Data, Journal of computational biology, Volume 7, Numbers 3/4, 2000, pp. 601-620.

[17] Schadt, et.al, *An Integrative Genomics Approach to Infer Causal Associations Between Gene Expression and Disease, Nature Genetics, vol.37, number 7, July 2005, pp, 710-717.*

[18] The EMBL Nucleotide Sequence Database (http://www.ebi.ac.uk/embl/).

[19] Liu, Y.; Wang, Y.; Liu, Y.;, Tan, Z. Data Integration of Bioinformatics Database Based on Web Services, International Journal of Web Applications, Volume 1, Number 3, 2009.

[20] UCLA-DOE Institute for Genomics and Proteomics. http://dip.doe-mbi.ucla.edu/dip/Main.cgi

[21] IntAct: open source database system and analysis tools for molecular interaction data.http://www.ebi.ac.uk/intact/

[22] GRID: http://www.moldiscovery.com/soft_grid.php/

[23] Zanzoni, A. Montecchi-Palazzi, L. Quondam, M. Ausiello, G. Helmer-Citterich, M. Cesareni, G. *MINT: A Molecular INTeraction database. Elsevier FEBS Letters, 2002, Volume 513, Issue 1, Pages 135-140.*

[24] Coessens B. et.al, *INCLUSive: A Web Portal and Service Registry for Microarray and Regulatory Sequence Analysis, Nucleic AciDS research, 2003, vol. 31, No.13. pp. 3468-3470.* http://tomcatbackup.esat.kuleuven.be/inclusive/

[25] Achard, F.; Vaysseix, G.; Barillot, E. XML, Bioinformatics, and Data Integration, Bioinformatics Review, Evry, France, 2001, pp. 115-125.

[26] Pathway Data List. http://cbio.mskcc.org/prl

[27] Hsing, M., Cherkasov, A. Integration of Biological Data with Semantic Networks, Current Bioinformatics, 2006, 1 000-000.

[28] Chung, M., Lim, M., Bae, M., Park, S. Customized Biological Database Integration for cDNA Microarray, RECOMB 2005, Research in Computational and Molecular Biology, Cambridge, 2005.

[29] Gopalcharyulu, P. Lindfors, E. et.al. Data integration and visualization system for enabling conceptual biology, BioInformatics, Vol.21, Suppl 1 2005, pp. i177-i185.

[30] Rzhetsky, A et.al, GeneWays: A System for Extracting, Analyzing, Visualizing and Integrating Molecular Pathway Data, Journal of Bioinformatics, 2004, 43-53.

[31] Zucker, J.,Luciano, J., Brandes, A. Lin, X. Semantic Aggregation Integration and Inference: Three case studies, ISMB 2005.

[32] Hu, Z., Mellor, J., Wu, J., Yamada, T., Holloway, D., DeLisi, C. VisANT: Data integrating visual framework for biological networks and modules, Nucleic AciDS research, 2005 vol. 33.

[33] Zhang Z.; Bajic, V.; Yu, J.; Cheung, K.; Townsend, J. Data Integration in Bioinformatics: Current Efforts and Challenges. Bioinformatics: Trends and Methodologies, Intech, 2011.

[34] Zhang, D. and Jing, L., *Context based Numerical information, IEEE conference on E-commerce Technology 2005*Arredondo, T., Seeger, M., Dombrovskaia, L., Avarias, J., Calderón, F., Candel, D., Muñoz, F., Latorre, V., Agulló, L., Cordova, M., and Gómez, L.: "Bioinformatics Integration Framework for Metabolic Pathway Data-Mining". In: Ali, M., Dapoigny, R. (eds): Innovations in Applied Artificial Intelligence. Lecture Notes in Artificial Intelligence, Vol. 4031. Springer-Verlag, Berlin (2006) pp. 917-926.

[35] PATIKA: http://www.iam.metu.edu.tr/research/groups/compbio/PATIKA_METU04.pdf

[36] INHO: http://www.inoh.org/

[37] TRANSPATH. http://www.ncbi.nlm.nih.gov/pubmed/12519957

[38] ReactomeSTKE. http://stke.sciencemag.org/

[39] MetaCyc. http://metacyc.org/

[40] Kher, S; Jianling Peng; SyrkinWurtele, E.; Dickerson, J. A Symbolic computing approach to evidence code mapping for biological data integration and subjective analysis for reference associations for metabolic pathways, Annual Meeting of the North American Fuzzy Information Processing Society, 2008, NAFIPS 2008. NY 2008. pp. 1-6.

[41] Kher, S; Dickerson, J; Rawat N. Biological pathway data integration trends, techniques, issues and challenges: A survey, Nature and biologically inspired computing, NaBIC 2010, Second World Congress, Fukuoka, Japan, 2010, pp.177 – 182.

[42] MetNetDB. http://www.metnetdb.org/MetNet_db.htm

[43] Karp, P. D., Paley, S., Krieger, C. J. An Evidence Ontology for Use in Pathway/Genome DS, Pacific Symposium on Biocomputing 2004, pp. 190-201, Singapore Bounsaythip, C., Lindfors, E., Gopalacharyulu, P., Hollmen, J., and Oresic, M. *Network Based Representation of Biological Data for Enabling Context Based Mining, Bioinformatics, vol.21, suppl 1. 2005, pp. 177-185.*

[44] Newman, M. E. J and Leicht, E. A *Mixture Models and Exploratory Analysis in Networks, Physics, May 2007.*

[45] Pearl. J. (2000) *Causality: Models, Reasoning, and Inference.*Cambridge University Press, 2000.

[46] Pearl, J. (1988). *Probabilistic Reasoning in Intelligent Systems: Networks of Plausible Inference.* San Mateo, CA, USA: Morgan Kaufmann Publishers.

[47] Christopher Nemeth, STOR-I, Hidden Markov Models with Applications to DNA Sequence Analysis.

[48] Crompton, S.; Matthews, B.; Gray, A.; Jones, A.; White, R. Data Integration in Bioinformatics Using OGSA-DAI, In Proceedings of Fourth All Hands Meeting, 2005.

[49] Cheung Kei-hoi; Qi, P; Tuck,D; Krauthammer,M. A Semantic Web Approach to Biological Pathway Data Reasoning and Integration, Elsevier Vol. 4, issue 3, Sep 2006, pp. 207-215.

[50] RDF-OWL. http://www.w3.org/RDF/

[51] BioPAX: http://www.biopax.org/

[52] Sun, J. and Zeng, A. , IdentiCS – Identification of coding sequence and *in silico* reconstruction of the metabolic network directly from unannotated low-coverage bacterial genome sequence, *BMC Bioinformatics* 2004, 5:112 doi:10.1186/1471-2105-5-112

[53] Pinney, J.W., Shirley, M.W., McConkey, G.A., Westhead, D.R. (2005) MetaSHARK: software for automated metabolic network prediction from DNA sequence and is application to the genomes of *Plasmodium falciparum* and *Eimeria tenella, Nucleic Acids Research*, 33, 1399-1409.

[54] Notebaart, R. A., F. H. van Enckevort, C. Francke, R. J. Siezen, and B. Teusink. 2006. Accelerating the reconstruction of genome-scale metabolic networks. BMC Bioinformatics 7:296

[55] Arredondo, T., Seeger, M., Dombrovskaia, L., Avarias, J., Calderón, F., Candel, D., Muñoz, F., Latorre, V., Agulló, L., Cordova, M., and Gómez, L.: "Bioinformatics Integration Framework for Metabolic Pathway Data-Mining". In: Ali, M., Dapoigny, R.(eds): Innovations in Applied Artificial Intelligence. Lecture Notes in Artificial Intelligence, Vol. 4031. Springer-Verlag, Berlin (2006) p. 917-926

Chapter 3

Systemic Approach to the Genome Integration Process of Human Lentivirus

Felipe García-Vallejo and Martha Cecilia Domínguez

Additional information is available at the end of the chapter

1. Introduction

The human genome is one of the most complex molecular structures ever seen in nature. Its extraordinary information content has revealed a surprising mosaicims between coding and non-coding sequences [1-4]. This highly regionalized structure introduces complex patterns for understanding the gene structure and repetitive DNA sequence composition providing a new scenario to study biological process such as Lentivirus cDNA integration into host genome. In the field of genome analysis, bioinformatics provides the key connection between all different forms of data gathered by new high-throughput techniques such as systematic sequencing, expression arrays, and high throughput screenings among others. Although the success of bioinformatics in the genome analysis is undeniable, in some cases has complicated the relationship of computation with experimental biology. There is a need to attend to our pressing needs of bioinformatics applications without forgetting other, perhaps less evident but equally important, aspects of computation in biology.

The study of particular systems is the source of inspiration that guides the formation of general ideas from specific cases to general principles. Therefore the systemic approach extends towards the study of fundamental biological questions, such as gene assembly, protein folding and the nature of functional specificity. Such issues extend beyond the current perception of bioinformatics as a support discipline and address aspects of biological complexity, including the simulation of molecular interaction networks.

2. An overview to human genome

The genome coding regions are defined, in part, by an alternative series of motifs responsible for a variety of functions that take place on the DNA and RNA sequences, such as, gene regulation, RNA transcription, RNA splicing, and DNA methylation. For example, sequencing of the human genome revealed a controversial number of interrupted genes (25,000-32,000) with their regulatory sequences [1, 2] representing about 2% of the genome. These genes are immersed in a giant sea of different types of non-coding sequences which make up around 98% of the genome. The non-coding regions are characterized by many kinds of repetitive DNA sequences, where almost 10.6% of the human genome consists of Alu sequences, a type of SINE (short interspersed elements) sequence [3]. [Alu] elements are not randomly distributed throughout the genome but rather are biased toward gene-rich regions [5]. They can act as insertional mutagens and the vast majority appears to be genetically inert (6). LINES, MIR, MER, LTRs, DNA transposons, and introns are other kinds of noncoding sequences, which together conform about 86% of the genome. In addition, some of these sequences are overlapped one to another, for example, the CpG islands (CGI), which complicates analysis of the genomic landscape. In turn, each chromosome is characterized by some particular properties of structure and function.

3. Human lentiviral integration

The two closely related human lentiviruses HIV-1 and HIV-2 are responsible for the 21th century AIDS pandemic [7-9]. Most current therapeutic approaches use combinations of antiviral drugs that inhibit activities of viral enzymes such as reverse transcriptase, protease and integrase; nevertheless none of those have succeeded in controlling infection [10-12]. One option to overcome the problem is to explore new therapies that include the study of the integration dynamics of human Lentiviruses because it would permit to understand the underpinnings behinds of alterations of cellular homeostasis when a cell is infected [13]. Additionally, analysis of integration process is important in HIV-induced disease and in Lentivirus-based gene therapy [14].

Integration is a crucial step in the life cycle of retrovirus permitting the incorporation of viral cDNA into the host genome [15-17]. cDNA integration is mediated by the virally encoded integrase enzyme and other viral and cellular proteins in a molecular complex called the pre-integration complex (PIC) [18]. One cellular factor involved in HIV targeting is the lens epithelium-derived growth factor (LEDGF) [19, 20], which binds to both HIV-1 integrase and chromatin, tethering the viral integration machinery to chromatin [21]. HIV-1 integration has been extensively studied using a wide array of molecular biology, biochemistry and structural biology approaches [22]. However, is critical to directly identify the viral distribution inside human genome in order to understand at genomic level the relationship between the composition and topology of chromatin and the target site selection.

As shown by previous studies, the preferences in target site selection for integration are not entirely random [23-26]; being pronounced favored and disfavored chromosomal regions which differ among retroviruses [27]. These preferential regions of host genomes are characterized by having a high frequency of integrational events, as known as "hotspot" and are distributed along the genome of host cell [28, 29]. In HIV-1, most of proviruses are localized into transcriptionally active regions not only in exons and introns, but also in sequences around start transcription sites [30, 31].

An additional related study performed by Felice et al, 2009 [32] compared and contrasted the chromosomal integration patterns between gamma retrovirus (Moloney Leukemia virus, MLV) and Lentivirus (human immunodeficiency virus type 1, HIV-1), finding that gamma-retroviral, but not lentiviral vectors, integrate in genomic regions enriched in cell-type specific subsets of transcription factors binding sites (TFBSs), independently from their relative position with respect to genes and transcription start sites. Therefore, is proposed that TFBSs could be differential genomic determinants of retroviral target site selection in the human genome.

Several *in vitro* and *in vivo* studies have shown that HIV-1 integrate predominantly in active transcription units and in genome zones with high gene density, high frequency of Alu elements, low content of CpG islands and open chromatin regions [33]. Notwithstanding this evidence, the identification of particular characteristics of local chromatin that facilitate integration in a wider genomic manner still remains to be elucidated.

The objective of the this chapter is to show the main results that our group of investigation have obtained of statistically testing those genomic variables that define a preferred genomic environment for human lentiviral integration and localize them in specific chromosome loci; moreover in the construction of gene/protein interaction networks among those cellular genes located around several Lentivirus integration sites in naturally infected humans as a systemic approach to better understand the lentiviral integration process.

To test our hypothesis we conducted *in silico* studies of the integration profile in the genomic DNA of peripheral blood mononuclear cells (PBMCs) and macrophages for both human Lentiviruses (HIV-1 and HIV-2) in a window size analysis of 100K. The statistical analyses included several genomic variables such as the chromosomal loci, the numbers of CpG Island, protein coding genes, transcripts and also the distribution of SINEs, LINEs, LTRs and others; moreover the exploration genomic regions in which epigenetics mechanisms would be associated with the integration process. Together, the results allow us to propose common genomic environments that favor the target chromatin zones for both human Lentiviruses.

4. Data mining and statistical analyses

A total of 352 human genome sequences flanking the 5′LTR of human Lentiviruses (176 sequences of HIV-1 [27] and 176 of HIV-2 [33] were obtained from GenBank (NCBI) under accession numbers: CL529260 to CL529766 (HIV-1) and DQ632388 to DQ632563 (HIV-2). Using the BLAST algorithm (NCBI; *http://blast.ncbi.nlm.nih.gov/Blast.cgi*), the sequences were aligned to the draft human genome (hg18) and those that met the following criteria were considered authentic integration sites: (i) contained the terminal 3′ end of the HIV-1 or HIV-2 LTR; (ii) had matching genomic DNA within five bp of the end of the viral LTR; (iii) had at least 95% homology to human genomic sequence across the entire sequenced region; (iv) matched a single human genetic locus with at least 95% homology across the entire sequenced region (v) had minimum size of 50 bp.

BLAST of NCBI and the BLAT algorithm of the Genome Browser (University of California, Santa Cruz, Human Genome Project) (*http://www.genome.ucsc.edu/*) were used to obtain information about coding protein genes (RefSeq), transcripts, CpG islands and repetitive elements. Additional genomic information included molecular process and molecular function, was obtained from Gene Ontology (GO) (*http://www.geneontology.org/index.shtml*), GenCard   (*http://www.genecards.org/cgi-bin/carddisp.pl*)   and   Gene   Entrez (*http://www.ncbi.nlm.nih.gov/ncbi/geneentrez*). The chromosomal localization of the HIV-1 and HIV-2 proviruses was identified using the G pattern banding of each chromosome, as proposed by the Paris Conference (1971) [35], with updating of 850 times resolution. As the highest number of HIV-1 and HIV-2 proviruses was recorded on chromosome 17, an extensive characterization of its chromatin structure was performed including the genomic information available in several platforms of the Genome Browser: shows the CpG islands and distribution of its methylation; of histone H3 in the Lysine 4 and 27 methylation data obtained from ENCODE Histone modification by University of Washington CHIP-seq; Nucleosoma occupancy probabilities from A375 by Washington University and DNase1 hypersensitivity (ENCODE University of Washington) in GM12878 cells. All statistical analyses were performed using STATISTICA 7 [35]. The Mann-Whitney test (Wilcoxon rank) was used to establish differences between HIV-1 and HIV-2 chromosomal integration. Differences in function, molecular process and cell localization were analyzed using the t-test for independent samples. The Kolgomorov-Smirnov test was used for determining normality of data. In order to avoid an erroneous significance level for multiple comparisons a Bonferroni correction test was applied. To calculate the significant association among CpG numbers, genes numbers and integrations multiple regression analyses were performed. CpG numbers and genes per Mpb per chromosomes were determined from the NCBI and Ensemble databases (update 2010).

5. Patterns of provirus distribution

No significant differences were observed in the integration lymphocytic profiles between HIV-1 and HIV-2 ($p>0.05$, Mann-Whitney test). The integrational events for both human Lentiviruses were recorded in all chromosomes except the Y (figure 1). However, significant differences between the number of HIV-1 and HIV-2 provirus were observed for chromosomes 4, 8, 9, 11 and 16 ($p<0.05$, X^2 test). Most of the total integrations (39/352) occurred in chromosome 17 (figure 1). A tendency to a differential distribution of provirus towards telomeric and subtelomeric regions of the most of human chromosomes was observed. In this sense, other authors showed that centromeric alphoid repeat regions are disfavored as integration sites [36]. Although proviruses were observed in all chromosomes, we identified some chromatin regions with only HIV-1 integrations in chromosomes 4, 6 and 9 and only HIV-2 in chromosome 21.

5.1. Functional characterization of genes flanking integration sites

The ontology of genes hosting HIV integrations events were analyzed using G.O (Gene Ontology from NCBI). 83% (146/176) of HIV-1 and 77% (135/176) of HIV-2 integrations occurred close to chromatin regions containing protein coding genes (p>0.05, t-student test). In a 100Kb extension of chromatin that harbored both HIV-1 and HIV-2 proviruses no differences were observed for the gene functional categories (p>0.05, Bonferoni´s correction). According to molecular function, 46% of HIV-1 integrations and 57% of HIV-2 were associated with molecular binding, while 19% and 18% respectively occurred in regions that code for genes associated with enzymatic function (figure 2a). Otherwise an exploring about the biological process revealed a preferential integration in a collection of genes involved in metabolism and gene expression for HIV-1 (36%) and HIV-2 (37%) (p>0.05, Bonferoni´s correction) (figure 2b).

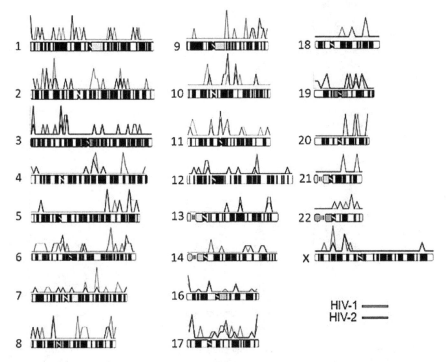

Figure 1. Chromosomal loci where 352 HIV-1 and HIV-2 cDNA have integrated into the human genome. Localization of chromosomal sequences matching both lentivirus are indicated in the graphics. Upper for each chromosome. Blue lines identify HIV-2 integrations and red lines identify HIV-1 integrations.

5.2. Distribution of the repetitive elements flanking integration sites

A low number of repetitive elements including SINEs, LINEs and LTRs were identified associated with provirus in an extension of 100Kb of flanking host chromatin. In general, there were no differences in the distribution of repetitive elements categories (SINEs, LINEs and LTRs) between HIV-1 and HIV-2 integrations (p>0.05, X² test). Our results showed that both lentiviruses had a preferential integration close to Alu elements which correspond to SINEs. Within LINEs, differences among L1, L2 and L3 were recorded. The other class of repetitive elements like LTR, simple repeats and low complexity represented a minor proportion of the integration associated chromatin (figure 3).

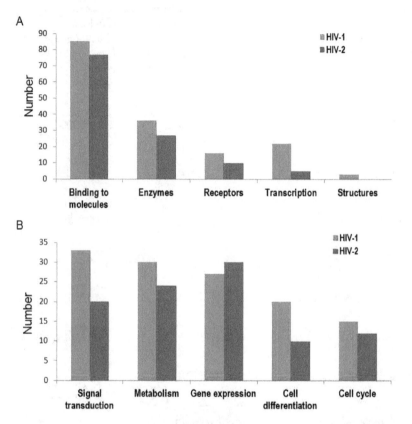

Figure 2. Functional characterization of the coding protein genes located in genome regions around 100 kb of human lentivirus. (a) Molecular function by GO of genes associated with HIV-1 and HIV-2 integration. (b) Biological process by GO of genes associated with HIV-1 and HIV-2 integration. Blue blocks correspond to HIV-1. Red blocks to HIV-2

5.3. Definition of the common genomic environment of integrations

As the integration do not follow a random model [23-25], some characteristics of the chromatin associated with regions with high level of provirus integration, support the hypothesis that a preferential integration is conditioned by structural and functional states of local chromatin; these states are defined by several genomic variables which were studied in this work, and together would define genomic environments.

The results of multiple-regression analysis conducted on the HIV-1 and HIV-2 data sets showed that there were differential distributions of CpG island, genes, and Alu elements that together conditioned a specific genomic environment per chromosome (R^2=0.91, $p<0.05$). Gene density was the independent variable contributed most in the prediction of the dependent variable (integrations) due to the highest regression coefficients (B= 0.83; $p<0.05$). The highest relative likelihood of hosting a lentiviral integration event in the human genome was registered in chromosome 17 (figure 4a). To test that integration events are favored by gene-rich regions in all chromosomes, a comparison between those variables was done indicating that a high gene density in chromatin regions determine a favorable environment for integration, even when the chromosome 17 is excluded   (Figure 4b). Because chromosome 17 registered the highest percentage of Lentiviral integration events, a detailed analysis of chromatin structure correlating several variables that give data about the cellular chromatin status was performed. In general the distal chromatin regions of p and q arms showed similarities in the distribution of methylation in CpG islands, methylation in several lysine residues of histone H3 (K4, K27 and K36) and variable levels of open chromatin and nucleosome occupancy (figure 5a and b).

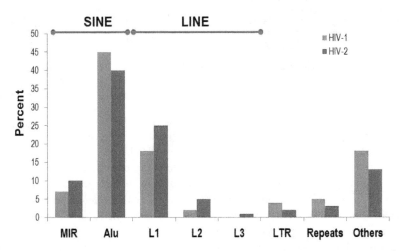

Figure 3. Frequencies of several repetitive elements associated with regions of 100 kb around the HIV-1 and HIV-2 proviruses. SINEs, short interspersed nuclear element; LINEs, long interspersed nuclear element.

Experimental studies have demonstrated that regulatory regions in general and promoters in particular, tend to be DNase sensitive and are target for integration of the majority of retroviruses [37, 38]. In 2006, the complete nucleotide sequence of chromosome 17 was published [39]. This chromosome is rich in protein coding genes, having the second highest gene density in the genome, (16.2 genes per Mb), with a relative excess of short interspersed elements (SINEs, 22.3%) and a deficit of long interspersed elements (LINEs, 14.4%). Likewise, this chromosome has high average CpG content (45.5%) and high euchromatin density [39] (figure 6). Our statistical analysis determined that chromosome 17 had the highest number of integrations, mainly concentrate towards the telomeres of both arms.

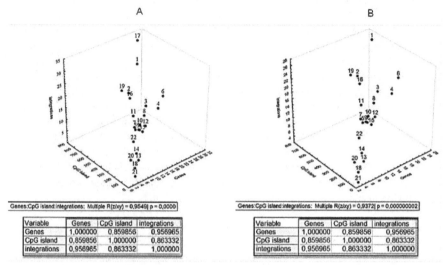

Figure 4. Multiple-regression analysis among gene density, CpG island number, and frequency of HIV-1 and HIV-2 proviruses including every human chromosome. A high statistical correlation is observed mainly for chromosome 17. (a) Analysis including all human chromosomes. (b) The same analysis but excluding chromosome 17.

The most relevant relationship was related to the conformational state of chromatin including the nucleosomes occupancy, methylation of CpG Islands, DNase hypersensitive regions and transcriptionally active genes that are found in open-decondensed chromatin regions. These regions provide the environment for DNA regulatory processes such as DNA replication, repairs and transcription. Albanese et al. (2008) [40], found histone and IN acetylation may favor integration by tethering the virus to acetylated/decondensed regions of the chromatin. We concluded that the structural characteristics and the epigenetic modifications observed in those regions with high frequency of cDNA viral integrations would synergistically configure a local "genomic environment" that facilitates the target site selection during the retroviral integration.

5.4. Construction of HIV-1 gene/protein networks

Host-virus interactions is a complex level of systems information that permits a thorough understanding of how the virus exploits the host cell and uses the cellular machinery to integrate into host genome. Recently, the HIV-1 Human Protein Interaction Database (HHPID) registered 3959 interactions among 1452 human proteins and nineteen HIV proteins (fifteen of them structural and four intermediate proteins) [41].

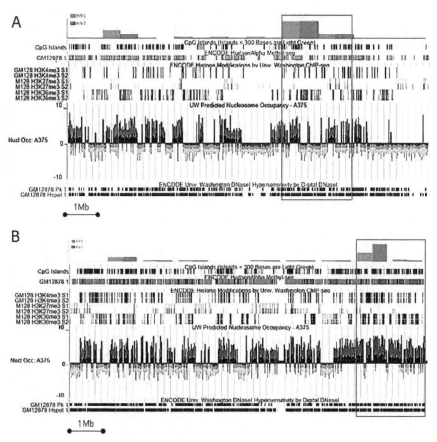

Figure 5. Flash image of the Genome Browser showing the distribution of several characteristics of the chromatin along 9.5 Mb of the p and q arm representing 25% of chromosome 17. (a) p arm, (b) q arm. The figure shows the GC percentage for each: 5pb (black), refseq Genes (black), CpG islands (several tones of gray), levels of open chromatin (ENCODE, Duke) in GM12878 cells with DNaseI and FAIRE (Formaldehyde Assisted Isolation of Regulatory Elements) (black), DNase1 hypersensitivity (ENCODE, University of Washington) in GM12878 cells (gray), pk (sites identified as signal peaks within FDR 0.5% hypersensitive zones), Hspots (zones identified using the HotSpot algorithm), and predicted nucleosome occupancy in A375 cells (black peaks).

Previous studies have identified most of human cell pathways been disturbed by at least one interaction with an HIV-1 protein during the virus life cycle [42-44]. Those interactions are of two types: either direct, via host cell protein-viral proteins or indirect, such as regulatory interactions that alter expression of human genes [45, 46]; the signaling network cc-cytokine is both disrupted and exploited by HIV at various stages of infection. 22 candidates human class E proteins were connected into coherent network by 43 different protein-protein interactions, in which AIP1 play a key role in linking complexes that act early (TSG101/ESCRT-I) and late (CHMP4/ESCRT-III) in the HIV infection pathways [47, 49]. Monocyte/macrophage infection is characterized by a viral dynamic substantially different from that of T lymphocytes. In fact, *in vivo* HIV infection of activated CD4-T lymphocytes accounts for the majority of the daily production of virus particles. However, a large number of lymphocytes are in a resting state, thus unable to sustain a complete and productive virus life cycle, and contribute only minimally to the daily virus production [50-52]. Because of the limited HIV-induced cytopathic effect and of their ability to accumulate high levels of HIV particles in intracellular compartments, HIV-infected macrophages serve as a potentially important reservoir, and as "Trojan horses" exploited by the virus to favor its dissemination in different tissues. [53, 54].

Cytoscape v.2.63 [55] was also used to construct a gene expression network from two kinds of files: The first one from gene expression profiles as a text file (.pvals) that were imported of expression data microarray experiments (GEO profiles, NCBI). The second, as data annotation in text files (.sif) that corresponds to each one gene-gene interactions (online databases). In the first one, gene expression values were collected from the microarray data series GSE19236 composed by two Agilent platforms (**GPL6480** and **GPL6848**) with 48 samples of monocytes to macrophages, macrophages and dendritic cells. These are available from the National Center for Biotechnology Information (NCBI) Gene Expression Omnibus (GEO) repository (accession number GEO: GSE19236) and for our analysis, we selected all macrophages expression samples (GSM476720, GSM476721, GSM476722, GSM476723, GSM476724, GSM476725). To identify which genes were significant among samples in microarrays; considering a p-value< 0.001 as significant, an ANOVA test was calculated. Additionally, a Hierarchical clustering analysis of the samples using Euclidean Distance Method and mean linking were performed. MultiExperiment Viewer v4.1 [56] was applied to make the corresponding statistical analyses. Using data from BOND (Biomolecular Network Data Bank, http://bond.unleashedinformatics.com/Action), BioGird (Biological General Repository for Interaction Datasets, http://thebiogrid.org/), KEEG (Kyoto Encyclopedia of Genes and Genomes, http://www.genome.jp/kegg/), available online, a new file with the interaction data of 28 genes located close to integration sites was constructed.

Cytoscape v2.6 was used for visualizing and analyzing the genetic interaction networks among 28 human macrophages genes and their interactions. BiNGO v2.6 plugin (Biological Networks Gene Ontology tool) was used to determine which Gene Ontology (GO) terms are significantly overrepresented in a set of genes. A hypergeometric test was applied to determine which categories were significantly represented (p-value< 0.01); significant value was adjusted for multiple hypotheses testing using the Bonferroni Family-wise error rate correction [57]. The network topology parameters were calculated using Network Analyzer plug-in, which includes network diameter, the number of connected pairs of nodes and average number of neighbors; it also analyses node degrees, shortest paths, clustering coefficients, and topological coefficients (Max Planck Institute Informatik).

To identify active sub-networks as highly connected regions of the main network we used j ActiveModules plug-in that grouped genes according with significant p-values of gene expression over particular subsets of samples. The result shows active modules, listed according to the number of nodes, and an associated Z-score. An active module with Z-scores greater than 3.0 indicated significant response upon the conditions of the experiment. We kept the standard default values, as being the most effective for initial analyses (58).

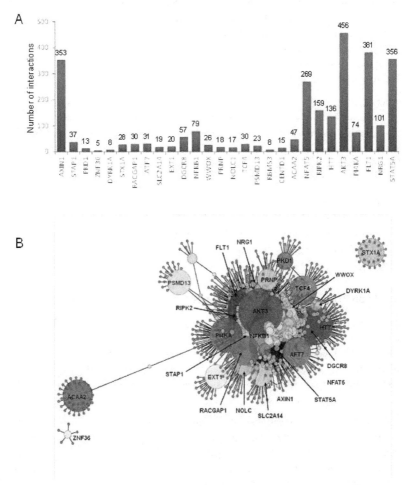

Figure 6. (A). Interaction values of 28 genes of human macrophages interrupted by HIV-1 cDNA integration. (B). Gene expression network in non HIV-1 infected macrophage. Visualization of gene network composed by 28 genes located close to regions with high frequency of HIV-1 provirus in human macrophages. These genes interact with 1202 genes through 2770 interactions. The network was constructed using Cytoscape. Each node corresponds to a gene and edges represent interactions among genes. The color gradient represents the expression values

Eleven thousand and seven hundred and thirteen (11,713) significant genes of 41,000 probes were clustered in two significant different groups of cells; one of them included only dendritic cells, meanwhile the second grouped monocyte to macrophages and macrophages which are sharing similar gene expression patterns. A total of 2,770 interactions among 28 genes which were located closed to HIV-1 proviruses in human macrophages were recorded. AKT3 was gene with highest number of interactions (456), followed by FLT1 (381), STAT5A (356) and AXIN1 (328) (figure 6a). In contrast ZNF36, DYRK1A and RBMS3 genes had the lowest number of gene interactions. The normal macrophage gene network showed tree components: the main cluster composed by 26 macrophages genes and its interactions and two minor clusters in which ZNF36 gene was the central node with five interactions; and STX1A as central node with twelve interactions (Figure 6a).

To further identify active sub-networks inside the main gene network, we performed an expression clustering analysis using p-values calculated by comparison of gene level expression among five macrophage samples. We found 5 subnetworks, in which the most significant active module was integrated by 222 genes with a score of 3.15 ($p<0.01$). Within them 12 genes related with provirus integration sites were found: AXIN1, NFAT5, STAT5A, FLT1, AKT3, HTT, RIPK2, DGCR8, WWOX, NRG1, DYRK1A and SLC2A14 (figure 6b).

The GO functional significant categories in this active module showed enrichment for positive regulation of biological process and cell proliferation. Most of the genes identified in this sub-network were associated with cellular pathways that play significant role by modulating cell signaling networks including Wnt signaling, MAPK signaling and ErbB signaling.

5.5. Effects on normal macrophage gene networks by HIV-1 integration

In order to better understand the alteration of macrophages homeostasis by the HIV-1 integration, our analyses were focused to simulate what are the effects of viral cDNA integration in the alteration of several gene expression networks in human macrophage. In general the topology of non-infected macrophage network gene was dramatically changed by the HIV-1 integration events that lead to turned off the expression of five genes by the integration of proviral cDNA (Figure 7).

The evaluation of the several topological parameters such as clustering coefficient, shortest paths, network heterogeneity, the centralization, average number of neighbors and characteristic path length, showed a changed in the values of HIV-1 macrophage infected gene network, compared with normal macrophage network. The non- altered network was more condensed, had more number of interactions, was wide open rich in shortest paths and also was composed by one major component and two minor clusters being more heterogeneous and multi-functional (table 1).

Statistical differences between the topology states of two networks were registered for topological coefficients, closeness centrality and neighborhood connectivity distribution (Kolgomorov-Smirnov test $p<0.05$), but not in average clustering coefficient distribution. These results indicate that normal network was significantly more central and densely connected in comparison with that of HIV-1 macrophage infected network.

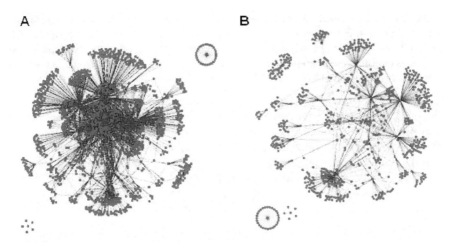

Figure 7. Effects in the topology gene expression network in macrophage by HIV-1 integration. (A) Normal macrophage genes expression network. (B) HIV-1 integration network when five macrophage genes were turned off.

Parameter	Normal macrophage	HIV-1 infected macrophage
Clustering coefficient	0.30	0.04
Connected components	3	3
Shortest paths	94%	90%
Network heterogeneity	5.63	3.75
Centralization	0.34	0.21
Avg. number of neighbors	4.2	2.70
Characteristic path length	3.30	4.13

Table 1. Comparison of network parameter values in normal and HIV-1 infected macrophages.

Using Random network plugin by Cytoscape we found the Clustering Coefficient of the non-infected Network and simulated infected Network in comparison with those generated at random showed not statistical differences (Kruskal-Wallis test, P= 0.317). The data confirmed that the topology of both reported networks have a strong support that the simulation of our gene network is valid.

We test our hypothesis that integration HIV-1 generate disturbs in the gene expression having a global effect in cellular networks and essential biological pathways. The enriched GO terms were categorized for normal and infected macrophages networks to identify the functional cellular change by HIV-1 integration. From all the GO categories covered by the 28 macrophages genes and its interactions, we have listed the ten most significant categories of the enriched GO terms in table 2.

The Gene Ontology (GO) enrichment analysis that normal network was composed by 423 significant functional categories of a total of 1190. These individual significant categories could be further classified into two major groups; cell function regulation and signaling of biological process. In contrast HIV-1 infected macrophage gene network was enriched with 10 significant functional categories of a total of 40. The significantly overrepresented categories indicated that this emergent new gene network was composed by genes involved in metabolic process and DNA repair process.

In this study we simulated at systemic level, the alterations of cellular pathways when HIV provirus integrates into genes by turning them off and produce dysregulation of several local signaling pathways. One of the target gene associated with HIV-1 integration was AKT3, also called PKB, which is a serine/threonine protein kinase family member. It is involved in a wide range of biological processes including cell proliferation, differentiation, apoptosis, stimulating cell growth, and regulating other biological responses (59, 60). Also, it have been identified playing important roles of regulation in the G2/M transition of the cell cycle.

Normal Network	p-value [b]	HIV-1 infected Network	p-value [b]
Signal transduction [GO-ID: 7165]	3,90E-123	Biopolymer biosynthetic process [GO-ID: 43284]	6,27E-05
Cell communication [GO-ID: 7154]	4,63E-120	Metabolic process [GO-ID: 8152]	8,00E-05
Positive regulation of cellular process [GO-ID: 51242]	1,39E-95	Macromolecule biosynthetic process [GO-ID: 9059]	1,40E-03
Positive regulation of biological process [GO-ID: 48518]	1,93E-92	Biosynthetic process [GO-ID: 9058]	2,43E-03
Biological regulation [GO-ID: 65007]	1,45E-88	alcohol metabolic process [GO-ID: 6066]	3,19E-03
Intracellular signaling cascade [GO-ID: 7242]	1,40E-86	Maintenance of fidelity during DNA-dependent DNA replication [GO-ID: 45005]	6,24E-03
Regulation of cellular process [GO-ID: 51244]	2,29E-85	Mismatch repair [GO-ID: 6298]	6,24E-03
Regulation of biological process [GO-ID: 50791]	2,65E-84	Furaldehyde metabolic process [GO-ID: 33859]	6,68E-03
Phosphate metabolic process [GO-ID: 6796]	3,01E-80	Age-dependent response to reactive oxygen species during chronological cell aging [GO-ID: 1320]	6,68E-03
phosphorus metabolic process [GO-ID: 6793]	3,01E-80	oxidation reduction [GO-ID: 55114]	6,90E-03

a. The description of the gene ontology biological processes and the corresponding gene ontology identifiers are given.
b. p-Value calculated as an exponential function.

Table 2. The top 10 of significant biological process of normal and HIV-1 infected macrophages networks [a].

AKT3 via JNK interacts with NFTA and Jun that are targets for the HIV-1 macrophage integration network and are included in the mitogen-activated protein kinase (MAPK) cascade which perform essential functions such as proliferation, survival and inflammation, apoptosis in all cell types. This pathway is associated with others that include the phosphatidylinositol signaling system, Wnt signaling pathway, ERK5 pathway, P53 signaling pathway. (61-63). According with these previous data, we propose that, when AKT3 is turned off by HIV-1 integration, the cross talk with others is disrupted leading to a signaling dysfunction of metabolic associated pathways. When AKT3 was inactive the direct interaction with MKK7 produce a disruption of JNK and after with JUN that would result in a non activation by phosphorilation of apoptotic and cell cycle process. On the other hand inactivation of the MAPK pathway in both macrophages and dendritic cells leads to inhibition of proinflammatory cytokine secretion, downregulation of co-stimulatory molecules such as CD80 and CD86, and ineffective T cell priming. The net result is an impaired innate and adaptive immune response (64, 65).

Recently it have been reported that HIV-1 infection triggers the activation of the PI3K/Akt cell survival pathway in primary human macrophages as reflected by decreased PTEN protein expression and increased Akt kinase activity and renders these cells resistant to cytotoxic insults (54, 61, 64, 65). As result of HIV-1 integration close to AKT3, PTEN, AKT1 and 2, FOXO 1 and MDM2 that are included into the macrophage gene network, would expected a disruption of the apoptotic process.

6. Conclusions

We can conclude that a general effect of HIV-1 integrations in macrophages DNA is to disrupt several signaling pathways that control the normal cell homeostasis. Comparison between normal and infected macrophages of top 10 GO function categories showed the dramatic change of one non-infected macrophage whose main cellular functions are devoted to maintain a cell signaling crucial functions, to one infected in which the most important function are macromolecular biosynthetic process, maintenance of fidelity during DNA-dependent DNA replication, mismatch repair, age-dependent response to reactive oxygen species during chronological cell aging and oxidation reduction. As HIV infected macrophage is an abnormal reservoir in which the metabolic cascades are altered, it is possible to propose that the metabolism of macrophage adapt to perform survival functions where the apoptotic process is interrupted and a SOS metabolism make that the macrophage change of its life style

In silico studies are based upon statistical calculations which permit the drawing of generalizations about a biological process; however since some variables could affecting the in toto process, in order to get a real history of Lentivirus integration it would be important to consider that there is another factors, including physiological process and cellular compartments that would be influencing the in vivo integration site selection. Some of these are cell-cycle phase, the transcriptional state of the cell, the topology of chromosomal DNA, cell type infected, and presence of co-helper molecules during the PIC complex conformation

By providing these new testable hypotheses we hope that our results will accelerate experimental efforts to define a reliable disturbing in the gene complex relationship by lentivirus integration in PBMC and macrophages which are critical immune cells responsible for a wide range of immune functions and play multifaceted roles in HIV pathogenesis

Author details

Felipe García-Vallejo
Physiological Sciences Department, Scientific Director of the Laboratory of Molecular Biology and Pathogenesis, School of Basic Sciences, Health Sciences Faculty, Universidad del Valle, Cali, Colombia

Martha Cecilia Domínguez
Laboratory of Molecular Biology and Pathogenesis, School of Basic Sciences, Health Sciences Faculty, Universidad del Valle, Cali, Colombia

7. References

[1] Lander ES, Linton LM, Birren B, Nusbaum C, Zody MC, Baldwin J, Devon K, Dewar K,Doyle M, FitzHugh W, Funke R, Gage D, Harris K, Heaford A, Howland J, Kann L, Lehoczky J, LeVine R, McEwan P, McKernan K, Meldrim J, Mesirov JP, Miranda C, Morris W, Naylor J, Raymond C, Rosetti M, Santos R, Sheridan A, Sougnez C, et al. (2001) Initial sequencing and analysis of the human genome. *Nature.* 409:860–921.
[2] Venter JC, Adams MD, Myers EW, Li PW, Mural RJ, Sutton GG, Smith HO, Yandell M, Evans CA, Holt RA, Gocayne JD, Amanatides P, Ballew RM, Huson DH, Wortman JR, Zhang Q, Kodira CD, Zheng XH, Chen L, Skupski M, Subramanian G, Thomas PD, Zhang J, Miklos G.L. Gabor, Nelson C, Broder S, Clark AG, Nadeau J, McKusick VA, Zinder N, et al. (2001) The sequence of the human genome. *Science.* 291:1304–1351.
[3] International human genome sequencing consortium. (2004) Finishing the euchromatic sequence of the human genome. *Nature.* 431: 931-945.
[4] Levy S, Sutton G, Ng PC, Feuk L, Halpern AL, Walenz BP, Axelrod N, Huang J, Kirkness EF, Denisov G, Lin Y, MacDonald JR, Pang AW, Shago M, Stockwell TB, Tsiamouri A, Bafna V, Bansal V, Kravitz SA, Busam DA, Beeson KY, McIntosh TC, Remington KA, Abril JF, Gill J, Borman J, Rogers YH, Frazier ME, Scherer SW, Strausberg RL, et al 2007 The diploid genome sequence of an individual human. *PLoS Biol.* 5:e254.
[5] Versteeg R, van Schaik BDC, van Batenburg MF, Roos M, Monajemi R, Caron H, Bussemaker HJ, van Kampen AHC (2003) The human transcriptome map reveals extremes in gene density, intron length, GC content, and repeat pattern for domains of highly and weakly expressed genes. *Genome Research* 13:1998-2004.
[6] DeCerbo J, Carmichael GG (2005) SINEs point to abundant editing in the human genome. *Genome Biology.* 216:1-4.

[7] United Nations AIDS Program on HIV/AIDS (2008). Report of the Global AIDS. UNAIDS/UN.

[8] Simon V, Ho DD.and Karim QA (2007) HIV/AIDS Epidemiology, Pathogenesis, Prevention and Treatment. Lancet. 368: 489-504

[9] Inciardi J.A. and Williams M.L Editor's introduction: (2005) The global epidemiology of HIV and AIDS. AIDS Care. 17 (suppl 1): S1–8

[10] Balakrishnan S (2009) Alternative paths in HIV-1 targeted human signal transduction pathways. BMC Genomics. 10 (Suppl 3), S30

[11] Wang YJ, McKenna PM, Hrin R, Felock P, Lu M, Jones KG, Coburn CA and Grobler JA (2010) Assessment of the susceptibility of mutant HIV-1 to antiviral agents. J. virol methods. 165: 230-237.

[12] Hanson K and Hicks C (2006) New antiretroviral drugs. Current HIV/AIDS Rep. 3: 93-101.

[13] Moore J.P. and Stevenson M : New Targets for Inhibitors of HIV-1 Replication. Nature Rev. 2000; 1: 40-49.

[14] Cereseto A, and Giacca M (2004) Integration site selection by retroviruses. AIDS Rev 6: 13-21.

[15] Coffin J.M: Retroviridae and their replication In Virology, ed. B.N. Fields et al., Raven Press, New York, 1996, pp. 1767–1848.

[16] Sierra S, Kupfer B and Kaiser R (2005) Basics of the virology of HIV-1 and its replication. J. Clin. Virol. 34: 233-244

[17] Hindmarsh P, Leis J (1999) Retroviral DNA integration. Microbiol mol. biol. rev. 63: 836-84

[18] Van Maele B, Busschots K, Vandekerckhove L, Christ F, and Debyser Z (2006) Cellular co-factors of VIH-1 integration. Trends biochem. sci. 31: 98–105.

[19] Bushman F, Lewinski M, Ciuffi A, Barr S, Leipzig J, Hannenhalli S. and Hoffmann C (2005) Genome-wide analysis of retroviral DNA integration. Na.t rev. microbiol. 3: 848-58.

[20] Ciuffi A, Llano M, Poeschla E, Hoffmann C, Leipzig J, Shinn P, Ecker JR and Bushman F (2005) A role for LEDGF/p75 in targeting HIV DNA integration. Nat. med. 11: 1287-9.

[21] Ciuffi A (2008) Mechanisms governing lentivirus integration site selection. Curr. gene. ther. 8: 419-29.

[22] Lewinski M, Yamashita M, Emerman M, Ciuffi A, Marshall H, and Crawford G (2006) Retroviral DNA Integration: Viral and Cellular Determinants of Target-Site Selection. PLoS pathog. 2: 0611-0622

[23] Ferris AL, Wu X, Hughes CM, Stewart C, Smith SJ, Milne TA, Wang GG, Shun MC, Allis CD, Engelman A and Hughes SH (2010) Lens epithelium-derived growth factor fusion proteins redirect HIV-1 DNA integration. Proc. natl. acad. sci. USA. 107: 3135-40

[24] Jordan A, Defechereux P, Verdin E (2001) The site of HIV-1 integration in the human genome determines basal transcriptional activity and response to Tat transactivation. The EMBO J. 20: 1726-1738

[25] Wu X, Li Y, Crise B, Burgess S.M (2003) Transcription start regions in the human genome are favored targets for MLV integration. Science. 300: 1749-1751

[26] Hematti P, Hong BK, Ferguson C, Adler R, Hanawa H, Sellers S, Ingeborg E (2004) Distinct Genomic Integration of MLV and SIV Vectors in Primate Hematopoietic Stem and Progenitor Cells. PLoS Biol. 2: E423

[27] Rick SM, Beitzel BF, Schroder AR, Shinn P, Chen H, Berry CC, Ecker JR, Bushman FD (2004) Retroviral DNA integration: ASLV, HIV, and MLV show distinct target site preferences. PLoS Biol .2: 1127-1137

[28] Maxfield L, Fraize C, Coffin JM (2005) Relationship between retroviral DNA-integration-site selection and host cell transcription. Proc natl. acad. Sci USA. 102: 1436-1441

[29] Soto J, Peña A, Salcedo M, Domínguez MC, Sánchez A, García-Vallejo F (2010) Caracterización Genómica de la Integración In vitro del VIH-1 en células mononucleares de sangre periférica, macrófagos, y células T de Jurkat. Infectio. 14: 20-30

[30] Schroder AR, Shinn P, Chen H, Berry C, Ecker JR, Bushman F (2002) HIV-1 integration in the human genome favors active genes and local hotspots. Cell. 110: 521–529

[31] Derse D, Crise B, Li Y, Princler G, Stewart C, Connor F, Hughes H, Munroe D, Wu X (2007) HTLV-1 integration target sites in the human genome: comparison with other retroviruses. J. virol. 81: 6731-6741

[32] Felice B, Cattoglio C, Cittaro D, Testa A, Miccio A, Ferrari G, Luzi L, Recchia A, Malivio, F (2009) Transcription Factors Binding Sites Are Genetic Determinants of Retroviral Integration in the Human Genome. PLoS One. 4: e4571

[33] MacNeil A, Sankale JL, Meloni S, Sarr A, Mboup S, Kanki P (2006) Genomic Sites of Human Immunodeficiency Virus Type 2 (HIV-2) Integration: Similarities to HIV-1 In Vitro and Possible Differences In Vivo. J. virol. 80: 7316–7321

[34] PARIS CONFERENCE. Supplement (1975) Standardization in human cytogenetic. Cytogenet. Cell Genet. 1971; 15: 203-238

[35] STATSOFT, INC: STATISTICA (data analysis software system), 2004, version 7. Available on: www.statsoft.com

[36] Carteau S, Hoffmann C, Bushman F (1998) Chromosome structure and human immunodeficiency virus type 1 cDNA integration: centromeric alphoid repeats are a disfavored target. J. virol. 72: 4005–4014.

[37] Taganov KD, Cuesta I, Daniel R, Cirillo LA, Katz RA (2004) Integrase specific enhancement and suppression of retroviral DNA integration by compacted chromatin structure in vitro. J. virol. 78: 5848–5855.

[38] Lander ES, Linton LM, Birren B, Nusbaum C, Zody MC, Baldwin J, Devon K, Dewar K, Doyle M, FitzHugh W, Funke R, Gage D, Harris K, Heaford A (2004) International Human Genome Sequencing Consortium. Finishing the euchromatic sequence of the human genome. Nature. 431: 931-945

[39] Zodyl MC, Garber M, Adams D, Sharpe T, Harrow J, Ames R, Nicholson C (2006) DNA sequence of human chromosome 17 and analysis of rearrangement in the human lineage. Nature. 440: 1045-1049

[40] Albanese A, Arosio D, Terreni M, Cereseto A (2008) HIV-1 Pre-Integration Complexes Selectively Target Decondensed Chromatin in the Nuclear Periphery. PLoS one. 3: e2413. doi:10.1371/journal.pone.0002413

[41] Fu W, Sanders-Beer BE, Katz KS, Maglott DR, Pruitt KD, Ptak RG (2009) Human immunodeficiency virus type 1, human protein interaction database at NCBI. Nucleic acid. res. 37(Database issue):D417-22

[42] Song, G, Ouyang G, Bao S (2005) The activation of Akt/PKB signaling pathway and cell survival. J. cell. mol. med. 9 (1): 59-71.

[43] Balakrishnan S, Tastan O, Carbonell J, Klein-Seetharaman J (2009) Alternative paths in HIV-1 targeted human signal transduction pathways. BMC Genomics. 10 (Suppl. 3):S30.

[44] Fu W, Sanders-Beer BE, Katz KS, Maglott DR, Pruitt KD, Ptak RG (2009) Human immunodeficiency virus type 1, human protein interaction database at NCBI. Nucleic acids res. 37: D417–D422.

[45] Perelson AS, Neumann AU, Markowitz M, Leonard JM, Ho DD (1996) HIV-1 dynamics in vivo: virion clearance rate, infected cell lifespan, and viral generation time. Science. 271 (5255):1582–1586.

[46] Sirskyj D, Thèze J, Kumar A, Kryworuchko M (2008) Disruption of the cc cytokine network in T cells during HIV infection. Cytokine. 43 (1): 1–14.

[47] von Schwedler UK, Stuchell M, Müller B, Ward DM, Chung HY, Morita E, Wang HE, Davis T, He GP, Cimbora DM, Scott A, Kräusslich HG, Kaplan J, Morham SG, Sundquist WI (2003) The protein network of HIV budding. Cell. 114 (6): 701–713.

[48] Bandyopadhyay S, Kelley R, Ideker T (2006) Discovering regulated networks during HIV-1 latency and reactivation. Pac. symp. biocomput. 354–366.

[49] Chun T, Carruth LM, Finzi D (1997) Quantification of latent tissue reservoirs and total body viral load in HIV-1 infection. Nature. 387:83–188.

[50] Bagnarelli P, Valenza S, Menzo R, Sampaolesi PE, Varaldo L, Butini M, Montoni CF, Perno S, Aquaro A, Mathez D (1996) Dynamics and modulation of human immunodeficiency virus type 1 transcripts in vitro and in vivo. J. virol. 70 (11):7603–7613.

[51] Perelson AS, Neumann AU, Markowitz M, Leonard JM, Ho DD (1996) HIV-1 dynamics in vivo: virion clearance rate, infected cell lifespan, and viral generation time. Science. 271(5255):1582–1586.

[52] Gendelman HE, Orenstein JM, Baca LM, Weiser B, Burger H, Kalter DC, Meltzer MS (1989) The macrophage in the persistence and pathogenesis of HIV infection. AIDS. 3:475–495.

[53] Herbein G, Gras G, Khan KA, Abbas W (2010) Macrophage signaling in HIV-1 infection. Retrovirology. 9:7–34.

[54] Shannon P, Markiel A, Ozier O, Baliga NS, Wang JT, Ramage D, Amin N, Schwikowski B, Ideker T (2003) Cytoscape: a software environment for integrated models of biomolecular interaction networks. Genome res. 13 (11):2498–2504.

[55] Saeed A, Bhagabati NK, Braisted JC, Liang W, Sharov W, Howe V, Li J, Thiagarajan M, White JA, Quackenbush J, (2006) TM4 microarray software suite. Methods enzymol. 411:134–193.

[56] Maere S, Heymans K, Kuiper M (2005) BiNGO: a cytoscape plug-in to assess overrepresentation of gene ontology categories in biological networks. Bioinformatics. 21 (16):3448–3449.

[57] Ideker T, Ozier O, Schwikowski B, Siegel AF (2002) Discovering regulatory and signalling circuits in molecular interaction networks. Bioinformatics. 18:S233–S240.

[58] Maxfield L, Fraize C, Coffin JM (2005) Relationship between retroviral DNAintegration-site selection and host cell transcription. Proc natl acad.sci. 102 (5):1436–1441.

[59] Schroder AR, Shinn P, Chen H, Berry C, Ecker JR, Bushman F (2002) HIV-1 integration in the human genome favors active genes and local hotspots. Cell. 110 (4):521–529.

[60] Dérijard B, Hibi M, Wu IH, Barrett T, Su B, Deng T, Karin M, Davis RJ (1994) JNK1: a protein kinase stimulated by UV light and Ha-Ras that binds and phosphorylates the c-Jun activation domain. Cell. 76:1025–1037.

[61] Mordret G, (1993) MAP kinase: a node connecting multiple pathways. Biol. cell. 79:193–207.

[62] Rao KM, (2001) MAP kinase activation in macrophages. J. Leukoc. Biol. 69 (1):3–10.

[63] Osaki M, Oshimura M, Ito M (2004) PI3K-Akt pathway: its functions and alterations in human cancer. Apoptosis. 9 (6):667–676.

[64] Chugh P, Bradel-Tretheway B, Monteiro-Filho CM, Planelles V, Maggirwar SB, Dewhurst S, Kim B (2008) Akt inhibitors as an HIV-1 infected macrophagespecific anti-viral therapy. Retrovirology. 5:11.

Sequence Analysis

Chapter 4

SeqAnt 2012: Recent Developments in Next-Generation Sequencing Annotation

Matthew Ezewudo, Promita Bose, Kajari Mondal, Viren Patel, Dhanya Ramachandran and Michael E. Zwick

Additional information is available at the end of the chapter

1. Introduction

The discovery of genome-wide genetic variation was central to the field of genomics [1,2]. Now, recent advances in second-generation sequencing technologies and better methods of targeted enrichment mean the detection of genome-wide patterns of genetic variation will soon be a routine operation [3,4]. Yet these advances in DNA sequencing have revealed a new bottleneck: the functional classification and interpretation of newly discovered genetic variation.

The scale of this problem is enormous. The high throughput and low cost of second-generation sequencing platforms now allow geneticists to routinely perform single experiments that identify tens of thousands to millions of variant sites in a single individual, but the methods that exist to annotate these variant sites using information from publicly available databases are too slow to be useful for the large sequencing datasets being generated. Because sequence annotation of variant sites is required before functional characterization can proceed, the lack of a high-throughput pipeline to annotate variant sites efficiently can be a major bottleneck in genetics research and clinical applications of genomics technologies.

To address this problem, we developed the Sequence Annotator (SeqAnt, http://seqant.genetics.emory.edu/), an open source web service and software package that rapidly annotates DNA sequence variants and identifies recessive or compound heterozygous loci in human, mouse, fly, and worm genome sequencing experiments [5]. Variants are characterized with respect to their functional type, frequency, and evolutionary conservation. Annotated variants can be viewed on a web browser, downloaded in a tab-delimited text file, or directly uploaded in a Browser Extensible Document (BED) format to the UCSC Genome Browser. To demonstrate the speed of SeqAnt, we annotated a series of publicly available datasets that ranged in size from 37 to 3,439,107 variant sites; the total time to annotate these data completely ranged from 0.17 seconds to 28 minutes 49.8 seconds.

1.1. Sequence annotation tools

Genome databases accessible via web browsers are very useful in the search for annotation information for DNA sequences. The UCSC Genome Browser web application has been a huge development of great value in analyzing and characterizing sequence information [6]. The application includes a variety of genomic tracks, assemblies, and browsers with genetic information from a host of species. The UCSC Genome Browser, with its various functionalities and annotation options, offers a one-stop shop for researchers, who can work directly on the web application by uploading their data, or they can download source codes of interest from the UCSC Genome Browser and run those locally. Despite its power, however, the main limitation we see in using the UCSC browser for sequence annotation lies in the limited amount of data that can be accessed at a given time, along with the need for human intervention. For example, it is time-consuming for geneticists who want annotation across multiple variant sites at once over different functional classes to use the browser comfortably. Ensembl is yet another superb broad-based web application with an expansive database, offering researchers choices on extracting specific regions of interest and annotating particular regions in the genome [7]. This application has various functionalities and tools that can accept uploaded data, convert formats of documents, and search for sequences of interest; still, like the UCSC browser, it is not the best choice for performing high-throughput sequencing annotation.

SNPnexus is a genetic variation tool developed to help determine functionally relevant SNPs for a given genomic region [8]. It has a user-friendly web interface that accepts inputs in the form of genomic positions, dbSNP id, or chromosomal region. The application database includes two different human genome assemblies: the hg19 and hg18 builds. SNPnexus generates calls on genomic mapping of variant sites, protein function consequences of such variants in the genome, the regulatory elements conserved within the region, and the conservation score of the variant site. The application also provides the genotype and allele frequencies estimation for known SNPs using data from the HapMap Project. This annotation tool, like so many others, is very useful for human variant annotation; however, it does not characterize variants in other species.

Since the development of SeqAnt in 2010, other software tools have come along to perform sequence annotation. Segtor is a tool designed to annotate large sets of genomic coordinates, intervals, single nucleotide variants (SNVs), indels, and translocations [9]. A more recent and very closely related annotation tool is AnnTools [10]. This is an open source web application that accepts user Inputs and queries their database for a full spectrum of variant site annotation, including single nucleotide variants, insertions and deletions, structural variants, and copy number variants. The application has a minimal memory footprint and likewise annotates variants quite rapidly. Nevertheless, AnnTools is restricted to human genome variant annotations and in this sense differs from SeqAnt, which annotates other species besides humans. There are also a number of other variant site annotation tools available either as downloadable command line applications or user interface web applications; these include snpEff (http://snpeff.sourceforge.net), MU2A[11], and Snat [12].

1.2. The distinction of SeqAnt

The uniqueness of SeqAnt versus all the other annotation tools we mentioned lies in three factors, which had been the key considerations for developing this technology to begin with. First, SeqAnt delivers annotations for multiple different species, ranging from primates to mammals, and now zebrafish and nematodes. Second, the web application has its own database updated from the UCSC website, which is a collection of binary files that drive the record speed with which large genomic data are annotated. Third, in addition to speed, the memory footprint is quite minimal, as data stored in binary files enable individuals from the public to download both the source file and database and locally run the application without elaborate computing apparatus. Some of the other tools mentioned have one or two of these unique features, but none have the robustness that comes from combining all three approaches to efficiently annotate variants and make meaningful functional calls across species, like SeqAnt does. Overall, we believe these represent important changes to SeqAnt that will be of broad utility to researchers using next-generation sequencing platforms in a wide variety of systems. SeqAnt will continue to be a fully open source web service and software package, and we believe it will prove especially useful for those investigators who lack dedicated bioinformatics personnel or infrastructure in their laboratories.

2. Upgraded features of SeqAnt 2.0

Since the initial publication of SeqAnt, we made a number of improvements that have been incorporated into SeqAnt 2.0 [5]. These modifications fall into four main categories. The first focused on updating the SeqAnt website (http://seqant.genetics.emory.edu). The second includes major changes made to the content and structure of the underlying binary databases that hold the annotation information. The third involves a significant redesign of the directory structure holding the output files. Finally, the last modification included substantial revisions to the number and content of output files themselves. Each of these updates will be described in greater detail in the sections that follow.

2.1. SeqAnt 2.0 - website updates

We undertook a major redesign of the SeqAnt web interface to make it more user-friendly. On the home page, we eliminated redundant tabs and buttons, simplified the overall design, and upgraded the graphic interface's color scheme (Figure 1). This page includes basic information about the original publication of SeqAnt [5], a link to contact the Zwick laboratory, and the web URL for the the SourceForge website (http://seqant.sourceforge.net), where the source code and associated binary libraries can be freely downloaded. From this page, the user is able to quickly access the three main types of input data accepted by SeqAnt. These include **SEQUENCE FILE**, **LIST OF VARIANTS**, and **SINGLE VARIANT**. In addition, the user can choose to view a **TUTORIAL** or select a set of **SAMPLE FILES** to gain experience performing analyses with the SeqAnt.

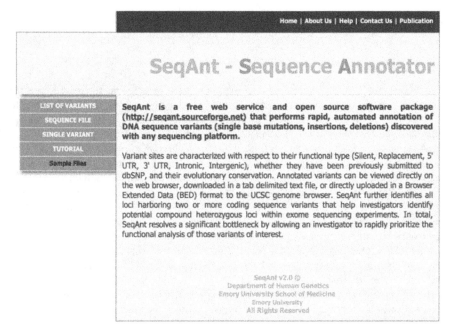

Figure 1. Screenshot of new SeqAnt 2.0 home page

Selecting the **SEQUENCE FILE** option returns the web interface shown in Figure 2. A typical use of this feature is when the user wants variation annotation information in a genomic region from a particular chromosome. Three different input files are accepted. The first is a reference sequence file in FASTA format of the entire genomic region being annotated. The second is a sequence file containing multiple FASTA sequences from a sequencing experiment, with each FASTA sequence representing a chromosomal region. The third is a genomic position file in the BED format which represents the coordinates for each of the chromosomal regions in the sequence file. The sequences in both the reference file and the sequence file should be in the positive orientation to ensure accurate annotation. The user is provided the option to choose a reference genome and assembly that will be used for annotating variant sites.

Selecting the **LIST OF VARIANTS** option returns the web interface shown in Figure 3. Only one input file is required to use this feature, the variations list file, which contains a listing of variant sites and the chromosomal regions of these sites, the minor allele and the reference allele. The variant list file is basically a pileup file, with a '.snp' or a '.txt' extension. If the PEMapper option were selected in this interface, the variation list file would be modified to include the sample ID for each individual within the experimental study where the sequence data was generated, if multiple individual samples were being analyzed. This particular (List of Variants) feature is very useful for researchers who want to perform genetic variation analysis (such as whole exome annotation) over a wide expanse of the genome.

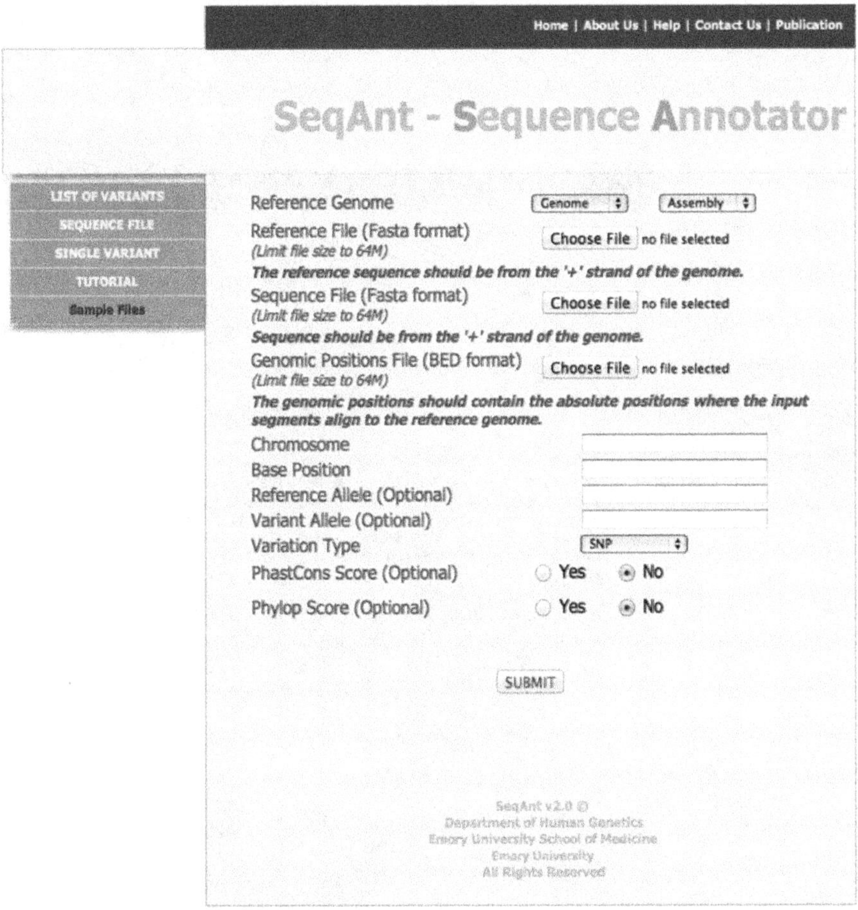

Figure 2. Screenshot of the SEQUENCE FILE page

Selecting the **SINGLE VARIANT** option returns the web interface shown in Figure 4. The user is provided the option to choose a reference genome and assembly that will be used for annotating a single variant site.The user then only needs to provide a chromosome and base position to obtain the annotation information.

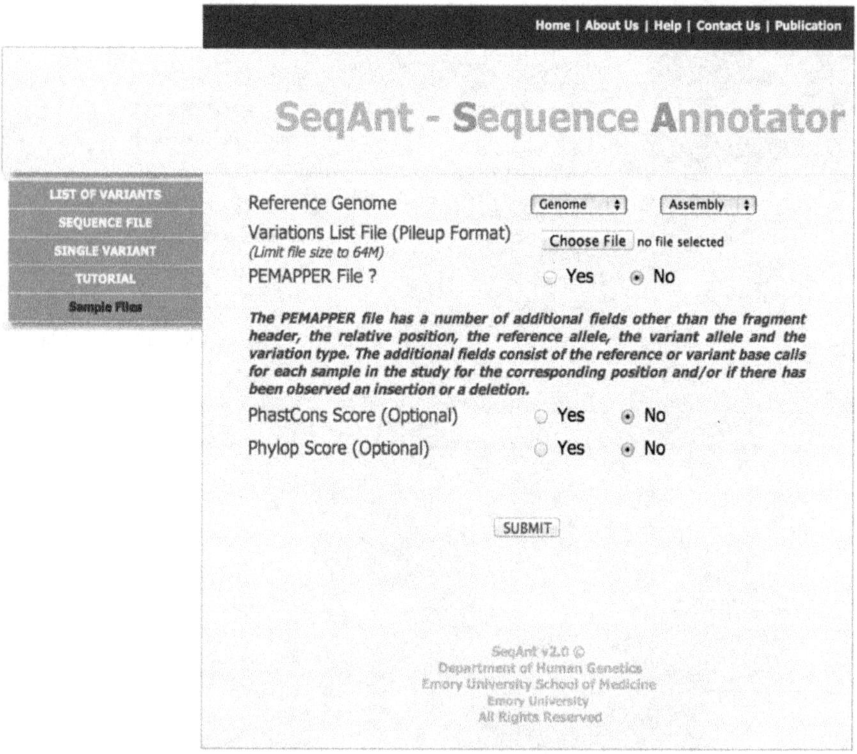

Figure 3. Screenshot of the LIST OF VARIANTS page

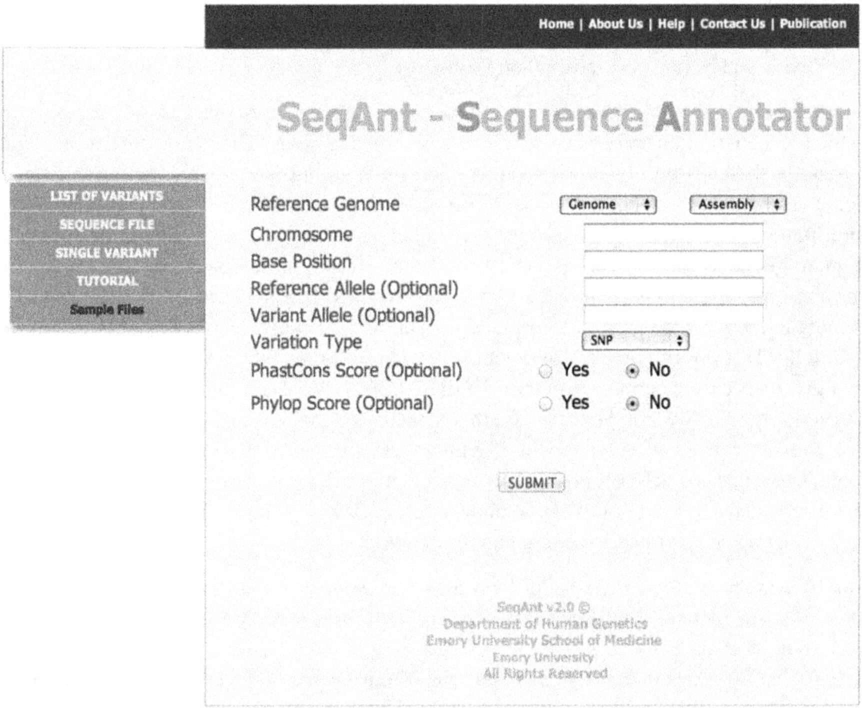

Figure 4. Screenshot of the SINGLE VARIANT page

2.2. SeqAnt 2.0 - Binary database upgrades

One of the unique features of SeqAnt is the ease and speed with which variant information is accessed from a set of customized binary databases. The SeqAnt binary databases are created from flat text table files obtained from the UCSC Genome Browser website [6]. Five main types of data constitute the SeqAnt binary databases. These include:

1. Reference Genome Sequence
2. RefGene Annotation
3. dbSNP Variation Data
4. PhastCons Evolutionary Conservation Scores
5. PhyloP Evolutionary Conservation Score

Standard queries, implemented through the web interfaces described above, are able to extract the annotation information from the binary databases. The actual structure of the binary databases is not directly visible to a SeqAnt user, but is worth examining in greater detail. The Reference Genome Sequence provides the basic backbone for other annotation information. Reference sequences for a given species are organized by different builds (i.e. human genome 18, human genome 19). Within each build, data are organized by chromosome, which reflects the structure of the flat files obtained from UCSC. The RefGene Annotation is the collection of information pertaining to known genes for a given species and build. This information is also organized by chromosome. The collection of variant sites in a given species is contained within the dbSNP Variation Data that is also organized by chromosome. Finally, the SeqAnt 2.0 binary databases include two different measures of evolutionary conservation for all sites in a given reference genome sequence. The PhastCons score is best used to detect functional elements in noncoding sequences, whereas the phyloP score provides a measure of the evolutionary conservation of single sites and is most useful for evaluating sites located in coding regions of genes.

Binary files are significantly smaller than their corresponding flat files, so querying binary files uses less memory than the same analysis performed with a flat file. Considering the vast amount of data that has to be accessed during sequence annotation of large genomic regions, the significant difference in the size of the binary files versus flat files helps to account for the speed with which information is processed using binary files. SeqAnt 2.0 updated a number of these specific binary files; a detailed description of the changes follows in the next sections.

2.2.1. Upgrade of dbSNP to SNP132 Track for hg19 Assembly (Homo sapiens)

The original goal of the dbSNP database (http://www.ncbi.nlm.nih.gov/projects/SNP/) was to develop a comprehensive catalog of common (>5% frequency) human genetic variation [13,14]. These variants were subsequently validated by genotyping in multiple human populations, and their patterns of statistical correlation among variants, known as linkage disequilibrium, were revealed in the HapMap project [15,16]. SeqAnt 1.0 included data from the SNP131 track from the dbSNP [17]. SeqAnt 2.0 was updated to the SNP132 build, which was characterized and uploaded to the UCSC Genome Browser in the summer of 2011. SNP132 has an expanded collection of variant sites that can help researchers determine whether an identical variant has been seen before in a different individual.

Results Directory
--Compound Replacement SNP
--Summary.txt
--Log

All_variations

--Exonic Indel
--Exonic Replacement SNP
--Exonic Silent SNP
--Intergenic Indel
--Intergenic SNP
--Intronic Indel
--Intronic SNP
--UTR Indel
--UTR SNP

Bed_Annotations

--Exonic Indel bed
--Intergenic Indel bed
--Intergenic SNP bed
--Intronic Indel bed
--Intronic SNP bed
--Replacement SNP bed
--Silent SNP bed
--UTR Indel bed
--UTR SNP bed
--UCSC bed

Unique_variations

--Unique Exonic Indel
--Unique Exonic Replacement SNP
--Unique Exonic Silent SNP
--Unique Intergenic Indel
--Unique Intergenic SNP
--Unique Intronic Indel
--Unique Intronic SNP
--Unique UTR Indel
--Unique UTR SNP

Figure 5. Contents of SeqAnt Output Directory. Directories are in bold; individual files shown in a standard font face.

2.2.2. Addition of PhyloP46way Conservation Score Database for hg19 Assembly (Homo sapiens)

The phyloP Evolutionary Conservation Score data type is a new addition to SeqAnt 2.0. Binary databases, including phylopP scores from a 46-way alignment of vertebrate species to the human genome, were included to complement the PhastCons Evolutionary Conservation Scores previously included in the application. The phyloP scores predict the probability of a given variant site having undergone evolution over time. The absolute phyloP values represent negative log p-values for the null hypothesis that there was no evolution across the regions annotated [18]. Regions that are more conserved tend to have more positive values, whereas sites believed to be fast evolving have negative values. The medium range of these scores for the 46-way alignment from the UCSC Genome Browser is between approximately -3 and +3. It should be noted that, unlike PhastCons, which takes into account flanking bases on a sequence in arriving at its final score for a given variant site, phyloP scores are computed by basically comparing the particular base in the sequence with aligned bases from other species [18]. Variations in highly conserved regions often suggest a significant change that could have functional implications. The PhyloP46way dataset we have on the upgraded SeqAnt web application is the most recent phyloP track in the UCSC, released in December 2009.

2.2.3. Addition of Full Genome Data Set by Chromosome of Zebrafish (danRer6 Assembly)

We selected zebrafish (*Danio rerio*) as the next species to be incorporated into the SeqAnt database because of its emergence as a model organism for a wide range of scientific studies, from behavioral genetics to drug modeling studies and integrative physiology [19,20]. SeqAnt 2.0 has now been updated to include binary files for the genome sequence of zebrafish. We derived binary databases for the first four data types from flat table files on the UCSC Genome Browser website. Flat table files for the phyloP evolutionary conservation score were not available and were therefore not included. The reference genome binaries use the danRer6 assembly, which annotated the datasets by chromosome and was released in December of 2008. The RefGene annotation and dbSNP variation data are relative to the danRer6 assembly. PhastCons evolutionary conservation scores were derived from multiple alignment between seven species and zebrafish. Including the zebrafish in SeqAnt 2.0 should prove valuable for researchers who work with this species.

2.3. SeqAnt 2.0: output directory structure and files

Significant changes to the number and types of output files are reflected in a new output directory structure in SeqAnt 2.0. The output from SeqAnt is contained within a Results directory that includes three subdirectories (Figure 5). This Results directory has the name of the original SeqAnt input file and a subscript '_Annotation_Files'. Within this directory, there are three distinct directories (All_Variations, BED_Annotation, Unique_Variations) holding the output of SeqAnt, which will be described in detail below. This directory also contains three other files of interest to a user. The first is a *.summary.txt file that provides a summary of all the variants annotated by SeqAnt. The second is a Compound.Replacement file that identifies variants, genes, and sample identifiers for those loci with two or more replacement variants. The collected list of variants includes those that could be compound recessive in a given individual, although since the phase of the variants is not determined, this would have to be validated by other means. This file may be useful when looking for genes that harbor variants that may fit a recessive loss-of-function model. The last is a *.log file generated by SeqAnt that records the major events that occur when SeqAnt processes a dataset.

2.3.1. All_variations directory

This directory contains the complete variant annotation files obtained from annotating input files with SeqAnt 2.0 (Figure 5). Two main types of genetic variation are annotated by SeqAnt: single nucleotide variants (SNPs) and insertions/deletions (INDELs). For SNPs, a given variant site when annotated belongs in one of five functional classifications. These include exonic.replacement, exonic.silent, untranslated region (UTR), intronic, or intergenic. For INDELs, a given variant when annotated belongs in one of four functional classifications. These include exonic, UTR, intronic, or intergenic. Overall, there are a total of nine files that contain the variants and their associated annotation information. These annotation files include all possible splice variants impacted by a given variant site. Thus, a given variant site may be listed multiple times in one of the nine output files.

2.3.2. BED_annotation directory

This directory contains files in BED format (http://genome.ucsc.edu/FAQ/FAQformat) that can be visualized on the UCSC Genome Browser or other viewer able to process files in this format. There are ten files total in this directory. Nine of the files include the variants and annotation information as described above; the tenth file (*.ucsc.bed) contains all the annotation information from each of the nine files in a single BED file for the entire genomic region to be visualized. These files can be uploaded to the UCSC browser as custom tracks to be visualized. They can also be visualized in other software packages that process BED files, such as the Integrative Genomics Viewer (Version 2.1) [21].

2.3.3. Unique_variations directory

In contrast to the annotation in the All_Variations directory, the Unique_Variations directory contains nine files that contain a single variant annotation for each SNP or INDEL. Thus, each variant is listed just once, regardless of the number of different splice variants it is predicted to impact. These files allow the user to quickly determine the total number of variants for any specific functional class.

2.4. SeqAnt 2.0 - Output files

2.4.1. Redesign of Result Columns for Annotation Files

We introduced a number of changes to the annotation fields contained within the SeqAnt output files. First, we rearranged the order of columns in the output files to aid users in evaluating their results. Second, we introduced additional feature columns to the output files. These included row 10, which depicts the transcript change that occurs for a coding sequence variant, row 14, which shows the concomitant amino-acid change for a coding sequence variant, and rows 21 and 22, which report the phyloP conservation score values for each variant position annotated. A summary of the annotation information provided by SeqAnt 2.0 is shown below in Table 1. A representation of an example output file is shown in Figure 6 below.

Field ID	Annotation Field	Description
1	Variation_Type	Type of variant
2	Functional Class	Annotated functional category for variant site
3	Chromosome	Chromosome containing variant site
4	Position	Absolute position of variant site on a chromosome
5	Gene_Name	Name of locus containing variant site
6	RefSeq_ID	Ref_Seq ID from UCSC track
7	Gene_Strand	Orientation of locus
8	Reference_Base	Reference allele at variant site
9	Input_Base	Minor allele at variant site
10	Transcript Change	Nucleotide base change on transcript
11	Original_Amino_Acid	Reference amino acid at variant site
12	Amino_Acid_Number	Position of amino acid on peptide chain
13	Modified_Amino_Acid	Modified amino acid due to variant site
14	Amino_Acid_Change	Amino acid change on peptide chain
15	dbSNP_IDs	dbSNP ID If variant site has been reported
16	Het_Rates	dbSNP heterozygosity of reported variant site
17	Orientation	dbSNP orientation of reported variant site
18	PhastCons_placentals	Placental PhastCons score for variant site (46way)
19	PhastCons_primates	Primate PhastCons score for variant site (46way)
20	PhastCons_vertebrate	Vertebrate PhastCons score for variant site (46way)
21	PhyloP_placental	Placental phyloP score for variant site (46way)
22	PhyloP_primates	Primate phyloP score for variant site (46way)
23	PhyloP_vertebrate	Vertebrate phyloP score for variant site (46way)

Table 1. Annotation information output by SeqAnt 2.0

Variation_Type	Functional Class	Chromosome	Position	Gene_Name	RefSeq_Id	Gene_Strand	Reference_Base	Input_Base	Transcript change	Original_Amino_Acid	Amino_Acid_Number	Modified_Amino_Acid
SNP	Replacement	chrX	3235724	MXRA5	NM_015419	-	C	T	c.5998C>T	G(1GGC)	2000	S
SNP	Replacement	chrX	3238733	MXRA5	NM_015419	-	G	A	c.4993G>A	P(1CCA)	1665	S
SNP	Replacement	chrX	3240343	MXRA5	NM_015419	-	G	A	c.3383G>A	A(2GCA)	1128	V
SNP	Replacement	chrX	3241256	MXRA5	NM_015419	-	T	C	c.2470T>C	I(1ATT)	824	V
SNP	Replacement	chrX	3241436	MXRA5	NM_015419	-	C	G	c.2290C>G	V(1GTG)	764	L
SNP	Replacement	chrX	3248104	MXRA5	NM_015419	-	C	T	c.664C>T	D(1GAT)	222	N
SNP	Replacement	chrX	3631167	PRKX	NM_005044	-	A	G	c.128A>G	V(2GTG)	43	A
SNP	Replacement	chrX	70236678	HDHD1	NM_001178135	-	G	A	c.263G>A	T(2ACG)	88	M
SNP	Replacement	chrX	70236678	HDHD1	NM_001135565	-	A	G	c.332G>A	T(2ACG)	111	M
SNP	Replacement	chrX	70236678	HDHD1	NM_012080	-	G	A	c.263G>A	T(2ACG)	88	M
SNP	Replacement	chrX	7268296	STS	NM_000351	+	C	G	c.1746C>G	S(3AGC)	582	R

Amino_Acid_Change	dbSNP_Ids	Het_Rates	Orientations	PhastCons_placental	PhastCons_primates	PhastCons_vertebrate	PhyloP_placental	PhyloP_primates	PhyloP_vertebrate	Num_Hom_SNPs	Sample_Ids	Num_Het_SNPs	Sample_Ids
G2000S	rs1635242,	0.407,	+,	0.673	0.217	0.929	1.331	0.512	1.228	44	SampleA	0	---
P1665S	rs1974522,	0.492,	+,	0.004	0.039	0.047	0.307	0.409	1.74	41	Sample B	0	---
A1128V	rs66465405,rs1635246,	0.000,0.467,	+,+,	0	0.016	0	-1.433	0.512	-0.512	42	Sample D	0	---
I824V	rs5983119,	0.322,	+,	0	0	0.004	0	-0.205	-0.409	45	Sample A	0	---
V764L	rs5983120,	0.060,	+,	0.012	0.016	0.004	1.433	0.512	0.921	1	Sample C	0	---
D222N	---	---	---	0	0.008	1	0.409	0.512	3.071	1	Sample E	0	---
V43A	rs3752362,	0.009,	+,	0	0.016	0.055	-0.307	-0.614	-0.717	28	Sample F	0	---
T88M	rs1131197,	0.367,	-,	0.917	0.63	0.996	0.512	-0.102	2.047	18	Sample G	0	---
T111M	rs1131197,	0.367,	-,	0.917	0.63	0.996	0.512	-0.102	2.047	18	Sample F	0	---
T88M	rs1131197,	0.367,	-,	0.917	0.63	0.996	0.512	-0.102	2.047	18	Sample L	0	---
S582R	---	---	---	0.004	0.008	0	0	-0.205	0.102	1	Sample M	0	---

Figure 6. Snapshot of Exonic Replacement Annotation Output File. The top half shows the data for fields 1 - 13. The bottom half of the figure shows the data from fields 14 - 23. The last four columns report the number of homozygous and heterozygous SNPs and associated sample IDs.

3. An application of SeqAnt 2.0: Targeted next-generation sequencing of *NLGN3* and *NLGN4X* in humans

The targeted sequencing of specific genes or genomic regions is a common experimental design that can benefit from the use of SeqAnt. Here we describe such a study. We sequenced the *NLGN3* and *NLGN4X* loci in a sample of 144 males with a diagnosis of autism. All the patient samples were obtained from the multiplex Autism Genetic Resource Exchange (AGRE) [22]. Raw base-calling data generated with an Illumina Genome Analyzer (IGA) were used as input for mapping and alignment. The total amount of sequence generated was 7.04 GB. Paired-end reads were mapped and variants were called using PEMapper (Cutler DJ et al, personal communication). In total, 99.7% of target bases had at least 8X coverage, with a median depth of coverage of 452. We identified a total of 208 sites of variation, with 176 single nucleotide polymorphisms and 32 insertions or deletions. Overall levels of variation were estimated at 5.8 x 10^{-4} (Θ_w per site [23]), which matched our expectation for loci from the human X chromosome. We also observed an excess of rare variants, as evidenced by a negative value for the Tajima's D test statistic (-0.27,[24]).

Single nucleotide variants (SNVs) and small insertions and deletions (INDELs) were annotated using SeqAnt [5]. For the SNPs, a total of 68, or 39%, had not been reported before (31 in *NLGN3* and 37 in *NLGN4X*, Table 2). For the INDELs, a total of 24, or 75%, had not been reported before (5 in *NLGN3* and 19 in *NLGN4X*, Table 3). As summarized in Figure 7, almost all common variation (>5% frequency in our sample) is contained in dbSNP, whereas most rare variants (<5%) have not been cataloged there.

Functional class	Total SNPs	SNPs in dbSNP	Novel SNPs	Novel SNPs at Evolutionary Conserved Sites
Replacement	1	1	0	0
Silent	3	3	0	0
UTR	18	10	8	2
Intron	134	78	56	9
Intergenic	20	16	4	0
Total	176	108	68	11

Table 2. Functional annotation of SNPs at the *NLGN3* and *NLGN4X* loci identified by next-generation sequencing of 144 males with autism.

Using SeqAnt to rapidly annotate our sequence data allows us to quickly draw four main conclusions. First, most common variation is already contained in dbSNP, while much of the rare variation remains undiscovered. Second, we did not see any novel replacement variants at either *NLGN3* or *NLGN4X*, suggesting that mutations at these loci are rare causes of autism. Third, we identified novel UTR variants at highly evolutionarily conserved sites, which could contribute to autism susceptibility. We focused on this set of variants for direct functional testing. Finally, we identified novel intronic variants at evolutionarily conserved sites that appear to be located in transcription factor binding sites. These variants are being followed up to determine whether they have a regulatory role that impacts the expression of *NLGN3* or *NLGN4X*. In summary, SeqAnt 2.0 allowed us to rapidly annotate all the sites of variation in our sample and rapidly focus attention on those variants most likely to be autism susceptibility alleles.

Functional Class	Total Indels	Indels in dbSNP	Novel Indels	Novel Indels at Evolutionary Conserved Sites
Coding	0	0	0	0
UTR	1	0	1	1
Intron	25	7	18	0
Intergenic	6	1	5	0
Total	32	8	24	1

Table 3. Functional annotation of INDELs at the *NLGN3* and *NLGN4X* loci identified by next-generation sequencing of 144 males with autism.

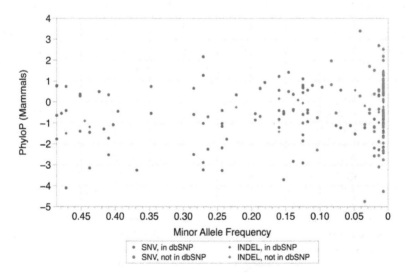

Figure 7. Summary of SNV and indel variation discovered at the *NLGN3* and *NLGN4X* loci in males with ASD. The frequency of SNVs and INDELs (minor alleles) in cases is plotted against their level of evolutionary conservation. Most common variation has already been discovered and exists in public databases (blue; circles and diamonds); most of the rare variation at both loci was discovered in our study and not contained in public databases (red; circles and diamonds).

4. An application of SeqAnt 2.0: Sequencing the *AFF2* locus and X chromosome exome in patients with autism

With improvements in methods of targeted enrichment and next-generation sequencing, the targeted sequencing of all genes on a specific chromosome has become feasible. Specific genes/genomic regions is a common experimental design that benefits from the use of SeqAnt [25]. Here we performed an experiment that combined targeted sequencing with chromosomal exome sequencing. We selected 127 males from the Autism Genetic Resource Exchange (AGRE) multiplex collection and 75 males from the Simons Foundation Autism Research Initiative (SFARI) Simplex Collection, New York, NY, USA (SSC) for target DNA amplification and DNA sequencing. From the AGRE collection, we chose multiplex families with two or more male affected sib-pairs who shared >99% of 76 genotyped SNPs in the *AFF2* genomic region [22]. One male was randomly chosen if both affected siblings were equally affected; otherwise, the male with autism was chosen over those boys with a diagnosis of not quite autism (NQA) or broad spectrum. From the SSC collection, we chose only those boys who were described as autistic and not reported to have any other syndromes. From the SSC collection, we chose 75 male children from different families with a diagnosis of ASD [26].

For the AGRE samples, we prepared target DNA for sequencing the AGRE samples by performing long PCR (LPCR) amplification of the *AFF2* genomic region, followed by sequencing on an Illumina Genome Analyzer. For the SSC samples, we prepared target DNA for Illumina sequencing by using RainDance Technology's (RDT) microdroplet-based technology to enrich for the human X chromosome exome, as described previously [25]. Following enrichment we performed 70-bp single-end multiplex sequencing on an Illumina Genome Analyzer (IGA). Nearly 20 GB of sequence was generated for AGRE samples, while ~55 GB of sequence was generated for the SSC samples. The *AFF2* reference sequence used for the AGRE samples consists of 10 discontiguous fragments covering 84.8 kb, and the SSC reference sequence consisted of the entire human X chromosome, which spanned 5748 discontiguous fragments covering 4.7 Mb. Raw base-calling data generated with the IGA were mapped and variants called using PEMapper (Cutler DJ et al, personal communication). For AGRE samples, 99% of the bases had more than 8X coverage. Median depth of coverage was in the range of 388-1548. For the SSC samples, between 83% and 97% of the targeted reference bases had more than 8X coverage. Median depth of coverage was in the range of 20-607. We identified a total of 286 sites of variation, with 269 single nucleotide polymorphisms (SNPs) and 17 insertions or deletions (INDELs). Overall levels of variation were similar between the two datasets (Θ_w per site [23]; AGRE - 6.0 x 10^{-4}, SSC - 6.7 x 10^{-4}), with an excess of rare variants as evidenced by a negative value for the Tajima's D test statistics for both sets of samples ([24]; AGRE: -1.46, SSC: -1.41).

We used SeqAnt to annotate the variants found at the *AFF2* locus in the total sample of 202 males with a diagnosis of autism (Mondal et al, in revision). We sought to test the hypothesis that rare variants at the *AFF2* locus can act as autism susceptibility alleles. Annotating our variants using the other web-based tools, like the UCSC Genome Browser or the Ensembl Genome Browser, would have been time-consuming and laborious. SeqAnt helped us rapidly annotate these SNPs and INDELs into different functional classes, as well as reported whether a variant had already been cataloged in the dbSNP database (Tables 4, 5). SeqAnt also reported the PhastCons and phyloP conservation scores, which are important in helping to determine whether a variant might cause a deleterious change in the protein structure/function, since variants in the well-conserved sites are likely to cause such changes. By using this feature of SeqAnt, we could easily identify our list of candidate variants that were rare, as well as likely to cause a damaging change.

Functional Class	Total SNPs	SNPs in dbSNP	Novel SNPs	Novel SNPs at Conserved Sites
Replacement	5	0	5	5
Silent	8	4	4	4
UTR	33	20	13	1
Intron	223	129	94	6
Total	269	153	116	16

Table 4. Functional annotation of single nucleotide polymorphisms at the *AFF2* locus identified by next-generation sequencing of 202 males with autism

Functional Class	Total Indels	Indels in dbSNP	Novel Indels	Novel Indels at Conserved Sites
Exonic	0	0	0	0
UTR	2	0	2	1
Intron	15	7	8	1
Total	17	7	10	2

Table 5. Functional annotation of indels at the *AFF2* locus identified by next-generation sequencing of 202 males with autism

As expected, almost all common variation (>5% frequency in our population) is contained in dbSNP, whereas most rare variants (<5%) are not cataloged in dbSNP (Figure 8). We found that, in our cases, there were five (2.5% of total cases sequenced) singleton nonsynonymous variants. This level of variation in our cases was significantly higher than that seen in a set of 5400 controls. Furthermore, we used SeqAnt to rapidly annotate 1006 X chromosome genes that had been sequenced in the 75 SSC samples, and ultimately showed that the excess mutations at *AFF2* were unusual compared to other X chromosome loci. Thus, the ability to rapidly annotate our sequence variants discovered from sequencing the entire X chromosome exome had a major impact on our ability to assess the role of *AFF2* as an autism susceptibility locus. Finally, SeqAnt helped us identify three rare noncoding UTR sequence variants, one of which was at an evolutionarily conserved site. Subsequent functional testing suggested that the variant at the conserved site acts to influence the level of *AFF2* expression. Thus, for this experiment, SeqAnt allowed us to rapidly focus on those sites of greatest interest for both statistical analyses and direct functional testing.

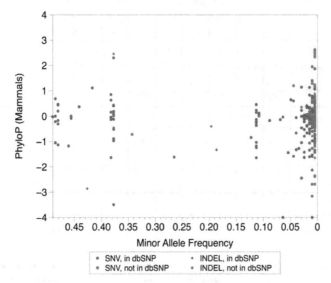

Figure 8. Summary of SNV and indel variation discovered at the *AFF2* locus in males with ASD. The frequency of SNVs and indels (minor alleles) in cases is plotted against their level of evolutionary conservation. Most common variation has already been discovered and exists in public databases (blue; circles and diamonds). Most of the rare variation at *AFF2* was discovered in our study and not contained in public databases (red; circles and diamonds).

5. An application of SeqAnt 2.0: Discovering new mutations from forward genetic screens in the mouse

Forward genetic screens in *Mus musculus* have been very informative, revealing unsuspected mechanisms governing basic biological processes [27-32]. In this approach, a potent chemical mutagens, such as *N*-ethyl-*N*-nitrosourea (ENU), is used to randomly induce mutations in mice. The mice are then bred and phenotypically screened to identify lines that disrupt a specific biological process of interest. Although identifying a mutation using the rich resources of mouse genetics is straightforward, it is unfortunately neither fast nor cheap.

To solve this problem, we developed a methodology that combines multiplex chromosome-specific exome capture, next-generation sequencing, rapid mapping, sequence annotation, and variation filtering to detect newly induced causal variants in a dramatically accelerated way [33]. Rapid sequence annotation and variation filtering are critical to this approach. We used SeqAnt as a part of this methodology for rapid annotation of variations obtained from mutant, parental, and background strains in a single experiment. By using SeqAnt, we first annotated all the variants into different functional classes. Next, by comparing variants identified in mutant offspring to those found in dbSNP, the unmutagenized background strains, and parental lines, we could immediately distinguish the induced putative causative mutations from preexisting variations or experimental artifacts (Table 6).

Mutant Line	Functional Classes	Total Homozygous Variants	In dbSNP	In Background Strains, Not in dbSNP	Remaining Variants	Replacement Variants Within Mapped Region
AB5	Replacement	96	80	13	3	1
AB5	Silent	157	143	12	2	-
AB5	UTR	331	191	135	5	-
AB5	Intronic	106	87	17	2	-
AB5	Intergenic	54	50	4	0	-
M2	Replacement	43	8	31	4	2
M2	Silent	19	11	7	1	-
M2	UTR	73	16	55	2	-
M2	Intronic	46	18	20	8	-
M2	Intergenic	40	4	36	0	-
X5	Replacement	128	59	63	6	2
X5	Silent	192	128	63	1	-
X5	UTR	387	231	152	4	-
X5	Intronic	205	116	86	3	-
X5	Intergenic	89	34	55	0	-
Y1	Replacement	17	1	14	2	1
Y1	Silent	5	0	4	1	-
Y1	UTR	14	2	11	1	-
Y1	Intronic	34	0	31	3	-
Y1	Intergenic	7	0	7	0	-

Table 6. Results of filtering homozygous variants sites for each mouse mutant line sequenced.

We demonstrated the use of this approach to find the causative mutations induced in four novel ENU lines identified from a recent ENU screen. In all four cases, after applying our method and combining with standard mapping data used to initially localize the variant to a chromosome, we found two or fewer putative mutations (and sometimes only a single one). Confirming that the variant was in fact causative was then easily achieved via standard segregation approaches. SeqAnt gave us the ability to rapidly annotate and screen variants of lesser interest (silent, UTR, intronic, intergenic), so we could instead focus our attention on those variants (replacement) that were most likely to account for the mutant phenotype.

6. An application of SeqAnt 2.0: Exome sequencing to discover mutations affecting neutrophil function in very-early-onset pediatric Crohn's disease

Children with very-early-onset (VEO) pediatric Crohn's disease (CD) are found to have high levels of neutrophil dysfunction. Neutrophils are an abundant type of white blood cell that play an essential role in innate immunity. We therefore hypothesized that children with very-early-onset Crohn's disease would exhibit an increased frequency of genetic mutations affecting neutrophil function. For an initial study we selected 45 VEO CD patients (median (range) age: 8.5 (5-10) years) with CBir1 sero-reactivity and moderate-to-severe clinical disease activity at diagnosis. We used the Roche NimbleGen SeqCap EZ Human Exome Library v2.0 on genomic DNA extracted from whole blood to capture the whole exome for each patient. Barcodes were used to prepare the libraries for whole-exome capture, which allowed us to sequence two whole exomes per lane of next-generation sequencing. We performed multiplexed 100 base-pair paired-end sequencing on an Illumina HiSeq 2000 instrument. We used PEMapper (Cutler and Zwick, in revision) to map raw sequence reads and identify variants sites relative to the ~30.8 Mb human exome reference sequence (NCBI37/hg19).

We then used SeqAnt to annotate all variant sites for functional significance, frequency, presence in databases like dbSNP, and measures of evolutionary conservation. Our central hypothesis was that early-onset (pediatric) forms of IBD would be substantially influenced by deleterious mutations found in the neutrophil pathway. If true, a straightforward evolutionary model of mutation-selection balance predicts that these variants ought to be rare in the general population, found at highly evolutionarily conserved sites, and have large effects on gene function. Thus, variants found in coding regions (replacement, nonsense, exonic insertions/deletions) that putatively alter protein structure and function will be the strongest candidates as contributors to IBD in pediatric patients. A number of lines of evidence specifically implicate loci involved in neutrophil functional pathways. We therefore proposed a strategy of first discovering variation in genes known to function in the neutrophil pathway, followed by direct functional testing of alleles from specific patients.

Gene	Location	Variants	Type	Position	Function	Frequency in VEO CD Patients	Frequency in Control Population
CSF2RA	chrX (p22.33)	0	-	-	GM-CSF signaling	-	-
CSF2RB	chr22 (q12.3)	1	SNP	37331455	GM-CSF signaling	0.02	0.0024
CYBB	chrX (p11.4)	1	SNP	37663322	oxidative burst	0.02	0.0032
DUOX1	chr15 (q21.1)	2	SNP SNP	45448069 45431655	enterocyte, H202	0.02 0.02	0.0003 0.0002
DUOX2	chr15 (q21.1)	1	Indel	45393428-30	enterocyte, H2O2	0.02	-
FCGR1A	chr1 (q21.2)	0	-	-	phagocytosis	-	-
FCGR2A	chr1(q23.3)	0	-	-	phagocytosis	-	-
FCGR2B	chr1 (q23.3)	0	-	-	phagocytosis	-	-
FCGR3A	chr1 (q23.3)	0	-	-	phagocytosis	-	-
FCGR3B	chr1 (q23.3)	0	-	-	phagocytosis	-	-
IL27RA	chr19 (p13.12)	1	Indel	14159807	IL-27 signaling	0.02	-
JAK2	chr9 (p24.1)	0	-	-	GM-CSF signaling	-	-
MPO	chr17 (q22)	0	-	-	bacterial killing	-	-
NCF1	chr7 (q11.23)	0	-	-	oxidative burst	-	-
NCF2	chr1 (q25.3)	0	-	-	oxidative burst	-	-
NCF4	chr22 (q12.3)	1	SNP	37273825	oxidative burst	0.02	0.0001
NLRP12	chr19 (q13.42)	0	-	-	chemotaxis	-	-
NOS2	chr17 (q11.2-q12)	3	Indel Indel Indel	26087106 26096042 26085975-76	reactive nitrogen intermediates	0.2 0.2 0.57	- - -
NOX1	chrX (q21.1)	0	-	-	oxidative burst	-	-
NOX3	chr6 (q25.3)	0	-	-	oxidative burst	-	-
NOX4	chr11 (q14.3)	2	SNP	89088208	oxidative burst	0.02	-

Gene	Location	Variants	Type	Position	Function	Frequency in VEO CD Patients	Frequency in Control Population
			SNP	89182666		0.02	0.0022
NOX5	chr15 (q23)	0	-	-	oxidative burst	-	-
PRAM1	chr19 (p13.2)	1	Indel	8564497-500	adhesion	0.02	-
RAC1	chr7 (p22.1)	0	-	-	oxidative burst	-	-
RAC2	chr22 (q12.3)	0	-	-	oxidative burst	-	-
SELPLG	chr12 (q24.11)	1	SNP	109017468	adhesion	0.11	-
SLC11A1	chr2 (q35)	2	Indel SNP	219247739 219254723	bacterial killing	0.02 0.02	- -
STAT3	chr17 (q21.2)	2	SNP SNP	40481429 40477064	IL-27 signaling	0.02 0.02	- 0.0002
STAT5A	chr17 (q21.2)	1	SNP	40461109	GM-CSF signaling	0.02	-
STAT5B	chr17 (q21.2)	0	-	-	GM-CSF signaling	-	-
VAV1	chr19 (p13.3)	0	-	-	oxidative burst	-	-
VAV2	chr9 (q34.2)	0	-	-	oxidative burst	-	-
VAV3	chr1 (p13.3)	0	-	-	oxidative burst	-	-

Table 7. Genetic variants found in genes that regulate neutrophil function.

We used SeqAnt to annotate all the sequence variations from the 45 exomes and identified a total of 60,682 variant sites of interest in coding regions (54,313 replacement SNPs, 2953 indels covering 6369 bases). For our exploratory genome-wide analysis of SNPs, we restricted our analysis to those variants with phyloP scores greater than 2.0, which corresponds to the top 1% of conserved sites in the human genome. Remaining were 12,575, of which 51% (6490) were not cataloged in dbSNP 132 and might constitute novel mutations contributing to early-onset IBD. We then restricted our analysis to 33 neutrophil genes. Table 6 contains a list of these 33 neutrophil genes with the number of rare putative functional variants (replacement SNPs or exonic indels). These variants are to be followed up using direct functional assays to assess function. Again, SeqAnt enabled us to rapidly annotate all variants, ignore those variants of lesser interest, and focus our attention on those most likely to contribute to the VEO CD in our sequenced patients.

7. Future directions

We have shown many useful features of SeqAnt and how it can be applied in a variety of experiments, yet we continue to develop SeqANt and plan to expand its functionalities going forward. Our goal is to create a one-stop online tool that readily accepts raw sequencing data and generates output through the annotation and functional characterization stages. Moreover, because our software and libraries are open source, they can be downloaded and optimized locally as part of a next-generation sequencing pipeline. SeqAnt is a truly dynamic application that is updated regularly to keep up with the constant flow of new sequencing data, genome assemblies, and improved annotation information available from public databases like those found at the UCSC Genome Browser.

Genomic sequence annotation requires an up-to-date and comprehensive database of DNA sequence information for a given organism. Our first aim is to continue adding to our database organisms whose genomic information could be annotated. We plan on including several other mammals, vertebrates, invertebrates, and ultimately bacteria strains in the near future. This will give researchers a web application they can use to speed their genetic studies of such organisms. We are also in the process of updating the dbSNP information contained in the SeqAnt database.

Another area of future focus is to broaden the types of input and output files that SeqAnt could work with, while embracing standards in broad use in the bioinformatics community. We intend to include the capability to directly annotate .vcf files as a standard input file format. Presently, all our output files are either text files or BED files. We also plan to provide the option of having the annotation output in .vcf format. Furthermore, we intend to modify SeqAnt to make the .map and .ped files (PLINK formats) from the snp variant file, which will be beneficial for substructure analysis and several other analyses that can be done using PLINK.

The inclusion of additional custom tracks from the UCSC browser to annotate for conserved and putatively functional sites will also be a future area of SeqAnt development. Our hope is that this will improve the effectiveness of downstream functional analysis. We also plan to have the application hosted in a cloud computing environment, side by side with other bioinformatics tools. This is relevant not only because of the wider accessibility it guarantees, but there is often the added ease of using other tools in the same environment to generate and modify input and output files from SeqAnt for further analysis.

SeqAnt was set up to be a dynamic application, and our improvements to this software make it possible to apply SeqAnt to different genomic variant analysis situations. Inevitable advances in sequencing technologies will spur continued demand for tools that can make sense out of the enormous raw sequence data generated, and we will work continually to make SeqAnt adaptable to these improvements and even more accessible to the wider public.

8. Conclusion

Great advances in targeted enrichment methods and DNA sequencing are beginning to allow individual investigators to sequence significant portions of many genomes; the bottleneck this has revealed lies with the annotation and interpretation of the resulting genomic variation data. SeqAnt is a software tool that directly addresses this bottleneck in a wide variety of potential applications. SeqAnt is an open source application that contains a number of unique features. The first is its ability to annotate data from many organisms, not just humans. Second, it is able to perform this analysis with a minimal memory footprint. Third, it completes this analysis in record time, thereby removing a significant bottleneck facing a researcher using the latest next-generation sequencing platforms.

The modifications we made to the application ensure we have the latest data tracks for the species we currently have in the SeqAnt binary databases. Furthermore, we have expanded the number of species that can now be annotated. Finally, with the addition of the PhyloP46Way conservation track, researchers can more confidently assess the evolution and significance of a particular variant site when the phyloP scores are viewed side by side with the PhastCons score values.

We have applied SeqAnt to various studies in our lab, from the work analysis of data on targeted sequencing of particular genes to the analysis of whole-exome data. We also used SeqAnt in the variant annotation of mouse genome and the adaptation of HapMap data for analyzing human exomes. The results from these various applications establish SeqAnt as a user-friendly tool that could help researchers in their work over a wide range of endeavors.

SeqAnt will continue to be an open source web application, which we will constantly update to meet the demands of changing and improving genomic and sequencing technologies. The future of genomics and variation studies lies in our ability to properly use the massive amounts of information we have obtained from DNA sequencing. Sequence annotation tools like SeqAnt that can efficiently turn such data into useable information will play a key role in this future.

Author details

Matthew Ezewudo, Promita Bose, Kajari Mondal, Viren Patel, Dhanya Ramachandran, and Michael E. Zwick*
Department of Human Genetics, Emory University School of Medicine, Atlanta, GA, 30322, USA

Acknowledgement

This work was supported by the National Institutes of Health/National Institutes of Mental Health (NIH/NIMH) and Gift Fund (grant number: MH076439, MEZ); the Simons Foundation Autism Research Initiative (MEZ); and the Training Program in Human Disease Genetics (grant number: 1T32MH087977, DR). We thank members of the Cutler and Zwick labs and Jennifer G. Mulle for discussion, Cheryl T. Strauss for editing, and the Emory-Georgia Research Alliance Genome Center (EGC), supported in part by PHS Grant UL1 RR025008 from the Clinical and Translational Science Award program, National Institutes of

* Corresponding Author

Health, National Center for Research Resources, for performing the Illumina sequencing discussed in this chapter. The ELLIPSE Emory High Performance Computing Cluster was used for the development of SeqAnt.

9. References

[1] Lander ES. 1996. The new genomics: global views of biology. *Science (New York, NY)* 274: 536-539.

[2] Chakravarti A. 2011. Genomic contributions to Mendelian disease. *Genome Res* 21: 643-644.

[3] Fledel-Alon A, Wilson DJ, Broman K, Wen X, Ober C, Coop G, Przeworski M. 2009. Broad-scale recombination patterns underlying proper disjunction in humans. *PLoS Genet* 5: e1000658.

[4] Bhangale TR, Rieder MJ, Nickerson DA. 2008. Estimating coverage and power for genetic association studies using near-complete variation data. *Nat Genet* 40: 841-843.

[5] Shetty AC, Athri P, Mondal K, Horner VL, Steinberg KM, Patel V, Caspary T, Cutler DJ, Zwick ME. 2010. SeqAnt: a web service to rapidly identify and annotate DNA sequence variations. *BMC Bioinformatics* 11: 471.

[6] Dreszer TR, Karolchik D, Zweig AS, Hinrichs AS, Raney BJ, Kuhn RM, Meyer LR, Wong M, Sloan CA, Rosenbloom KR, Roe G, Rhead B, Pohl A, Malladi VS, Li CH, Learned K, Kirkup V, Hsu F, Harte RA, Guruvadoo L, Goldman M, Giardine BM, Fujita PA, Diekhans M, Cline MS, Clawson H, Barber GP, Haussler D, James Kent W. 2012. The UCSC Genome Browser database: extensions and updates 2011. *Nucleic Acids Res* 40: D918-23.

[7] Flicek P, Amode MR, Barrell D, Beal K, Brent S, Chen Y, Clapham P, Coates G, Fairley S, Fitzgerald S, Gordon L, Hendrix M, Hourlier T, Johnson N, Kahari A, Keefe D, Keenan S, Kinsella R, Kokocinski F, Kulesha E, Larsson P, Longden I, McLaren W, Overduin B, Pritchard B, Riat HS, Rios D, Ritchie GR, Ruffier M, Schuster M, Sobral D, Spudich G, Tang YA, Trevanion S, Vandrovcova J, Vilella AJ, White S, Wilder SP, Zadissa A, Zamora J, Aken BL, Birney E, Cunningham F, Dunham I, Durbin R, Fernandez-Suarez XM, Herrero J, Hubbard TJ, Parker A, Proctor G, Vogel J, Searle SM. 2011. Ensembl 2011. *Nucleic Acids Res* 39: D800-6. PMC3013672.

[8] Chelala C, Khan A, Lemoine NR. 2009. SNPnexus: a web database for functional annotation of newly discovered and public domain single nucleotide polymorphisms. *Bioinformatics* 25: 655-661.

[9] Renaud G, Neves P, Folador EL, Ferreira CG, Passetti F. 2011. Segtor: rapid annotation of genomic coordinates and single nucleotide variations using segment trees. *PLoS ONE* 6: e26715.

[10] Makarov V, O'Grady T, Cai G, Lihm J, Buxbaum JD, Yoon S. 2012. AnnTools: A Comprehensive and Versatile Annotation Toolkit for Genomic Variants. *Bioinformatics*

[11] Garla V, Kong Y, Szpakowski S, Krauthammer M. MU2A – Reconciling the genome and transcriptome to determine the effects of base substitutions.

[12] Jiang J, Jiang L, Zhou B, Fu W, Liu J-F, Zhang Q. 2011. Snat: a SNP annotation tool for bovine by integrating various sources of genomic information. *BMC genetics* 12: 85.

[13] Sachidanandam R, Weissman D, Schmidt SC, Kakol JM, Stein LD, Marth G, Sherry S, Mullikin JC, Mortimore BJ, Willey DL, Hunt SE, Cole CG, Coggill PC, Rice CM, Ning Z, Rogers J, Bentley DR, Kwok PY, Mardis ER, Yeh RT, Schultz B, Cook L, Davenport R, Dante M, Fulton L, Hillier L, Waterston RH, McPherson JD, Gilman B, Schaffner S, Van Etten WJ, Reich D, Higgins J, Daly MJ, Blumenstiel B, Baldwin J, Stange-Thomann N, Zody MC, Linton L, Lander ES, Altshuler D, Group ISNPMW. 2001. A map of human genome sequence variation containing 1.42 million single nucleotide polymorphisms. *Nature* 409: 928-933.

[14] Mitchell AA, Zwick ME, Chakravarti A, Cutler DJ. 2004. Discrepancies in dbSNP confirmation rates and allele frequency distributions from varying genotyping error rates and patterns. *Bioinformatics* 20: 1022-1032.

[15] Consortium IH, Frazer KA, Ballinger DG, Cox DR, Hinds DA, Stuve LL, Gibbs RA, Belmont JW, Boudreau A, Hardenbol P, Leal SM, Pasternak S, Wheeler DA, Willis TD, Yu F, Yang H, Zeng C, Gao Y, Hu H, Hu W, Li C, Lin W, Liu S, Pan H, Tang X, Wang J, Wang W, Yu J, Zhang B, Zhang Q, Zhao H, Zhao H, Zhou J, Gabriel SB, Barry R, Blumenstiel B, Camargo A, Defelice M, Faggart M, Goyette M, Gupta S, Moore J, Nguyen H, Onofrio RC, Parkin M, Roy J, Stahl E, Winchester E, Ziaugra L, Altshuler D, Shen Y, Yao Z, Huang W, Chu X, He Y, Jin L, Liu Y, Shen Y, Sun W, Wang H, Wang Y, Wang Y, Xiong X, Xu L, Waye MMY, Tsui SKW, Xue H, Wong JT-F, Galver LM, Fan J-B, Gunderson K, Murray SS, Oliphant AR, Chee MS, Montpetit A, Chagnon F, Ferretti V, Leboeuf M, Olivier J-F, Phillips MS, Roumy S, Sallée C, Verner A, Hudson TJ, Kwok P-Y, Cai D, Koboldt DC, Miller RD, Pawlikowska L, Taillon-Miller P, Xiao M, Tsui L-C, Mak W, Song YQ, Tam PKH, Nakamura Y, Kawaguchi T, Kitamoto T, Morizono T, Nagashima A, Ohnishi Y, Sekine A, Tanaka T, Tsunoda T, Deloukas P, Bird CP, Delgado M, Dermitzakis ET, Gwilliam R, Hunt S, Morrison J, Powell D, Stranger BE, Whittaker P, Bentley DR, Daly MJ, de Bakker PIW, Barrett J, Chretien YR, Maller J, McCarroll S, Patterson N, Pe'er I, Price A, Purcell S, Richter DJ, Sabeti P, Saxena R, Schaffner SF, Sham PC, Varilly P, Altshuler D, Stein LD, Krishnan L, Smith AV, Tello-Ruiz MK, Thorisson GA, Chakravarti A, Chen PE, Cutler DJ, Kashuk CS, Lin S, Abecasis GR, Guan W, Li Y, Munro HM, Qin ZS, Thomas DJ, Auton A, Bottolo L, Cardin N, Eyheramendy S, Freeman C, Marchini J, Myers S, Spencer C, Stephens M, Donnelly P, Cardon LR, Clarke G, Evans DM, Morris AP, Weir BS, Tsunoda T, Mullikin JC, Sherry ST, Feolo M, Skol A, Zhang H, Zeng C, Zhao H, Matsuda I, Fukushima Y, Macer DR, Suda E, Rotimi CN, Adebamowo CA, Ajayi I, Aniagwu T, Marshall PA, Nkwodimmah C, Royal CDM, Leppert MF, Dixon M, Peiffer A, Qiu R, Kent A, Kato K, Niikawa N, Adewole IF, Knoppers BM, Foster MW, Clayton EW, Watkin J, Gibbs RA, Belmont JW, Muzny D, Nazareth L, Sodergren E, Weinstock GM, Wheeler DA, Yakub I, Gabriel SB, Onofrio RC, Richter DJ, Ziaugra L, Birren BW, Daly MJ, Altshuler D, Wilson RK, Fulton LL, Rogers J, Burton J, Carter NP, Clee CM, Griffiths M, Jones MC, McLay K, Plumb RW, Ross MT, Sims SK, Willey DL, Chen Z, Han H, Kang L, Godbout M, Wallenburg JC, L'Archevêque P, Bellemare G, Saeki K, Wang H, An D, Fu H, Li

Q, Wang Z, Wang R, Holden AL, Brooks LD, McEwen JE, Guyer MS, Wang VO, Peterson JL, Shi M, Spiegel J, Sung LM, Zacharia LF, Collins FS, Kennedy K, Jamieson R, Stewart J. 2007. A second generation human haplotype map of over 3.1 million SNPs. *Nature* 449: 851-861.

[16] Consortium IH. 2005. A haplotype map of the human genome. *Nature* 437: 1299-1320.

[17] Sherry ST, Ward MH, Kholodov M, Baker J, Phan L, Smigielski EM, Sirotkin K. 2001. dbSNP: the NCBI database of genetic variation. *Nucleic Acids Res* 29: 308-311.

[18] Pollard KS, Hubisz MJ, Rosenbloom KR, Siepel A. 2010. Detection of nonneutral substitution rates on mammalian phylogenies. *Genome Res* 20: 110-121.

[19] Briggs JP. 2002. The zebrafish: a new model organism for integrative physiology. *Am J Physiol Regul Integr Comp Physiol* 282: R3-9.

[20] Norton W, Bally-Cuif L. 2010. Adult zebrafish as a model organism for behavioural genetics. *BMC Neurosci* 11: 90. PMC2919542.

[21] Thorvaldsdóttir H, Robinson JT, Mesirov JP. 2012. Integrative Genomics Viewer (IGV): high-performance genomics data visualization and exploration. *Briefings in bioinformatics*

[22] Geschwind DH, Sowinski J, Lord C, Iversen P, Shestack J, Jones P, Ducat L, Spence SJ, Committee AGRES. 2001. The autism genetic resource exchange: a resource for the study of autism and related neuropsychiatric conditions. *Am J Hum Genet* 69: 463-466.

[23] Watterson GA. 1975. On the number of segregating sites in genetical models without recombination. *Theor Pop Biol* 7: 256-276.

[24] Tajima F. 1989. Statistical method for testing the neutral mutation hypothesis by DNA polymorphism. *Genetics* 123: 585-595.

[25] Mondal K, Shetty AC, Patel V, Cutler DJ, Zwick ME. 2011. Targeted sequencing of the human X chromosome exome. *Genomics* 98: 260-265.

[26] Fischbach GD, Lord C. 2010. The Simons Simplex Collection: a resource for identification of autism genetic risk factors. *Neuron* 68: 192-195.

[27] Caspary T, Anderson KV. 2006. Uncovering the uncharacterized and unexpected: unbiased phenotype-driven screens in the mouse. *Dev Dyn* 235: 2412-2423.

[28] Cook MC, Vinuesa CG, Goodnow CC. 2006. ENU-mutagenesis: insight into immune function and pathology. *Curr Opin Immunol* 18: 627-633.

[29] Acevedo-Arozena A, Wells S, Potter P, Kelly M, Cox RD, Brown SD. 2008. ENU mutagenesis, a way forward to understand gene function. *Annu Rev Genomics Hum Genet* 9: 49-69.

[30] Beutler B, Moresco EM. 2008. The forward genetic dissection of afferent innate immunity. *Curr Top Microbiol Immunol* 321: 3-26.

[31] Caspary T. 2010. Phenotype-driven mouse ENU mutagenesis screens. *Methods Enzymol* 477: 313-327.

[32] Stottmann RW, Moran JL, Turbe-Doan A, Driver E, Kelley M, Beier DR. 2011. Focusing forward genetics: a tripartite ENU screen for neurodevelopmental mutations in the mouse. *Genetics* 188: 615-624. PMC3176541.

[33] Sun M, Mondal K, Patel V, Horner VL, Long AB, Cutler DJ, Caspary T, Zwick ME. 2012. Multiplex Chromosomal Exome Sequencing Accelerates Identification of ENU-Induced Mutations in the Mouse. *G3 (Bethesda, Md)* 2: 143-150.

High-Performance Computing

Chapter 5

Hardware Accelerated Molecular Docking: A Survey

Imre Pechan and Béla Fehér

Additional information is available at the end of the chapter

1. Introduction

Hardware acceleration is the general concept of applying a specialized hardware for a given problem instead of an ordinary CPU in order to get lower processing time. General purpose CPUs can be considered as a totally general platform suitable for executing virtually any software or algorithm. Application specific accelerators have a custom architecture that fits the needs of a certain family of algorithms. As a consequence, they are able to outperform CPUs by orders of magnitude in a special application area but they are unfit for other, more general tasks. In contrast to normal CPUs, which are essentially serial machines executing instructions sequentially, hardware accelerators use parallel architectures which allow them to exploit the parallelism available in the given application by performing independent operations simultaneously.

The most important examples of hardware accelerators are graphics processing units (GPUs) and field-programmable gate array devices (FPGAs). GPUs are special many-core processors optimized for 3D rendering and image processing purposes. GPU devices are nowadays part of any desktop PC configurations and they can be programmed with general purpose programming languages. These facts make them an easily accessible and cost-effective accelerator platform and explain why they are used more and more frequently even in applications that are not graphics-related (general purpose GPU programming). FPGAs are programmable logic devices consisting of hundreds of thousands of general logic elements whose interconnection can be configured by the user. Thus FPGAs have a highly flexible architecture that allows to implement a totally custom digital hardware without the enormous cost of designing and manufacturing an application-specific integrated circuit (ASIC). When using an FPGA as a hardware accelerator a custom logic device is realized in the FPGA whose only purpose is to execute the algorithm to be accelerated as effectively as possible; thus the algorithm is usually implemented as pure hardware instead of software.

Hardware accelerators such as GPUs or FPGAs are utilized in many scientific applications, when the time-consuming operations make it impractical or even impossible to use ordinary CPUs. Bioinformatics is not an exception; it includes many problems and algorithms which are computationally expensive due to the large amount of data to be processed or the complex operations involved. Typical examples are different sequence alignment algorithms, protein structure prediction algorithms and molecular dynamics simulations which were implemented on various accelerator platforms several times.

Molecular docking is another key field of bioinformatics whose purpose is to determine the binding geometry of molecules and is used by the pharmaceutical industry for identifying drug candidate compounds. Docking algorithms are usually computationally demanding since they consist of generating and evaluating a large amount of different molecule conformations and placements. However, these different placements can often be processed simultaneously and evaluating a single placement usually offers further parallelization possibilities. These facts make molecular docking an ideal target for hardware acceleration. In accordance with this, several GPU- and FPGA-based docking implementations were reported applying different approaches for hardware acceleration. In this chapter our purpose is to give a general overview of the most interesting implementations and to compare them with respect to the applied parallelization, applicability and achieved speedup. The remainder of this chapter is organized as follows. Section 2 surveys the concept and methods of molecular docking. Section 3 gives a general overview of FPGA and GPU devices. Section 4 and 5 introduce the existing FPGA- and GPU-based docking implementations, respectively. Finally, Section 6 surveys the current state and perspectives of hardware accelerated molecular docking.

2. Overview of molecular docking

Molecular docking is a computer simulation technique for determining the possible binding position and binding energy of molecules whose initial 3D spatial structure is known. Many docking methods and software exist, which may be different in several respects such as the size and number of molecules involved, the applied docking algorithm, the applied chemical model or the modeling of molecular flexibility.

Molecular docking usually refers to docking a molecule to another one, that is, to determine the binding pose of the former relative to the latter. In case of protein-protein docking both of the molecules are large macromolecules. The more typical case is the protein-ligand docking when one of them is a small ligand molecule whose binding pose needs to be determined within the active site of a receptor. Since the computational complexity (the number of atoms, the size of the search space, etc.) differ by orders of magnitude, protein-protein and protein-ligand docking usually require different approaches. Although the number of molecules involved in the docking problem is generally two, some protein-ligand docking software allow to dock more than one ligand to a macromolecule simultaneously. For some software a good starting position has to be provided manually which is then refined by the algorithm; other ones are totally automated and try to find the docked position without any a priori knowledge.

Another important aspect is how the docking algorithm takes into account molecular flexibility. Rigid-body docking methods keep the structure of the molecules rigid, flexible algorithms consider one or both of the molecules flexible allowing their conformation to change. The two approaches correspond to the lock-key and the induced fit model, respectively. Rigid docking methods are usually much faster but may easily fail to find the proper binding position in case of molecules that actually undergo a conformational change upon binding. The most obvious way to model flexibility is to consider some bonds rotatable by allowing their torsional angle to change during docking. This method is effective in case of small ligands, but greatly increases the number of degrees of freedom and the computational complexity of the docking problem when applied for a large protein. As a consequence, protein flexibility is often taken into account only partially (allowing a few bonds of some side chains to rotate) or is modeled differently. One example is the soft receptor technique which allows small atomic collisions between neighboring protein and ligand atoms by reducing the repulsion energy term. The method is based on the assumption that the highly flexible protein could avoid the collision in practice by a low energy conformational change. Modeling flexibility in this way is computationally economic but may easily lead to invalid docked positions. Another straightforward technique is to keep the protein structure rigid and repeat the docking process with different pre-generated (or experimentally determined) protein conformations. Ultimately, this enables taking into account both protein and ligand flexibility even in case of rigid-body docking methods. The approach is also useful for considering the flexibility of rings within the ligand, which cannot be modeled with rotatable bonds; instead, a set of pre-generated, valid substructure conformations can be used during docking.

Although there are numerous different molecular docking algorithms, essentially each of them consists of two important components: a scoring function and a search method. The scoring function represents a chemical model and usually estimates the free energy of a geometrical arrangement of the molecules, thus it scores the given placement. The search method tries to find the ideal arrangement by sampling the search space according to a strategy. Docking can be viewed as an optimization problem where the global optimum of the scoring function is to be identified and the degrees of freedom are the variables describing the position, orientation and conformation of the molecules. Some docking methods apply one of the standard force fields as scoring function such as AMBER or CHARMM [1-4]. Other ones use empirical scoring functions that consist of a sum of terms representing different interaction types between the molecules; the term types are weighted with values determined empirically from a set of protein-ligand complexes [5, 6]. Knowledge-based functions are also typical which are derived from the statistical analysis of a large database containing molecular structures [7, 8]. The search methods applied by the different docking methods are also very diverse. One example is incremental reconstruction applied by the docking tools DOCK [4] and FlexX [9], which split the ligand to be docked and place the fragments one-by-one at the binding site. AutoDock [6] and GOLD [10] use genetic algorithms as global optimization methods. AutoDock Vina [11] applies a quasi-Newton BFSG algorithm along with Monte Carlo simulation. Other standard algorithms such as simulated annealing, tabu search or particle swarm optimization techniques are also common. A good overview of the general terms and concepts of molecular docking can be found in references [12-14].

The most important application area of molecular docking is computer-aided, structure-based drug design. Docking can be used for identifying drug candidates (potential inhibitors) for a given target receptor molecule. During virtual screening the members of a large ligand database are docked one by one to the target; promising compounds are subjected to further experiments. Virtual screening is extremely time-consuming; accelerating it can make the drug design process more effective. Trivially, this can be done by executing the docking runs of different molecules in parallel utilizing a lot of CPU cores. The other method is to accelerate the applied docking algorithm itself, potentially by an FPGA- or GPU-based hardware accelerator.

3. Accelerator platforms

3.1. FPGA devices

A field-programmable gate array is a programmable logic device - an integrated circuit with a flexible hardware architecture that can be configured to implement a specific functionality. FPGAs represent a trade-off between highly flexible, general purpose microprocessors and high-performance application-specific integrated circuits (ASICs). FPGA devices execute the required computation with a specific hardware architecture just like ASICs. Although they are not as efficient in terms of performance and power consumption, implementing a custom hardware in a 100-1000$ FPGA does not require to manufacture a new chip which is affordable only in case of large-scale production. In addition, FPGAs can be reconfigured many times. Thus they can be considered general-purpose similarly to CPUs but due to the applied custom architecture they can be orders of magnitude faster in case of a specific application.

The two major FPGA vendors, Xilinx and Altera offer a wide range of FPGAs and FPGA families with different capabilities, the performance and complexity of the devices is also continuously growing; however, the basic architecture remains the same. FPGA devices consist of a large number of similar basic logic blocks or cells arranged usually in rows and columns on the chip and a configurable interconnect structure. Figure 1. shows a simplified diagram of the basic logic block (slice) of a Xilinx Virtex-4 FPGA. The slice consists of two 4-input LUTs (look-up tables), two D flip-flops, carry logic supporting chaining of neighboring slices for high-performance arithmetic operations and routing resource configurable by multiplexers. A 4-input look-up table is a simple $2^4 = 16$ bit memory element that can realize any four-variable logic functions when initialized with the truth table of the corresponding function. D flip-flops are 1-bit registers that capture and store the value of the D input at every active CLK clock edge. Thus LUTs are the basic resources of the FPGA for implementing combinational logic and D flip-flops for sequential logic, respectively. In addition to the general logic resources FPGAs usually include special purpose cells such as dedicated memory blocks or DSP (digital signal processing) blocks consisting of adders and multipliers for arithmetic-intensive applications. FPGA-based accelerator cards are usually equipped with high-capacity external memory modules and high-speed interfaces like PCIe in addition to the FPGA.

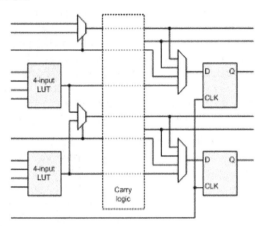

Figure 1. Virtex-4 slice

FPGA devices have an inherently parallel architecture which makes them suitable for high-performance computing applications. Different parts of an algorithm are executed by different hardware elements or modules; the execution can be simultaneous if the operations are independent. In data-parallel applications, where the same steps need to be performed on different data elements, the data can be distributed among many identical processing elements in the FPGA. In this case the achievable parallelism is limited only by the capacity of the device and the speed of the interface providing the input data. Another typical design concept is to apply a pipeline consisting of serially connected stages, which execute different steps of the same algorithm on different independent data elements.

Implementing an algorithm in an FPGA instead of a CPU may lead to a much shorter execution time; however, it usually requires more programming time and effort. The FPGA configuration can be defined with hardware description languages (HDL) such as VHDL and Verilog. HDLs allow the designer to describe the operation and interconnection of general digital circuits at a relatively high level (called register-transfer level). The HDL description is then mapped to the FPGA architecture by automatic tools. Further information regarding FPGA architectures, programming languages and design methodologies can be found in references [15-16].

3.2. GPU devices

Graphics processing units are massively parallel processors consisting of hundreds of processing cores, thus capable of executing hundreds of threads in parallel. Their architecture is optimized for data-parallel applications, which consist of instructions that have to be carried out on many different data elements. GPU operation is akin to the SIMD (single instruction multiple data) behavior – the parallel threads execute the same code but process independent input data. There are two main GPU manufacturers, AMD and NVIDIA, and although there are differences between the GPU architectures, the basic concepts are very similar. The same is true for the two widely used programming languages, CUDA and OpenCL. The former is developed by NVIDIA and is applicable to NVDIA devices only. OpenCL in turn is a standard parallel programming language supporting not only both GPU architectures but also multicore CPUs and heterogeneous platforms in general. The remainder of this section gives an overview of NVIDIA GPUs and CUDA since this is used by the majority of the GPU-based molecular docking implementations introduced in Section 5. However, the basic methodology and design patterns are very similar in case of OpenCL, only the terminology differs.

CUDA (Compute Unified Device Architecture) is the computing architecture of NVIDIA GPUs, which defines a parallel programming model based on high-level programming languages. CUDA C gives minimal extensions to the standard C language and provides an API, which enable the user to write a CUDA program consisting of serial code and special parallel functions called kernels. The former runs on the host CPU, the latter are executed K-times parallel by K different CUDA threads on the GPU. Threads of a kernel are grouped into thread blocks; the blocks in turn form a grid. Threads within the same block can communicate and synchronize with each other. This is not possible between different blocks of threads, since these are scheduled and executed in a random, non-deterministic order based on run-time decisions. This leads to automatic scalability; among ideal circumstances a GPU with twice as many processing cores can execute the same kernel twice faster.

The simplified hardware architecture can be seen on Figure 2. An NVIDIA GPU consists of multiprocessors. Each multiprocessor includes several processing cores, a large amount of registers, shared memory and a scheduler. In addition, each multiprocessor can access the external memory and has caches for texture and constant data access. When a kernel is launched, a certain number of thread blocks is assigned to every multiprocessor and becomes active. A multiprocessor executes its active blocks logically in parallel, and it manages, schedules and executes the threads of its active blocks in groups of 32 threads called warps. Warps are executed physically in parallel, that is, a multiprocessor is able to execute the same operation of every 32 thread within a warp simultaneously in one or a few clock cycle. However, if threads of a warp take different execution paths after a conditional branch statement, the different instructions get serialized, that is, they are executed sequentially (warp divergence).

Keeping the number of active blocks and warps high is important since this helps keeping every multiprocessor of the GPU busy as well as since the scheduler can hide the instruction and memory access latencies by switching between active warps. The maximal number of blocks that can be active on a multiprocessor is limited by the register and shared memory usage of the block since these resources are split among the active blocks. On the other hand, internal register and shared memory access is very fast. Threads can access their own registers in parallel; shared memory is divided into banks, and can be accessed also in parallel, as long as parallel threads access different memory banks. This suggests that data should be stored in registers and shared memory whenever possible. External memory access is much slower, but if threads of a warp read from or write to a contiguous memory space, the memory operations can be coalesced and executed as a single access, which can greatly increase the effective memory bandwidth. Constant data access is faster than ordinary memory read operations since it is cached. All of the aspects mentioned above have to be taken into account when choosing data storage areas, grid and block sizes. Further information about GPU architectures and programming can be found in references [17-19].

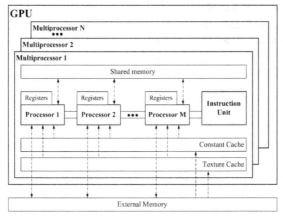

Figure 2. NVIDIA GPU architecture

4. Molecular docking on FPGA platforms

We believe that there are only three FPGA-based docking implementations which have been published until now. This chapter introduces all of them: a docking engine using 3D correlation, its successor, the FPGA-based implementation of the PIPER [20] docking program, and the FPGA-based acceleration of AutoDock.

4.1. Docking with 3D correlation

This implementation is described in references [21, 22]. The applied algorithm uses 3D correlation which is a common rigid-body docking technique. The molecules to be docked are represented with 3D grids whose voxels consist of pre-calculated values expressing some property of the molecule at the corresponding spatial location related to the binding affinity. In order to evaluate an arrangement the two grids are shifted relative to each other, then the voxels are multiplied pairwise and the values are summed to get the final score. By calculating the whole correlation array every possible translational position is evaluated.

This process has to be repeated for each orientation to be investigated, which requires the rotation of one of the grids periodically. In case of correlation-based docking methods the applied search method is essentially exhaustive search. Obviously the molecules are treated rigid during docking, since their structure is hard-coded in the grids.

The CPU-based docking programs using correlation usually replace it with Fourier transformation (FFT) and multiplication, which can be much faster on serial machines. The described FPGA-based implementation, however, performs direct correlation which can be effectively implemented with a highly parallel systolic chain in the FPGA. Another advantage of this method is that, by avoiding FFT, the operation for determining the voxel-voxel interaction is not restricted to multiplication; even non-linear functions can be used. In order to exploit this the implementation has a flexible structure; the design can be easily configured to adapt different scoring schemes. The initial implementation [21] used a very simple voxel type consisting of only two bits that distinguish molecule interiors from exteriors and mark the surface of the molecules. The final version allows using voxels with tuple data type that represent different effects including directional interactions like hydrogen bonding.

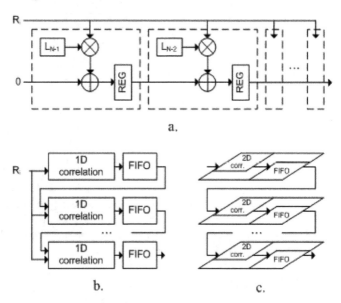

Figure 3. Systolic 3D array architecture [22, 23]

The core element of the implementation is a systolic 3D correlation array consisting of cells. Each cell stores one voxel of the grid corresponding to the smaller (ligand) molecule. The receptor grid is stored in external memory. Instead of rotating the ligand at the beginning of each new correlation cycle, rotated orientation is obtained by reading the receptor voxels in rotated order. Thus rotation is performed on the fly by the address logic and uses only little of the FPGA resources. The receptor voxels read from the memory are also rotated in case of directional data types; then they are passed to the systolic array. Figure 3/a shows a 1D correlation array consisting of pipelined cells. Each cell executes a pairwise operation (in this case, a multiplication) defined by the scoring method on its ligand voxel (L_i) and the receptor voxel (R_i) available at its input, then adds it to the sum received from the previous cell and stores the result in a register. 1D correlation arrays are connected by FIFO delay lines to form a 2D correlation plane; planes in turn are connected by delay planes to obtain the 3D correlation array (Figure 3/b and 3/c). Due to the pipeline-based structure, the systolic array produces the result of one position evaluation (correlation) in each clock cycle, and the achieved parallelism is proportional to the number of ligand grid voxels. Due to the large amount of output data the resulting grids are not sent to the host machine directly. Instead, a data reduction filter module detects the best score (local maximum) within each subblock of the correlation array; only these promising docked positions are returned for further analysis. Certain parts of the FPGA design are configurable according to the applied voxel word with and type, score data type, and the applied pairwise scoring operation in order to support various force laws and scoring schemes.

Performance tests were carried out with a Xilinx Virtex-II Pro XC2VP70-5 FPGA. Results were compared to a software running on a 3 GHz Xeon CPU. The software applied direct correlation since FFT proved to be slower for the applied small problem sizes. FPGA speedup varied between ×100-1000 according to the scoring method used.

4.2. PIPER on FPGA

The docking engine described in reference [23] is a modified, extended version of the docking core introduced in Section 4.1 and implements the PIPER software [20]. PIPER is based on 3D correlation and calculates it with the standard FFT method. The scoring function of PIPER consists of the weighted sum of different terms represented with separate grids; as a consequence, several independent forward FFTs have to be performed during evaluation. In addition to the van der Waals repulsion and attraction terms and the electrostatic interaction, desolvation effect is taken into account as well. The latter is described by a pairwise potential which is transformed to correlation grids with eigenvalue-eigenvector decomposition. Grids corresponding to low eigenvalues are often discarded which reduces computational complexity but retains the accuracy of the algorithm [20].

The original implementation described in Section 4.1 was modified in a variety of ways to support multiple energy grids as well as to allow docking of larger molecules which would not fit in the systolic 3D array, thus permitting even protein-protein docking. The basic cell element of the systolic array is extended to process the independent grids in parallel; as a consequence, each correlation is performed simultaneously. At the end of every 1D correlation array a new weighted scorer module sums the partial correlation results with respect to the weights defined in PIPER. New FIFOs are used to propagate the output of a scorer module to the input of the next one. Calculating the weighted sum at the end of every

1D array requires a balanced amount of multipliers and FIFOs (block RAMs) of the FPGA keeping the resource utilization optimal. To support large molecules both the receptor and the ligand are stored in external memories. The ligand grid is partitioned into subgrids small enough to fit the size of the correlation array. Correlation is performed piece-wise; each subgrid is first loaded to the FPGA, then the receptor voxels are streamed through the array.

The docking engine was implemented on an Altera Stratix-II EP2S180 and was validated against the original PIPER software. FPGA performance, however, was determined with post place-and-route simulations supposing an Altera Stratix-III EPSL340. Performance was compared to the original PIPER code, its multithreaded version, as well as a GPU-based implementation of PIPER (introduced in Section 5.1). The host CPU was a quad-core Intel Xeon 2 GHz CPU, the GPU code run on an NVIDIA Tesla C1060 device. The measured FPGA speedup depended greatly on the ligand grid size. In case of a 4^3 ligand grid speedup of the correlation task only and that of the whole application was almost ×1000 and ×37, respectively, compared to the single-core PIPER. However, it dropped exponentially with respect to the ligand size, decreasing below the ×16 speedup of the GPU at grid edge size 16 and below the ×3 speedup of the quad-core version at grid edge size 32. The reason for this is that the FFT method applied by the CPU and the GPU became greatly superior to direct convolution at this problem sizes.

4.3. AutoDock on FPGA

References [24, 25] introduce our own FPGA-based docking implementation, the acceleration of the AutoDock [6] docking software. AutoDock is applicable basically for protein-ligand docking and models molecular flexibility with rotatable bonds. AutoDock uses a semi-empirical scoring function that consists of weighted terms representing van der Waals and electrostatic interactions, hydrogen bonding and desolvation. The scoring function gives the energy contribution of one non-bonded atom pair; this value has to be summed over all movable atom pairs of the system to determine the score. To reduce computational complexity AutoDock represents the rigid part of the receptor molecule with pre-calculated potential grids. Thus the energy contribution of a given ligand atom and the whole receptor can be determined with trilinear interpolation and iterating over the receptor atoms is not necessary. AutoDock uses a standard genetic algorithm (GA) as search method. Genetic algorithms generate sets of potential solutions (generations of entities) iteratively. Solutions are represented with values of the degrees of freedom (called genes) and are created by combining the genes (crossover) of selected previous entities (selection) and altering them randomly (mutation). In addition to the genetic algorithm AutoDock subjects some selected entities of each generation to an iterative local search method (LS) similar to hill climbing, which greatly increases the effectiveness of the algorithm.

AutoDock was implemented on the SGI RASC RC100 module on a Xilinx Virtex-4 LX200 FPGA. The design consists of four main blocks organized as a three stage pipeline (Figure 4). The first pipeline stage executes the genetic algorithm, that is, it generates the genes of a new entity periodically. The second stage calculates the positions of the atoms of the ligand based on the input gene values. This step consists mainly of performing atomic rotations according to the positions of rotatable bonds and to the orientation of the ligand. The third stage includes two modules. One of them determines the receptor-ligand interaction energy based on the potential grids stored in external memory, that is, it performs a trilinear interpolation for each ligand atom; the other one calculates the energy contribution of each movable ligand atom pair by evaluating the scoring function directly. Each of the four modules consists of massively parallel, fine-grained internal pipelines; as a consequence, all of them are able to produce a new result of the realized operation in each clock cycle. The first module generates a new gene value, the second one performs the rotation of an atom, the other ones calculate the interaction energy of a ligand atom and the receptor molecule or that of an internal ligand atom pair in every clock cycle.

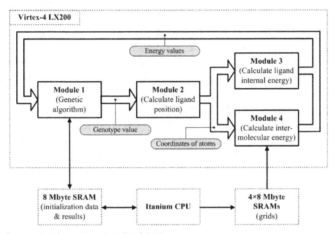

Figure 4. FPGA core implementing AutoDock [24]

In order to increase the performance of the docking engine the implemented algorithm slightly differs from the original AutoDock code and uses fixed-point arithmetic that fits better the FPGA architecture. According to test runs these differences does not degrade the accuracy of docking. Performance tests showed that the FPGA-based implementation yields an average speedup of ×23 over AutoDock running on a 3.2 GHz Intel Xeon CPU; the actual speedup varied between ×10-40 according to the structure and size of the molecules.

5. GPU-based implementations

Compared to the relatively small number of FPGA-accelerated docking engines, quite a lot of GPU-based solutions have been reported, which clearly indicates the advantages of GPUs over FPGAs in terms of accessibility and programming effort. It is neither reasonable nor possible to introduce every one of them. Instead, we aim at describing a wide variety of different approaches, and we tried to select the most promising implementations. Two of the docking codes introduced in the following subsections were implemented also on FPGA.

5.1. PIPER on GPU

The authors of the FPGA-based PIPER (Section 4.2) published also a GPU-based version [26]. In case of the FPGA the FFT applied in PIPER was replaced with direct correlation, which can be executed by a very effective standard structure in the FPGA. On GPU, both FFT and direct correlation were implemented and they proved to be advantageous at different ligand grid sizes. Other steps such as summing the grids and filtering the results by identifying local maxima also run on the GPU; although they comprise only a few percent of total PIPER runtime, executing them on the CPU would have limited the achievable speedup. The only exception is re-calculation of the ligand grid according to the current orientation and charges, which run on the host CPU.

3D correlation includes a lot of parallelism which can be exploited on a GPU as easily as on FPGA. Each voxel of the result grid can be calculated by a different thread simultaneously; in addition, correlation of grids representing different terms can be performed in parallel. In this implementation two different approaches are applied whose performance turned out to be similar: assigning each 2D plain to a different tread block, and assigning the same part of each 2D plain to a thread block. Receptor grid is stored in the external memory of the GPU due to its size and since it has to be available for each thread block (multiprocessor). Ligand grid is stored in shared or constant memory if possible; if the grid is small enough grids corresponding to multiple ligand orientations are stored and processed in parallel, which leads to further performance improvement.

Forward and inverse FFT is executed with the standard NVIDIA CUFFT library consisting of optimized FFT-related CUDA functions. Receptor grids are calculated by the CPU, moved to the GPU memory and transformed by the GPU only once at initialization. Ligand grids are re-calculated, copied and transformed for each ligand orientation. Voxels of the transformed receptor and ligand grids are multiplied pairwise by the GPU. The CUDA implementation is trivial, since each voxel pair can be processed independently by a different thread. Finally the product grid is inverse transformed.

The final step of each orientation evaluation is to sum the result grids according to the PIPER coefficients and find the voxels with the best scores corresponding to the best translational poses. PIPER uses several different sets of weights; these are assigned to different thread blocks in the GPU. Each block performs averaging according to the given set of weights. Individual threads process different parts of the grid. During averaging each thread identifies the best score of the grid part assigned to it and stores it in shared memory. Finally a single thread iterates over the scores to find the best one. Clearly the last filtering step could be implemented on the GPU the less effectively; if the number of coefficient sets is less than that of the multiprocessors, certain processors are not utilized, and serial steps such as finding the very last best score leads to idle threads. The majority of the algorithm, however, suits well the GPU architecture.

Performance tests were carried out on the platforms already mentioned in Section 4.2; the CUDA code run on a Tesla C1060 GPU and was compared to the FPGA-based version and to PIPER running on a single core and on all the four cores of a 2 GHz Intel Xeon CPU. Speedup of the correlation task was about ×300 compared to the single core version at a minimal ligand grid size of 4, but decreased exponentially with respect to ligand size similarly to the FPGA-based implementation. FPGA speedup was about ×1000 in case of a 4^3 ligand grid, so in case of direct correlation the FPGA outperformed the GPU. The FFT-based GPU code achieved a speedup of about ×30 regardless the ligand size and proved to be faster than GPU-based direct correlation above ligand grid size 8^3. Worst-case speedup of the whole GPU application was ×17.7 and ×6.1 versus single core and quad-core PIPER, respectively, and was faster than the FPGA accelerated version if ligand grid size was above 8^3.

5.2. A general FFT-based approach

In reference [27] another CUDA implementation is presented that applies FFT for performing the correlation-based rigid docking algorithm. The approach is very similar to the one described in Section 5.1. The scoring function is very simple; it consists of two terms which represent the shape of the molecules and the electrostatic field. These terms are calculated over the 3D grid for the receptor and for each orientation of the ligand. Again, FFT is executed with the CUDA library.

The test environment consisted of a dual-core AthlonX2 3600+ CPU and an NVIDIA GeForce9800GT GPU. The GPU speedup proved to be about ×3-4, depending on the grid size and the angle step size between different ligand orientations. That is, for the same search space size a finer discretization of the grids (meaning higher number of grid voxels) and a finer discretization of the ligand orientation (leading to more different orientations to be evaluated) resulted higher speedup. The reason is that in this case the FFT-grid multiplication-IFFT steps became more dominant compared to the whole GPU algorithm, and these can be executed the most effectively on the GPU.

The achieved GPU performance seems to be lower with respect to the GPU-based PIPER (Section 5.1). Although the applied algorithms and implementation methods are similar, the achieved speedups are hard to compare due to the different hardware platforms. The GeForce 9800 GT includes about half the number of multiprocessors than Tesla C1060. CPU frequencies are the same but the architectures are very different; the applied AMD CPU is older than the Intel used in case of PIPER. The other possible explanation of the different performance improvements is that in case of PIPER several grids has to be processed during docking, which leads to more parallelism and requires more FFT computation; thus the advantages of the GPU can be exploited more effectively.

5.3. AutoDock on GPU

AutoDock is one of the best-known docking software; it was the most cited docking program in the ISI Web of Science database in 2005 [28]. This explains why it is a popular subject for GPU-based acceleration. There is even a related SourceForge project called gpuautodock. The following subsections focus on three different AutoDock implementations; each of them maps different parts of the original algorithm to the GPU architecture.

5.3.1. Acceleration based on profiling

This AutoDock implementation is described in a case study [29]. The authors followed a traditional way – they profiled the original code in order to identify the most time-consuming functions and ported only these to GPU. Two functions were selected – eintcal() and trilininterp() – which together accounted for about 63% of the total runtime. The former calculates the internal energy of the ligand molecule, that is, it evaluates the scoring function for each ligand atom pair whose distance can change due to rotatable bonds. The latter is called for each ligand atom during the calculation of receptor-ligand intermolecular energy to perform interpolation based on the pre-calculated potential grids.

Each time these functions are called the corresponding CUDA kernel is executed instead of the original function. In both cases the number of threads within the kernel equals to the number of ligand atoms. This molecule usually consists of a few tens of atoms, which is a very low number compared to the GPU capabilities leading to a poor GPU utilization ratio. In addition, before each kernel call some data is transferred from the main memory to the GPU according to the current ligand position; these frequent memory transfer operations further decrease the performance.

According to test runs, which were executed on an NVIDIA GeForce GTX 280 GPU, the GPU accelerated application could not achieve speedup but was slower than the CPU for typical ligand sizes. Performance improvement was obtained only if the number of atoms (threads) was in the range of 10^4, which is not a realistic use case. The reasons are mentioned above. Accelerating only a few computationally expensive functions without restructuring the original code is straightforward and does not require much programming effort; however, it does not allow to exploit all the parallelism available in the algorithm, and also limits the maximal achievable speedup according to Amdahl's law.

5.3.2. Acceleration excluding local search

AutoDock includes further parallelism that is not exploited by the implementation described in Section 5.3.1. It uses a genetic algorithm as search method, which can be parallelized easily; each entity of the next generation can be created and evaluated simultaneously by different processing cores. The default population size is 150, which makes this approach promising with respect to GPU-based acceleration. However, AutoDock also applies an iterative local search method in addition to the GA, which is executed only on a few percent of the population (6%, that is, averagely 9 entities by default). Executing local search of different entities in parallel is possible, but would lead to low GPU utilization. In addition, performing the local search algorithm on an entity may consist of hundreds of iterations (energy evaluations); that is, executing the whole LS on CPU would greatly reduce the achievable speedup.

To overcome this problem, the authors of reference [30] chose to exclude the local search from the algorithm, but implement virtually every other part of AutoDock (the genetic algorithm, the ligand position calculation and the scoring function evaluation) on the GPU. Although the genetic algorithm (generating the degrees of freedom according to the GA rules) is usually not time-critical, leaving it on the host CPU would require periodic CPU-GPU memory transfer operations, which is avoided if it is executed by the GPU.

The main idea behind the implementation is to assign a different thread block to each entity of the new generation, whose threads cooperatively execute the different steps on the given entity. Another scheme was also tried where different entities were assigned to different threads, but this leads to low GPU utilization in case of typical population sizes – using default size, the number of parallel threads would be only 150 instead of 150 multiplied by the thread block size. The coordinates of ligand atoms are stored in the fast shared memory, which is crucial since every step of the scoring function evaluation modifies or reads this data and each thread of the block has to access it. During evaluation, each thread block first determines the atom positions (using two kernels for calculating the ligand conformation and orientation). Independent rotations of different atoms can be executed by different threads of the block. Then each thread performs trilinear interpolation for a different ligand atom (determining the atom-receptor intermolecular energy), and each thread evaluates the scoring function directly for a different ligand-ligand atom pair. Trilinear interpolation offers a further optimization, since NVIDIA GPUs support the fast access of 3D data by hardware.

Parallelization of the GA operators (selection, crossover and mutation) is also straightforward. Selection requires to calculate the relative score (fitness) of the entities compared to the average score, which can be performed for each entity simultaneously. Genes of the new entities can be generated by crossover and mutation in parallel by threads of the block assigned to the entity.

The test platform included an AMD Athlon 2.4 GHz and an NVIDIA Tesla C1060. Validation of the CUDA code was performed by using the same random seeds and comparing the output to that of original AutoDock. The results differed slightly only due to the single precision arithmetic applied in the GPU. The speedup of the different kernels depended highly on the population size. At default size speedup of the scoring function evaluation proved to be ×50, the selection and crossover ×1.25 and ×2.75. In case of mutation no speedup was obtained. The overall speedup of the algorithm was ×10 for a population size 50, it increased to ×20 for the default size and become saturated at 10000 yielding a speedup of ×47 over the CPU. On one hand, the GA operators could be implemented on the GPU much less effectively than the fitness evaluation. The probable reason is that they are much more control-intensive than the different steps of the scoring function evaluation consisting of a lot of arithmetic operations. On the other hand, executing GA on the CPU would certainly decrease the speedup due to the additional transfer operations between the CPU and GPU memory.

5.3.3. Acceleration including local search

Implementing AutoDock on CUDA without local search as in Section 5.3.2 clearly offers a straightforward parallelization scheme that avoids GPU underutilization. However, the local search process usually increases docking accuracy of AutoDock significantly [31]. In order to include the LS in the implemented algorithm and simultaneously achieve a high speedup we ported AutoDock to CUDA exploiting a further high-level parallelization possibility [25]. Due to the heuristic nature of the search algorithm, often several (10-100) different docking runs are performed with AutoDock for the same receptor-ligand complex. This increases the reliability of the results as well as helps identifying multiple valid docked poses. Since these docking runs are totally independent from each other, they can be executed in parallel.

Our implementation includes two CUDA kernels. In each generational cycle, first Kernel A is launched that creates and evaluates a whole population; then Kernel B is launched for performing LS on the selected entities. The two kernels call the same CUDA functions for scoring function evaluation; they differ only in how the degrees of freedom are generated (using either GA or LS rules). Basically, our implementation is quite similar to the one introduced in Section 5.3.2. Each thread block of the kernels is assigned to a different entity. Threads within a thread block generate different gene values, calculate independent rotations, and process different ligand atoms or atom pairs during scoring function evaluation. However, in case of kernel A a thread block is launched for each new entity of every independent docking run; in case of kernel B a block is launched for each entity of every run which is selected for local search.

The advantage of this method is that local search is included which allows preserving docking accuracy, and even significant performance improvement can be achieved if the number of independent runs is high enough. The performance improvement, however, depends strongly on this number and in case of too few parallel runs the GPU is underutilized during LS, which leads to a low speedup.

Test runs were carried out on an NVIDIA GeForce GTX 260 GPU; performance was compared with that of AutoDock running on a 3.2 GHz Intel Xeon CPU. In case of only one docking run the GPU achieved a low, ×2-5 speedup depending on the ligand structure and size. In case of 10 and 100 independent runs the average speedup proved to be ×30 and ×65, respectively, for a large set of ligands.

Our FPGA-based AutoDock implementation described in Section 4.3 achieved an average speedup of ×23. This value does not depend on the number of docking runs since the FPGA executes only one at a time. Due to the applied three stage pipeline (Figure 4) only three entities are processed simultaneously in the FPGA. On the contrary, the GPU applies a brute force approach by processing each entity of every run in parallel. The low level (per rotation, per atom, etc.) parallelization possibilities are exploited by fine-grained pipelines in the FPGA very effectively; this allows the FPGA-based implementation to achieve a significant speedup regardless the number of runs. As a consequence, the FPGA is faster than the GPU for a low number of runs. Further advantage of the FPGA architecture is that implementing local search is not problematic. However, if the number of runs is high enough, the GPU outperforms the FPGA; that is, similarly to the FPGA and GPU-based PIPER (Section 4.2 and 5.1) the two platforms are advantageous at different parameter ranges.

5.4. MolDock on GPU

Reference [32] describes the GPU-based acceleration of the MolDock [33] docking software. MolDock is very similar to AutoDock: it models molecular flexibility with rotatable bonds, its scoring function consists of the summation of pairwise energy terms, it uses pre-calculated potential grids for representing the receptor during docking and it applies a genetic (evolutionary) algorithm as search method. Differences are the actual form of the energy terms (which is virtually irrelevant from the point of view of parallelization) and the lack of local search.

Due to the similar algorithms the basic implementation schemes are practically the same as the ones described in Section 5.3.2 and 5.3.3; the gene values and atoms of every entity are distributed among the threads and are processed in parallel. Although no local search process is used, independent docking runs are performed in parallel to increase GPU utilization ratio (like in Section 5.3.3). Due to these similarities the implementation is not described here in more details. However, we would like to emphasize an apparent difference regarding how different jobs are aligned to the threads of the kernel.

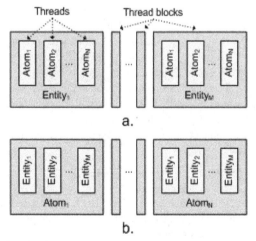

Figure 5. Job alignment comparison

In the GPU-based AutoDock implementations each thread block processes a different entity. In case of receptor-ligand energy calculation, for example, threads within the block perform trilinear interpolation for different atoms of the same ligand orientation (Figure 5/a). On the contrary, in this implementation threads within the same block perform interpolation for the same ligand atom of different entities (orientations) (Figure 5/b). Parallelization of other steps (genetic operators, internal energy calculation, etc.) also follows this scheme. This makes orientation calculation more effective; its disadvantage is that data corresponding to a given entity has to be stored in external GPU memory.

Performance tests were carried out using a 2.66 GHz Intel Core 2 Quad CPU and an NVIDIA GeForce 8800 GT. Average GPU speedup was ×5, ×27 and ×33 for 1, 10 and 20 parallel docking runs, respectively. The speedup, that is, GPU utilization showed a similar saturating tendency as in case of our GPU-based AutoDock implementation (Section 5.3.3).

5.5. PLANTS on GPU

PLANTS [34] stands for Protein-Ligand ANT System; it is a docking software using ant colony optimization (ACO) as search method. ACO is an optimization technique that mimics the behavior of ants when they collectively found the shortest path between the food source and the nest. At initialization, the degrees of freedom of the problem are discretized, and the same probability (pheromone level) is assigned to each discrete value of every degree of freedom. Then in each iteration a set of ants (potential solutions of the problem) choose a value for each degree of freedom according to the probability distribution. At the end of the iteration most of the probabilities are decreased (pheromone evaporation), but the ones corresponding to the best solution (shortest route) of the current iteration are increased, making it more likely that these values will be chosen by the ants in the next iteration. In PLANTS each solution is subjected to a local search algorithm at the end of each ACO iteration; then in a refinement step the LS is repeated for the best solution, which potentially further increases its fitness. PLANTS models flexibility with rotatable bonds and uses two different empirical scoring functions. One of them includes terms for protein-ligand steric interactions, torsions and clashes of the ligand (representing ligand internal energy), in addition, steric interactions and side-chain clashes of the protein (representing protein internal energy). The other scoring function is similar but models hydrogen bonds as well. The protein is represented with 3D grids during docking making the protein-ligand energy calculation more effective. From the point of view of parallelization ACO is similar to genetic algorithms: the ants can be generated, evaluated and subjected to local search in parallel like the entities of the GA.

The GPU accelerated PLANTS is described in reference [35]. The authors followed the traditional way of GPU programming using OpenGL and the NVIDIA Cg shading language. This method is less flexible than using CUDA; input data has to be encoded as textures, and functionality is implemented as shader programs processing these textures. The receptor grids, for example, are stored in a four channel (red, green, blue and alpha) 3D texture; the channels correspond to the four atom types which the scoring function of

PLANTS distinguishes. The optimization algorithms run on the CPU. The degrees of freedom are generated for each ant, then they are mapped to textures and moved to the GPU memory. Different shader programs calculate the coordinates of atoms, the protein-ligand interaction energy (by exploiting the interpolation capabilities of the GPU), the ligand clash and torsional energy terms. Finally a shader sums the partial energy terms. These steps are executed for each ant of the current ACO or LS iteration in parallel.

In order to exploit the capabilities of the GPU effectively the optimization algorithm was modified. The default value of ant colony size is 20 in PLANTS; to increase the number of solutions than can be evaluated in parallel multiple colonies are used, which sometimes exchange information by modifying the pheromone values of every colony according to the currently best solution. The refinement step was removed since it involves only one solution; in addition, the termination criterion of the LS was modified to prevent the parallel LS iterations from stopping after different number of steps. Although these modifications were necessary to achieve a high GPU utilization ratio, the altered algorithm turned out to be less effective than the original one; it requires a higher number of evaluations for finding the same solutions.

Test runs were performed on a 3.0 GHz dual core Pentium 4 CPU and an NVIDIA GeForce 8800 GTX GPU. For protein-ligand complexes the speedup of GPU accelerated steps was ×2-6 in case of 100 parallel solutions (5 colonies) and ×7-16 in case of 4000 parallel solutions (200 colonies), depending on the ligand structure. For protein-protein complexes with higher arithmetic intensity the speedup was ×10-20 and ×40-50 for 100 and 4000 parallel ants, respectively. The speedup of the whole GPU-based application with typically 400-500 parallel solutions proved to be about ×4 over the original PLANTS. This is an average value for a large set of protein-ligand complexes; in case of large and highly flexible ligands speedups over ×7 were observed.

5.6. Other approaches

As we mentioned, it is not possible to introduce every GPU-based docking solution reported; instead we try to give a general overview of the diverse methods applied in this field. In this subsection some further GPU-based implementations are mentioned, which in a way are different from the solutions described above. Instead of introducing these in details, we focus on the differences.

5.6.1. Hex on GPU

Reference [36] describes the GPU-based acceleration of the Hex [37] program. Hex uses the FFT-correlation technique for docking. Instead of the ordinary Cartesian grids and translational correlation, however, Hex applies the spherical polar Fourier method based on rotational correlations, which allows to traverse not just the translational but also the orientational search space with FFT. The docking can be executed both with multiple 3D and with multiple 1D FFTs. Using 1D FFTs turned out to be much more advantageous on the GPU, since it has a better memory read pattern than 3D FFT. The measured speedup on an NVIDIA GeForce GTX 285 was about ×45 compared to running Hex with 1D FFTs on a single CPU core.

5.6.2. Calculating pairwise potentials

Reference [38] focuses on the acceleration of calculating the pairwise potentials between the protein-ligand atoms. In many docking applications this is performed with pre-calculated grids which reduces the $O(N_{prot}*N_{lig})$ complexity to $O(N_{lig})$ during docking (where N denotes the number of atoms of the molecule). This implementation, however, calculates the double sum directly; one protein atom is assigned to each CUDA thread, which iterates over the ligand atoms and calculates the corresponding potential values. Although the effectiveness of the approach is uncertain due to the increased complexity, it is interesting since it fits the GPU architecture perfectly. The number of protein atoms is usually high enough to keep the multiprocessors of the GPU busy; it is not necessary to evaluate multiple ligand positions simultaneously. In addition, the amount of input data is smaller (the number of protein atoms is usually lower than that of the grid points), making this approach less memory-intensive. Depending on the molecule sizes, speedups between ×10-260 were observed on an NVIDIA Tesla C1060 GPU, compared to the same algorithm running on an Intel Xeon E5530 CPU.

5.6.3. Using multiple GPUs

Similarly to the previous section, reference [39] deals with accelerating only the pairwise potential calculation on GPU. The scoring function consists of two usual terms representing the van der Waals and electrostatic interaction. However, in this implementation two separate GPU devices are used; one of them calculates the van der Waals, the other one the electrostatic term. In a real docking application this approach would be probably impractical due to the required CPU-GPU memory transfer operations. Still, the applicability of multiple GPUs to the docking problem is intriguing; the most trivial way of utilizing them is to perform independent runs on the different devices. In case of this implementation overall speedup factors between ×118-193 were achieved; the test platform consisted of a 2.4 GHz Intel Core 2 Quad CPU and an NVIDIA GeForce 8800 GTX GPU.

6. Conclusion

Three FPGA-based and several GPU-based molecular docking implementations were surveyed in the previous sections. Although molecular docking algorithms are quite diverse in general, the methods introduced in this chapter actually fall into two categories. Both categories represent a docking approach which is easily parallelizable and thus suits well the architecture of accelerator platforms.

The first group includes the correlation-based methods (Section 4.1, 4.2, 5.1, 5.2 and 5.6.1). As it was shown, correlation is a massively parallel operation and can be implemented effectively in FPGA; on GPU in turn it can be performed with optimized FFT kernels. This makes correlation-based docking algorithms ideal for hardware acceleration; the limitation is that they support only rigid-body docking.

The second group includes docking algorithms based on a global optimization algorithm which is inherently parallel (Section 4.3, 5.3-5.5). Both the evolutionary algorithms used by AutoDock and MolDock, and the ant colony optimization method of PLANTS operate on sets of potential solutions, which allows members of the set to be processed in parallel. The usual pairwise scoring functions applied by these programs offer further parallelization at the level of atoms or atom pairs. In addition, these methods support modeling of molecular flexibility, too.

Many of the introduced, accelerator-based docking implementations achieved significant speedup over single or even multi-core CPUs. The actual speedup value is always a matter of reference platform, of course; still, the results prove that molecular docking can effectively accelerated by hardware and often a performance improvement of 1-2 orders of magnitude can be obtained. However, this improvement is usually not constant; in many cases it was shown that it strongly depends on input parameters (number of atoms, size of search space, search exhaustiveness, etc.), making accelerators usually more suitable for larger problem sizes.

It should also be noted that performance improvement may come at a price: in some cases (4.3, 5.3.2, 5.5) the original algorithm had to be altered to make it more suitable for parallelization. Typically these changes were related to the local search in these cases, which is essentially a sequential algorithm. Such modifications are often necessary, however, they change the behavior and accuracy of the algorithm, which is sometimes unacceptable. Another typical necessity is that in addition to the computationally intensive but parallelizable steps that suit well the accelerator architecture, other parts must also be mapped to the accelerator in order to avoid that the host-accelerator bandwidth becomes a bottleneck. This, however may greatly increase the required programming effort.

Another interesting point is the applicability and performance of FPGAs vs. GPUs. In case of the PIPER implementations (Section 4.2, 5.1) the FPGA outperformed the GPU when both executed correlation directly; but due to the effective FFT-based approach the GPU implementation seemed to be more suitable since its performance scaled well with the problem size. In case of AutoDock (Section 4.3, 5.3.3) the GPU outperformed the FPGA in practical cases, although the latter exploited the low-level parallelism of the docking algorithm more effectively and thus was faster than the GPU if the number of parallel runs was low. All these results confirm that GPU devices represent a real competitor of FPGAs even when considering only performance. In addition, as it was mentioned in Section 3, FPGA programming usually requires hardware skills while GPUs can be programmed in C-like languages (although there are high-level C-based HDLs they are usually not as effective as VHDL or Verilog). GPU cards are cheaper by far than high-performance FPGA accelerators, and often they are already available in the desktop PC. All these facts suggest that GPUs are a better choice as accelerator platform than FPGAs in case of floating point-intensive applications like the majority of the docking algorithms, although clearly there are problem domains where FPGAs remain superior.

Author details

Imre Pechan
evopro Informatics and Automation Ltd, Budapest, Hungary

Béla Fehér
Department of Measurement and Information Systems,
Budapest University of Technology and Economics, Budapest, Hungary

Acknowledgement

We would like to thank evopro Informatics and Automation Ltd for supporting our work and providing access to the necessary hardware and software tools.

7. References

[1] Brooks BR, Bruccoleri RE, Olafson BD, States DJ, Swaminathan S, Karplus M (1983) CHARMM: A Program for Macromolecular Energy, Minimization, and Dynamics Calculations. J. Comput. Chem. 4: 187-217.

[2] Cornell WD, Cieplak P, Bayly CI, Gould IR, Merz KM, Ferguson DM, Spellmeyer DC, Fox T, Caldwell JW, Kollman PA (1995) A Second Generation Force Field for the Simulation of Proteins, Nucleic Acids, and Organic Molecules. J. Am. Chem. Soc. 117: 5179-5197.

[3] Grosdidier A, Zoete V, Michielin O (2011) Fast docking using the CHARMM force field with EADock DSS. J. Comput. Chem. 32: 2149-2159.

[4] Ewing TJA, Makino S, Skillman AG, Kuntz ID (2001) DOCK 4.0: Search Strategies for Automated Molecular Docking of Flexible Molecule Databases. J. Comput. Aided Mol. Des. 15: 411-428.

[5] Friesner RA, Banks JL, Murphy RB, Halgren TA, Klicic JJ, Mainz DT, Repasky MP, Knoll EH, Shelley M, Perry JK, Shaw DE, Francis P, Shenkin PS (2004) Glide: A New Approach for Rapid, Accurate Docking and Scoring. 1. Method and Assessment of Docking Accuracy. J. Med. Chem. 47: 1739-1749.

[6] Huey R, Morris GM, Olson AJ, Goodsell DS (2007) A Semiempirical Free Energy Force Field With Charge-Based Desolvation. J. Comput. Chem. 28: 1145-1152.

[7] Muegge I, Martin YC (1999) A General and Fast Scoring Function for Protein-Ligand Interactions: A Simplified Potential Approach. J. Med. Chem. 42: 791-804.

[8] Gohlke H, Hendlich M, Klebe G (2000) Knowledge-Based Scoring Function to Predict Protein-Ligand Interactions. J. Mol. Biol. 295: 337-356.

[9] Rarey M, Kramer B, Lengauer T (1997) Multiple Automatic Base Selection: Protein–Ligand Docking Based on Incremental Construction Without Manual Intervention. J. Comput. Aided Mol. Des. 11: 369-384.

[10] Jones G, Willett P, Glen RC, Leach AR, Taylor R (1997) Development and Validation of a Genetic Algorithm for Flexible Docking. J. Mol. Biol. 267: 727-748.

[11] Trott O, Olson AJ (2010) AutoDock Vina: Improving the Speed and Accuracy of Docking with a New Scoring Function, Efficient Optimization, and Multithreading. J. Comput. Chem. 31: 455-461.

[12] Teodoro ML, Phillips GN, Kavraki LE (2001) Molecular Docking: A Problem With Thousands of Degrees of Freedom. IEEE Int. Conf. on Robotics and Automation, 2001 May 21-26, Seoul, Korea.

[13] Dias R, de Azevedo WF (2008) Molecular Docking Algorithms. Curr. Drug Targets 9: 1040-1047.

[14] Kavraki LE (2007) Protein-Ligand Docking, Including Flexible Receptor-Flexible Ligand Docking. Receptor 1-19. Available: http://cnx.org/content/m11456/latest/. Accessed 2012. 04. 29.

[15] Hauck S, DeHon A (2007) Reconfigurable Computing - The Theory and Practice of FPGA-Based Computation. Morgan Kaufmann. 944 p.

[16] Kilts S (2007) Advanced FPGA Design - Architecture, Implementation, and Optimization. Wiley. 352 p.

[17] NVIDIA CUDA C Programming Guide. Available: http://developer.nvidia.com/nvidia-gpu-computing-documentation. Accessed 2012. 04. 29.

[18] Sanders J, Kandrot E (2010) Cuda by Example - An Introduction to General-Purpose GPU Programming. Addison-Wesley. 312 p.

[19] AMD Accelerated Parallel Processing OpenCL Programming Guide. Available: http://developer.amd.com/sdks/AMDAPPSDK/documentation/Pages/default.aspx. Accessed 2012. 04. 29.

[20] Kozakov D, Brenke R, Comeau SR, Vajda S (2006) PIPER: An FFT-Based Protein Docking Program with Pairwise Potentials. Proteins 65: 392-406.

[21] VanCourt T, Gu Y, Herbordt MC (2004) FPGA Acceleration of Rigid Molecule Interactions. 12th Ann. IEEE Symp. on Field-Programmable Custom Computing Machines, 2004 Apr. 20-23, Napa, USA.

[22] VanCourt T, Gu Y, Mundada V, Herbordt MC (2006) Rigid Molecule Docking: FPGA Reconfiguration for Alternative Force Laws. EURASIP J. on Applied Signal Processing 2006: 1-10.

[23] Sukhwani B, Herbordt MC (2010) FPGA Acceleration of Rigid-Molecule Docking Codes. IET Comput. Digit. Tech. 4: 184-195.

[24] Pechan I, Fehér B, Bérces A (2010) FPGA-Based Acceleration of the AutoDock Molecular Docking Software. Conf. on Ph.D. Research in Microelectronics and Electronics, 2010 July 18-20, Berlin, Germany.

[25] Pechan I, Fehér B (2011) Molecular Docking on FPGA and GPU Platforms. Int. Conf. on Field Programmable Logic and Applications, 2011 Sept. 5-7, Chania, Greece.

[26] Sukhwani B, Herbordt MC (2009) GPU Acceleration of a Production Molecular Docking Code. 2nd Workshop on General Purpose Processing on Graphics Processing Units, 2009 Mar. 8, Washington, USA.

[27] Feng Z, Tian X, Chang S (2010) A Parallel Molecular Docking Approach Based on Graphic Processing Unit. 4th Int. Conf. on Bioinformatics and Biomedical Engineering, 2010 June 18-20, Chengdu, China.

[28] Sousa SF, Fernandes PA, Ramos MJ (2006) Protein-Ligand Docking: Current Status and Future Challanges. Proteins 65: 15-26.

[29] Micevski D, Kuiper M (2009) Optimizing Autodock with CUDA. VPAC Case Study. Available: http://www.vpac.org/?q=node/290. Accessed 2012. 04. 29.

[30] Kannan S, Ganji R (2010) Porting Autodock to CUDA. IEEE Cong. on Evolutionary Computation, 2010 July 18-23, Barcelona, Spain.

[31] Morris GM, Goodsell DS, Halliday RS, Huey R, Hart WE, Belew RK, Olson AJ (1998) Automated Docking Using a Lamarckian Genetic Algorithm and an Empirical Binding Free Energy Function. J. Comput. Chem. 19: 1639-1662.

[32] Simonsen M, Pedersen CNS, Christensen MH, Thomsen R (2011) GPU-Accelerated High-Accuracy Molecular Docking Using Guided Differential Evolution. 13th Ann. Conf. on Genetic and Evolutionary Computation, 2011 July 12-16, Dublin, Ireland.

[33] Thomsen R, Christensen MH (2006) MolDock: A New Technique for High-Accuracy Molecular Docking. J. Med. Chem. 49: 3315-3321.

[34] Korb O, Stützle T, Exner TE (2007) An Ant Colony Optimization Approach to Flexible Protein–Ligand Docking. Swarm Intell. 1: 115-134.

[35] Korb O, Stützle T, Exner TE (2011) Accelerating Molecular Docking Calculations Using Graphics Processing Units. J. Chem. Inf. Model. 51: 865-876.

[36] Ritchie DW, Venkatraman V (2010) Ultra-Fast FFT Protein Docking on Graphics Processors. Bioinformatics 26: 2398-2405.

[37] Ritchie DW, Kozakov D, Vajda S (2008) Accelerating and Focusing Protein-Protein Docking Correlations Using Multi-Dimensional Rotational FFT Generating Functions. Bioinformatics 24: 1865-1873.

[38] Guerrero GD, Sánchez HP, Wenzel W, Cecilia JM, García JM (2011) Effective Parallelization of Non-bonded Interactions Kernel for Virtual Screening on GPUs. 5th Int. Conf. on Practical Applications of Computational Biology & Bioinformatics, 2011 Apr. 6-8, Salamanca, Spain.

[39] Roh Y, Lee J, Park S, Kim J (2009) A Molecular Docking System Using CUDA. Int. Conf. on Hybrid Information Technology, 2009 Aug. 27-29, Daejeon, Korea.

Chapter 6

Towards a Hybrid Federated Cloud Platform to Efficiently Execute Bioinformatics Workflows

Hugo Saldanha, Edward Ribeiro, Carlos Borges, Aletéia Araújo, Ricardo Gallon, Maristela Holanda, Maria Emília Walter, Roberto Togawa and João Carlos Setubal

Additional information is available at the end of the chapter

1. Introduction

Current generation of high-throughput DNA sequencing machines [1, 35, 66] can generate large amounts of DNA sequence data. For example, the machine HiSeq 2000 from the company Illumina, a current workhorse of genome centers, is capable of generating 600 Giga base-pairs of sequence in one single run [35]. The Human Microbiome project (https://commonfund.nih.gov/hmp) and the 1000 Genomes project (http://www.1000genomes.org) are two examples of projects that are generating terabyte-scale amounts of DNA sequence.

Such vast amounts of data can only be handled by powerful computational infrastructures (also known as cyberinfrastructures), sophisticated algorithms, efficient programs, and well-designed boinformatics workflows. As a response to this challenge, a large ecosystem composed by different technologies and service providers has emerged in recent years with the paradigm of cloud computing [2, 58, 63, 71]. In this paradigm users have transparent access to a wide variety of distributed infrastructures and systems. In this environment, computing and data storage necessities are accomplished in different and unanticipated ways to give the user the illusion that the amount of resources is unrestricted.

In this scenario, cloud computing is an interesting option to control and distribute processing of large volumes of data produced in genome sequencing projects and stored in public databases that are widespread in distinct places. However, considering the constant growing of computational and storage power needed by different bioinformatics applications that are continously beeing developed in different distributed environments, working with one single cloud service provider can be restrictive for bioinformatics applications. Working with more than one cloud can make a workflow more robust in the face of failures and unanticipated needs. Cloud federation [11, 14, 15] is one such solution. Cloud federation offers other advantages over single-cloud solutions. Bioinformatics centers can profit from participation in a cloud federation, by having access to other center programs, data, execution and storage capabilities, in a collaborative environment. The federation can abstract cloud-specific mechanisms, thus potetially making the use of such a resource more user-friendly and easier to install and customize. This is particularly valuable for small and medium centers that can enlarge their hardware resources and software tools using machines and programs of other centers integrating a federated system.

In this work, we propose a hybrid federated cloud computing platform that aims at integrating and controlling different bioinformatics tools in a distributed, transparent, flexible and fault tolerant manner, also providing highly distributed processing and large storage capability. The objective is to make possible the use of tools and services provided by multiple institutions, public or private, that can be easily aggregated to the cloud. We also discuss a use case of this platform, a bioinformatics workflow for identifying differentially expressed genes in cancer tissues.

2. Federated cloud computing

There are many distinct definitions of cloud computing. According to [29], cloud computing could be defined as "*a computational paradigm highly distributed, directed by a scale economy, in which the computational power, storing, abstract platforms and services, virtualized, managed and dinamically scalable are provided on demand by external users through the Internet*".

[71], using all the characteristics collected from the literature, proposed a definition of clouds as "*a big pool of virtualized resources, easily usable. The resources can be reconfigured dinamically according to a variable load, allowing optimized using. This pool is typically explored by a pay-per-use model in which guarantees are offered by the infrastructure provider, following a service contract*". These authors attempted to define cloud computing using only common characteristics in cloud providers, but they did not find features that were mentioned by all providers. The most common were scalability, pay-per-use model and virtualization.

From these definitions we can state that the goal of cloud computing is to offer to users the idea that they have unrestricted resources, but they have to pay only for those effectively used (model pay-per-use). Another significant advantage of clouds is the management of the computational infrastructure, relieving users from concerns such as power failures and backups. The property of allocating computational resources depending on user needs is called elasticity.

Cloud services can be deployed by providers in different ways [48]:

- Private cloud: operated for the use of a single organization. It can be managed by the organization itself or by external ones.
- Community Cloud: shared by several organizations and used as a tool for a specific group of users with common interests.
- Public Cloud: available to the general public or a large corporate group that is part of the organization that sells this service.
- Hybrid cloud: composed of two or more clouds (private, community or public) that remain separate entities, but that are bound together by standardized or proprietary technologies that enable portability of data and applications.

In clouds, one of the key technologies adopted to execute bioinformatics programs is the Apache Hadoop framework [6], in which the MapReduce [25] model and its distributed file system (HDFS) [13] are used as infrastructure to distribute large scale processing and data storage. In the MapReduce model parallelization does not require communication among simultaneously processed tasks, since they are independent from one another.

Bittman [11] claimed that the evolution of cloud computing market could be divided in three phases. In phase 1 (Monolithic), cloud computing services were based on proprietary architectures, or cloud services were delivered by megaproviders. In phase 2 (Vertical Supply Chain), some cloud providers leveraged services from other providers, i.e. independent software vendors (ISVs) developed applications as a service using an existing cloud infrastructure. Clouds were still proprietary, but ecosystems construction started. In phase 3 (Horizontal Federation), smaller providers would horizontally federate to gain economy of scale and efficient use of their assets. Projects would leverage horizontal federation to enlarge their capacibilities, more choices at each cloud computing layer would be provided, and discussion about standards would begin.

In general, cloud computing intends to increase efficiency in service delivery, dealing with services including infrastructure, platforms and software, and treating with distinct users like a single user, other clouds, academic institutions and large companies. Besides public clouds maintained by large organizations, hundreds of smaller heterogeneous and independent clouds, private or hybrid, are being developed. In this scenario, cloud federation becomes an interesting way to optimize the use of the resources offered by various organizations. In particular, in this chapter, we are interested in horizontal cloud federation, also called federated cloud computing, inter-cloud [14] or cross-cloud [15].

Federated cloud computing can be defined as a set of cloud computing providers, public and private, connected through the Internet [14, 15]. Among its objectives we distinguish the seemingly availability of unrestricted resources, independence of a single infrastructure provider, and optimization when using a set of distinct resource providers.

Thus, federation allows each cloud computing provider to increase its processing and storage capabilities by requesting more resources to other clouds in the federation when needed. This means that a local cloud provider is able to satisfy user requests beyond its capabilities, since idle resources from other providers can be used. Furthermore, if a provider fails, resources can be requested to another one, providing more fault tolerance.

Although the advantages of federated cloud computing are obvious, its implementation is not trivial, since the participating clouds present heterogeneous and frequently changing resources. Therefore, traditional models of federation are not useful [15]. Typically, federated models are based on *a priori* agreements among their members, noting that these agreements can be inappropriate according to the particular characteristics of a cloud provider. Thus, to make possible the creation of a federated cloud environment, it is necessary to achieve the following requirements [14, 15]:

- **Automatism**: a cloud member of the federation, using discovery mechanisms, should be able to identify the other clouds in the federation together with their resources, responding to changes in a transparent and automatic way;

- **Application behavior prediction**: the system implementing the federation has to be able to predict demands and behaviors of the offered applications, so that its load balancing mechanism can have its efficiency improved;

- **Mapping services to resources**: the services offered by the federation must be mapped to available resources in a flexible manner so that it can achieve the highest levels of efficiency and cost/benefit. In other words, the schedule must choose the best hardware-software combination to ensure the quality of service at lowest cost, taking into account the uncertainty of the availability of resources;

- **Interoperable security model**: federation must allow the integration of different security technologies so that a cloud member does not need to change its security policies when entering the federation;

- **Scalability in monitoring components**: considering the possible large number of participants, the federation must be able to handle multiple task queues and the largest number of requests, so that management can guarantee that the various cloud providers of the federation will mantain scalability and performance.

It is noteworthy that issues to choose an appropriate cloud provider and lack of common cloud standards hinder the interoperability across these federated cloud providers. Thus, nowadays the user is faced with the challenging problem of selecting the appropriate cloud that fits his or her needs. To address this problem, the BioNimbus platform offers to users a federated platform that can execute bioinformatics applications in a transparent and flexible manner. This is possible because BioNimbus offers standardized interfaces and intermediate services to manage the integration of different cloud providers. Moreover, as will be seen next, BioNimbus was designed to incorporate the requirements defined by [15].

3. BioNimbus: a federated cloud platform

As mentioned before, cloud computing is a promising paradigm for bioinformatics due to its ability to provide a flexible computing infrastructure on demand, its seemingly unrestricted resources, and the possibility to distribute execution in a large number of machines leading to a significant reduction in processing time due to the high degree of achieved parallelism. Some bioinformatics tools have been implemented in cloud environments belonging to several infrastructures of physically separated institutions, which makes it difficult for them to be integrated.

BioNimbus [12, 62] is a federated cloud platform designed to integrate and control different bioinformatics tools in a distributed, flexible and fault tolerant manner, providing rapid processing and large storage capabilities, transparently to users. BioNimbus joins physically separate platforms, each modelled as a cloud, which means that independent, heterogenous, private/public clouds providing bionformatics applications can be used as if they were a single system. In BioNimbus, resources of each cloud can be maximally explored, but if more are required, other clouds can be requested to participate, in a transparent manner. BioNimbusis thus able to satisfy further service allocation requests sent by its users. The objective is to offer an environment with apparently unrestricted computational resources given that computing and storage space demands are always provided on demand to the users.

3.1. BioNimbus architecture

All the components of BioNimbus architecture together with their funcionalities are defined such that it allows simplicity, speed and eficiency when a new cloud provider enters in the federation. Another key characteristic is the communication among the BioNimbus components that is realized through a Peer-to-Peer (P2P) [67] network, guaranteeing the following properties:

- Fault tolerance, since there is not a single fail point. Thus, even if some nodes fail, the others can work;

- Efficiency, since there is not a single bottleneck. Then, messages are end-to-end and not routed by a single node;

- Flexibility, since clouds can operate independently or in a coordinated manner;

- Scalability, since the use of a P2P network allows integration of thousands of interconnected machines.

BioNimbus (Figure 1) architecture enables the integration of different cloud computing platforms, meaning that independent, heterogeneous, private or public providers may offer their bioinformatics services in an integrated manner, while maintaining their particular characteristics and internal policies. BioNimbus is composed of three layers: application layer, core layer and cloud provider layer.

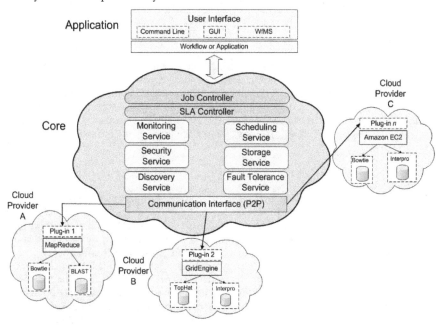

Figure 1. The architecture of BioNimbus hybrid federated cloud.

3.1.1. Application layer

This layer provides the service of interaction with users, which can be implemented by web pages, command lines, graphical interfaces (GUI) or workflow management systems (WfMS). Users can execute workflows or a single application, choosing among available services. Job controller service has the function of collecting user requests and sending the input data to the core layer. Moreover, this layer is responsible for showing to each user the current status of his running applications. Users can list the files stored in the federation, upload or download files, create and execute workflows in the BioNimbus cloud environment.

3.1.2. Cloud provider layer

This layer encompasses the cloud providers belonging to BioNimbus. The previous described core layer ensures a unified view of the cloud, which allows users to see all the resources available on each cloud as if they were one unified system.

A plug-in service is used to integrate a cloud provider (public or private) in the federation. Each plug-in service is an interface that aims at communicating the BioNimbus core with each cloud provider. Cloud providers can communicate among themselves also using the core layer. Each plug-in needs to map the requests sent by the core components to the corresponding actions that have to be realized in each cloud provider. This implies that each cloud requires a special plug-in service. Furthermore, to integrate distinct providers (public or private), each plug-in needs to treat three different kinds of requests: information about the provider infrastructure, task management and file transfer.

3.2. Core layer

This layer is responsible for managing the federated environment. Among their functions are: identification of new providers with their corresponding hardware and software resources; task scheduling and controlling; definition, establishment and monitoring of SLA (Service Level Agreement); storage and managing of input and output files; maintainance of the online environment; and the election of new coordinators for each requested service. To each function implemented in this layer, a controller service was included in the architecture, as described next.

3.2.1. Discovery service

This service identifies the cloud providers integrating the federation, and consolidates information about storage and processing capabilities, network latency, availability of resources, available bioinformatics tools, details of parameters and input and output files. To realize this, the discovery service waits for information published by providers about their infrastructure and available tools. To consolidate these data, the discovery service maintains a data structure that is updated whenever new data is received. Furthermore, the discovery service has a policy of controlling each provider, removing from the federation those providers not regularly sending updated information, which guarantees the correct and update task execution on the federated cloud. Regarding to the entrance of a cloud provider in BioNimbus, *a priori*, at any time a peer participating in the P2P network can start the process of publishing its resources (storage and processing capabilities) and available bioinformatics applications. However, for security and controlling purposes, permission to join the federation as a provider must be verified with the support of the security service whenever any information about a new provider arrives to the discovery service.

As can be seen from the above description, an efficient resource discovery mechanism plays a central role in our federated cloud, since the information gathered by this service is essential to other services to properly perform their functions. According to [49], in large-scale distributed services, a resource discovery infrastructure has to meet the following key requirements: it must be scalable so it can handle thousands of machines without being unavailable or losing performance; it must be able to handle both static and dynamic resources; and it must be flexible enough so its queries could be extended in order to handle different types of resources. Possible implementations of a resource discovery service could be developed using central or hierarchical approaches, but these are known to have serious limitations of scalability, fault-tolerance and network congestion [56].

In BioNimbus, we plan to use a publish/subscribe mechanism, in which providers publish information about their resources to a decentralised resource discovery system. This system will use a Distributed Hash Table (DHT) data structure [7] in order to achieve low management costs and network overhead, efficient resource searching and fault-tolerance. For resource information handling, we plan to use serializable and extendable formats such as the JSON format [23]. In this way it will be possible for the federated cloud to deal with different types of information, thus causing the least impact possible.

3.2.2. Job controller

The job controller links the core and the application layers of BioNimbus. It first calls the security service to verify if a user has permission (authentication) to execute jobs in BioNimbus and what are the credentials of this user. Moreover, the job controller's main function is to manage distinct and simultaneously running workflows, noting that the workflows may belong to the same or to different users. Thus, for each accepted workflow, the job controller generates an associated ID and controls each workflow execution using this ID.

3.2.3. SLA controller

According to [74], SLA is a formal contract between service providers and consumers to guarantee that consumers' service quality expectations can be achieved. In BioNimbus, the SLA controller is responsible for implementing the SLA lifecycle, which has six steps: discovers service providers, defines SLA, establishes agreement, monitors SLA violation, terminates SLA and enforces penalties for violation. A SLA template represents, among others, the QoS parameters that a user has negotiated with BioNimbus. The user can populate, through an user interface, a suitable template with required values or even define a new SLA from scratch in order to describe functional (e.g. CPU cores, memory size, CPU speed, OS type and storage size) and non-functional (e.g. response time, budget, data transfer time, availability and completion time) service requirements. In bioinformatics, functional requirements are number of cores, amounts of memory and storage, CPU speed, bioinformatics programs and databases and respective versions. Non-functional requirements are latency (transfer rate) and uptime (reliability, in the sense that it measures how frequently a cloud provider is running tasks or if it is not entering and leaving the federation).

The SLA controller has the responsibility to investigate whether the SLA template submitted by the user can be supported by the federated cloud platform. For this, the SLA controller retrieves the SLA level published through the provider plug-in (e.g. gold, silver or bronze SLA level).

So, if the service agreement required by the SLA template can not be satisfied, a negotiation phase starts. The SLA negotiation phase is done as follows: the user submits a service request with the new SLA template to the job controller. Next, after parsing the SLA definition, the SLA controller asks the monitoring service if it could execute the service with the specified requirements. In order to respond to this request, the monitoring service requests the scheduling service to find the best suitable provider by matching the gathered resource properties to the service requirements by applying predefined scheduling algorithms. If none of the providers can be matched, the monitoring service enables the discovery service, which must seek new cloud providers to be integrated into the federated environment, aiming at satisfying the SLA template requested by the user. However, if this is not possible, the mentioned steps must be repeated for renegotiation, with a new SLA template, until reaching an agreement.

After establishing an agreement, the SLA controller generates an ID for the agreement, and sends the ID to the job controller, which records this ID agreement. Then, the job controller forwards both the request and the agreement ID to the monitoring service, which sends the tasks for the scheduling service. The monitoring service is responsible for checking if a violation of the agreement occurred and in this case it immediately has to inform the SLA controller, which terminates the SLA and enforce penalties for violation.

3.2.4. Monitoring service

This service verifies if a requested service is available in a cloud provider, searching for another cloud in the federation if it is not; receives the tasks to be executed from the job controller, and sends them to the scheduling service that will distribute them, guaranteeing that all the tasks of a process are correctly executed; and informs the job controller when a task successfully finishes its execution. To ensure the monitoring of all the requested tasks, this service periodically sends messages to the clouds that are executing tasks, and informs the user the current status of each submitted task.

To perform the activities described above, the monitoring service must be able to gather information about resource allocation and task execution, which depends on the application being executed [28]. Therefore, we have to establish some criteria about the frequency that data are obtained and their corresponding format, so that the decision-making process performed by this service can be made with reliability with respect to data timeliness and flexibility towards distinct applications. In BioNimbus, the monitoring service was planned to send messages at regular intervals to all the federation members or whenever needed. The latter case happens when a decision has to be taken for a specific federation member or when data update is necessary. All information exchange is done with timestamps so only the updated data are sent in order to save network bandwidth. We also plan to use an extensible and flexible format, such as JSON [23], like in the discovery service.

In federated clouds the monitoring service must have other characteristics, such as: scalability, to handle a large number of resources and tasks to be monitored; elasticity, to handle addition and removal of resources in a transparent manner; and federation, to handle entering and leaving providers [20]. In order to meet these requirements, we propose to use a decentralized information indexing infrastructure, which would be the same DHT available to the discovery service. Furthermore, as previously described, the monitoring service has to verify agreement violations.

3.2.5. Storage service

This service decides how to distribute and replicate data among the cloud providers integrating the federation [8, 39, 73], particularly model the storage strategy of the files consumed and produced by the jobs executed in BioNimbus. To realize this, the storage service can communicate with the discovery service to access information about the federation, since the discovery service knows the actual storage conditions of each provider integrating the federation. Thus a storage policy is defined, so that this choice can be made based on receiving information about the file (FileInfo) and returns at least one cloud provider (PluginInfo) to store this file.

Some characteristics of biological data for bioinformatics applications are: large volume; it is not necessary to guarantee the ACID transaction properties since there are no users simultaneously updating data during execution; according to a particular bioinformatics application, fragmentation and replication can use different models; and data provenance is essential.

Considering these characteristics, the BioNimbus storage service proposal is based on the HBase NoSQL (Not only SQL) database. Among distinct noSQL databases, like HBase [38], Dynamo [26], Bigtable [17], Cassandra [41], PNUTS [22], monogDB [19] and cloudDB [5], we adopted HBase since its basic data storage is Apache's Hadoop Distributed File System (HDFS) [13] and it is a column-oriented database [24, 50, 51], which allows joining data (biological data file) and sets of information (e.g. data provenance).

Replication will be done copying data to at most three clouds in order to ensure recovery in case of failure. Total or partial fragmentation depends on the biological data and the application. On the top of HBase, we propose to create an Analyzer module, which will decide where the replication has to be done. The objective of the Analyzer module is to reduce data transfers among the cloud providers, based on three criteria: disk space, geographic position and data transfer speed. The most important analysis is the available space, which should be sufficient to store input and output. The geographic position criterion has the objective of reducing data transfer on the network, being the closer clouds used first if possible. Finally, the Analyzer module uses data transfer speed, which must be computed using the time to transfer packages.

3.2.6. Security service

This service guarantees integrity among the distinct tasks executed in the federated clouds. A federated cloud needs to include the security policies of each cloud provider while avoiding strong inter-dependency among the clouds. A security context can be partitioned into three main topics: authentication, authorization and confidentiality. We address those requirements using standard algorithms and protocols as described next.

- **Authentication**: The descentralized federated cloud infrastructure should not make a centralized authentication, which is a not a good choice because it limits the scalability and creates a strong interdependency among the clouds. We intend to use a Single Sign-On (SSO) protocol [52] so that no central authority is in charge of its users' authentication, which prevents a single point of failure and allows scalability according to the number of users. We chose the OpenID standard [57] as our SSO mechanism, since it has been used by corporate and academic sites around the world. OpenID allows each "site" (e.g. a cloud) to provide an authentication facility to its users so that they do not need to authenticate with each other cloud integrating the federation. Instead, each cloud provider acts as an identity provider for user credentials, so that each user should authenticate with its affiliated provider. Once this user is authenticated, each time his/her credentials are required, OAuth [10] allows a user's site to forward authorization without exposing the user account or login information.

- **Authorization**: The authorization of a federated cloud resource is provided by the Access Control Lists (ACLs) [69] provided by each cloud provider. An ACL determines who can access a given resource, e.g. disk storage, CPU cycles and bioinformatics services. Therefore, each cloud is able to determine access patterns so that it can control its resource's uses.

- **Confidentiality**: Communication between each two cloud providers is established using TLS/SSL [68] connection. The use of secure connections between two clouds in the federation is not enforced by our model, but it can be provided as well. As far as we know, few cloud systems provide secure intra-cloud communication. Each cloud should provide a certificate that will be used by hosts in two clouds to establish a secure connection. As we improve BioNimbus, we plan to include audit trails so that each required resource can be available when needed.

3.2.7. Fault tolerance service and high availability

This service guarantees that all the core services are always available. In a cloud environment, machine failures occur, and it is well known among the cloud community that those failures are the norm rather than the exception. Thus, any federated cloud should be designed for fault recovering and system availability. Therefore, a fault tolerance service is an essential part of our federated cloud, and has the objective of providing high availability and resiliency against periodic or transient failures.

There are extensive studies in the literature on failure detection systems [16, 31, 45, 70]. On the other hand, few systems are designed to scale with a large number of nodes as those found on clouds. Thus, an important requirement of our fault detection service is to be scalable with a large number of machines. We adopted a modified gossip based failure detector proposed by Renesse et al [70], which works as described. Each host runs the gossip failure detector service, which maintains a list of known hosts in the cloud. Every $T_{seconds}$, a host increases a heartbeat, and at random chooses a set of nodes for sending a list of known nodes. When received, each list is merged with the host current list, assuming the largest heartbeat for each node in the list. If a node does not update its heartbeat for a $T_{elapsed}$ time, then it will be marked as failed. Note that a node may be marked as failed due to slow network links or even in presence of a fractioned network. But our failure detection service is conservative so that it only purges a host from the list after a $T >= 2 * T_{elapsed}$.

Besides using this gossip based failure detector, we use a coordination service based on atomic broadcast protocol [59]. The open source system Apache Zookeeper [34] runs on each cloud and allows our system to detect node failures and realize an election of leaders among the cloud machines, in order to guarantee the services availability, including discovery and fault tolerance services. Zookeeper is used to elect some of the nodes that are known as gossip servers. Those servers are dinamically chosen so that they can exchange the list of nodes among the cloud providers. This helps to reduce the bandwidth between two clouds to a few servers.

3.2.8. Scheduling service

This service dynamically distributes tasks among the cloud providers belonging to the federation, maintaining a register for the allocated tasks, controlling load of each cloud provider, and redistributing the tasks when resources are overloaded. The scheduling service is responsible for receiving the tasks created from the user requests, and maintaining a record about the status of each executed task. Before being executed in a cloud provider, a task is sent to the scheduling service, which uses one or more scheduling policies to choose the cloud provider that will execute this task, according to the negotiated SLA. Each policy receives a list of tasks to be scheduled and an agreement ID, and returns a mapping of the tasks and the cloud providers where these tasks will be executed. To do this, the scheduling policy communicates with the discovery service. The scheduling policy should consider the SLA QoS parameters and the margin values accepted by the cloud providers (e.g. gold, silver and bronze SLA level). These parameters are important for a matching of a cloud provider that is done by the scheduling policy, and therefore the user needs to give reasonable values for them. Some typical SLA parameters used in context of a cloud provider are CPU cores, CPU speed, memory size, in/ou bandwidth, OS type, storage size, response time, budget, data transfer time, completion time and availability. In BioNimbus, the scheduling service can be easily modified to use different scheduling policies.

We implemented a new *DynamicAHP* algorithm in BioNimbus [12]. The key idea of DynamicAHP is to map available resources of the cloud providers to the requested tasks, then associating a cloud to execute each task. This algorithm is based on a decision making strategy proposed by [61]. DynamicAHP worked well on a first BioNimbus prototype, since it was capable to dinamically scale using only the knowledge about the length of each task input file, while performing load balancing among the cloud providers. Since BioNimbus stores information about the cloud providers such as network latency and wait time in the execution queues, DynamicAHP reduced costs and execution time of the tasks. The promising results obtained from developing DynamicAHP in BioNimbus showed that good scheduling algorithms can really lower the time to execute bioinformatics applications in federated clouds.

It is interesting to investigate new scheduling metrics, mainly related to costs. For example, a public cloud can be associated to a lower priority due to its associated costs, when compared to other public clouds integrating the federation. Another idea is to assign weights to the metrics that could set a priority order among them. To develop and analyze a model capable of storing information about the executed tasks, such that the scheduling service could combine this information to estimate the execution time of a particular task is another challenging project.

3.3. Performing tasks in BioNimbus

Figure 2 shows how BioNimbus works. Initially (step 1), the user interacts with BioNimbus through an interface, which could be a command line or a web interface, for example. The user informs details of the application (or workflow) to be executed, and these information are sent to the job controller in form of jobs to be executed. Then, the job controller verifies the availability of the informed applications and input files, sending a response message to the user accordingly. Afterwards, these jobs' features are analyzed by the security service (step 2), which verifies the user permission to access the resources of the federation, and sends a response to the job controller (step 3).

If the requested jobs can be executed, a message is sent to the SLA Controller (step 4) that investigates whether the SLA template submitted by the user can be identified by BioNimbus. If the user request can be executed, the SLA controller sends a message to the monitoring service (step 5), which stores the jobs in a pending task list. This service is responsible for informing to the scheduling service that there are pending jobs waiting to be scheduled.

Next (step 6), the scheduling service starts when the monitoring service informs that there are pending jobs. The scheduling policy adopted in BioNimbus can be easily changed, according to the characteristics of a particular application. The scheduling service gets information about the resources using the discovery service (steps 9 and 10), which periodically updates the status of the federation infrastructure, and stores these information in a management data structure. This information is used to generate the list of ordered resources, and to assign the more demanding jobs to the best resources, according to the scheduling policy.

With the resource and job ordered lists, the scheduling service communicates with the storage service to ensure that all the input files are available to the providers chosen to execute the jobs (steps 7 and 8).

Next, the scheduler distributes instances of jobs (tasks) to be executed by the plug-ins and their corresponding clouds (steps 11 and 12).

The scheduling service decision is then passed to the monitoring service (step 13) so that it can monitor each job status until it is finished. When the jobs are all completed, the monitoring service informs the SLA Controller (step 14), which sends a message to the job controller (step 15). Finally, the job controller communicates with the user interface (step 16) informing that the jobs were completed, which closes one execution cycle in BioNimbus.

The BioNimbus architecture follows [3], who claims that high-throughput sequencing technologies have decentralized sequence acquisition, which increases demands for new and efficient bioinformatics tools that have to be easy to use, portable across multiple platforms, and scalable for high-throughput applications.

4. A case study

A federation with two cloud providers, one nonpublic (University of Brasilia) and one public (EC2 Amazon), were created in order to study BioNimbus when applied to a simple workflow with real data.

A prototype of BioNimbus containing all the main controller services was implemented: *monitoring and scheduling service, discovery service* and a simple *storage service*, using an open

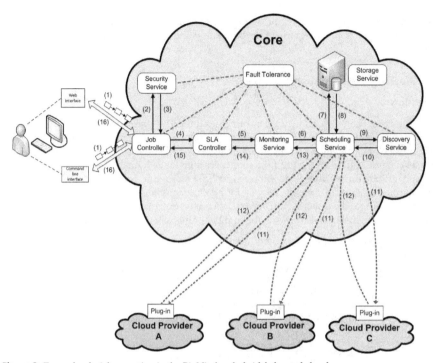

Figure 2. Example of a job execution in the BioNimbus hybrid federated cloud.

source implementation of the Zab protocol [59], which allows a distributed consensus among a group of processes. We also implemented Hadoop infrastructure plug-ins. Each plug-in provides information about the current status of its respective infrastructure, like number of cores, processing and storage resources and bioinformatics tools that can be executed in BioNimbus, as well as information of input and output files. The interaction of the user and the platform was implemented by a command line that sends requests. Services and plug-ins communicate through a P2P network based on the Chord protocol [67] .

In order to study the runtime performance of a workflow involving real biological data, we created a three-phase workflow in BioNimbus. The objective was to compare the time of a workflow running in a federated cloud to a single cloud.

4.1. Cloud providers

At the University of Brasilia, a Hadoop cluster was implemented with 3 machines, each one with two Intel Core 2 Duo 2.66Ghz (so a total of 6 cores), 4 GB RAM and 565 GB of storage. The Hadoop cluster executed Bowtie [44] with the Hadoop MapReduce (Hadoop streaming), with storage implemented with the Hadoop Distributed FileSystem (HDFS).

In addition, at Amazon EC2, a Hadoop cluster Cluster Hadoop was implemented with 4 virtualized machines, each one with two Intel Xeon 2.2 7Ghz (so a total of 8 cores), 8 GB RAM, and 1.6 TB of storage. The cluster also executed Bowtie.

Two Perl scripts implementing the workflow (SAM2BED and genome2interval) and the coverageBed program (integrating the BEDTolls suite [54]) were installed in each cloud provider.

4.2. Workflow, tools and data

Workflow

Now we describe the workflow used as our case study. The objective of the workflow was to identify differentially expressed genes in human kidney and liver cancerous cells [47, 60], with fragments of genes sequenced with Illumina technology [35]. The workflow consists of four phases (Figure 3): (i) mapping the input sequences onto the 24 human chromosome sequences; (ii) converting format from SAM (Bowtie) to BED (a specific format of the CoverageBED program); (iii) generating fixed intervals for all chromossomes based on their length, since this is the input for the CoverageBED program; and (iv) executing the CoverageBED program, which generates histograms showing the number of mappings for each interval.

The *mapping phase* has the objective of identifying the region of a reference genome where each input sequence was located. A set of sequences mapping in the same region allows the inferences that these sequences have the same structural organization of the reference genome.

The *CoverageBED* program [54] allowed the study of the expression level of the cancerous genes using histograms of the mapped input sequences onto the human reference genome, so that differentially expressed genes between kidney and liver cancer genes could be identified.

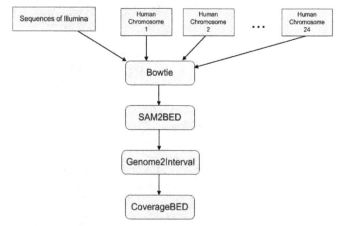

Figure 3. The workflow investigated the expression level of liver and kidney genes (generated by Illumina) mapping them to 24 human chromosome sequences.

Tools

Four tools were implemented in each cloud provider: Bowtie [44], SAM2BED (a Perl script), genome2interval (another Perl script) and coverageBed [54].

Data

The 24 human chromosome sequences were downloaded from HG19:

ftp://ftp.ncbi.nih.gov/genomes/H_sapiens/Assembled_chromosomes/seq/

The reference site is:

http://www.ncbi.nlm.nih.gov/genome/assembly/293148/

Finally, the names of the files followed the format:

hs_ref_GRCh37.p5_chr*.fa.gz.

4.3. Implementation details

A message module allowed the communication among the services, having been created using the Nettycommunication library [36], which is responsible for the TCP connection event manager. Messages were serialized using both JSON format [23] and Jackson library [21], and file transfer was accomplished through the HTTP protocol GET and PUT methods. Message and file communications were realized using an unique TCP port, which avoided the necessity to create complex firewall rules. Besides, the message module is capable of multiplexing both message and file traffic. A simplified version of the *Chord* [67] protocol was implemented for the P2P network and plug-ins. We developed plug-in prototypes for Apache Hadoop and SunGridEngine. Java was the language used to implement the BioNimbus prototype.

Next, we briefly describe somefeatures of the services implemented on our BioNimbus prototype (Figure 4):

- Discovery service: this implementation used two execution threads. The first one is responsible for updating and cleaning the data structure storing information about the cloud providers. The second thread waits for P2P network messages that have to be treated by the discovery service. A data structure **map** was used for storing information about each federated cloud provider using a unique identifier. Besides, each cloud has a *timestamp* for its last mapping. To update the infrastructure, the first thread is executed in intervals of 30 seconds in order to send messages to all the BioNimbus members. The response of each plug-in is treated by the second thread, which updates the mapping with the received new information and corresponding *timestamp* for each execution. The first thread removes from the **map** those pieces of information that did not have their date modified in the last 90 seconds, which indicates that those cloud providers left the federation. The second thread also treats the requisition about the federation clouds, using the **map** maintained by the discovery service.

- Monitoring and scheduling service: to realize the work of receiving, monitoring and scheduling user jobs, three main data structures of type **map** were used. The first one, called PendingJobs, maps each job identifier to its information and also represents those jobs waiting to be scheduled. The second one, named RunningJobs, maps each executing task identifier to its information and the job to which it belongs. The third data structure, called CancelingJobs, maps the task identifier to its corresponding job and to the user requiring its cancelation.

  In the monitoring service, there is a thread responsible for waiting the user requests and responses received from other services of the infrastructure. When a request initiates a

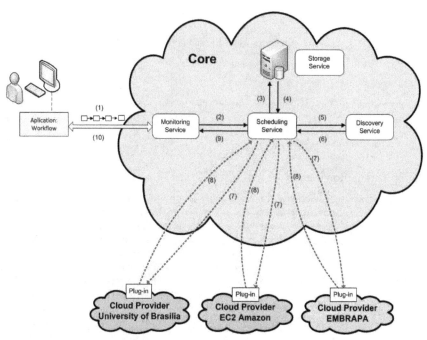

Figure 4. The services implemented for our case study, noting that we used two cloud providers in the BioNimbus prototype.

job (`JobStartReq`) is received, this thread generates an unique identifier for this job and saves this informaticon in the `PendingJobs` map. Next, it calls the scheduling policy, which returns a mapping among the jobs and the plug-ins that can execute them. Thus, when the jobs are all scheduled, this thread sends requests in order to create tasks (`TaskStartReq`) that have to be executed in the cloud providers, and waits for their corresponding outputs (`TaskStartReply`). When an output is received, the service removes the job from the `PendingJobs` map and creates an input in the `RunningJobs` map, with information about the job and its corresponding tasks, removing a job when all its tasks finish. As previouly mentioned, a new *DynamicAHP* algorithm was implemented in BioNimbus [12], which is based on on a decision making strategy proposed by [61].

Another thread in the monitoring service, executed at intervals of 15 seconds, is responsible for following the jobs. First, it sends status requests (`TaskStatusReq`) to each job registered in `RunningJobs`. The response (`TaskStatusReply`), treated by the previous described thread, can again initiate the scheduling service according to some parameters. Cancelling messages (`TaskCancelReq` and `TaskCancelReply`) will be scnt, and the job will be reinserted in the `PendingJobs` map and removed from the `RunningJobs`. This thread also verifies whether there are pending jobs in `PendingJobs`, initiating another scheduling process in this case, and sending query messages to the discovery service (`CloudReq`) and to the storage service (`ListReq`), whose responses (`CloudReply` and `ListReply`) will be received by the first thread and used by the scheduling policy when needed.

- Storage service: two threads were used for its implementation. The first one waits for the requests sent by other services. To treat the request of saving files (`StoreReq`), the storage service executes the storage policy adopted in BioNimbus. For this case study, we used a method based on a round-robin of the plug-ins that informed having enough space to store the file. When a cloud is chosen, a response (`StoreReply`) is sent to the service making the request, which will send the file to the cloud indicated by the storage service. When this transfer finishes, the plug-in receiving the file storage sends a special message (`StoreAck`), which contains information that will keep correct the federation file table.

  In the case study, a simple backend was implemented to maintain the federation file table. Every time a new confirmation is received by the storage service, it adds an input in the map file with the file identifier containing information such as name, size and storage cloud. This mapping is stored in JSON format [23] in a file in the federation file system of the cloud where the service will be executed. When initiating its execution, the storage service verifies if the map file left and load in memory the federation file table last status.

  The other two types treated by the first thread are file list (`ListReq`) and localization (`GetReq`). For the first case, the thread builds a response (`ListReply`) with the mapping loaded in memory. For localization, it builds a response (`GetReply`) searching for the cloud information in the map using the request identifier.

  Finally, another thread is executed at intervals of 30 seconds requesting to the discovery service the current configuration of the federation (`CloudReq` message). The received information is used by the storage policy.

4.4. Results

We executed the workflow at the University of Brasilia and the Amazon EC2, and on both cloud providers (Table 1).

Cloud Providers	hour:minute:second
University of Brasilia (UnB)	1:11:47
Amazon EC2	1:18:44
Both clouds (UnB and EC2)	1:09:07

Table 1. Workflow execution time on each cloud and on the BioNimbus federated cloud.

We measured how the file transfer time affected the job execution total time. Table 2 and Figure 5 shows the total and file transfer times of the 18 longest jobs of the workflow, as well as the percentage of the file transfer time related to the total time. These percentages show that file transfer represents at least 50% of the total time of this job execution. This means that in federated clouds executing data-driven bioinformatics applications, storage services have to be especially designed to minimize as much as possible huge file transfers.

We also investigated how the time execution of a job was affected when sent to execution in a cloud provider, taking a long time, being cancelled and returning to the list of pending jobs to be executed again. There were seven jobs cancelled, the first seven jobs in Table 2 with the longest times to be executed. When making an experiment without cancelling jobs, we obtained greater times, when compared to the experiment with cancelling since they were sent to clouds almost idle.

We mention now some points that can affect BioNimbus performance: (i) the scheduler does not consider jobs being transferred and identifies CPUs involved in these transfers as idle; (ii)

Total time (seconds)	File transfer time (seconds)	Percentage of file transfer time related to the total time
4230.297	2114.996	50.0%
4123.492	2264.552	54.9%
4098.571	2337.454	57.0%
4030.492	2297.580	57.0%
3807.501	2229.992	58.6%
3145.645	2168.201	68.9%
3113.729	2116.199	68.0%
3066.488	2058.771	67.1%
3032.701	2018.942	66.6%
3001.165	2137.157	71.2%
2952.875	2087.761	70.7%
2849.506	2074.117	72.8%
2801.489	2023.309	72.2%
2680.382	1892.002	70.6%
2587.076	2006.842	77.6%
2579.184	1959.727	76.0%
2533.254	1928.888	76.1%
2405.470	1899.626	79.0%

Table 2. Total and file transfer times of the longest jobs executed in BioNimbus.

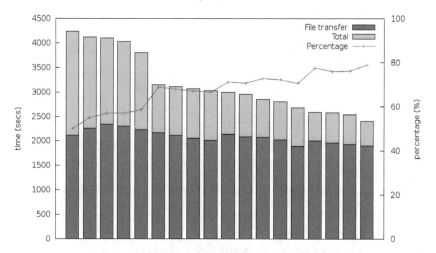

Figure 5. Comparing the total and file transfer times of the longest jobs executed in BioNimbus. The file transfer time is colored red, while its percentage related to the total time is shown in blue.

the input files are all simultaneously downloaded, i.e. there are no priorities for downloads; (iii) jobs are now canceled based only on the wait time in the pending jobs list, i.e. the file transfering time is not considered; and (iv) jobs with small input files that were sent to a cloud provider after jobs with large input files got executed earlier, while the later were still downloading their input data.

Table 3 and Figure 6 show the number of jobs executed in a single cloud provider and on both. Note that, including the transfer time, jobs with smaller inputs execute faster on two cloud providers, since the possibility to cancel delayed jobsthat are running and scheduling them again lowered the total execution time. Besides, when files are small, the time to transfer files is rapid, while when they are large the transfer time strongly affects the total execution time (as shown in Table 2). Thus, for large files, the storage policy has to be very carefully designed using replication and fragmentation in order to significantly decrease file transfer time.

Cloud Providers	until 200 seconds	between 200 seconds and 1000 seconds	above 1000 seconds
University of Brasilia	34	30	32
EC2 Amazon	37	27	32
UnB and EC2	64	8	24

Table 3. Number of executed jobs, where time includes the file transfer time.

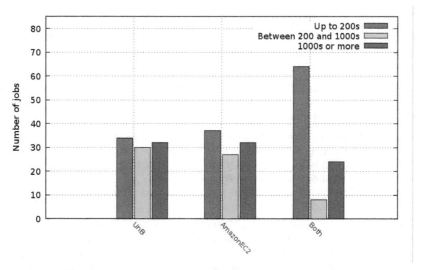

Figure 6. Comparing the number of executed jobs in BioNimbus, where time (in seconds) includes the file transfer time.

5. Related work

In this section, we discuss cloud projects designed to accelerate execution and increase the amount of storage available to bioinformatics applications. When compared to BioNimbus, these projects are dedicated to particular applications or are executed in a single cloud environment. BioNimbus intends to integrate public and private centers offering bioinformatics applications in one single platform using the hybrid federation cloud paradigm.

Cloudburst [64] parallel algorithm is optimized for mapping DNA fragments, also known as short read sequences (SRSs), to a reference genome. The execution time varies almost linearly with the increase in the number of processors. The mapping of millions of SRSs to the human genome, executed in 24 cores, is thirty times faster when compared to other non-distributed applications [44, 65]. CloudBurst uses the MapReduce model.

Crossbow [43] is a pipeline developed in the infrastructure provided by the Apache Hadoop streaming mode. It combines the Bowtie [43] SRS mapping tool, performed during the map phase, with the SOAPsnp [46] tool to identify SNPs, processed during the reduce phase. During the execution of the workflow, the SRSs are sent as input to the nodes of the Hadoop cluster, which executes the map phase. In this phase, the SRSs are mapped to a reference genome using Bowtie. Afterwards, the mappings are joined with parts of the reference genome, and each group is sent to a node that executes the reduce phase. The SOAPsnp tool is used to detect SNPs in the already analyzed parts of the genome. The execution time for about 2.6 billion SRSs and the entire human genome used as a reference took a little more than 3 hours in a 320 core cluster of the Amazon EC2 [2] infrastructure. The experiments cost less than US$ 100.

Myrna [42] identifies differentially expressed genes in large sets of sequenced data. The workflow combines a mapping phase with a statistical analysis phase, performed with R [55], which is able to analyze more than one billion SRSs in a little more than 90 minutes, using 320 cores and costing around US$ 75.

The RSD (Reciprocal Smallest Distance) comparative genomics algorithm, composed of different bioinformatics tools, was adapted to be executed in the Amazon EC2 infrastructure, having obtained expressive results [72].

[3] created the Cloud Virtual Resource (CloVR), a desktop application for automated sequence analysis using cloud computing resources. CloVR is implemented as a single portable virtual machine (VM) that provides several automated analysis pipelines for microbial genomics, whole genome and metagenome sequence analysis. The CloVR VM runs on a personal computer, uses local computer resources and addresses problems arising in constructing bioinformatics workflows.

[4] noted that genomic applications are limited by the "bioinformatics bottleneck", due to computational costs and infrastructure needed to analyze the enormous amounts of SRSs. They presented benchmark costs and runtimes for microbial genomics applications, microbial sequence assembly and annotation, metagenomics and large-scale BLAST. They also analyzed workflows (also called pipelines) implemented in the CloVR virtual machine running in Amazon EC2, having achieved cost-efficient bioinformatics processing using clouds, and thereby claiming that this is an interesting alternative to local computing centers.

[53] adapted a particular peptide search engine called X!Tandem to Hadoop MapReduce. Their MR-Tandem application runs on any Hadoop cluster, but it was especially designed to run on Amazon Web Services. They modified the X!Tandem C++ program and created a Python script for driving Hadoop clusters, which includes the Amazon Web Services (AWS) Elastic Map Reduce (EMR) used by the modified X!Tandem as a Hadoop streaming mapper and reducer.

[75] worked on pathway-based or gene set analysis of expression data, having developed a gene set analysis algorithm for biomarker identification in a cloud. Their YunBe tool is ready

to use on the Amazon Web Services. YunBe performed well when compared to desktop and cluster executions. YunBe is open-source and freely accessible within the Amazon Elastic MapReduce service.

[27] ported two bioinformatics applications, a pairwise Alu sequence alignment application and an Expressed Sequence Tag (EST) sequence assembly program, to the cloud technologies Apache Hadoop and Microsoft DryadLINQ. They studied the performance of both applications in these two cloud technologies, comparing them with traditional MPI implementation. They also analyzed how non-homogeneous data affected the scheduling mechanisms of the cloud technologies, and compared performance of the cloud technologies under virtual and nonvirtual hardware platforms.

[32] used cloud computing for scientific workflows, and discussed a case study of a widely used astronomy application.

The Bio-Cloud Computing platform [9] was designed to support large-scale bioinformatics processing. It has five main bio-cloud computing centers, with a total peak performance up to 157 Teraflops, 33.3 TB memory and 12.6 PB storage.

Recently, many bioinformatics applications have been ported to clouds [33, 37, 40], noting that they offer user-friendly web interfaces and efficiency in the execution of tools that extensively use memory and storage resources.

6. Conclusion and future work

In this work, we proposed a hybrid federated cloud computing platform called BioNimbus, which aims at integrating and controlling different bioinformatics tools in a distributed, transparent, flexible and fault tolerant manner, also providing highly distributed processing and large storage capability. The objective was to make possible the use of tools and services provided by multiple institutions, public or private, that could be easily aggregated to the federated cloud. We also discussed a case study in a prototype of BioNimbys including two cloud providers, in order to verify its performance in practice. We created a bioinformatics workflow for identifying liver and kidney cancerous differentially expressed genes, and measured its total time execution on each single cloud provider and on all of them.

The next step is to study different scheduling strategies for the *scheduling service*, in order to improve its efficiency when choosing a cloud provider to execute jobs. Our results showed that the execution time is strongly affected by the file transfer time, implying that we have to carefully design the *storage service*; we plan to use data replication and fragmentation to address this problem. A *fault tolerance service* to check the cloud providers and other services status will be developed and evaluated. We also plan to use an adaptive fault monitoring algorithm, as proposed by [18, 30] and [70], which are more adaptable to be used in a large-scale distributed environment. It is also important to include a *security service* and an *SLA service* in the federated platform. Finally, we will investigate the use of a Workflow Management System (WfMS) in BioNimbus.

Acknowledgments

M.E.M.T.Walter would like to thank to FINEP (Project number 01.08.0166.00) and all the authors would like to thank Daniel Saad for having written the Perl scripts for the workflow.

Author details

Hugo Saldanha, Edward Ribeiro, Carlos Borges, Aletéia Araújo, Ricardo Gallon, Maristela Holanda and Maria Emília Walter
University of Brasília, Brasil

Roberto Togawa
Embrapa/Genetic Resources and Biotechnology, Brasil

João Carlos Setubal
University of São Paulo, Brasil

7. References

[1] 454 [2012]. 454 life sciences. roche diagnostics corporation, http://www.454.com/.
[2] Amazon [2012]. Amazon Elastic Compute Cloud (Amazon EC2), http://aws.amazon.com/ec2/.
[3] Angiuoli, S. V., Matalka, M., Gussman, A., Galens, K., Vangala, M., Riley, D. R., Arze, C. & White, J. R. [2011]. Clovr: A virtual machine for automated and portable sequence analysis from the desktop using cloud computing, *BMC Bioinformatics* 12(356): 1–15.
[4] Angiuoli, S. V., White, J. R., Matalka, M., White, O. & Fricke, W. F. [2011]. Resources and costs for microbial sequence analysis evaluated using virtual machines and cloud computing, *PLoS ONE* 6(10): e26624.
[5] Apache [2011]. The Apache Software Foundation: Apache, http://couchdb.apache.org/.
[6] Apache [2012]. Apache Hadoop, http://hadoop.apache.org/.
[7] Balakrishnan, H., Kaashoek, M. F., Karger, D., Morris, R. & Stoica, I. [2003]. Looking up data in p2p systems, *Commun. ACM* 46(2): 43–48.
URL: *http://doi.acm.org/10.1145/606272.606299*
[8] Bermbach, D., Klems, M., Tai, S. & Menzel, M. [2011]. Metastorage: A federated cloud storage system to manage consistency-latency tradeoffs, *IEEE International Conference on Cloud Computing (CLOUD)*, IEEE, pp. 452–459.
[9] BGI [2012]. Bio-Cloud Computing, http:www.genomics.cn/en/navigation/show_navigation?nid=4143.
[10] Bhandari, A. & Singh, M. [2010]. 2010 the oauth 1.0 protocol, internet engineering task force (ietf), rfc:5849.
URL: *http://tools.ietf.org/html/rfc5849*
[11] Bittman, T. J. [2008]. Th evolution of the cloud computing market, http://blogs.gartner.com/thomas_bittman/2008/11/03/the-evolution-of-the-cloud-computing-market.
[12] Borges, C. A. L., Saldanha, H. V., Ribeiro, E., Holanda, M. T., Araujo, A. P. F. & Walter, M. E. M. T. [2012]. Task scheduling in a federated cloud infrastructure for bioinformatics applications, *in* INSTICC (ed.), *2nd International Conference on Cloud Computing and Services Science ()*, CLOSER 2012, Porto, Portugal, pp. 1–7.
[13] Borthakur, D. [2008]. The Apache Software Foundation: HDFS Architecture, http://hadoop.apache.org/common/docs/r0.20.2/hdfs_design.pdf.
[14] Buyya, R., Ranjan, R. & Calheiros, R. N. [2010]. Intercloud: Utility-oriented federation of cloud computing environments for scaling of application services, *Proceedings of the*

10th International Conference on Algorithms and Architectures for Parallel Processing (ICA3PP 2010), Springer, pp. 21–23.

[15] Celesti, A., Tusa, F., Villari, M. & Puliafito, A. [2008]. How to enhance cloud architectures to enable cross-federation, *3rd IEEE International Conference on Cloud Computing (IEEE Cloud 2010)*, Miami, Florida, USA, pp. 337–345.

[16] Chandra, T. D. & Toueg, S. [1996]. Unreliable failure detectors for reliable distributed systems, *Journal of the ACM* 43: 225–267.

[17] Chang, F., Dean, J., Ghemawat, S., Hsieh, W., Wallach, D., Burrows, M., Chandra, T., Fikes, A. & Gruber, R. [2008]. Bigtable: A distributed storage system for structured data, *ACM Transactions on Computer Systems (TOCS)* 26(2): 1–26.

[18] Chen, W. [2000]. On the quality of service of failure detectors, *IEEE Transactions on Computers* 51: 561–580.

[19] Chodorow, K. & Dirolf, M. [2010]. *MongoDB: the definitive guide*, O'Reilly Media, Inc.

[20] Clayman, S., Galis, A., Chapman, C., Toffetti, G., Rodero-Merino, L., Vaquero, L. M., Nagin, K. & Rochwerger, B. [2010]. Monitoring Service Clouds in the Future Internet, *Towards the Future Internet - Emerging Trends from European Research*, IOS Press.

[21] Codehaus [2012]. Jackson Java JSON-Processor, http://jackson.codehaus.org.

[22] Cooper, B., Ramakrishnan, R., Srivastava, U., Silberstein, A., Bohannon, P., Jacobsen, H., Puz, N., Weaver, D. & Yerneni, R. [2008]. PNUTS: Yahoo!'s hosted data serving platform, *Proceedings of the VLDB Endowment*, VLDB Endowment, pp. 1277–1288.

[23] Crockford, D. [2006]. The application/json Media Type for JavaScript Object Notation (JSON), RFC 4627 (Informational).
URL: *http://www.ietf.org/rfc/rfc4627.txt*

[24] da Silva, C. A. R. F. O. [2011]. *Data modeling with NoSQL: How, When and Why*, Master's thesis, University of Porto.

[25] Dean, J. & Ghemawat, S. [2004]. MapReduce: simplified data processing on large clusters, *6th Conference on Symposium on Operating Systems Design & Implementation*, USENIX Association, Berkeley, CA, EUA, pp. 10–10.

[26] DeCandia, G., Hastorun, D., Jampani, M., Kakulapati, G., Lakshman, A., Pilchin, A., Sivasubramanian, S., Vosshall, P. & Vogels, W. [2007]. Dynamo: amazon's highly available key-value store, *SIGOPS Oper. Syst. Rev.* 41(6): 205–220.
URL: *http://doi.acm.org/10.1145/1323293.1294281*

[27] Ekanayake, J., Gunarathene, T. & Qiu, J. [2011]. Cloud technologies for bioinformatics applications, *IEEE Transactions on Parallel and Distributed Systems* 22(6): 998–1011.

[28] Elmroth, E. & Larsson, L. [2009]. Interfaces for placement, migration, and monitoring of virtual machines in federated clouds, *Proceedings of the 2009 Eighth International Conference on Grid and Cooperative Computing*, GCC '09, IEEE Computer Society, Washington, DC, USA, pp. 253–260.
URL: *http://dx.doi.org/10.1109/GCC.2009.36*

[29] Foster, I., Zhao, Y., Raicu, I. & Lu, S. [2008]. Cloud Computing and Grid Computing 360-Degree Compared, *Grid Computing Environments Workshop GCE '08*, pp. 1–10.

[30] Hayashibara, N., Défago, X., & Rami Yared, T. K. [2004]. The phi Accrual Failure Detector, *23rd IEEE International Symposium on Reliable Distributed Systems*, pp. 66–78.

[31] Hayashibara, N., Défago, X., Yared, R. & Katayama, T. [2004]. The ϕ accrual failure detector, *RR IS-RR-2004-010, Japan Advanced Institute of Science and Technology*, pp. 1–16.

[32] Hoffa, C., Mehta, G., Freeman, T., Deelman, E., Keahey, K. a. B. B. & Good, J. [2008]. On the use of cloud computing for scientific workflows, *3rd International Workshop on Scientific Workflows and Business Workflows Standards in e-Science*, SWBES 2008, IEEE Digital Library, pp. 640–645.

[33] Hong, D., Rhie, A., Park, S.-S., Lee, J., Ju, Y. S., Kim, S., Yu, S.-B., Bleazard, T., Park, H.-S., Rhee, H., Chong, H., Yang, K.-S., Lee, Y.-S., Kim, I.-H., Lee, J. S., Kim, J.-I. & Seo, J.-S. [2012]. FX: an RNA-Seq analysis tool on the cloud, *Bioinformatics* 28(5): 721–723.
URL: *http://dx.doi.org/10.1093/bioinformatics/bts023*

[34] Hunt, P., Konar, M., Junqueira, F. P. & Reed, B. [2010]. Zookeeper: wait-free coordination for internet-scale systems, *USENIX conference on USENIX annual technical conference*, USENIXATC'10, USENIX Association, pp. 11–11.

[35] Illumina [2012]. Illumina life sciences, `http://www.illumina.com`.

[36] Inc., R. H. [2012]. Netty - the Java NIO Client Server Socket Framework, `http://www.jboss.org/netty`.

[37] Jourdren, L., Bernard, M., Dillies, M.-A. A. & Le Crom, S. [2012]. Eoulsan: A Cloud Computing-Based Framework Facilitating High Throughput Sequencing Analyses., *Bioinformatics (Oxford, England)* .
URL: *http://dx.doi.org/10.1093/bioinformatics/bts165*

[38] Khetrapal, A. & Ganesh, V. [2006]. Hbase and hypertable for large scale distributed storage systems, Dept. of Computer Science, Purdue University, http://www.uavindia.com/ankur/downloads/HypertableHBaseEval2.pdf.

[39] Kossmann, D., Kraska, T., Loesing, S., Merkli, S., Mittal, R. & Pfaffhauser, F. [2010]. Cloudy: a modular cloud storage system, *Proceedings of the VLDB Endowment*, VLDB Endowment, pp. 1533–1536.

[40] Krampis, K., Booth, T., Chapman, B., Tiwari, B., Bicak, M., Field, D. & Nelson, K. [2012]. Cloud BioLinux: pre-configured and on-demand bioinformatics computing for the genomics community, *BMC Bioinformatics* 13(1): 42+.
URL: *http://dx.doi.org/10.1186/1471-2105-13-42*

[41] Lakshman, A. & Malik, P. [2010]. Cassandra: a decentralized structured storage system, *SIGOPS Oper. Syst. Rev.* 44(2): 35–40.
URL: *http://doi.acm.org/10.1145/1773912.1773922*

[42] Langmead, B., Hansen, K. & Leek, J. [2010]. Cloud-scale RNA-sequencing differential expression analysis with Myrna, *Genome Biology* 11(8): R83.

[43] Langmead, B., Schatz, M. C., Lin, J., Pop, M. & Salzberg, S. [2009]. Searching for SNPs with cloud computing, *Genome Biology* 10(11): R134.

[44] Langmead, B., Trapnell, C., Pop, M. & Salzberg, S. [2009]. Ultrafast and memory-efficient alignment of short DNA sequences to the human genome, *Genome Biology* 10(3): R25.

[45] Larrea, M., Fernandez, A., Arevalo, S., Carlos, J. & Carlos, J. [2002]. Eventually consistent failure detectors, *Brief Announcement, 14th International Symposium on Distributed Computing (DISC'2000)*, pp. 326–327.

[46] Li, R., Li, Y., Fang, X., Yang, H., Wang, J., Kristiansen, K. & Wang, J. [2009]. SNP detection for massively parallel whole-genome resequencing, *Genome Research* 19(6): 1124–1132.
URL: *http://dx.doi.org/10.1101/gr.088013.108*

[47] Marioni, J. C., Mason, C. E., Mane, S. M., Stephens, M. & Gilad, Y. [2008]. Rna-seq: An assessment of technical reproducibility and comparison with gene expression arrays,

Genome Research 18: 1509–1517.
URL: *http://genome.cshlp.org/cgi/content/full/18/9/1509*

[48] Mell, P. & Grance, T. [2009]. The NIST Definition of Cloud Computing, *National Institute of Standards and Technology* 53(6): 50.
URL: *http://csrc.nist.gov/groups/SNS/cloud-computing/cloud-def-v15.doc*

[49] Oppenheimer, D., Albrecht, J., Patterson, D. & Vahdat, A. [2004]. Scalable wide-area resource discovery, *Technical Report UCB/CSD-04-1334*, EECS Department, University of California, Berkeley.
URL: *http://www.eecs.berkeley.edu/Pubs/TechRpts/2004/5465.html*

[50] Orend, K. [2010]. *Analysis and classification of nosql databases and evaluation of their ability to replace an object-relational persistence layer*, Master's thesis, Fakultät für Infoormatik, Technische Universität München.

[51] Padhy, R., Patra, M. & Satapathy, S. [2011]. Rdbms to nosql: Reviewing some next-generation non-relational databases, *International Journal of Advanced Engineering Science and Technologies* 11(1): 15–30.

[52] Pashalidis, A. & Mitchell, C. J. [2003]. A taxonomy of single sign-on systems, *Information Security and Privacy, 8th Australasian Conference, ACISP 2003*, Springer-Verlag, pp. 249–264.

[53] Pratt, B., Howbert, J. J., Tasman, N. & Nilsson, E. J. [2011]. MR-Tandem: Parallel X!Tandem using Hadoop MapReduce on Amazon Web Services, *Bioinformatics* 8: 1–12.

[54] Quinlan, A. R. & Hall, I. M. [2010]. BEDTools: a flexible suite of utilities for comparing genomic features, *Bioinformatics* 26(6): 841–842.
URL: *http://bioinformatics.oxfordjournals.org/content/26/6/841.abstract*

[55] R Development Core Team [2011]. *R: A Language and Environment for Statistical Computing*, R Foundation for Statistical Computing, Vienna, Austria. ISBN 3-900051-07-0.
URL: *http://www.R-project.org*

[56] Ranjan, R., Chan, L., Harwood, A., Karunasekera, S. & Buyya, R. [2007]. Decentralised resource discovery service for large scale federated grids, *Proceedings of the Third IEEE International Conference on e-Science and Grid Computing*, E-SCIENCE '07, IEEE Computer Society, Washington, DC, USA, pp. 379–387.
URL: *http://dx.doi.org/10.1109/E-SCIENCE.2007.27*

[57] Recordon, D. & Reed, D. [2006]. Openid 2.0: a platform for user-centric identity management, *Proceedings of the second ACM workshop on Digital identity management*, DIM '06, ACM, New York, NY, USA, pp. 11–16.

[58] Redkar, T. [2011]. *Windows Azure Platform*, Vol. 1, 2th edn, Apress, Berkeley, CA, USA.

[59] Reed, B. & Junqueira, F. P. [2008]. A simple totally ordered broadcast protocol, *2nd Workshop on Large-Scale Distributed Systems and Middleware*, LADIS'08, ACM, New York, NY, USA, pp. 2:1–2:6.

[60] Robinson, M. & Oshlack, A. [2010]. A scaling normalization method for differential expression analysis of RNA-seq data, *Genome Biology* 11(3): R25+.
URL: *http://dx.doi.org/10.1186/gb-2010-11-3-r25*

[61] Saaty, T. L. [1990]. How to make a decision: The analytic hierarchy process, *European Journal of Operational Research* 48(1): 9 – 26.

[62] Saldanha, H. V., Ribeiro, E., Holanda, M., Araujo, A., Rodrigues, G., Walter, M. E. M. T., Setubal, J. C. & Davila, A. [2011]. A cloud architecture for bioinformatics workflows,

in L. INSTICC (ed.), *1st International Conference on Cloud Computing and Services Science,* CLOSER 2011, pp. 1–8.

[63] Sanderson, D. [2009]. *Programming Google App Engine: Build and Run Scalable Web Apps on Google's Infrastructure,* 1st edn, O'Reilly Media, Inc.

[64] Schatz, M. C. [2009]. CloudBurst: Highly Sensitive Read Mapping with MapReduce, *Bioinformatics* 25: 1363–1369.

[65] Smith, A., Xuan, Z. & Zhang, M. [2008]. Using quality scores and longer reads improves accuracy of Solexa read mapping, *BMC Bioinformatics* 9(1): 128.

[66] Solid [2012]. Life technologies & applied biosystems, `http://www.appliedbiosystems.com/`.

[67] Stoica, I., Morris, R., Liben-Nowell, D., Karger, D. R., Kaashoek, M. F., Dabek, F. & Balakrishnan, H. [2003]. Chord: a scalable peer-to-peer lookup protocol for internet applications, *IEEE/ACM Trans. Netw.* 11(1): 17–32.

[68] Tanenbaum, A. S. [2002]. *Computer Networks (International Edition),* fourth edn, Prentice Hall.

[69] Tolone, W., Ahn, G.-J., Pai, T. & Hong, S.-P. [2005]. Access control in collaborative systems, *ACM Comput. Surv.* 37(1): 29–41.

[70] van Renesse, R., Minsky, Y. & Hayden, M. [1998]. A gossip-style failure detection service, *Proceedings of the IFIP International Conference on Distributed Systems Platforms and Open Distributed Processing,* Middleware '98, Springer-Verlag, London, UK, pp. 55–70.

[71] Vaquero, L. M., Rodero-Merino, L., Caceres, J. & Lindner, M. [2008]. A break in the clouds: towards a cloud definition, *SIGCOMM Comput. Commun. Rev.* 39: 50–55.

[72] Wall, D., Kudtarkar, P., Fusaro, V., Pivovarov, R., Patil, P. & Tonellato, P. [2010]. Cloud computing for comparative genomics, *BMC Bioinformatics* 11(1): 259.

[73] Wang, J., Varman, P. & Xie, C. [2011]. Optimizing storage performance in public cloud platforms, *Journal of Zhejiang University-Science C* 12(12): 951–964.

[74] Wu, L. & Buyya, R. [2010]. Service level agreement (sla) in utility computing systems, *CoRR* abs/1010.2881.

[75] Zhang, L., Gu, S., Wan, B., Liu, Y. & Azuaje, F. [2011]. Gene set analysis in the cloud, *Bioinformatics* 13: 1–10.

Molecular Modeling

Using Molecular Modelling to Study Interactions Between Molecules with Biological Activity

María J. R. Yunta

Additional information is available at the end of the chapter

1. Introduction

To better understand the basis of the activity of any molecule with biological activity, it is important to know how this molecule interacts with its site of action, more specifically its conformational properties in solution and orientation for the interaction. Molecular recognition in biological systems relies on specific attractive and/or repulsive interactions between two partner molecules. This study seeks to identify such interactions between ligands and their host molecules, typically proteins, given their three-dimensional (3D) structures. Therefore, it is important to know about interaction geometries and approximate affinity contributions of attractive interactions. At the same time, it is necessary to be aware of the fact that molecular interactions behave in a highly non-additive fashion. The same interaction may account for different amounts of free energy in different contexts and any change in molecular structure might have multiple effects, so it is only reliable to compare similar structures. In fact, the multiple interactions present in a single two-molecule complex are a compromise between attractive and repulsive interactions. On the other hand, a molecular complex is not characterised by a single structure, as can be seen in crystal structures, but by an ensemble of structures. Furthermore, changes in the degree of freedom of both partners during an interaction have a large impact on binding free energy [Bissantz et al., 2010].

The availability of high-quality molecular graphics tools in the public domain is changing the way macromolecular structure is perceived by researchers, while computer modelling has emerged as a powerful tool for experimental and theoretical investigations. Visualisation of experimental data in a 3D, atomic-scale model can not only help to explain unexpected results but often raises new questions, thereby affecting future research. Models of sufficient quality can be set in motion in molecular dynamic (MD) simulations to move beyond a static picture and provide insight into the dynamics of important biological processes.

Computational methods have become increasingly important in a number of areas such as comparative or homology modelling, functional site location, characterisation of ligand-binding sites in proteins, docking of small molecules into protein binding sites, protein-protein docking, and molecular dynamic simulations [see for example Choe & Chang, 2002]. Current results yield information that is sometimes beyond experimental possibilities and can be used to guide and improve a vast array of experiments.

To apply computational methods in drug design, it is always necessary to remember that to be effective, a designed drug must discriminate successfully between the macromolecular target and alternative structures present in the organism. The last few years have witnessed the emergence of different computational tools aimed at understanding and modelling this process at the molecular level. Although still rudimentary, these methods are shaping a coherent approach to help in the design of molecules with high affinity and specificity, both in lead discovery and in lead optimisation. Moreover, current information on the 3D structure of proteins and their functions provide a possibility to understand the relevant molecular interactions between a ligand and a target macromolecule. As a consequence, a comprehensive study of drug structure–activity relationships can help identify a 3D pharmacophore model as an aid for rational drug design, as a pharmacophore model can be defined as 'an ensemble of steric and electronic features that is necessary to ensure the optimal supramolecular interactions with a specific biological target and to trigger (or block) its biological response', and a pharmacophore model can be established either in a ligand-based manner, by superposing a set of active molecules and extracting common chemical features that are essential for their bioactivity, or in a structure-based manner, by probing possible interaction points between the macromolecular target and ligands.

Molecular recognition (MR) is a general term designating non-covalent interactions between two or more compounds belonging to host-guest, enzyme-inhibitor and/or drug-receptor complexes. A rigorous approach to an MR study should involve the adoption of a computational method independent from the chemical intuition of the researcher. Drug design purposes prompt another challenging feature of such an ideal computational method, the ability to make sufficiently accurate thermodynamic predictions about the recognition process.

2. Molecular modelling methods and their usefulness

Molecular recognition is a central phenomenon in biology, for example, with enzymes and their substrates, receptors and their signal inducing ligands, antibodies and antigens, among others. Given two molecules with 3D conformations in atomic detail, it is important to know if the molecules bind to each other and, if it is so, what does the formed complex look like ("docking") and how strong is the binding affinity (that can be related to the "scoring"functions).

Molecules are not rigid. The motional energy at room temperature is large enough to let all atoms in a molecule move permanently. That means that the absolute positions of atoms in a molecule, and of a molecule as a whole, are by no means fixed, and that the relative location of substituents on a single bond may vary with time. Therefore, any compound containing one or several single bonds exists at every moment in many different conformers, but generally only low energy conformers are found to a large extent [Kund, 1997, as cited in Tóth et al., 2005].

The biological activity of a drug molecule is supposed to depend on one single unique conformation amongst all the low energy conformations, the search for this so-called bioactive conformation for compound sets being one of the major tasks in Medicinal Chemistry. Searching for all low energy conformations is possible with molecular modelling studies, since molecular modelling is concerned with the description of the atomic and molecular interactions that govern microscopic and macroscopic behaviours of physical systems. These molecular interactions are classified as: (a) bonded (stretching, bending and torsion), (b) non-bonded (electrostatic (including interactions with metals), van der Waals and π-stacking), and (c) derived, as they result from the previous ones (hydrogen bonds and hydrophobic effect).

Protein-ligand or, in general, molecule-molecule binding free energy differences can *a priori* be computed from first principles using free energy perturbation techniques and a full atomic detailed model with explicit solvent molecules using molecular dynamics simulations. However, these are computationally demanding. More affordable approaches use end-point molecular dynamic simulations and compute free energies accounting for solvent effects with continuum methods, such as MM-PBSA (molecular mechanics Poisson-Boltzman surface area) or MM-GBSA (generalized Born surface area) [Kollman et al., 2000; Wang et al., 2005]. One of the first approaches was comparative molecular field analysis (CoMFA) [Cramer et al., 1988], which enabled interpretation and understanding of enzyme active sites when the crystal structure was absent. However, this type of analysis was not possible until *in vitro* drug-drug interaction studies were widely used (through the 1990s).

2.1. Molecular mechanics, molecular dynamics and docking

Molecular mechanics (MM) is often the only feasible means with which to model very large and non-symmetrical chemical systems such as proteins and polymers. Molecular mechanics is a purely empirical method that neglects explicit treatment of electrons, relying instead on the laws of classical physics to predict the chemical properties of molecules . As a result, MM calculations cannot deal with problems such as bond breakage or formation, where electronic or quantum effects dominate. Furthermore, MM models are wholly system-dependent. MM energy predictions tend to be meaningless as absolute quantities, as the zero or reference value depends on the number and types of atoms and their connectivity, and so they are generally useful only for comparative studies. A force field is an empirical approximation for expressing structure-energy relationships in molecules and is usually a compromise between speed and accuracy.

Molecular mechanics have been shown to produce more realistic geometry values for the majority of organic molecules, owing to the fact that they are highly parameterised. Parameterisation of structures should be performed with care and non-"standard" molecules will need to have new parameters. This is usually done by analogy for bonded terms and assigning charges by a procedure consistent with the used force field.

There are many levels of theory in which computational models of 3D structures can be constructed. The overall aim of modelling methods is often to try to relate biological activity to structure. An important step towards this goal is to be able to compute the potential energy of the molecule as a function of the position of the constituent atoms. Once a method for evaluating the molecular potential energy is available, it is natural to search for an optimum molecular geometry by minimising the energy of the system. In a biological macromolecule, the potential energy surface is a complicated one, in which there are many local energy minima as well as a single overall energy minimum. All the energy minimisation algorithms commonly used have a marked tendency to locate only a local energy minimum that is close to the starting conformation. For a biological macromolecule, the number of conformations that have to be searched rises exponentially with the size of the molecule; hence, systematic searching is not a practical method for large molecules.

Molecular dynamics (MD) is a conformation space search procedure in which the atoms of a biological macromolecule are given an initial velocity and are then allowed to evolve in time according to the laws of Newtonian mechanics [van Gunsteren & Berendsen, 1977]. Depending on the simulated temperature of the system, the macromolecule can then overcome barriers at the potential energy surface in a way that is not possible with a minimisation procedure. One useful combination of molecular dynamics and minimisation schemes is a method known as simulated annealing [Kirkpatrick et al, 1983, Černý, 1985]. This method uses a molecular dynamics calculation in which the system temperature is raised to a high value to allow for a widespread exploration of the available conformational space. The system temperature is then gradually decreased as further dynamics are performed. Finally, a minimisation phase may be used to select a minimum energy molecular conformation.

One of the most important applications of molecular modelling techniques in structural biology is the simulation of the docking of a ligand molecule onto a receptor. These methods often search to identify the location of the ligand binding site and the geometry of the ligand in the active site, to get the correct ranking when considering a series of related ligands in terms of their affinity, or to evaluate the absolute binding free energy as accurately as possible. To select a force field and the adequate modelling methodology for a given task, it is important to appreciate the range of molecular systems to which it is applicable and the types of simulations that can be performed.

2.2. Most used existing force fields

AMBER (Assisted Model Building with Energy Refinement) developed by Kollman et al. [http://ambermd.org/] was originally parameterised specifically for proteins and nucleic acids [Weiner et al., 1984, 1986; Cornell et al., 1995], using 5 bonding and non-bonding terms along with a sophisticated electrostatic treatment and with no cross terms included. The results obtained with this method can be very good for proteins and nucleic acids, but less so for other systems, although parameters that enable the simulation of other systems have been published [for examples see Doshi & Hamelberg, 2009; Zgarbová et al., 2011].

CHARMM (Chemistry at HARward Macromolecular Mechanics) developed by Karplus et al. [http://www.charmm.org] was originally devised for proteins and nucleic acids [Brooks et al., 1983], and is now used for a range of macromolecules, molecular dynamics, solvation, crystal packing, vibrational analysis and QM/MM (quantum mechanics/molecular mechanics) studies. It uses five valence terms, one of which is electrostatic and is a basis for other force fields (e.g., MOIL [Elber et al., 1995]).

GROMOS (Groningen Molecular Simulation) developed at the University of Groningen and the ETH (Eidgenössische Technische Hochschule) of Zurich [http://www.igc.ethz. ch/GROMOS/index] is quite popular for predicting the dynamical motion of molecules and bulk liquids, also being used for modelling biomolecules. It uses five valence terms, one of which is electrostatic [van Gunsteren and Berendsen., 1977]. Its parameters are currently being updated [Horta et al., 2011].

MM1-4 (Molecular Mechanics) developed by Allinger [1976] are general purpose force fields for monofunctional organic molecules. The first version of this method was the MM1 [Allinger, 1976]. MM2 was parameterised for a lot of functional groups while MM3 [Allinger & Durkin, 2000; Allinger & Yan, 1993] is probably one of the most accurate ways of modelling hydrocarbons. MM4 is the latest version with several improvements [Allinger et al., 1996].

MMFF (Merck Molecular Force Field) developed by Halgren [1996] is also a general purpose force field mainly for organic molecules. MMFF94 [Halgren, 1996] was originally designed for molecular dynamics simulations, but has also been widely used for geometrical optimisation. It uses five valence terms, one of which is electrostatic and another is a cross term. MMFF was parameterised based on high level *ab initio* calculations. MMFF94 contains parameters for a wide variety of functional groups that arise in Organic and Medicinal Chemistry.

OPLS (Optimized Potential for Liquid Simulations) developed by Jorgensen at Yale [http://zarbi.chem.yale.edu] was designed for modelling bulk liquids [Jorgensen & Tirado-Rives, 1996] and has been extensively used for modelling the molecular dynamics of biomolecules. It uses five valence terms, one of which is an electrostatic term and none of them is a cross term.

TRIPOS (Sybil force field) is a commercial method designed for modelling organics and biomolecules. It is often used for CoMFA analysis and uses five valence terms, one of which is an electrostatic term.

CVFF (Consistent Valence Force Field) developed by Dauber-Osguthorpe is a method parameterised for small organic (amides and carboxylic acids, among others) crystals and gas phase structures [Dauber-Osguthorpe et al., 2004]. It handles peptides, proteins and a wide range of organic systems. It was primarily intended for studies of structures and binding energies, although it predicts vibrational frequencies and conformational energies reasonably well.

2.3. Popular docking programs

One of the most important and useful areas of application of molecular modelling is the approach of docking a protein onto a second molecule, typically a small ligand. This is of interest because it models the possible interactions between the protein and the ligand in the formation of a biologically important protein-ligand complex. To perform a computational docking, experimental or model 3D structures of both the protein and ligand molecules are required together with the charge distribution for each molecule.

There are several software programs that are available for carrying out docking calculations, only some of them will be considered here. The DOCK program suite [Kuntz, 1992] is one of the best known. First of all, a set of overlapping spheres are used in the program to construct a negative image of a specified site on the protein or another macromolecule, and the negative image is then matched against structures of potential ligands. Matches can be scored in this program by the quality of the geometric fit, as well as by the molecular mechanics interaction energy [Meng et al., 1992] and can lead to protein-binding ligands that have micromolecular levels of binding affinity [Kuntz et al., 1994]. It has also been used for modelling protein-protein docking [Shoichet & Kuntz, 1996].

The program GRID [Goodford, 1985] identifies likely protein binding sites for ligands [Reynolds et al., 1989; Cruciani & Goodford, 1994] using a 3D grid around the protein.

The program AutoDock developed by Morris et al.; [http://www.scripps.edu/pub/olson-web/doc/autodock/] uses a grid-based scheme for energies of individual atoms, allowing a quick computation of the interaction energy of the protein-ligand complex as the interaction between the ligand and the grid.

GLIDE software [Friesner et al., 2004, 2006; Halgren et al., 2004] also uses a grid-based scheme to represent the shape and properties of the receptor and then uses a systematic search algorithm to produce a set of initial conformations, using a OPLS-AA force field for ligand minimisation in the field of the receptor.

SURFLEX [Jain, 2003, 2007] is a fully automatic flexible molecular docking algorithm that presents results evaluated for reliability and accuracy in comparison with crystallographic experimental results on 81 protein/ligand pairs of substantial structural diversity.

In a recent study, comparison of seven popular docking programs [Plewczynski et al., 2011] clearly showed that the ligand binding conformation could be identified in most cases by using the existing software. Yet, there is still the lack of universal scoring function for all types of molecules and protein families. One can always hope that incremental improvements in current techniques will gradually lead to major advances in this field.

3. The solvent and how to model it

Solvation plays an important role in ligand-protein association and has a strong impact on comparisons of binding energies for dissimilar molecules. The binding affinity of a ligand for a receptor (ΔG_{bind}) depends on the interaction free energy of the two molecules relative to their free energy in solution:

$$\Delta G_{bind} = \Delta G_{interact} - \Delta G_{solv,L} - \Delta G_{solv,R} \qquad (1)$$

where $\Delta G_{interact}$ is the interaction free energy of the complex, $\Delta G_{solv,L}$ is the free energy of desolvating the ligand, and $\Delta G_{solv,R}$ is the free energy of occluding the receptor site from the solvent. Various methods have been proposed to evaluate or estimate these terms. The problem is difficult because the energy of each component on the right hand side of Equation 1 is large while the difference between them is small.

An accurate way to calculate relative binding energies is with free-energy perturbation techniques, although they are usually restricted to calculating the differential binding of similar compounds and require extensive computation, making it impractical as an initial screen, but quite useful sometimes [Buch et al., 2011; Reddy & Erion, 2007]. Several authors have described force fields that consider the bound and solvated states [see for example Chen et al., 2008; Moon & Howe, 1991], successfully predicting new ligands and also the structures of ligand-receptor complexes [Wilson et al., 1991].

When calculating interactions in congeneric series, the cost in electrostatic free energy of desolvating both the enzyme binding site and the burial part of the ligand (ΔG_{desolv}) is roughly constant within the series. This is particularly true when the calculation is done partitioning the electrostatic free energy contributions into a van der Waals term from the molecular mechanics force field, and an electrostatic contribution computed using a continuum method [Checa et al., 1997]. For that reason, it has been proposed to neglect ΔG_{desolv} in earlier studies.

The binding energy between ligand and receptor is approximated to the interaction enthalpy calculated by means of empirical energy functions that represent van der Waals repulsion, dispersion interactions by a Lennard-Jones term, and electrostatic interactions in the form of a Coulomb term that uses atom-centred point charges [Ajay & Murcko, 1995]. In most cases, these calculations of molecular mechanics are performed on a structure that is taken to represent the ensemble average of each complex. Entropy contributions are usually ignored although solvation terms are sometimes added to the scoring function by calculating changes in buried nonpolar surface area [Viswanadhan et al., 1999] or differences in the ease of desolvation of both the ligand and the binding site upon complex formation [Checa et al., 1997]. Molecular mechanics-based QSAR studies on ligand-receptor complexes can benefit greatly from proper incorporation of solvation effects into a COMBINE framework based on residue-based interaction energy decomposition [Pérez et al., 1998].

The relevance of solvation in modulating the biological activity of drugs is well known [Orozco & Luque, 2000]. In the last years, theoretical methods have been developed to calculate fragment contributions to the solvation free energy, particularly in the framework of quantum mechanical (QM) continuum solvation methods [Klamt et al., 2009]. Thus, fractional methods based on GB/SA methods have been developed [Cramer & Truhlar,

2008], as well as those based on the MST(Miertus-Scrocco-Tomasi) solvation method model [Soteras et al., 2004].

An explicit solvent model includes individual solvent molecules and calculates the free energy of solvation by simulating solute-solvent interactions. It requires an empirical interaction potential between the solvent and the solute, and between the solvent molecules, usually involving Monte Carlo (MC) calculations and/or molecular dynamics. MC calculations can be used to compute free energy differences and radial distribution functions, among others, and cannot be used to compute time-dependent properties such as diffusion coefficients or viscosity. MD simulations, on the other hand, can be used to compute free energies and time-dependent properties, transport properties, correlation functions, and others.

An implicit solvent model treats solvent as a polarisable continuum with a dielectric constant, ε, instead of explicit solvent molecules. The charge distribution of the solute polarises the solvent, producing a reaction potential that alters the solute. This interaction is represented by a solvent reaction potential introduced into the Hamiltonian. As interactions should be self consistently computed, they are also known as self-consistent reaction field (SCRF) methods [Onsager, 1936]. These models are significantly easier than explicit solvent models, but cannot model specific interactions such as hydrogen bonds.

Changes in hydration free energy during complex formation are a crucial element of binding free energies [Gilson & Zhou, 2007]. With the use of methods to predict binding free energies becoming common-place in the field of drug design, there is still a need for solvation methods that are both quick and accurate [Mancera, 2007], although much research has been carried out on the improvement of existing methods and development of new solvation models at many levels of theory [Chambers et al., 1996; Gallicchio et al., 2002; Palmer et al., 2011].

Explicit solvation models such as free energy perturbation (FEP), thermodynamic integration (TI) [Gilson & Zhou, 2007; Khavertskii & Wallquist, 2010] and the faster linear interaction energy (LIE) [Aqvist et al., 1994; Carlson & Jorgensen, 1995] offer detail on the distinct nature of water around the solute and are transferable across a wide range of data sets, although there is a lack of throughput in the field of drug design.

Implicit solvation models offer a faster alternative to explicit models by replacing the individual water molecules with a continuous medium [Baker, 2005; Chen et al., 2008], combining the hydration free energy density and group contribution [Jäger & Kast, 2001], or, more recently, calculating solvation free energy directly from the molecular structure [Delgado & Jaña, 2009]. For small organic molecules, the loss of molecular detail of the solvent results in relatively small differences between hydration free energy prediction accuracies calculated with explicit solvent models relative to the explicit treatment [Mobley et al., 2009; Nicholls et al., 2009]. To cope with some of these pitfalls, the variational implicit solvent model (VISM) has been proposed for calculating the solute/water interface where established models fail [Dzubiella et al., 2006a, 2006b].

It is sometimes possible to get quite accurate results with very simple models, such as the case of the molecular modellisation of phenethylamine carriers conducted in our lab. Calculations were carried out using chloride anion to mimic the picrate anion used in experimental measurements and with no explicit solvent molecules. The chloroform environment was simulated by a constant dielectric factor, as this solvent has a low dielectric constant and thus, interactions should not end quickly with the distance [Campayo et al., 2005]. When complexation takes place in water as the solvent, the environment is simulated by a distance-dependent dielectric factor, as it takes into account the fact that the intermolecular electrostatic interactions should vanish with distance faster than in the gas phase. This assumption proves to work as it gives theoretical results in good agreement with experimental transportation values [Miranda et al., 2004; Reviriego et al., 2008]. Results for theoretical interactions have been supported by NMR experiments.

When applied to complex biomolecular systems, this loss of detail may become problematic in locations where water does not behave as a continuum medium, for example, the individual water molecules occurring in concave pockets at the surfaces of proteins [Li & Lazaridis, 2007]. The ELSCA (Energy by Linear Superposition of Corrections Approximation) method [Cerutti et al., 2005] has also been proposed for the rapid estimation of solvation energies. This procedure calculates the electrostatic and apolar solvation energy of bringing two proteins into close proximity or into contact compatible with the AMBER ff99 parameter set. The method is most useful in macromolecular docking and protein association simulations.

Solvent treatment is also of considerable interest in MD simulations as the solvent molecules (usually water, sometimes co-solvent and counterions/buffer or salt for electrolyte solutions) enter pockets and inner cavities of the proteins through their conformational changes. This is a very slow process and nearly as difficult to model as protein solving. One solution to this problem is using an efficient coupling of molecular dynamics simulation with the 3D molecular theory of solvation (3D-RISM-KH), contracting the solvent degrees of freedom [Luchko et al., 2010] or using free energy perturbation and OPLS force field together with molecular dynamics [Shivakumer et al., 2010].

4. Molecule-molecule or ion-molecule interactions in active molecule design

Non-covalent interactions are central to biological structure and function. In considering potential interactions of molecules and/or ions and their receptor, the focus has been on hydrophobic interactions, hydrogen bonding and ion pairing. Although hydrogen bonds are by far the most important interactions in biological recognition processes, the cation-π interaction is a general, strong, non-covalent binding force that occurs throughout nature, being energetically comparable or stronger than a typical hydrogen bond.

Cooperativity in multiple weak bonds (hydrogen bond and ion-π interactions among others) has been considered and studied at the MP2/6-311++ G(d,p) computational level

[Alkorta et al., 2010]. Due to the presence of a great number of aromatic rings containing heteroatoms in biological systems, this effect might be important and help to understand some biological processes where the interplay between both interactions may exist.

Computer-assisted drug design (CADD) has contributed to the successful discovery of numerous novel enzyme inhibitors, having been used to predict the binding affinity of an inhibitor designed from a lead compound prior to synthesis [Reddy & Erion, 2005]. A free energy simulation technique known as the thermodynamic cycle perturbation (TCP) approach [Reddy et al., 2007], used together with calculations of molecular dynamics, offers a theoretically precise method to determine the binding free energy differences of related inhibitors.

Many small molecules are transported across cell membranes by large integral membrane proteins, which are referred generically as transporters. Selection among competing alternatives is always interesting and cation-π interactions are strongly involved in substrate recognition by many transporters. Drug transporters are able to carry small molecules or ions across membranes, being an important target for pharmaceutical development [Zacharias & Dougherty, 2002].

The regulation of metal ions plays a major role in enzymes, allowing to catalyse a range of biological reactions. Identification and characterisation of the metal ion binding sites and their selectivity have received immense attention over the past few decades [Ma & Dougherty, 1997]. It is evident from earlier studies that metal ions can bind to aromatic groups in a covalent as well as non-covalent fashion. Non-covalent interactions between metal ions and an aromatic ring, which are considered strong cation-aromatic interactions, are increasingly being recognised as an important binding force relevant to structural biology [Meyar et al., 2003; Elguero et al., 2009]. However, in many cases, the cation is the side chain protonated nitrogen of a basic amino acid. Reddy et al. have made available a web-based cation-aromatic database (CAD) including metal ions and basic amino acids [Reddy et al., 2007b].

Macrocyclic entities that act as ion receptors and carriers exhibit a large number of conformations in crystals and solutions, depending on the nature of their environments and of the complexed ion. To ensure the formation of the most favourable cavity for a given ion, as well as to enhance the binding and release of the ion during transport at interfaces, flexibility in the ligand structure is of utmost importance.

Complexation studies of ions with macrocycles are well documented in the literature. Some representative trends in these studies would include the following: taking into account the existence of hydrogen-bonded water molecules [Hill & Feller, 2000; Durand et al., 2000; Fantoni, 2003] and sometimes using molecular dynamics and free energy perturbation studies [Varnek et al., 1999]. The complexation phenomena have also been studied in cases where the ligand can exist as different conformers able to complex the cation [Hashimoto & Ikuta, 1999].

One of the most important aspects of ion complexation is ion selectivity, which is considered in terms of the more or less favourable binding energies. The binding energy (BE) is defined as the difference between the energy of the complex and the energy of the free ligand and ion:

$$BE = E_{complex} - (E_{ion} + E_{ligand}) \tag{2}$$

Metal ion affinity is enhanced if the host molecule has a unique conformation that is optimal for complexation, that is, with all the binding sites positioned to structurally complement the metal ion [Lumetta et al., 2002].

Density functional theory based on electronic structure calculations is computationally affordable. It has very good predictability power for various structural and thermodynamic properties of a molecular system, and has therefore been used to model M^+-crown ether complexes [Ali et al., 2008] and collarenes acting as ionophores and receptors [Choi et al., 1998]. In both cases, the most stable equilibrium structure for complexes are estimated based on PM3 semi-empirical calculations followed by B3LYP calculations using the G-311++G(d,p) basis set of functions. Currently, the Protein Data Bank (PDB) contains over 25,000 structures that contain a metal ion. Thus, methodologies to incorporate metal ions into the AMBER force field have been developed there [Hoops et al., 1991; Reichert et al., 2001; Peters et al., 2010].

Molecular modellisation of Cu(II) and Zn(II) coordination complexes has been studied by our research group, among many others. The parameters used by us were checked against a known X-ray structure and the data obtained agreed quite well with similar deviations published for other theoretical results [Miranda et al., 2005]. The models obtained were useful in explaining the differences observed among the complexes obtained in different environments. Our cation metal parameters have also been used to help in the data elucidation of coordination metal complex structures [Rodríguez-Ciria, 2000; Rodríguez-Ciria et al., 2002].

Coordination and complexation of ions by aromatic moieties have been studied, taking into account the different characteristics of the electronic charge distribution on the aromatic frame as an addition of coulombic potentials [Albertí et al., 2010]. This type of interaction is quite common in biology as signalling in the nervous system is generally mediated by the binding of small molecules (neurotransmitters) to the appropriate receptors, which usually contain a cationic group at physiological pH.

An organic ammonium ion never exists as a sole cation; an anion is always associated with it. Depending on the polarity and hydrogen donor/acceptor abilities of the solvent, the association strength is different [Marcus & Hefter, 2006]. Strongly coordinating counter ions such as chloride generally lead to weaker binding constants upon recognition of the associated cation, when compared to weakly coordinating counterions such as iodide or perchlorate [Gevorkyan et al., 2001].

5. Selective formation of complexes

There are several examples of molecular modelling studies on complexes between cyclic receptors and ammonium ions, calixarenes [Choe & Chang, 2002] and crown ethers being the most used. As an example, it is noteworthy to mention the theoretical studies on calix[4]crown-5 and a series of alkyl ammonium ions [Park et al., 2007], having shown that the energy of complex formation depends on the number of amine groups in the alkyl chain as well as on the number of methylene groups between the primary and secondary amine groups, results that agree with experimental measurements. Although the calculations are performed under quite different conditions of vacuum compared with the experimental conditions of the phase system of chloroform-water, the binding properties of calixarene-type compounds towards alkyl ammonium ions have been successfully simulated, providing general and useful explanations for the molecular recognition behaviour.

Complex formation of compounds containing benzene rings with ammonium cations has also been theoretically studied using many computational techniques, including *ab initio* calculations [Kim et al., 2000]. It has been shown that two types of NH-aromatic π and CH-aromatic π interactions, which are important in biological systems, are responsible for binding, and that charged hydrogen bonds versus cation-π interaction is the origin of the high affinity and selectivity of novel receptors for NH_4^+ over K^+ ions [Oh et al., 2000]. Organic molecules complexed with metal cations have also been studied by MM2 molecular modelling [Mishra, 2010]. The search for metal ion selectivity is of interest in the field of biomimetic models of metalloenzymes and molecular modelling helps in the design of new ligands with this purpose [Kaye, 2011].

Molecular modelling has been used to suggest possible contributions of carrier effectivity and selectivity to complex formation in accordance with experimental results [Chipot et al., 1996; Ilioudis et al., 2005]. Our research group has evaluated the possible cation-receptor interactions involved in the complexes with ammonium and metal cations of selective carriers using the Amber force field with appropriate parameters developed by us. The complexation energies obtained are in reasonable agreement with experimental values, taking into account that complexation/decomplexation processes have a great influence on transport rates and are not equally favoured in cyclic and acyclic carriers [Campayo et al., 2004].

Both binding and selectivity in binding can be understood through the combined efforts of several non-covalent interactions, such as hydrogen bonding, electrostatic interactions, hydrophobic interactions, cation-π interactions, π-π stacking interactions and steric complementarity [Späth & König, 2010]. Formation of complexes is also possible in the case of neutral ligands. For example, the interactions between cholesterol and cyclodextrins have been theoretically studied to investigate their 1:1 and 1:2 complexes [Castagne et al., 2010], while the formation of stable complexes between trehalose and benzene compounds have been investigated by the general Amber force field (GAFF) and Gaussian 03 for MP2/6G-31G** calculation of atomic charges [Sakakura et al., 2011].

Docking of a ligand into a receptor may occur via an automated procedure [Subramanian et al., 2000] or manually [Filizola et al., 1999]. In both cases, docking is a combination of two components: a search strategy and a scoring function [Taylor et al., 2002]. The computational method MOLINE (Molecular Interaction Evaluation) was created to study complexes in an unbiased fashion [Alcaro et al., 2000]. It is based on a systematic, automatic and quasi-flexible docking approach that prevents the influence of the chemist's intuition on generating the configuration. This method has been used with acceptable results in studying inclusion complexes [Alcaro et al., 2004].

It would be adequate at this point to remember that testing the 'drug-receptor complexation' for a receptor model against available experimental data usually involves the use of site-directed mutagenesis experiments. This fact provides information on the amino acids involved in ligand binding and receptor activation. However, it should be noted that the results of mutagenesis studies are not necessarily related to receptor-ligand interactions. In fact, mutations can also alter the 3D structure of a receptor and therefore, modify the binding profile of a ligand by this mechanism. Besides that, efficient binding to a receptor does not guarantee that a ligand will produce a pharmacological action, given that the ligand may act as an agonist or antagonist.

6. Interaction of molecules with DNA

Anthracycline antibiotics such as doxorubicin and its analogues have been in common use as anticancer drugs for around half a century. There has been intense interest in the DNA-binding sequence specificity of these compounds in recent years, with the hope of identifying a compound that can modulate gene expression or exhibit reduced toxicity. Cashman and Kellog have studied models of binding for doxorubicin and derivatives [Cashman & Kellog, 2004], looking for sequence specificity and the effects of adding aromatic or aliphatic ring substituents or additional amino or hydroxyl groups. They performed a hydropathic interaction analysis using the HINT program (a Sybyl program module, Tripos Inc.) and four double base pair combinations. Interaction of some intercalators with two double DNA base pairs have also been studied with the density functional based tight binding (DFTB) method [Riahi et al., 2010], despite DFT methods being known to be inherently deficient in calculating stacking interactions, and the Amber force field and then AM1 to dock the intercalator between DNA base pairs [Miri et al., 2004].

Studies on sequence-selectivity of DNA minor groove binding ligands have shown that the most reliable results for AT-rich DNA sequences are obtained when MD simulations are performed in explicit solvent, when the data are processed using the MM-PB/SA approach, and when normal mode analysis is used to estimate configurational entropy changes [Shaikh et al., 2004; Wang & Laughton, 2009]. Use of the GB/SE model with a suitable choice of parameters adequately reproduces the structural and dynamic characteristics in explicitly solvated simulations in approximately a quarter of the computational time, although limitations become apparent when the thermodynamic properties are evaluated [Sands & Laughton, 2004]. Water molecules taking part in the complexation have been studied using the MMX force field and then PMB for gas phase optimisation, followed by re-optimisation in aqueous phase with the PM3 method using the AMSOL package [Silva & Jayasundera, 2002]. Optimisation geometries with AM1 and the use of implicit solvent have been taken into account when considering intercalation versus insertion into the minor or major groove [Bendic & Volanschi, 2006].

Calculating the curvature radius of molecular DNA structures has been reported [Slickers et al., 1998] as a new method for understanding the dependence of binding affinity on ligand structure, assuming that strong binders should have a shape complementary to the DNA minor groove. A method for predicting sequence selectivity and minor groove binding, based on MD simulations on DNA sequences with and without the bound ligand, to obtain an approximate free energy of binding has been proposed [Wang & Laughton, 2010].

Amber force field, developing the necessary parameters, has also been used together with electrostatic potential-derived (ESP) charges and explicit solvent molecules to study bisintercalation into DNA. The targeted molecular dynamics (tMD) approach has been considered for comparing the relative energetic cost involved in creating the intercalation sites and also studying the mechanisms of action [Braña et al., 2004]. It has been found that the electrostatic contribution is a critical characteristic of binding selectivity [Marco et al., 2005]. Reports on duplex and triplex formation of oligonucleotides by stacking aromatic moieties in the major groove, using Amber force field and the GB/SA solvation model in molecular dynamic simulations, can be found in the literature [Andersen et al., 2011]. Studies on docking using GOLD [Kiselev et al., 2010] to optimise the starting structures with the MMFF94 force field have also been performed.

Most of the published molecular modelling studies use two double base pairs or more than eight double base pairs to represent DNA. In our opinion, molecular modelling of DNA intercalation complexes should be done using at least the two base pairs of the intercalation site and an additional base pair at the two strand ends to maintain DNA shape and avoid distortion leading to inaccurate results. That means four base pairs for monointercalation studies and five or six base pairs for bisintercalation ones should be used. Using these DNA models, our studies on the mono and bisintercalation of benzo[g]phthalazine derivatives strongly suggest the possibility of bisintercalation and the important role played by an N-methyl group in stabilising the DNA complex of one of the compounds, throwing some light over the experimental results obtained [Rodríguez-Ciria et al., 2003]. The possibility of bisintercalation for a 1,4-disubstituted piperazine has been studied on duplexes of five and six base pairs, obtaining much better results in the case of five base pairs, in accordance with the theoretical calculations of binding mode not conforming to the neighbouring exclusion principle proposed by different authors [Veal et al., 1990].

7. Interaction of small molecules with enzymes

The potential of molecular simulations to enhance our understanding of drug behaviour and resistance relies ultimately on their ability to achieve an accurate ranking of drug binding affinities at clinically relevant time scales. Several computational approaches exist to estimate ligand binding affinities and selectivities, with various levels of accuracy and computational expense: free energy perturbation (FEP), thermodynamic integration (TI), lineal response (LR), and molecular mechanics Poisson-Boltzman surface area (MM/PBSA). Identification of conformational preferences and binding site residues, as well as structural and energetic characterisation, is possible using MD simulations [Anzini et al., 2011; Dastidor et al., 2008; Stoika et al., 2008]. It is also possible to estimate conformational energy penalties for adopting the bioactive conformation identified by using a pharmacophore model [Frølund et al., 2005].

A model based on van der Waals intermolecular contribution from Amber and electrostatic interactions derived from the Poisson-Boltzman equation has been used to predict the change in the apparent dissociation constant for a series of six enzyme-substrate complexes during COMBINE analysis [Kmunicek et al., 2001]. In COMBINE analysis, binding energies are calculated for the set of enzyme-substrate complexes using the molecular mechanics force field. The total binding energy, ΔU, may be assumed to be the sum of five terms: the intermolecular interaction energies between the substrate and each enzyme residue, E_{inter}^{ES}, the change in the intramolecular energy of the substrate upon binding to the enzyme, ΔE^S, the change in the intramolecular energy of the enzyme upon binding, ΔE^E, the desolvation energy of the substrate, E_{desolv}^S, and the desolvation energy of the enzyme, E_{desolv}^E.

$$\Delta U = E_{inter}^{ES} + \Delta E^S + \Delta E^E + E_{desolv}^S + E_{desolv}^E \tag{3}$$

When the substrate is a rather small molecule, there is no evidence for large differences in the structure of the enzyme when different substrates are bound and so the second and third are neglected. This method identifies the amino acid residues responsible for modulating enzyme activity [Kmunicek et al., 2005].

Molecular modelling of proteins is sometimes directed towards homology modelling, enabling progress in understanding the mechanisms of action despite the lack of detailed information on the 3D structure of a protein. Molecular dynamic simulations are usually used to test the stability of the complete structure derived from homology modelling [Srinivas et al., 2006].

Molecular docking examples can be used to compare relative stabilities of the complexes, but not calculate binding affinities, since changes in entropy and solvation effects are not taken into account [Pastorin et al., 2006; Tschammer et al., 2011]. In any case, docking calculations are common studies on novel drugs, Autodock being one of the most used docking programs [see for example Venskutonyte et al., 2011]. Docking programs treat enzymes and substrates as rigid entities, but flexible docking is also possible, if several different protein conformations extracted from molecular dynamic simulations are used [Roumen et al., 2010].

In our laboratory, molecular modelling has been tentatively used to study the trypanosomicidal activity of some phthalazine derivatives. Results obtained with Amber force field implemented in HyperChem 8.0 plus our own necessary parameters, and with AutoDock 4.2 using the PDB structure for *T. cruzi* Fe-SOD enzyme, were in accordance with experimental data, helping to explain the experimental results obtained. However, if there is no PDB structure for the desired enzyme and only a model of the active site, as for *Leishmania* Fe-SOD enzyme, results obtained with our calculations do not agree with the experimental ones when compared to the *T. cruzi* ones. This indicates that the interaction with the external part of the enzyme plays an important role as it might collaborate in, or make access to the active site difficult, since the enzyme shape and conformation plays a crucial role in its activity [Sanchez-Moreno et al., 2011; Yunta, unpublished results].

8. Conclusion

Modern molecular modelling techniques are remarkable tools in the search for potentially novel active agents by helping to understand and predict the behaviour of molecular systems, having assumed an important role in the development and optimisation of leading compounds. Moreover, current information on the 3D structure of proteins and their functions provide a possibility of understanding the relevant molecular interactions between a ligand and a target macromolecule. Although improvements are still needed in the techniques used, they have been shown to be invaluable in structure–activity relationship research.

On the basis of the current improved level of understanding of molecular recognition and the widespread availability of target structures, it is reasonable to assume that computational methods will continue to aid not only the design and interpretation of hypothesis-driven experiments in disease research, but also the fast generation of new hypotheses.

Author details

María J. R. Yunta
Universidad Complutense, Madrid, Spain

Acknowledgement

Financial support from the Spanish MEC project (CGL2008-0367-E/BOS) and the MCINN projects (CTQ2009-14288-C04-01 and CONSOLIDER INGENIO 2010 CSD2010-00065) are gratefully acknowledged.

9. References

Ajay, & Murcko, M.A. (1995). Computational methods to predict binding free energy in ligand-receptor complexes. *J. Med. Chem.*, Vol. 38, No. 26, (December 1995), pp. 4953-4967. ISSN: 0022-2623

Albertí, M., Aguilar, A., Lucas, J.M. & Pirani, F. (2010). A generalized formulation of ion-π electron interactions: role of the nonelectrostatic component and probe of the potential parameter transferability. *J. Phys. Chem. A*, Vol. 114, No. 44, (November 2010), pp. 11964-11970. ISSN: 1089-5639

Alcaro, S., Battaglia, D. & Ortuso, F. (2004). Molecular modeling of β-cyclodextrin inclusions complexes with pharmaceutical compounds. *Arkivoc*, Vol. 2004, No. 5, (February 2004), pp. 107-117. ISSN: 1424-6376

Alcaro, S., Gasparrini, F. Incani, O., Mecucci, S., Misiti, D., Pierini, M. & Villani, C. (2000). A 'quasi-flexible' automatic docking processing for sudying stereoselective recognition mechanisms. Part 1. Protocol validation. *J. Comput. Chem.*, Vol. 21, No. 7, (May 2000), pp. 515-530. ISSN: 1096-987X

Ali, Sk.M., Mainly, D.K., De, S. & Shenoi, M.R.K. (2008). Ligands for selective metal ion extraction: a molecular modeling approach. *Desalination*, Vol. 232, No. 1-3, (November 2008), pp. 181-190. ISSN: 0011-9164

Alkorta, I., Blanco, F., Deyà, P.M., Elguero, J., Estarellas, C, Frontera, A. & Quiñonero, D. (2010). Cooperativity in multiple unusual weak bonds. *Theor. Chem. Acc.*, Vol. 126, No. 1-2, (May 2010), pp.1-14. ISSN: 1432-2234

Allinger, N.L. (1976). Calculation of molecular structure and energy by force field methods, In: *Advances in Physical Organic Chemistry*, Vol. 13. Gold, V & Bethell, D. (Eds.), pp. 1-82, Elsevier, ISBN: 978-0120335138, Amsterdam

Allinger, N.L., Chen, K. & Lii, J.H. (1996). An improved force field (MM4) for saturated hydrocarbons. *J. Comput. Chem.*, Vol. 17, No. 5-6, (April 1996), pp. 642-668. ISSN: 1096-987X

Allinger, N.L. & Durkin, K.A. (2000). Van der Waals effects between hydrogen and first row atoms in molecular mechanics (MM3/MM4). *J. Comput. Chem.*, Vol. 21, No. 14 (November 2000), pp. 1229-1242. ISSN: 1096-987X

Allinger, N.L. & Yan, Q.L. (1993). Molecular mechanics (MM3) - calculations of vinyl ethers, and related compounds. *J. Am. Chem. Soc.*, Vol. 115, No. , (1993), pp. 11918-11925. ISSN: 0002-7863

Andersen, N.K., Døssing, H., Jensen, F., Vester, B. & Nielsen, P. (2011). Duplex and triplex formation of mixed pyrimidine oligonucleotides with stacking of phenyl-triazole moieties in the major groove. *J. Org. Chem.*, Vol. 76, No. 15, (August 2011), pp. 6177-6187. ISSN: 0022-3263

Anzini, M., Valenti, S., Braile, C., Cappelli, A., Vomero, S., Alcaro, S., Ortuso, F., Marinelli, L., Limongelli, V., Novellino, E., Betti, L., Giannaccini, G., Lucacchini, A., Daniele, S., Martini, C., Ghelardini, C., Mannelli, L.D.C., Giorgi, G., Mascia, M.P. & Biggio, G. (2011). New insight into the central benzodiazepine receptor-ligand interactions: design, synthesis, biological evaluation, and molecular modeling of 3-substituted 6-phenyl-4*H*-imidazo[1,5-*a*][1,4]benzodiazepines and related compounds. *J. Med. Chem.*, Vol. 54, No. 16, (August 2011), pp. 5694-5711. ISSN: 0022-2623

Aqvist, J., Medina, C. & Samuelson, J.E. (1994). A new method for predicting binding affinity in computer aided drug design. *Protein Eng.* Vol. 7, No. 3, (March 1994), pp. 385-391. ISSN: 0269-2139

Baker, N.A. (2005). Improving implicit solvent simulations: a poisson-centric view. *Curr. Opin. Struct. Biol.*, Vol. 15, No. 2 (April 2005), pp. 137-143. ISSN: 0959-440X

Bendic, C. & Volanschi, E. (2006). Molecular modeling of the interaction of some phenoxazone-antitumoral drugs with DNA. *Int. Elect. J. Mol. Des.*, Vol. 5, No. 6, (June 2006), pp. 320-330. ISSN: 1538-6414

Bissantz, C., Kuhn, B. & Stahl, M. (2010). A medicinal chemist's guide to molecular interactions. *J. Med. Chem*, Vol. 53, No. 14, (July 2010), pp. 5061-5084. ISSN: 0022-2623

Braña, M.F., Cacho, M., García, M.A., Pascual-Teresa, B., Ramos, A., Dominguez, M.T., Pozuelo, J.M., Abradelo, C., Rey-Stolle, M.F., Yuste, M.,Bañez-Coronel, M. & Lacal, J.C. (2004). New analogues of amonafide and elinafide, containing aromatic heterocycles: synthesis, antitumor activity, molecular modeling, and DNA binding properties. *J. Med. Chem.*, Vol. 47, No. 6 (March 2004), pp. 1391-1399. ISSN: 0022-2623

Brooks, B.R., Bruccoleri, R.E., Olafson, B.D., Stales, D.J., Swaminathan, S. & Karplus, M. (1983). CHARMM: A program for macromolecular energy, minimization and dynamic calculations. *J. Comput. Chem.*, Vol. 4, No. 2, (July 1983), pp. 187-217. ISSN: 1096-987X

Buch, I., Sadig, S.K. & DeFabritiis, G. (2011). Optimized potential of mean force calculations for standard binding free energies. *J. Chem. Theory Comp.*, Vol. 7, No. 6, (June 2011), pp. 1765-1772. ISSN: 1549-9626

Campayo, L., Calzado, F., Cano, M.C., Yunta, M.J.R., Pardo, M., Navarro, P., Jimeno, M.L., Gómez-Contreras, F. & Sanz, A.M. (2005). New acyclic receptors containing pyridazine units. The influence of π-stacking on the selective transport of lipophilic phenethylamines. *Tetrahedron*, Vol. 61., No. 50 (December 2005), pp. 11965-11975. ISSN: 0040-4020

Campayo, L., Pardo, M., Cotillas, A., Jaúregui, O., Yunta, M.J.R., Cano, M., Gómez-Contreras, F., Navarro, P. & Sanz, A.M. (2004). A new series of heteroaromatic receptors containing the 1,3-bis(6-oxopyridazin-1-yl)propane unit: their selective transport ability towards NH_4^+ in relation to Na^+, K^+ and Ca^{2+}. *Tetrahedron*, Vol. 60, No. 4, (January 2004), pp. 979-986. ISSN: 0040-4020

Carlson, H.A. & Jorgensen, W.L. (1995). An extended linear response method for determining free energies of hydration. *J. Phys. Chem.*, Vol. 99, No. 26, (June 1995), pp. 10667-10673. ISSN: 0022-3654

Cashman, D.J. & Kellogg, G.E. (2004). A computational model for anthracycline binding to DNA: Tuning groove-binding intercalators for specific sequences. *J. Med. Chem.*, Vol. 47, No. 6, (March 2004), pp. 1360-1374. ISSN: 0022-2623

Castagne, D., Dive, G., Evrad, B., Frédérich, M. & Piel, G. (2010). Spectroscopic studies and molecular modeling for understanding the interactions between cholesterol and cyclodextrins. *J. Pharm. Pharmaceut. Sci.*, Vol. 13, No. 3, (July 2010), pp. 362-367. ISSN: 1482-1826

Černý, V. (1985). Thermodynamical approach to the traveling salesman problem: An efficient simulation algorithm. *J. Optimization Theory and Applications*, Vol 45, No 1, (January 1985): pp. 41–51. ISSN: 0022-3239.

Cerutti, D.S., Ten Eyck, L.F. & McCammon, J.A. (2005). Rapid estimation of solvation energy for simulations of protein-protein association. *J. Chem. Theory Comput.*, Vol. 1, No. 1, (January 2005), pp. 143-152, ISSN: 1549-9626

Chambers, C.C., Hawkins, G.D., Cramer, C.J. & Truhlar, D.G. (1996). Model for aqueous solvation based on class IV atomic charges and first solvation shell effects. *J. Phys. Chem.*, Vol. 100, No. 40, (October 1996), pp. 16385-16398. ISSN: 0022-3654

Checa, A., Ortiz, A.R., Pascual-teresa, B. & Gago, F. (1997). Assessment of solvation effects on calculated binding affinity differences: Trypsin inhibition by flavonoids as a model system for congeneric series. *J. Med. Chem.*, Vol. 40, No. 25, (December 1997), pp. 4136-4145. ISSN: 0022-2623

Chen, J., Brooks, C.L. III & Khandogin, J. (2008). Recent advances in implicit solvent-based methods for biomolecular simulations. *Curr. Opin. Struct. Biol.*, Vol. 18, No. 2 (April 2008), pp. 140-148. ISSN: 0959-440X

Chipot, C., Maigret, B., Pearlman, D.A. & Kollman, P.A. (1996). Molecular dynamics potential of mean force calculations: a study of the toluene-ammonium π-cation interactions. *J. Am. Chem. Soc.*, Vol. 118, No. 12, (March 1996), pp. 2998-3005. ISSN: 0002-7863

Choe, J.I. & Chang, S.K. (2002). Molecular modeling of complexation behavior of *p-tert*-butylcalix[5]arene derivative toward butylammonium ions. *Bull. Korean Chem. Soc.*, Vol. 23, No. 1, (January 2002), pp. 48-52. ISSN: 0253-2964

Choi, H.S., Suh, S.B., Cho, S.J. & Kim, K.S. (1998). Ionophores and receptors using cation-π interactions: collarenes. *Proc. Natl. Acad. Sci. USA*, Vol. 95, No 21, (October 1998), pp. 12094-12099. ISNN: 1091-6490

Cornell, W.D., Cieplak, P., Bayly, C.I., Gould, I.R., Merz, K.M. Jr., Ferguson, D.M., Spellmeyer, D.C., Fox, T., Caldwell, J.W. & Kollman, P.A. (1995). A second generation force field for thr simulation of proteins and nucleic acids. *J. Am. Chem. Soc.*, Vol. 117, No. 19, (May 1995), pp. 5179-5197. ISSN: 0002-7863

Cramer, C.J. & Truhlar, D.G. (2008). A universal approach to solvation modeling. *Acc. Chem. Res.*, Vol. 41, No. 6, (June 2008), pp. 760-768. ISSN: 0001-4842

Cramer, R.D., Patterson, D.E. & Bunce, J.D. (1988). Comparative molecular field analysis (CoMFA). 1. Effect of shape on binding of steroids to carrier proteins. *J. Am. Chem. Soc.*, Vol. 110, No. 18, (August 1998), pp. 5959-5967. ISSN: 0002-7863

Cruziani, G. & Goodford, P.J. (1994). A research for specificity in DNA-drug interactions. *J. Mol. Graph.*, Vol. 12, No. 2, (June 1994), pp. 116-129. ISSN: 0263-7855

Dastider, S.G., Lane, D.P. & Verma, C.S. (2008). Multiple peptide conformations give rise to similar binding affinities: molecular simulations of p53-MDM2. *J. Am. Chem. Soc.*, Vol. 130, No. 41, (October 2008), pp. 13514-13515. ISSN: 0002-7863

Dauber-Osguthorpe, P., Roberts, V.A., Osguthorpe, D.J., Wolff, J., Genest, M. & Hagler, A.T. (2004). Structure and energetics of ligand binding to proteins: *E. coli* dihydrofolate reductase- trimethoprim, a drug-receptor system. *Proteins*, Vol. 4, No. 1, (February 2004), pp. 31-47. ISSN: 0887-3585

Delgado, E.J. & Jaña, G.A. (2009). Quantitative prediction of solvation free energy in octanol of organic compounds. *Int. J. Mol. Sci.*, Vol. 10, No. 3, (March 2009), pp. 1031-1044. ISSN: 1422-0067

Doshi, U. & Hamelberg, D. (2009). Reoptimization of the AMBER force field parameters for peptide bond (omega) torsions using accelerated molecular dynamics. *J. Phys. Chem. B*, Vol. 113, No. 52, (December 2009), pp. 16590-16595. ISSN: 1089-5647

Durand, S., Dognon, J.P., Guiband, P., Rabbe, C. & Wipff, G. (2000). Lanthanide and alkaline-earth complexes of EDTA in water: a molecular dynamics study of structures and binding selectivities. *J. Chem. Soc., Perkin Trans. 2*, Vol. 2000, No. 4, (April 2000), pp. 705-714. ISSN: 1364-5471

Dzubiella, J., Swanson, J.M.J. & McCammon, J.A. (2006a). Coupling nonpolar and polar solvation free energies in implicit solvent models. *J. Chem. Phys.*, Vol. 124, (February 2006), pp. 084905. ISSN: 0021-9606

Dzubiella, J., Swanson, J.M.J. & McCammon, J.A. (2006b). Coupling hydrophobicity dispersion, and electrostatics in continuum solvent models. *Phys. Rev. Lett.*, Vol. 96, No. 8, (March 2006), pp. 087802. ISSN: 1079-7114

Elber, R., Rotberg, A., Simmerling, C., Goldstein, R., Li, H., Verkhivker, G., Keasar, C., Zhang, J. & Ulitsky, A. (1995). MOIL: A program for simulations of macromolecules. *Comp. Phys. Comm.*, Vol. 91, No. 1-3, (September 1995), pp. 159-189. ISSN: 1815-2406

Elguero, J. Alkorta, I., Claramunt, R.M., López, C., Sanz, D. & Santa María, D. (2009). Theoretical calculations of a model of NOS indazole inhibitors: Interaction of aromatic compounds with Zn-porphyrins. *Bioorg. Med. Chem.*, Vol. 17, No. 23, (December 2009), pp. 8027-8031. ISSN: 0968-0896

Fantoni, A.C. (2003). Molecular dynamics study of geometrical isomers of a pyridinocalix[4]arene in methanol solution: solvation and alkali metal cation binding properties. *J. Mol. Struct. (Theochem)*, Vol. 693, No. 1, (August 2003), pp. 1-6. ISSN: 0166-1280

Filizola, M., Carteri-Farina, M. & Perez, J.J. (1999). Molecular modeling study of the differential ligand-receptor interaction at the μ, δ and κ opioid receptors. *J. Comput. Aid. Mol. Des.*, Vol. 13, No. 4, (July 1999), pp. 397-407. ISSN: 1573-4951

Friesner, R.A., Banks, J.L., Murphy, R.B., Halgren, T.A., Klicic, J.J., Mainz, D.T., Repasky, M.P., Knoll, E.H., Shelley, M., Perry, J.K., Shaw, D.E., Francis, P. & Shenkin, P.S. (2004). Glide: A new approach for rapid, accurate docking and scoring. 1. Method and assessment of docking accuracy. *J. Med. Chem.*, Vol. 47, No. 7, (March 2004), pp. 1739-1749. ISSN: 0022-2623

Friesner, R.A., Murphy, R.B., Repasky, M.P., Frye, L.L., Greenwood, J.R., Halgren, T.A., Sanschagrin, P.C. & Mainz, D.T. (2006). Extra precision Glide: Docking and scoring incorporating a model of hydrophobic enclosure for protein-ligand complexes. *J. Med. Chem.*, Vol. 49, No. 21, (October 2006), pp. 6177-6196. ISSN: 0022-2623

Frølund, B., Jensen, L.S., Guandalini, L., canillo, C., Vestergarard, H.T., Kristiansen, U., Nielsen, B., Stensbøl, T.B., Madsen, C., Krogsgaard-Larsen, P. & Liljefors, T. (2005). Potent 4-aryl- or 4-arylalkyl-substituted 3-isoxazolol GABAA antagonists: synthesis, pharmacology, and molecular modeling. *J. Med. Chem.*, Vol. 48, No. 2, (January 2005), pp. 427-439. ISSN: 0022-2623

Galisteo, J., Navarro, P., campayo, L., Yunta, M.J.R., Gómez-Contreras, F., Villa-Pulgarin, J.A., Sierra, B.G., Mollinedo, F., Gonzalez, J. & García-España, E. (2010). Synthesis and cytotoxic activity of a new potential bisintercalator: 1,4-bis{3-[N-(4-chlorobenzo[g]phthalazin-1-yl)aminopropil]}piperazine. *Bioorg. Med. Chem.*, Vol. 18, No. 14 (July 2010), pp. 5301-5309. ISSN: 0968-0896

Gallicchio, E. & Levy, R.M. (2004). AGBNP: An analytical implicit solvent model suitable for molecular dynamics simulations and high-resolution modeling. *J. Comput. Chem.*, Vol. 25, No. 4, (March 2004), pp. 479-499. ISSN: 1096-987X

Gallicchio, E., Zhang, L.Y. & Levy, R.M. (2002). The SGB/NP hydration free energy model based on the surface generalized born solvent reaction field and novel nonpolar hydration free energy estimators. *J. Comput. Chem.*, Vol. 23, No. 5, (April 2002), pp. 517-529. ISSN: 1096-987X

Gevorkyan, A.A., Arakelyan, A.S., Esayan, V.A., Petrosyan, K.A. & Torosyan, G.O. (2001). Ionic character of the ammonium-counterion bond and catalytic activity of ammonium salts in elimination reactions. *Gen. Chem.*, Vol. 71, No. 8, (August 2001), pp. 1327-1328. ISSN: 1070-3632

Gilson, M.K. & Zhou, H.X. (2007). Calculation of protein-ligand binding affinities. *Annu. Rev. Biophys. Biomol. Struct.*, Vol. 36, (June 2007), pp. 21-42. ISSN: 1056-8700

Goodford, P.J. (1985). A computational procedure for determining energetically favorable binding sites on biologically important macromolecules. *J. Med. Chem.*, Vol. 18, No. 8, (August 1985), pp. 849-857. ISSN: 0022-2623

Halgren, T.A. (1996). Merck molecular force field. 1. Basis, form, scope, parameterización, and performanceof MMFF94. *J. Comput. Chem.*, Vol. 17, No. 5-6, (April 1996), pp. 490-519. ISSN: 1096-987X

Halgren, T.A., Murphy, R.B., Friesner, R.A., Beard, H.S., Frie, L.L., Pollard, W.T. & Banks, J.L. (2004). Glide: A new approach for rapid, accurate docking and scoring. 2. Enrichment factors in database screening. *J. Med. Chem.*, Vol. 47, No. 7, (March 2004), pp. 1750-1759. ISSN: 0022-2623

Hashimoto, S. & Ikuta, S. (1999). A theoretical study on the conformations, energetics, and solvation effects on the cation-π interaction between monovalent ions Li$^+$, Na$^+$ and K$^+$ and naphthalene molecules. *J. Mol. Struct. (Theochem)*, Vol. 468, No. 1-2, (August 1999), pp. 85-94. ISSN: 0166-1280

Hill, S.E. & Feller, D. (2000). Theoretical study of cation/ether complexes: 15-crown-5 and its alkali metal complexes. *Int. J. of Mass Spect.*, Vol. 201, No. 1-3, (December 2000), pp. 41-58, ISSN: 1387-3806

Hoops, S.C., Anderson, K.W. & Merz, K.M. Jr. (1991). Force field design for metalloproteins. *J. Am. Chem. Soc.*, Vol. 113, No. 22, (October 1991), pp. 8262-8270. ISSN: 0002-7863

Horta, B.A.C., Fuchs, P.F.J., van Gunsteren, W.F. & Hunenberger, P.H. (2011). New interaction parameters for oxygen compounds in the GROMOS force field: improved pure-liquid and solvation properties for alcohols, ethers, aldehydes, ketones, carboxylic acids and esters. *J. Chem. Theory Comp.*, Vol. 7, No. 4, (April 2011), pp. 1016-1031. ISSN: 1549-9626

Ilioudis, C.A., Bearpark, M.J. & Stead, J.W. (2005). Hydrogen bonds between ammonium ions and aromatic rings exist and have key consequences on solid-state and solution phase properties. *New J. Chem.*, Vol. 29, No. 1, (January 2005), pp. 64-67. ISSN: 1144-0546

Jager, R. & Kast, S.M. (2001). Fast prediction of hydration free energies from molecular interaction fields. *J. Mol. Graphs. Mod.*, Vol. 20, No. 1, (February 2001), pp. 123-131, ISSN: 1093-3263

Jain, A.N. (2003). Surflex: Fully automatic flexible molecular docking using a molecular similarity-based search engine. *J. Med. Chem.*, Vol. 46, No. 4, (February 2003), pp. 499-511. ISSN: 0022-2623

Jain, A.N. (2007). Surflex-Dock 2.1: Robust performance from ligand energetic modeling, ring flexibility, and knowledge-based search. *J. Comput. Aid. Mol. Des.*, Vol. 21, No. 5, (May 2007), pp. 281-306. ISSN: 1573-4951

Jorgensen, W.L. & Tirado-Rives, J. (1996). Monte Carlo vs molecular dynamics for conformational sampling. *J. Phys. Chem.*, Vol. 100, No. 34, (August 1996), pp. 14508-14513. ISSN: 0022-3654

Kaye, P.T. (2011). Designer ligands: The search for the metal ion selectivity. *S. Afr. J. Sci.*, Vol. 107, No. 3-4, (March 2011), pp. 439-446. ISSN: 0038-2353

Khavretskii, I.V. & Wallquist, A. (2010). Computing relative energies of solvation using single reference thermodynamic integration augmented with Hamiltonian replica exchange. *J. Chem. Theor. Comput.*, Vol. 6, No. 11, (2010), pp. 3427-3441. ISSN: 1549-9626

Kim, K.S., Lee, J.Y. & Tarakeshwar, P. (2000). Molecular clusters of π-systems: Theoretical studies of structures, spectra, and origin of interaction energies. *Chem. Rev.*, Vol. 100, No. 11, (November, 2000), pp. 4145-4186. ISSN:0009-2665

Kirkpatrick, S.; Gelatt, C. D.; Vecchi, M. P. (1983). Optimization by Simulated Annealing. *Science*, Vol 220, No 4598, (May 1983) pp. 671–680. ISSN: 0036-8075.

Kiselev, E., Dexheimer, T., Pommier, Y. & Cushman, M. (2010). Design, synthesis, and evaluation of dibenzo[*c*,*h*][1,6]naphthyridines as topoisomerase I inhibitors and potential anticancer agents. *J. Med. Chem.*, Vol. 53, No. 24 (December 2010), pp. 8716-8726. ISSN: 0022-2623

Klamt, A., Mennucci, B., Tomasi, J., Barone, V., Curutchet, C., Orozco, M. & Luque, F.J. (2009). On the performance of continuum solvation methods. A comment on 'universal approaches to solvation modeling'. *Acc. Chem. Res.*, Vol. 42, No. 4, (April 2009), pp. 489-492. ISSN: 0001-4842

Kmunicek, J., Luengo, S., Gago, F., Ortíz, A.R., Wade, R.C. & Damborský, J. (2001). Comparative binding energy analysis of the substrate specificity of haloalkane dehalogenase from *Xanthobacter autotrophicus* GJ10. *Biochem.*, Vol. 40, No. 30, (July 2001), pp. 8905-8917. ISSN: 006-2960

Kmunicek, J., Hyncová, K., Jedlicka, T., Nagata, Y., Negri, A., Gago, F., Wade, R.C. & Damborský, J. (2005). Quantitative analysis of substrate specificity of haloalcane dehalogenase Lin B from *Sphingomonas paucimobilis* UT26. *Biochem.*, Vol. 44, No. 10, (March 2005), pp. 3390-3401. ISSN: 006-2960

Kollman, P.A., Massova, I., Reyes, C., Kuhn, B., Huo, S. (2000). Calculating structures and free energies of complex molecules: combining molecular mechanics and continuum models. *Acc. Chem. Res.*, Vol. 33, No. 12, (December 2000), pp.889-897. ISSN: 0001-4842

Kuntz, I.D. (1992). Structure based strategies for drug design and discovery. *Science*, Vol. 257, No. 8, (August 1992), pp. 1078-1082. ISSN: 0036-8075

Kuntz, I.D., Meng, E.C. & Shoichet, B.K. (1994). Structure based molecular design. *Acc. Chem. Res.*, Vol. 27, No. 5, (May 1994), pp. 117-123. ISSN: 0001-4842

Li, Z. & Lazaridis, T. (2007). Water at biomolecular binding interfaces. *Phys. Chem. Chem. Phys.*, Vol. 9, No. 5, (February 2007), pp. 573-581. ISSN: 1463-9076

Lin, F. & Wang, R. (2010). Systematic derivation of AMBER force field parameters applicable to zinc-containing systems. *J. Chem. Theory Comput.*, Vol. 6, No. 6, (June 2010), pp. 1852-1870. ISSN: 1549-9626

Luchko, T., Gusarov, S., Roe, D.R., Simmerling, C., Case, D.A., Tuszynski, J. & Kovalenko, A. (2010). Three-diemnsional molecular theory of solvation coupled with molecular dynamics in Amber. *J. Chem. Theory Comput.*, Vol. 6, No. 3, (March 2010), pp. 607-624. ISSN: 1549-9626

Lumetta, G.J., Rapko, B.M., Garza, P.A. & Hay, B.P. (2002). Deliberate design of ligand architecture yields dramatic enhancement of metal ion affinity. *J. Am. Chem. Soc.*, Vol. 124, No. 20, (May 2002), pp. 5644-5645. ISSN: 0002-7863

Ma, J.C. & Dougherty, D.A. (1997). The cation-π interaction. *Chem. Rev.*, Vol. 97, No. 5, (August 1997), pp. 1303-1324. ISSN: 0009-2665

Mancera, R.L. (2007). Molecular modeling of hydration in drug design. *Curr. Opin. Drug. Discov. Dev.*, Vol. 10, No. 3, (May 2007), pp. 275-280. ISSN: 1367-6733.

Marco, E., Negri, A., Luque, F.J. & Gago, F. (2005). Role of staking interactions in the binding sequence preferences of DNA bis-intercalators: insight from thermodynamic integration free energy simulations. *Nuc. Ac. Res.*, Vol. 33, No. 19 (November 2005), pp. 6214-6224. ISSN: 0305-1048

Marcus, Y. & Hefter, G. (2006). Ion pairing. *Chem. Rev.*, Vol. 106, No. 11, (November 2006), pp. 4585-4621. ISSN: 0009-2665

Meng, E.C., Shoichet, B.K. & Kuntz, I.D. (1992). Automated docking with grid-based energy evaluation. *J. Comput. Chem.*, Vol. 13, No. 4, (May 1992), pp. 505-524. ISSN: 1096-987X

Meyar, E.A., Castellano, R.K. & Diederich, F. (2003). Interactions with aromatic rings in chemical and biological recognition. *Angew. Chem. Int. Ed.*, Vol. 42, No. 11, (March 2003), pp. 1210-1250. ISSN: 1433-7851

Miranda, C., Escartí, F., Lamarque, L., Yunta, M.J.R., Navarro, P., García-España, E. & Jimeno, M.L. (2004). New 1*H*-pyrazole-containing polyamine receptor sable to complex L-glutamate in wáter at physiological pH values. *J. Am. Chem. Soc.*, Vol. 126, No. 3, (January 2004), pp. 823-833. ISSN: 0002-7863

Miranda, C., Escartí, F., Lamarque, L., García-España, E., Navarro, P., Latorre, L., lloret, F., Jimenez, H.R. & Yunta, M.J.R. (2005). Cu^II and Zn^II coordination chemistry of pyrazole-containing poliamine receptors – Influence of the hydrocarbon side chain length on the metal coordination. *Eur. J. Inorg. Chem.*, Vol. 2005, No. 1, (January 2005), pp. 189-208. ISSN: 1434-1948

Miri, R., Javidnia, K., Hemmateenejad, B., Azarpira, A. & Amirghofran, Z. (2004). Synthesis, cytotoxicity, QSAR, and intercalation study of new diindenopyridine derivatives. *Bioorg. Med. Chem.*, Vol. 12, No. 10, (May 2004), pp. 2529-2536. ISSN: 0968-0896

Mishra, P. (2010). Biocoordination and computational modeling of streptomycin with Co(II), Ni(II), In(II) and inorganic Sn(II). *Int. J. Pharm. Sci.*, Vol. 2, No. 2, (June 2010), pp. 87-97. ISSN: 0976-044X

Mobley, D.L., Bayly, C.I., Cooper, M.D. Shirts & Dill, K.A. (2009). Small molecule hydration free energies in explicit solvent: an extensive test of fixed-cahrge atomistic simulations. *J. Chem. Theory Comput.*, Vol. 5, No. 2, (February 2009), pp. 350-358. ISSN: 1549-9626

Moon, J.B. & Howe, W.J. (1991). Computer design of bioactive molecules: a method for receptor-based de novo ligands design. *Proteins*, Vol. 11, No.4 , (December 1991), pp. 314-328. ISSN: 0887-3585

Nicholls, A., Wlodek, S. & Grant, J.A. (2009). The SAMP1 solvation challenge: Further lessons regarding the pitfalls of parameterization. *J. Phys. Chem. B*, Vol. 113; No. 14, (April 2009), pp. 4521-4532. ISSN: 1089-5647

Oh, K.S., Lee, C.W., Choi, H.S., Lee, S.J. & Kim, K.S. (2000). Origin of the high affinity and selectivity of novel receptors for NH_4^+ over K^+: Charged hydrogen bonds vs cation-π interaction. *Org. Lett.*, Vol. 2, No. 17, (August 2000), pp. 2679-2681. ISSN: 1523-7052

Onsager, L. (1936). Electric moments of molecules in liquids, *J. Am. Chem. Soc.*, Vol. 58, No. 8, (August 1936), pp. 1486-1493. ISSN: 0002-7863

Orozco, M. & Luque, F.J. (2000). Theoretical methods for the description of the solvent effect in biomolecular systems. *Chem. Rev.*, Vol. 100, No. 11, (November 2000), pp. 4187-4226. ISSN: 0009-2665

Palmer, D.S., Frolov, A.I., Ratkova, E.L. & Fedorov, M.V. (2011). Toward a universal model to calculate the solvation thermodynamics of druglaike molecules: The importance of new experimental databases. *Mol. Pharm.*, Vol. 8, No. 4 (August 2011), pp. 1423-1429. ISSN:0026-895X

Park, J.Y., Kim, B.C. & Park, S.M. (2007). Molecular recognition of protonated polyamines at calix[4]crown-5 self-assembled monolayer modified electrodes by impedance measurements. *Anal. Chem.*, Vol. 79, No. 5, (March 2007), pp. 1890-1896. ISSN: 0003-2700

Pastorin, G., Da Ros, T., Bolcato, C., Montopoli, C., Moro, S., Cacciari, B., Baraldi, P.G., varani, K., Borea, P.A. & Spalluto, G. (2006). Synthesis and biological studies of a new series of 5-heteroarylcarbamoylaminopirazolo[4,3-*e*]1,2,4-triazolo[1,5-*c*]pyrimidines as human A3 adenosine receptor antagonists. Influence of the heteroaryl substituent on binding affinity and molecular modeling investigations. *J. Med. Chem.*, Vol. 49, No. 5, (March 2006), pp. 1720-1729. ISSN: 0022-2623

Perez, C., Pastor, M., Ortiz, A.R. & Gago, F. (1998). Comparative binding energy analysis of HIV-1 protease inhibitors: incorporation of solvent effects and validation as a powerful tool in receptor-based drug design. *J. Med. Chem.*, Vol. 41, No. 6, (March 1998), pp. 836-852. ISSN: 0022-2623

Peters, M.B., Yang, Y., Wang, B. Füsti-Molnár, L. Weaver, M.N. & Merz, K.M. Jr. (2010). Structural survey of zinc-containing proteins and development of the zinc AMBER forcefield (ZAFF). *J. Chem.Theory Comput.* Vol. 6, No. 9, (September 2010), pp. 2935-2947. ISSN: 1549-9626

Plewczynski, D., Lazniewski, M., Augustyniac, R. & Ginalski, K. (2011). Can we trust docking results? Evaluation of seven commonly used programs on PDB bind database. *J. Comput. Chem.*, Vol. 32, No. 4, (March 2011), pp. 742-755. ISSN: 1096-987X

Reddy, M.R., Erion, M.D. & Agaewal, A. (2000). Use of free energy calculations in drug design, In: *Reviews in computational chemistry 2*. K.B. Lipkowitz & D.B. Boyd (Eds.), pp. 217-304. ISBN: 978-0471188100

Reddy, M.R. & Erion, M.D. (2005). Computer aided drug design strategies used in the discovery of fructose 1,6-biphosphate inhibitors. *Curr. Pharm. Des.*, Vol. 11, No. 3, (February 2005), pp. 283-294. ISSN: 1381-6128

Reddy, A.S., Sastry, G.M. & Sastry, G.N. (2007). Cation-aromatic database. *Proteins*, Vol. 67, No. 4, (March 2007), pp. 41-58, ISSN:0887-3585

Reddy, M.R. & Erion, M.D. (2007). Relative binding affinities of fructose-1,6-bisphosphatase inhibitors calculated using a quantum mechanics-based free energy perturbation method. *J. Am. Chem. Soc.*, Vol. 129, No. 30, (August 2007), pp. 9296-9297. ISSN: 0002-7863

Reichert, D.E., Norrby, P-O. & Welch, M.J. (2001). Molecular modeling of bifunctional chelate peptide conjugates. 1. Copper and indium parameters for the Amber force field. *Inorg. Chem.*, Vol. 40, No. 20, (September 2001), pp. 5223-5230. ISSN: 0020-1669

Reviriego, F., Navarro, P., García-España, E., Albelda, M.T., frias, J.C., Domènech, A., Yunta, M.J.R., Costa, R. & Ortí, E. (2008). Diazatetraester 1*H*-pyrazole crowns as fluorescent chemosensors for AMPH, METH, MDMA(Ecstasy) and dopamine. *Org. Lett.*, Vol. 10, No. 22, (November 2008), pp. 5099-5102. ISSN: 1523-7060

Reynolds, C.A., Wade, R.C. & Goodford, P.J. (1989). Identifying targets for bioreductive agents: using GRID to predict selective binding regions of proteins. *J. Mol. Graph.*, Vol. 7, No. 2, (June 1989), pp. 103-108. ISSN: 0263-7855

Riahi, S., Eynollahi, S., Ganjali, M.R. & Norouzi, P. (2010). Computational modeling of interaction between Camphothecin and DNA base pairs. *Int. J. Electrochem. Sci.*, Vol. 5, No. 8, (August 2010), pp. 1151-1163. ISSN: 1452-3981

Rodríguez-Ciria, M. (2000). Síntesis de 1-amino y 1,4-diamino derivados de benzo[g]ftalazina, evaluación de sus propiedades complejantes frente a cationes metálicos y catecolaminas involucrados en mecanismos de neurotrnasmisión. *Ph.D. Thesis*, Universidad Complutense, Madrid

Rodríguez-Ciria, M., Sanz, A.M., Gómez-Contreras, F., Navarro, P., Pardo, M., Yunta, M.J.R., Castiñeiras, A. & Cano, M.C. (2002). Benzo[*g*]phthalazine ligands as tyrosinase mimetics: the influence of the polyaminic side-chains size and nature on the complexation of Cu(II). *Proceedings of 8ᵗʰ International symposium on the chemistry and pharmacology of pyridazines*, Ferrara (Italy), October 2002

Rodríguez-Ciria, M., Sanz, A.M., Yunta, M.J.R., Gómez-Contreras, F., Navarro, P., Fernández, I., Pardo, M. & Cano, M. (2003). Synthesis and cytostatic activity of *N,N*-bis-{3-[*N*-(4-chlorobenzo[*g*]-phthalazin-1-yl]aminopropil}-*N*-methylamine: a new potential DNA bisintercalator. *Bioorg. Med. Chem.*, Vol. 11, No. 10 (May 2003), pp. 2143-2148. ISSN: 0968-0896

Roumen, L., Peeters, J.W., Emmen, J.M.A., Bengels, I.P.E., Custers, E.M.G., de Gooyer, M, Plate, R., Pieterse, K., Hilbers, P.A.J., Smits, J.F.M., Vekemans, J.A.J., Leysen, D., Ottenheijm, H.C.J., Janssen, H.M. & Hermans, J.J.R. (2010). Synthesis, biological evaluation, and molecular modeling of 1-benzyl-1H-imidazoles as selective inhibitors of aldosterone synthase (CYP11B2). *J. Med. Chem.*, Vol. 53, No. 4, (February 2010), pp. 1712-1725. ISSN: 0022-2623

Sakakura, K., Okabe, A., Oku, K. & Sakurai, M. (2011). Experimental and theoretical study on the intermolecular complex formation between trehalose and benzene compounds in aqueous solution. *J. Phys. Chem. B*, Vol. 115, No. 32, (August 2011), pp.9823-9830. ISSN: 1089-5647

Sanchez-Moreno, M., Sanz, A.M., Gómez-Contreras, F., Navarro, P., Marín, C., Ramírez-Macías, I., Rosales, M.J., Olmo, F., García-Aranda, I., Campayo, L., Cano, C., Arrebola, F. & Yunta, M.J.R. (2011). *In vivo* Trypanosomicidal activity of imidazole-or pyrazole-based venzo[g]phthalazine derivatives against acute and chronic phases of chagas disease. *J. Med. Chem.*, Vol. 54, No. 4, (February 2011), pp. 970-979. ISSN: 0223-5234

Sands, Z.A. & Laughton, C.A. (2004). Molecular dynamics simulations of DNA using the generalized Born solvation model: quantitative comparisons with explicit solvation results. *J. Phys. Chem. B*, Vol. 108, No. 28, (July 2004), pp. 10113-10119. ISSN: 1089-5647

Shaikh, S.A., Ahmed, S.R. & Jayaram, B. (2004). A molecular thermodynamic view of DNA-drug interactions: A case study of 25 minor-groove binders. *Arch. Biochem. Biophys.*, Vol. 429, No. 1, (September 2004), pp. 81-99. ISSN: 0003-9861

Shivakumar, D., Williams, J. Wu, Y., Damm, W., Shelley, J. & Sherman, W. (2010). Prediction of absolute solvation free energies using molecular dynamics free energy perturbation and the OPLS force field. *J. Chem. Theory Comput.*, Vol. 6, No. 5, (May 2010), pp. 1509-1519. ISSN: 1549-9626

Shoichet, B.K. & Kuntz, I.D. (1996). Predicting the structure of protein complexes: a step in the right direction. *Chem. and Biol.*, Vol. 3, No. 3, (March 1996), pp.151-156. ISSN: 1074-5521

Silva, S.J. & Jayasundera, K. (2002). Quantitative structure activity relationships for guanidiniothiazole carboxamides using theoretically calculated molecular descriptors. *J. Natn. Sci. Found. Sri Lanka*, Vol. 30, No. 3-4, (December 2002), pp. 171-184. ISSN: 1391-4588

Simonson, T. (2001). Macromolecular electrostatics: continuum models and their growing pains. *Curr. Opin. Struct. Biol.*, Vol. 11, No. 2 (April 2001), pp. 243-252. ISSN: 0959-440X

Slickers, P., Hillebrand, M., Kittler, L., Löber, G. & Sühnel, J. (1998). Molecular modeling and footprinting studies of DNA minor groove binders: bisquaternary ammonium heterocyclic compounds. *Anti-Cancer Drug Des.*, Vol. 13, No. 5, (September 1998), pp. 463-488. ISSN: 0266-9536

Soteras, I., Morreale, A., López, J.M., Orozco, M. & Luque, F.J. (2004). Group contributions to the solvation free energy from MST continuum calculations. *Braz. J. Phys.*, Vol. 34, No. 1, (March 2004), pp. 48-57. ISSN: 1678-4448.

Späth, A. & König, B. (2010). Molecular recognition of organic ammonium ions in solution using synthetic receptors. *Beilstein J. Org. Chem.*, Vol. 6, No. 32, (April 2010), pp. 1-111. ISSN: 1860-5397

Srinivas, E., Murthy, J.N., Rao, A.R.R. & Sastry, G.N. (2006). Recent advances in molecular modeling and medicinal chemistry aspects of phosphor-glycoprotein. *Curr. Drug Metabol.*, Vol. 7, No. 2, (February 2006), pp. 205-217. ISSN: 1389-2002

Stoika, I., Sadiq, S.K. & Coveney, P.V. (2008). Rapid and accurate prediction of binding free energies for saquinavir-bound HIV-1 proteases. *J. Am. Chem. Soc.*, Vol. 130, No. 8, (February 2008), pp. 2639-2648. ISSN: 0002-7863

Subramanian, G., Paterlini, M.G., Portoghese, P.S. & Ferguson, D.M. (2000). Molecular docking reveals a novel binding site model for fentanyl at the μ-opioid receptor. *J. Med. Chem.*, Vol. 43, No. 3, (February 2000), pp. 381-391. ISSN: 0022-2623

Taylor, R.D., Jewsbury, P.J. & Essex, J.W. (2002). A review of protein-small molecule docking methods. . *J. Comput. Aid. Mol. Des.*, Vol. 16, No. 3, (March 2002), pp. 151-166. ISSN: 1573-4951

Tóth, J., Remko, M. & Nagy, M. (2005). The ability of molecular modeling methods to reproduce the structure of flavonoids. *Acta Facul. Pharm. Univ. Comenianae*, Vol. LII, (2005), pp. 218-225. ISSN: 0301-2298

Tschammer, N., Elsner, J. Goetz, A., Ehrlich, K., Schuster, S., Ruberg, M., Kühhorn, J., Thompson, D., Whistler, J., Hübner, H. & Gmeiner, P. (2011). Highly potent 5-aminotetrahydropyrazolopyridines: enantioselective dopamine D_3 receptor binding, functional selectivity, and analysis of receptor-ligand interactions. *J. Med. Chem.*, Vol. 54, No. 7, (April 2011), pp. 2477-2491. ISSN: 0022-2623

van Gunsteren, W.F. & Berendsen, H.J.C. (1977). Algorithms for macromolecular dynamics and constraint dynamics. *Mol. Phys.*, Vol. 34, No. 5, (August 2006), pp.1311-1327. ISSN: 1362-3028

Varnek, A. Wipff, G., Bilyk, A. & Harrowfield, J.M. (1999). Molecular dynamics and free energy perturbation studies of Ca^{2+}/Sr^{2+} complexation selectivities of the macrocyclic ionophores DOTA and TETA in water. *J. Chem. Soc. Dalton Trans.*, Vol. 1999, No. 23, (December 1999), pp. 4155-4164. ISSN: 1472-7773

Veal, J.M., Li, X., Zimmerman, S.C., Lambenmon, C.R., Cory, M., Zon, G. & Wilson, W.D. (1990). Interaction of a macrocyclic bisacridine with DNA. *Biochem.*, Vol. 29, No. 49, (December 1990), pp. 10918-10927. ISSN: 0006-2960

Venskutonyte, R., Butini, S., Coccone, S.S., Gemma, S., Brindisi, M., Kumor, V., Guarino, E., Maramai, S., Amir, A., Valades, E.A., Frydenvang, K., Kastrup, J.S., Novellino, E., Campiani, G. & Pickering, D.S. (2011). Selective kainite receptor (Gluk1) ligands structurally based upon 1H-cyclopentapyrimidin-2,4(1H,3H)-dione: Synthesis, molecular modeling, and pharmacological and biostructural characterization. *J. Med. Chem.*, Vol. 54, No. 13, (July 2011), pp. 4793-4805. ISSN: 0022-2623

Viswanadhan, V.N., Ghose, A.K., Sing, U.C. & Wendoloski, J.J. (1999). Prediction of solvation free energies of small organic molecules:additive-constitutive models based on molecular fingerprints and atomic constants. *J. Chem. Inf. Comput. Sci.*, Vol. 39, No. 2, (March 1999), pp. 405-412. ISSN: 0095-2338

Wang, J., Kang, X., Kuntz, I.D. & Kollman, P.A. (2005). Hierarchical database screenings for HIV-1 reverse transcriptase using a pharmacophore model, rigid docking and MM-PB/SA. *J. Med. Chem.*, Vol. 48, No. 8, (April 2005), pp. 2432-2444. ISSN: 0022-2623

Wang, H. & Laughton, C.A. (2009). Evaluation of molecular modeling methods to predict the secuence-selectivity of DNA minor groove binding ligands. *Phys. Chem. Chem. Phys..* Vol. 11, No. 45, (December 2009), pp. 10722-10728. ISSN: 1463-9076

Wang, H. & Laughton, C.A. (2010). Molecular modeling mrthods to quantitative drud-DNA interactions, In: *Drug-DNA interaction protocols, Methods in molecular biology*, Vol. 613, pp. 19-31, Humana Press, Germany. ISBN: 978-1-60327-417-3

Weiner, S.J., Kollman, P.A., Case, D.A., Singh, V.C., Ghio, C., Alagona, G., Profeta, S. Jr. & Weiner, P. (1984). A new force field for molecular mechanical simulation of nucleic acids and proteins. *J. Am. Chem. Soc.*, Vol. 106, No. 3, (February 1984), pp. 765-784. ISSN: 0002-7863

Weiner, S.J., Kollman, P.A., Nguyen, D.T. & Case, D.A. (1986). An all atom force field for simulations of proteins and nucleic acids. *J. Comput. Chem.*, Vol. 7, No. 2, (April 1986), pp. 230-252. ISSN: 1096-987X

Wilson, C., Mace, J.E. & Agard, D.A. (1991). A computational method for designing enzymes with altered substrate specifity. *J. Mol. Biol.*, Vol. 220, No. 2, (July 1991), pp. 495-506. ISSN: 0022-2836

Woods, R.J., Dwek, R.A., Edge, C.J. & Fraser-Reid, B. (1995). Molecular mechanical and molecular dynamical simulations of glycoproteins and oligosaccharides. 1. GLYCAM_93 parameter development. *J. Phys. Chem.*, Vol. 99, No. 11, (March 1995), pp. 3832-3846. ISSN: 0022-3654

Yang, L., Tan, C., Hsieh, M-J., Wang, J., Duan, Y., Cieplak, P., Caldwell, J., Kollman, P.A. & Luo, R. (2006). New generation Amber united-atom force field. *J. Phys. Chem. B*, Vol. 110, No. 26, (July 2006), pp. 13166-13176. ISSN: 1089-5647

Zacharias, N. & Dougherty, D.A. (2002). Cation-π interactions in ligand recognition and catalysis. *Trends Pharm. Sci.*, Vol. 23, No. 6, (June 2002), pp. 281-287. ISSN: 0165-6147

Zgarbová, M., Otyepka, M., Sponer, J., Mládek, A., Banés, P., Cheatham, T.E. III & Jurecka, P. (2011). Refinement of the Cornell et al. nucleic acids force field based on reference quantum chemical calculations of glycosidic torsion profiles. *J. Chem. Theory Comp.*, Vol. 7, No. 9, (September 2011), pp. 2886-2902, ISSN: 1549-9626

Incorporating Molecular Dynamics Simulations into Rational Drug Design: A Case Study on Influenza a Neuraminidases

Ly Le

Additional information is available at the end of the chapter

1. Introduction

Nowadays, information about targeted diseases needed for structure-based drug design can be accessed easily. There are more than 80,000 coordinate entries of macromolecules revealed by X-ray, NMR, and Electron Microscopy techniques available in the Brookhaven Protein Data Bank. Many new target proteins whose 3D structures have not been solved experimentally can also be easily predicted by homology modelling with adequate reliability. Similarly, thousands of compounds including their drug-like properties are provided in free chemical databases such as the NCI Diversity set, ZINC, and the Drug Bank. Therefore, it is crucial to applied suitable tools to take advantages of these promising resources for rational drug design. Molecular dynamics (MD) simulation has proven itself as a complement to lab experiments to fill in the gaps in our knowledge between 3D structures of biological targets and their potential inhibitors (Rognan et al., 1998 & Jacob et al., 2011). MD can be simply understood as a simulation of physical movements of particles like atoms in atomistic simulation or a group of atoms in coarse-grained simulation. These particles are allowed to move and interact with each others. Their motions are described by Newton's equations, in which forces between the particles and potential energy are obtained from empirical data or quantum mechanical calculations. There are quite several MD simulation packages that are free for academics such as NAMD (Phillips et al., 2005), AMBER (Case et al., 2005), GROSMOS (Christen et al., 2005) and CHARMM (Brooks et al., 1983). The method was introduced by Alder and Wainwright in the late 1950's (Alder and Wainwright, 1957) for the study of the behaviour of simple liquids and the first protein simulation, bovine pancreatic trypsin inhibitor was done successfully twenty years later (McCammon et al., 1977). After that, MD simulation has been used wildly for investigating, interpreting and discovering the dynamics of biological macromolecules, not only fast internal motions but also slow conformational changes and even whole folding processes of some small proteins. MD simulation has become important complement to experimental procedures in structure-function determination of targeted diseases and rational design of their inhibitors. In the lead discovery stage, thousands of compounds from free chemical databases are docked against the rigid structures of receptors. Such screening processes are fast but are associated with a high number of false positives and false negatives. Flexible docking has improved the outcome of this process, but to a very limited degree. A recent method that significantly increases the accuracy of the lead identification process is called ensemble-based docking. This method combines the docking algorithm (Morris et al., 1998) with the dynamic structure of proteins taken from MD simulations as well as statistical analysis of binding energy (Amaro et al., 2008). Another important aspect of rational drug design is to understand all drug-protein interactions at an atomistic level and how these interactions are ruptured by certain mutations, leading to drug resistance. Thorough understanding of drug resistant mechanisms is crucial for the design of new agents effective against current drug-resistant strains. MD simulation is also an important tool in identifying drug binding pathway. However, this could be one of the most challenging tasks in computer-aided drug design due to the limitation of MD simulation time scale. One of the solutions is to combine electrostatic surface potential analysis with steered MD (SMD) simulation (Isralewitz et al., 2001). Forces can be applied to drug molecules in order to pull it along possible pathways predicted from electrostatic surface potential. The findings of drug binding pathway are highly important for investigation on non-active site mutations which possibly prevent drugs from entering binding site by rupture the structure of binding pathway as well as for the rational design of new drugs with good binding kinetics.

In this chapter we highlight the successes in using MD simulations to speed up the rational design of antiviral drugs. Due to their ability to mutate quickly, the viruses can easily survive people's immune systems and resist current drugs. Currently, there are two pathogenic viruses, the 2003 avian flu (H5N1) virus(Ford Stephen et al., 2006) and the 2009 swine flu (H1N1pdm) virus (Butler et al., 2009), which share the same subtype 1 (N1) of neuraminidase. Neuraminidase, a glycoprotein component on a flu virus' surface that cleaves the alpha-ketosidic linkage of sialic acid (SA) located on human cells to release new virions that then infect nearby healthy cells, is the most important target for antiviral drug design. Oseltamivir functions as a neuraminidase inhibitor that binds competitively to the Sialic Acid (SA) binding site (Laver et al., 2006). Unfortunately, oseltamivir resistance has been a big concern to public health since 2005 and thus continues effort to gain insight of drug resistant mechanism and designing new effective medicine become highly significant.

2. Ensemble-based docking

2.1. Receptor

2.1.1. MD simulation of ionized oseltamivir-neuraminidase complex

The molecular model of H1N1pdm used in MD simulation was built from the crystal structure of avian H5N1 and the amino acid sequence of swine flu H1N1pdm from

GenBank Locus ID CY041156. All simulations were performed using NAMD 2.720 and the CHARMM31 force field with the CMAP correction. The ionized systems were minimized for 10,000 integration steps and equilibrated for 20 ns with a 1 fs time step. Following this, a 20 ns unconstrained equilibration production run was performed for subsequent trajectory analysis, with frames stored after each picosecond (every 1000 time steps). Constant temperature (T = 300 K) was enforced using Langevin dynamics with a damping coefficient of 1 ps−1. Constant pressure (p = 1 atm) was enforced using the Nosé-Hoover Langevin piston method. Van der Waals interaction cut-off distances were set at 12 Å (smooth switching function beginning at 10 Å) and long-range electrostatic forces were computed using the particle-mesh Ewald (PME) summation method. The trajectories from our 20ns production run of EQ simulation of H1N1pdm neuraminidase with oseltamivir bound, were clustered as shown in Figure 1, and then used for ensemble based docking.

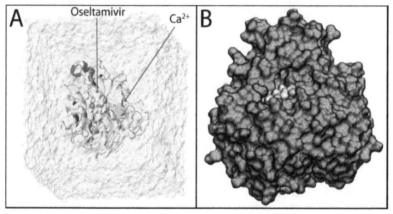

Figure 1. Schematic representations of drug-bound simulation systems. Shown here as a representative example of simulated systems is H1N1pdm bound to oselvamivir. In A), the simulation system is shown in the full explicit solvation box with oseltamivir and the active-site calcium ion labelled. In B), oseltamivir is shown buried in the SA binding pocket of H1N1pdm rendered in surface view

2.1.2. RMSD clustering to extract receptor ensembles from an all-atom MD simulation

The holo system with oseltamivir removed was used for RMSD clustering and the docking experiments. Clustering analyses were performed on 20 ns MD trajectories using the g_cluster tool in the Gromacs package. In brief, snapshots at every 10 ps over the 20 ns simulation were recorded. 2000 resulting structures were superimposed, using all Cα atoms to remove possible rotational and translational movements of the whole system. We have visually verified that the binding-site residues of avian H5N1 neuraminidase, which cover the active site and are responsible for interaction with putative inhibitors, can also be used for the swine flu H1N1pdm neuraminidase. The four most populated clusters are shown in Figure 2. The RMSD clustering analysis was performed on this subset (117-119, 133-138, 146-152, 156, 179, 180, 196-200, 223-228, 243-247, 277, 278, 293, 295, 344-347, 368, 401, 402, and 426-441) using all-atoms (including side chains and hydrogen atoms) with the cut-off of 1.5 Å. A total of 13 representative clusters were obtained, which account for 96.2% of the configuration space from the 20 ns MD trajectories. These 13 clusters were used in the docking experiments.

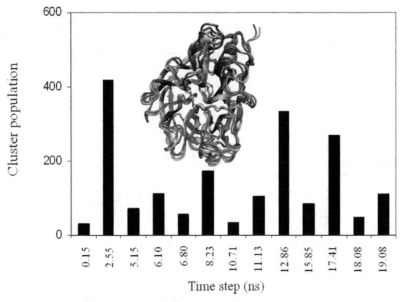

Figure 2. 13 representative ensembles resulting from clustering analysis, accounting for 96.2% of the configuration space, are ordered by the corresponding simulation time. The four largest cluster ensembles account for over 66% of the configuration space from the 20 ns MD simulation. The most dominant cluster is colored in orange, the second one in silver, the third one in blue and the fourth one in cyan.

2.2. Ligands

The high percentage sequence identity (91.47 %) of swine H1N1pdm compared to avian H5N1 neuraminidase, and similarities in 3D structures (active-site 150-loop and SA binding site residues) explain why oseltamivir, which has been developed for the H5N1 virus, is also effective against the swine flu virus H1N1pdm. These facts also suggest that top-binding ligands of avian H5N1 are likely to have high affinity to the swine flu H1N1pdm neuraminidase. Therefore, the 27 top hits for H5N1 neuraminidase (Cheng et al., 2008) and six known drugs for avian H5N1 namely: SA, N-acetyl neuraminic acid, aka, NANA or Neu5Ac), DANA (2,3-didehydro-2-deoxy-N-acetyl neuraminic acid), oseltamivir, zanamivir, peramivir (clinical trial phase 3 drug candidate) and SK (shikimic acid) were selected for our study. Ligand structures were obtained from the NCI and optimized by the MOPAC (Stewart, 2007). Our selection of ligands for docking is based on the high sequence identity and observation that mutations mainly appear on the H1N1 neuraminidase surface not its active site (Le et al., 2009). However, further screening for all the entries of the NCI is suggested to avoid false positives and false negatives.

2.3. Molecular docking

In the docking experiments, the 13 most representative configurations were used as receptors. AutoDockTools 1.5.2 was used to add polar hydrogens, assign Gasteiger charges11 and create grid binding boxes. The volume of each grid box was 72 x 72 x 72, with the default 0.375 Å spacing. The binding box was positioned to encompass all three possible binding sites, namely the SA, 150 and 430 cavities (Cheng et al., 2008). AutoGrid version 4.2.1 was used to calculate the binding affinities using the following atom types: A (aromatic carbon), C, N, NA (hydrogen bond accepting N), OA (hydrogen bond accepting O), P, S, SA (hydrogen bond accepting S), Cl, HD (polar hydrogen) and e (electrostatics). AutoDockTools version 1.5.2 was also used to merge nonpolar hydrogens, add Gasteiger charges and visually set up rotatable bonds for each ligand via AutoTors. For screening larger ligand libraries, Autodock Vina (Trott et al., 2010), which run more efficiently than this version, is highly suggested. The Lamarckian genetic algorithm was used to do the docking experiments using AutoDock 4.2.1.16 Docking parameters were chosen to reproduce structures of 13 corresponding oseltamivir–neuraminidase complexes in the MD simulation. Other parameters are as follows: trials of 100 dockings, population size of 200, random starting position and conformation, translation step range of 2.0 Å, rotation step range of 50 degrees, maximum number of generations of 27000, elitism of 1, mutation rate of 2%, crossover rate of 80%, local search rate of 6%, 8 million energy evaluations, unbound model was "same as bound", and docked conformations were clustered with the tolerance of 2.0 Å RMSD. Docking results were sorted by the lowest binding energy of the most populated cluster in cases of convergence. In the case of no dominant cluster, docking results were visually analyzed using VMD (Humphrey et al., 1996) to choose the best binding pose. Hydrogen bond analysis utilized a distance and angle cut-off of 3.5 Å and 45 degrees, respectively.

The appearance frequency (AF) of important hydrogen bonds is calculated as follows:

$$AF = \frac{\sum_{i=1}^{13} n_i h_i}{\sum_{i=1}^{13} n_i} \qquad (1)$$

Where i is the index number of each ensemble; ni the size of each ensemble; and hi = 1 if hydrogen bond exists, and 0 otherwise. After the dockings, statistical calculations were performed to obtain the final binding energies for compound ranking, using the arithmetic mean (AM) and harmonic mean (HM) binding energies as defined in the previous study. The arithmetic means were calculated directly from the binding energies

$$AM = \frac{\sum_{i=1}^{13} n_i E_i}{\sum_{i=1}^{13} n_i} \qquad (2)$$

Where Ei is the binding energy of each ensemble with the standard deviation

$$SD = \sqrt{\frac{\sum_{i=1}^{13} n_i \left(E_i - AM \right)^2}{\sum_{i=1}^{13} n_i}} \tag{3}$$

The harmonic means were calculated by first converting the binding energies into inhibition constant K_i

$$K_i = e^{\frac{1000 E_i}{RT}} \tag{4}$$

Where R is the Boltzmann constant and T is the temperature (298.15K). The harmonic means were calculated using below equation then converted back to HM binding energies.

$$\overline{K_i} = \frac{\sum_{i=1}^{13} n_i}{\sum_{i=1}^{13} \frac{n_i}{K_i(i)}} \tag{5}$$

2.4. Results

The obtained docking scores reveal that 6 compounds, specifically NSC211332, NSC141562, NSC109836, NSC350191, NSC1644640, and NSC5069, have higher binding affinity to the H1N1pdm neuraminidase protein than oseltamivir does.

Rank / Comp. ID	NSC	HM mean energy (kcal/mol)	Predicted Ki (μM)	AM mean energy (kcal/mol)	Standard deviation (kcal/mol)	Structure
1	211332	-12.05	0.001	-11.73	0.61	
2	141562	-10.14	0.037	-9.87	0.63	

Rank / Comp. ID	NSC	HM mean energy (kcal/mol)	Predicted Ki (μM)	AM mean energy (kcal/mol)	Standard deviation (kcal/mol)	Structure
3	109836	-9.74	0.072	-9.50	0.47	
4	350191	-9.56	0.099	-8.77	0.68	
5	164640	-8.95	0.274	-8.78	0.42	
6	5069	-8.85	0.326	-8.23	1.11	

Rank / Comp. ID	NSC	HM mean energy (kcal/mol)	Predicted Ki (µM)	AM mean energy (kcal/mol)	Standard deviation (kcal/mol)	Structure
7	Oseltamivir	-8.69	0.429	-8.57	0.35	

Table 1. Docking results ranked by harmonic mean of binding energy. The first column is the final rank and also the compound ID. The predicted Ki calculated according to the harmonic mean binding free energies are also shown, as well as the arithmetic mean binding free energies and their corresponding standard deviations.

The results also confirm the observed effectiveness of oseltamivir against both the swine H1N1pdm and H5N1 flu. Detailed analysis on the hydrogen bond networks between top binding candidates with the swine H1N1pdm neuraminidase protein reveals that the mutations H274Y and N294S do not have any direct interactions with these compounds, and thus suggest the possibility of using the present top hit compounds for further computational and experimental studies to design new antiviral drugs against swine H1N1pdm flu virus and its variants (Hung et al., 2009). Furthermore, a more complete virtual screening using the full NCI diversity set (NCIDS) or larger sets from the ZINC database should be done to identify drug candidates that may have been missed in this study. The NCIDS has over 2000 compounds thus the full screening should be done with parallel automatic pipeline.

3. Investigation of drug resistant mechanism by MD simulation

Genetics study of influenza H5N1 virus isolated from patients who died despite being given oseltamivir showed that mutations H274Y or N294S confer high-level resistance to oseltamivir (De Jong et al., 2005 & Le et al., 2005)). There is even emerging evidence that these drug-resistant mutants pose the same risk with H1N1pdm, as shown by reported cases of the H274Y mutation of H1N1pdm (Guo et al, 2009). The rapid emergence of oseltamivir resistance in avian flu has already motivated numerous studies, both experimental and theoretical, to uncover the mechanisms of how point mutations in neuraminidase alter drug binding. Despite initial inroads, the current understanding of drug resistance remains incomplete and some conclusions are conflicting. For example, in one study, it was reported that the H274Y mutation disrupts the E276-R224 salt bridges, but in a separate study the same salt bridges were observed to be stable. We characterize the drug-protein interactions of oseltamivir bound forms of wild type avian H5N1 and swine H1N1pdm neuraminidases and how their mutations, H274Y and N294S, rupture these interactions to confer drug resistance through molecular modelling and atomistic MD simulation.

3.1. Computational details

The coordinates for the H5N1 neuraminidase bound with oseltamivir was taken from a monomer of the Protein Data Bank (PDB) structure 2HU4 (tetramer), while those of mutants H274Y and N294S were taken from structures 3CL0 (monomer) and 3CL2 (monomer) respectively. Even though the biological form of neuraminidase is tetrameric, its monomer contains a functionally complete active site and yields reasonable results in a prior study using MD simulations. The position for oseltamivir bound to H1N1pdm was adopted from its corresponding location in H5N1, as the two proteins' binding pockets differ only by residue 347 (which is Y in H5N1 and N in H1N1pdm), located on a loop at the periphery of the active site. Oseltamivir-mutant complexes of H1N1pdm were built by mutating H274Y and N294S of the H1N1pdm wild type model. In total, 6 systems were modelled and simulated for oseltamivir bound H5N1, and H1N1pdm wild type and H274Y and N294S mutants. Crystallographically resolved water molecules and a structurally relevant calcium ion near the native binding site for SA were retained and modelled in all simulated systems. The protein complexes were then solvated in a TIP3P water box and ionized by NaCl (0.152M) to mimic physiological conditions.

All simulations were performed using NAMD 2.7 and the CHARMM31 force field with CMAP correction. The ionized systems were minimized for 10,000 integration steps and equilibrated for 20 ns with 1 fs time steps. Following this, a 20 ns unconstrained equilibration production run was performed for subsequent trajectory analysis, with frames stored after each picosecond (every 1000 time steps). Constant temperature (T = 300 K) was enforced using Langevin dynamics with a damping coefficient of 1 ps−1. Constant pressure (p = 1 atm) was enforced using the Nosé-Hoover Langevin piston method. Van der Waals interaction cut-off distances were set at 12 Å (smooth switching function beginning at 10 Å) and long-range electrostatic forces were computed using the particle-mesh Ewald (PME) summation method.

Analysis included the calculation of an averaged electrostatic potential field over all frames of the trajectory using RMSD-aligned structures. Maps of the electrostatic potential field were calculated on a three-dimensional lattice. The long-range contributions to the electrostatics were approximated using the multilevel summation method (MSM), which uses nested interpolation of the smoothed pairwise interaction potential, with computational work that scales linearly with the size of the system. The calculation was performed using the molecular visualization program VMD that provides a graphics processing units (GPU) accelerated version of MSM to produce the electrostatic potential map. The GPU acceleration of MSM (Hardy et al., 2009) provided a significant speedup over conventional electrostatic summation methods such as the Adaptive Poisson Boltzman Solver (APBS), achieving a benchmark processing time of 0.2s per frame versus 180 seconds per frame (on a conventional CPU) using APBS69 for a 35,000 atom system, offering a speedup factor of about 900. The use of GPU acceleration enabled averaging the electrostatic potential field over all frames of the simulation trajectories. Hydrogen bond analysis utilized a distance and angle cut-offs of 3.5 Å and 60 degrees, respectively.

3.2. Results and discussion

Hydrogen bonds which form the primary interactions between oseltamivir and H5N1/ H1N1pdm neuraminidases were shown in figure 4 and figure 5 accordingly. While the SA binding sites of H5N1 and H1N1pdm appear to differ mainly in the sequence of loop residue 347, it is not well understood whether antiviral drugs bind to each protein in the same manner, or if the drug resistant H274Y and N294S mutations disrupt critical hydrogen bonds. To address this question, the hydrogen bonds which form between oseltamivir and the residues lining the SA binding pockets of H5N1 and H1N1pdm were calculated for all simulation trajectories. R292 and R371 were observed to hydrogen bond with oseltamivir's carboxyl moiety, and E119 and D151 with oseltamivir's amino group (NH_3^+). The H274Y mutation, however, appeared to disrupt the hydrogen bonding of oseltamivir's acetyl group with R152, an interaction which was seen in the wild type and N294S systems for both simEQ1 and simEQ2. Prior analyses of crystallographic data alone suggested that Y347 forms a stable hydrogen bond with oseltamivir's carboxyl group and is the source of oseltamivir-resistance in the N294S mutant.

Our MD simulations however, reflect statistics collected from long timescale simulations which produce a dynamic picture of molecular interactions in greater detail and resolution than can be seen from a static crystal structure. In our simulations oseltamivir's carboxyl group primarily forms hydrogen bonds with R292 and R371, having little involvement with Y347. In fact, residue Y347 undergoes rotation to interact strongly with residue W295. Therefore, the speculation from previous studies, that the N294S mutation in the case of H5N1 actually destabilizes the hydrogen bonding between oseltamivir and Y347 to induce drug resistance, is not supported in our simulations.

The notable difference between H5N1 and H1N1pdm neuraminidases is the replacement of Y347 by N347 at the drug binding pocket. No conserved drug-protein hydrogen bond was observed for N347 in any of the three H1N1pdm simulations. Given the transient nature of even the N294S mutant induced hydrogen bond involving residue 347 in the case of H5N1, and the lack of interaction with residue 347 in any of the other simulations, it is highly unlikely that the single residue change (Y347 to N347), between the H5N1 and H1N1pdm strains significantly alters the drug-protein stability in regard to the hydrogen bond network involved. H274Y mutation induced disruption of the stable hydrophobic packing of oseltamivir's pentyl group in both H5N1 and H1N1pdm neuraminidases.

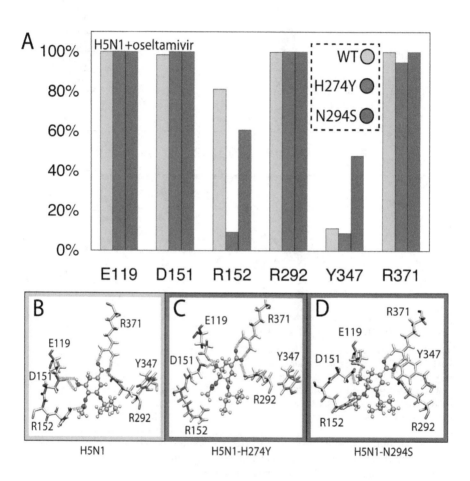

Figure 3. Network and occupancy of hydrogen bonds stabilizing oseltamivir in the SA binding pocket of wild type and drug-resistant mutant avian H5N1 neuraminidases, in simEQ1, simEQ3, and simEQ5.(A) shows histograms of the percent of hydrogen-bond occupancies for interactions between oseltamivir and residues E119, D151, R152, R292, Y347, and R371 across each simulation run. (B) through (D) are schematic views depicting the orientation of protein sidechains which form protein-drug hydrogen bonds.

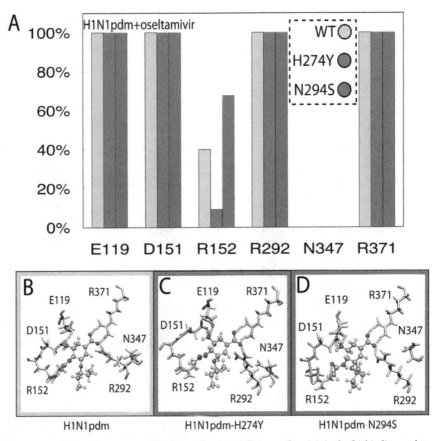

Figure 4. Network and occupancy of hydrogen bonds stabilizing oseltamivir in the SA binding pocket of wild type and drug-resistant mutant avian H1N1pdm neuraminidases, in simEQ2, simEQ4, and simEQ6. (A) are histograms of the percent of hydrogen-bond occupancies for interactions between oseltamivir and residues E119, D151, R152, R292, N347, and R371 across each simulation run. (B) through (D) are schematic views depicting the orientation of protein sidechains which form protein-drug hydrogen bonds.

Beyond disrupting the drug-protein hydrogen-bonding network, another mechanism through which protein mutations may induce drug resistance is by disruption of the hydrophobic packing of the drug into the protein binding pocket. Through inspection of the static crystal structures of the H274Y and N294S mutants of H5N1, it has been speculated that the mutations disrupt favourable hydrophobic packing interactions necessary for strong binding of oseltamivir. In our wild type simulations for both the H5H1 and H1N1pdm systems, the packing of oseltamivir's pentyl moiety tended to favour close association with residues I222, R224, A246, and E276. To test the effect of mutations H274Y and N294S on hydrophobic interactions of oseltamivir's pentyl group with the proteins, we calculated the solvent accessible surface area (SASA) of oseltamivir's pentyl group for all simulation trajectories. While there was no significant change to the pentyl group SASA (henceforth referred to as PG-SASA) in the wild type and N294S mutant for either H5N1 or H1N1pdm neuraminidases, an outward rotation of the pentyl group was observed in the H274Y mutant simulations, visible in oseltamivir's binding pose and evident in a notably higher calculated PG-SASA. The PG-SASAs for all simulated systems are plotted in Figure 5, with inset images of oseltamivir's binding pose in simEQ2 (Figure 5A) and simEQ4 (Figure 5B) illustrating the rotation of the pentyl group towards the open mouth of the binding pocket.

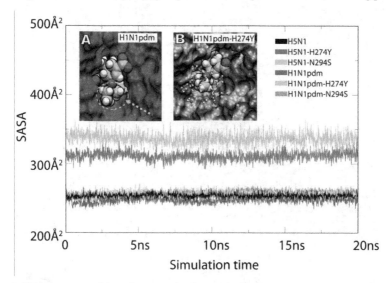

Figure 5. The solvent accessible surface area of oseltamivir's pentyl group (PG-SASA) in H5N1 and H1N1pdm wild type and mutant simulations. The PG-SASA in the N294S mutant simulation (simEQ5 and simEQ6) did not vary significantly from wild type simulations (simEQ1 and simEQ2). However, there was a huge loss of hydrophobic interaction between drug and protein in the case of the H274Y mutant simulations (simEQ3 and simEQ4), resulting in an increase in measured PG-SASA.

Previously published MD simulations performed over relatively short time scales (3 to 6 ns) have suggested two possible mechanisms: 1) that the H247Y mutation reduces the size of the hydrophobic pocket within the SA binding pocket near Oseltamivir's pentyl moiety (Malaisree et al., 2008), and 2) that the H274Y mutation breaks a critical salt bridge between E276 and R224 to disrupt drug binding(Wang et al., 2009). Our longer (40ns) simulations were able to corroborate the former suggested mechanism (as shown by the increase in PG-SASA in the case of the H274Y mutant simulations) but not the latter. In fact, in all six of our simulations, E276 maintains stable charge-charge interactions (salt bridging) with R224 despite displacement of the drug from the protein I222-R224-A246-E276 pocket in the case of H274Y mutants. This drug displacement increases water penetration into the I222-R224-A246-E276 pocket (Figure 5B). Evidence from our simulations therefore supports predictions from earlier studies of a possible mechanism for the H274Y mutation-induced drug resistance through water infiltration and destabilization of favourable drug packing. However, because no change in PG-SASA was observed during our simulations in the case of N294S for either protein, N294S induced drug resistance is probably due to a different mechanism.

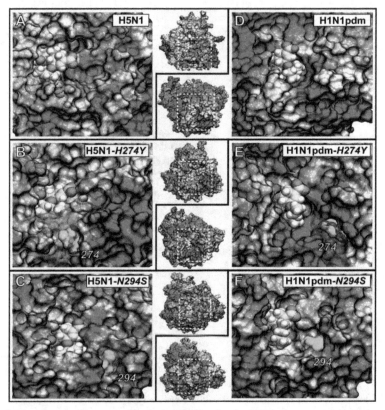

Figure 6. Electrostatic surface potential of avian H5N1 and swine H1N1pdm neuraminidases in oseltamivir-bound simulations, revealing a positively charged pathway into the binding pocket. (A) through (C) show oseltamivir bound to H5N1 wild type, H274Y, and N294S drug-resistant mutant structures, respectively. (D) through (F) show oseltamivir bound to wild type, H274Y, and N294S drug-resistant mutant structures, respectively. The outer columns show a close-up view of the binding pocket, highlighted as a subset of the enter protein shown in the central column. The positions of the mutant residues are shown in green for residue 274 and 294 in the mutant systems

While alterations in hydrophobic sidegroup packing may explain in part the mechanism behind H274Y mutation-induced drug resistance, they fail to shed light on the role that the N294S mutation plays for oseltamivir binding inhibition. Initial investigations of the electrostatic surface potentials of drug-bound N1 neuraminidases have proposed that drug binding affinity is closely related to favourable charge-charge interactions with the electrostatic potential of the binding pocket wall, which exhibits a weak negative charge. In order to understand whether charge-charge interactions may play a role in mutation induced drug resistance, the electrostatic potentials were calculated and mapped onto the surfaces of the proteins. Even though prior studies have investigated the possible role of the electrostatic surface potential for drug binding in neuraminidases, the extensive electrostatic calculations required for fully understanding role of this phenomenon over a long simulation trajectory has not yet been done. The electrostatic surface potentials of the equilibrated systems were calculated and averaged across every trajectory frame in six equilibrium simulations. Extensive electrostatic calculations for the six systems show that the mouth of the binding pocket is positively charged, except for a narrow pathway of negative surface charge that seems to direct a possible binding pathway through which the drug may access the binding pocket. In Figure 6, the electrostatic surface potentials calculated from all six simulations is shown for the SA binding pocket with oseltamivir bound.

Mutation H274Y in the H1N1pdm virus shares the same sources of oseltamivir resistance as H5N1, including loss of hydrogen bonds with R152 and reduction of hydrophobic interaction of oseltamivir's pentyl group. This leads to our suggestion to replace the pentyl group by a more hydrophilic one by adding a few hydroxyl groups on this bulky hydrophobic group. Our results do not support previous suggestions that the N294S mutation of H5N1 destabilizes the hydrogen bonding between oseltamivir and Y347, or that it disrupts the hydrophobic pocket, leading to drug resistance. Sources of drug resistance in mutant N294S remain unclear. Quantitative analysis of drug binding to the pocket is surrounded by a highly positive potential ring (colored blue). Simulations revealed the presence of a negatively charged pathway at the mouth of the binding pocket which may play a role for drug binding and mutation induced resistance, as the position of residue 294 maps directly onto the pathway while position of residue 274 is positioned on or adjacent(Le et al., 2009). WT and the mutants will be importantly complementary to obtained results in this chapter. Since the two mutations are nonactive-site, endpoint interactions alone cannot account for all drug resistance. Kinetics of drug binding is therefore also important for drug resistant mechanism. Especially, based on the decrease in association rate constants (K_{on}) of oseltamivir with H5N1 neuraminidase mutants (2.52 μM-1s-1 in the WT, 0.24 2.52 μM-1s-1 in H274Y and 1.1 2.52 μM-1s-1 in N294S mutants), we speculate that mutations also prevent drugs from entering the SA binding site. It is hoped that our observation of a possible binding pathway for oseltamivir will encourage further investigations that test the hypothesis posed here, by identifying whether the actual drug binding pathway follows this route.

4. Identification of drug binding pathway

4.1. Characteristics of the electrostatic surface potential of N1 neuraminidases shed light for further study on drug binding and drug resistance

Up to this point, all proposed mechanisms for oseltamivir resistance have focused on the effects of the mutations on the SA binding site but little has been known about the effects of those mutations on the kinetics of drug binding. Since both H274Y and N294S are nonactive site mutations, prior studies which focused on endpoint interactions between drug and proteins have been unable to provide a full understanding of how these mutations directly impact drug binding. In fact, given that the drug binding kinetics of H5N1 mutants are significantly diminished, it is possible that these mutations alter the binding process, and not necessarily just the specific endpoint interactions. It is well known that electrostatic surface potential of a protein can be an important driving force directing the diffusion of ligands into a protein's active site. The resulting electrostatic maps shown in Figure 7A for H5N1 and Figure 7B for H1N1pdm reveal a highly negatively charged column of residues that forms a pathway 10 Å in length between the SA binding site and the edge of the binding cavity mouth. Electrostatic calculations also reveal that oseltamivir has a highly positive electrostatic surface potential, illustrated in Figure 7C. The question arises whether the negatively charged surface column plays a role in the binding and unbinding of oseltamivir, given a possible mutual attraction between oseltamivir and this column. To answer this question, we employed SMD simulations (described in the Methods section) to pull oseltamivir out of the SA binding site and probe possible unbinding pathways. Such simulations have

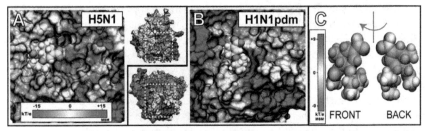

Figure 7. Electrostatic surface potential of the SA binding pocket of H1N1pdm and oseltamivir. Shown in A) and B) are closeup views of the SA binding pocket with drug bound H1N1pdm and avian H5N1 neuraminidase, respectively. The region of the binding pocket where the drug bound possesses a highly negative potential (colored red), whereas the opening of the pocket is surrounded by a highly positive potential ring (colored blue). In C), a detailed surface electrostatic potential for oseltamivir. Shown are the "front" side facing the annulus of the binding pocket, and "back" side facing the interior of the binding pocket is shown.

4.2. Computational details

Six systems were modelled and simulated for oseltamivir bound H5N1, and H1N1pdm wild type and H274Y and N294S mutants. In simSMD1, steered molecular dynamics (SMD) simulations were used to remove oseltamivir from its stable binding site in H5N1 neuraminidase. In simFEQ1-10, equilibration simulations used a starting point generated from simSMD1 in which Oseltamivir has undergone an axial rotation such that it is partially displaced from its binding site. In total, 680 ns of simulations were carried out on system sizes of approximately 35,000 atoms.

The "Ensemble" column lists the variables held constant during the simulations; N, p, T, and V correspond to the number of atoms, pressure, temperature, and volume respectively.

Under "Type", EQ denotes equilibration, and SCV denotes constant velocity SMD simulation with the speed of 0.5 Å/ns. SimSMD1 is a steered MD simulation with the starting structure from equilibrated simEQ1 ("preflip" drug position). In simFEQ1 to simFEQ10, the starting structure reflected a "flipped" position of oseltamivir from simSMD1 after 7.5ns of simulation, whereas several of its main stabilizing hydrogen bonds to the protein had already been ruptured. Crystallographically resolved water molecules and a structurally relevant calcium ion near the native binding site for SA were retained and modelled in all simulated systems. The protein complexes were then solvated in a TIP3P water box 23 and ionized by NaCl (0.152M) to mimic physiological conditions.

All simulations were performed using NAMD 2.7 and the CHARMM31 force field (Mackerrel et al., 1998). The ionized systems were minimized for 10,000 integration steps and equilibrated for 20 ns with 1 fs time steps. Following this, a 20 ns unconstrained equilibration production run was performed for subsequent trajectory analysis, with frames stored after each picosecond (every 1000 time steps). Constant temperature (T = 300 K) was enforced using Langevin dynamics with a damping coefficient of 1 ps−1. Constant pressure (p = 1 atm) was enforced using the Nose'-Hoover Langevin piston method with a decay period of 100 fs and a damping time constant of 50 fs. Van der Waals interaction cut-off distances were set at 12Å, (smooth switching function beginning at 10 Å) and long-range electrostatic forces were computed using the particle-mesh Ewald (PME) summation method with a grid size of less than 1Å, along with the pencil decomposition protocol where applicable. SMD simulations fixed the center of mass of neuraminidase -carbons and applied a force to the center of mass of oseltamivir, along a vector connecting the two centers of masses. In simSMD1, a constant velocity protocol was employed, with stretching velocity of 0.5Å/ns. For the SMD spring constant we chose k_{SMD} = 3kBT/Å2 which corresponds to an RMSD value of $(pkBT/k_{SMD})1/2$ < 0.6 Å.

4.3. Results

To simulate the binding of the drug would be the most natural approach, but the computations would be rather expensive. It is possible to the put drug in front of the receptor active site and the attraction forces between the drug and the receptor will drive it to the binding site. This process usually requires microsecond simulations and there is a high chance that the drug will fluctuate around the water box. Unbinding simulations however are feasible and may also reveal features that are characteristic for binding. In simSMD1, a pulling force was applied to rupture all the stabilizing hydrogen bonds between H5N1 and oseltamivir, in order to draw the drug away from the SA binding site. The results of simSMD1 show that the behaviour of oseltamivir under effect of a pulling force can be divided into three distinct stages: 1) from 0 to 8 ns, a buildup of forces during which hydrogen bonds between oseltamivir with E119, D151 and R152 are destabilized; 2) at 8 ns where the remaining stable hydrogen bonds with R292 and R371 rupture; 3) after 8 ns during which the drug is pulled out of the binding pocket. Figure 8 shows the force dependent rupture of hydrogen bonds in simSMD1 by plotting both hydrogen bond stability and (in inset) the force vs. time curve. To our surprise, it was observed that

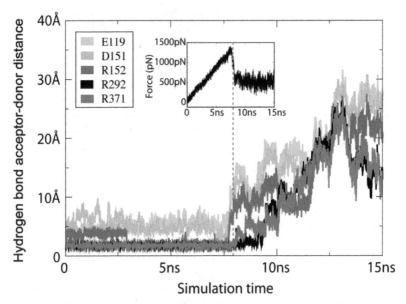

Figure 8. Distances between hydrogen bond acceptor-donor pairs between oseltamivir and active site amino acids vs. simulation time in simSMD1. Most hydrogen bonds were quickly broken by the pulling force except for those with R292 and R371, which fully ruptured only after 8 ns, corresponding to the peak of the curve of the applied force vs. simulation time (shown in inset). Position of oseltamivir and all its possible hydrogen bonding pairs with residues located along this pathway, it was seen that nonspecific electrostatic attractions formed the predominant interactions between drug and protein.

Oseltamivir followed a lateral escape path through strong interaction with the negatively charged column of residues indentified via electrostatic mapping above, despite application of force to pull the drug straight out of the binding pocket. This divergent path taken by the drug is shown in Figure 9A-D. A second notable observation in simSMD1 was that just before rupture of hydrogen bonds between oselvamivir's carboxyl functional group and residues R292 and R371 of the binding pocket, the drug underwent a rather significant rotation due to the destabilization of hydrogen bonds with E119, D151 and R152. It is likely that this rotation or "flip" is crucial for placing oseltamivir in a position which permits it to leave the SA binding site. Despite application of force to pull oseltamivir straight out of its binding pocket, the drug followed a somewhat lateral path through the electrostatically charged funnel. The "preflip" or stably bound state for oseltamivir in H5N1 is shown in Figure 10A1, 10A2, 10A3, and the flipped transition state shown in Figure 10B1 and 10B2, 10B3.

It was observed in simSMD1 that following the transition to the flipped state, very little force was then required to subsequently draw oseltamivir out of its binding pocket in neuramidase. This result suggests that one may be able to probe the unbinding pathway via diffusion, if the starting state consists of oseltamivir already in its flipped orientation. We therefore performed additional equilibrium simulations (simFEQ1-10) with oseltamivir already in this flipped state. From these simulations, we were able to observe two distinct outcomes: 1) oseltamivir is able to escape the binding pocket by interacting favourably with the charged binding funnel and 2) the drug returns, not unexpectedly, to its stably bound "preflip" state. Each simulation for FEQ1-10 was run long enough to observe either outcome, with the exception of FEQ5. SimFEQ5 was a special case in which the drug, after following the binding funnel to escape the protein, actually rebound to the SA active site through the same binding funnel after we extended the simulation to follow its movement. A summary of observed outcomes from these simulations is shown in Table 2. In simFEQ1-5, oseltamivir successfully escaped the SA binding site, whereas in simFEQ6-10, oseltamivir returned to its stably bound "preflip" state. Oseltamivir was observed to diffuse out of the SA active site after strong interaction with the electrostatically charged binding funnel (described above) in five out of ten equilibrium simulations we performed (simFEQ1-5).

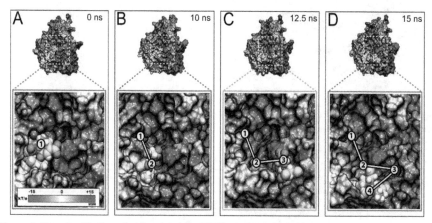

Figure 9. Forced unbinding of oseltamivir from H5N1 neuraminidase. Shown here are the relative positions of oseltamivir on the electrostatic surface of avian H5N1 neuraminidase during simSMD1.At 0 ns (A), oseltamivir was stably bound within the active site, as seen in simEQ1. Application of force ruptured the stabilizing hydrogen bonds between H5N1 and oseltamivir (see Figure 9), drawing the drug away from its stable binding site within 10 ns, as shown in B. Over the next 2.5 ns of pulling, oseltamivir followed the charged binding funnel (shown in C) until it was completely free of the protein binding pocket after 15 ns, as shown in D).

In four of the cases (simFEQ1-3, 5) oseltamivir was observed to diffuse along the full length of the binding funnel before disassociating with neuraminidase. In simFEQ5 we observed not only a diffusion of oseltamivir through the charged binding funnel, but also the re-entry.

Snapshots from each of these events in FEQ5 are shown in Figure 10. Analysis of interactions of the newly rebound oseltamivir with active site residues from 50 to 100 ns revealed that the drug was stabilized by hydrogen bonds with Y406, R292, D151, E119, and R118, even though the pentyl group had not yet moved to its requisite hydrophobic pocket (I222-R224- A246-E276).

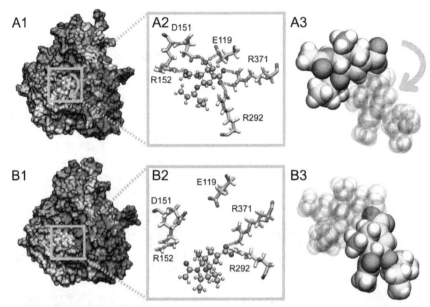

Figure 10. Oseltamivir in "flipped" position (position of oseltamivir at 7.5ns in simSMD1) in comparison with its stable equilibrium position,

Name	Result	Time (ns)
simFEQ1	Drug escape via binding funnel	15
simFEQ2	Drug escape via binding funnel	10
simFEQ3	Drug escape via binding funnel	15
simFEQ4	Drug interaction with binding funnel but escape via 430-cavity	50
simFEQ5	Drug escape and rebind into SA pocket via binding funnel	100
simFEQ6	Drug returned to "preflip" position	10
simFEQ7	Drug returned to "preflip" position	15
simFEQ8	Drug returned to "preflip" position	50
simFEQ9	Drug returned to "preflip" position	50
simFEQ10	Drug returned to "preflip" position	50

Table 2. Summary of FEQ1-10 simulations starting from "flipped" position of oseltamivir taken from simSMD1 at 7.5 ns.

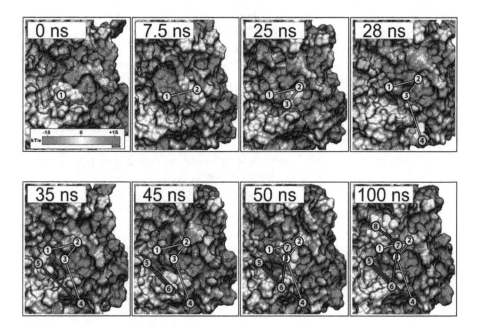

Figure 11. Escape and rebinding of oseltamivir through the electrostatic binding funnel in H5N1 neuraminidase during simFEQ5. Shown here are snapshots of simFEQ5, in which oseltamivir first diffused out of the SA active site through interaction with the electrostatic binding funnel within the first 25ns of simulation. Between 28 and 35ns, oseltamivir diffuses and approaches the periphery of the binding pocket away from the binding funnel, but is prohibited from entering due to electrostatic repulsion (45ns). However, between 45 and 50ns, oseltamivir was observed to approach and enter the neuraminidase binding pocket through the binding funnel, adopting a stable position within the SA binding pocket through hydrogen bonds with Y406, R292, D151, E119, and R118.

The result has shed light on the important role of the electrostatic surface potentials in directing the diffusion of oseltamivir into the SA binding site. From our simulations, it is clear that the negatively charged funnel serves as a prominent binding and unbinding pathway for oseltamivir in the wild type systems investigated with SMD and followup equilibrium simulations in simSMD1 and simFEQ1-10. It turns out also that the binding funnel may possibly play a crucial role in drug resistance caused by mutations. The conspicuous location of residue 294, which maps directly onto this negatively charged pathway, may play a key role in the N294S mutation for disrupting the proper guidance of the drug into its binding pocket. Thus, it is possible that the 274 and 294 mutations may confer drug resistance by not only disrupting the end-point interactions of oseltamivir but also its entry into the binding pocket by interfering with the binding funnel. While sources of end-point interactions, including hydrogen bonds, hydrophobic packing and solvent infiltration, of oseltamivir resistance have been thoroughly studied, little is known about the kinetics of the drug binding in mutants at atomic level. The idea that drug resistant mutants actually disrupt entry of oseltamivir into the SA active site of neuraminidase through disruption of an electrostatic binding funnel is in part supported by experiments which have noted reduced drug binding kinetics in H5N1 H274Y and N294S mutants. Even though the oseltamivir-resistant mutations were seen located in or adjacent to the funnel, clearly additional study is still needed for a full understanding of how the H274Y and N294S mutations weaken the binding of the drug. Furthermore, the mutations might not only affect the electrostatic gradient but also the geometry of the drug binding and unbinding path. Future or followup studies should therefore focus on the specific drug entry/exit pathways for oseltamivir-resistant mutant systems, sampling timescales great enough (such as in the case of simFEQ5 described above) to capture both the binding.

5. Challenges and opportunities

We have presented three important applications of MD simulation in drug design against influenza A virus. While MD simulation has been proven as a powerful tool complement to experiment in drug discovery processes, the problems in accuracy of drug parameter and limitation in time scale of MD simulation definitely affect applications of this tool. The challenge in drug force field development is that, unlike uniformed amino acids or nucleotides, each drug has its own structure and requires separate parameter. Since force field for general macromolecules have been well developed, attention should be shifted to development of adequately accurate drug force field (Wang et al., 2004; Zoete et al., 2012). Another challenge in MD simulation is limitation of time scale. Several important phenomena which are important for drug design application happen in the time scales that can't be done by even the biggest supercomputers in the world. Over the past decade several methods were developed to speed up classical MD simulation including SMD, accelerated MD (Hamelberg et al., 2009), coarse-grained MD simulation (Izvekov et al., 2005). Last but not least, the implementations of specialized hardware including CBE, GPU, and FPGA architectures are important to broaden application of MD simulation to modern drug discovery (Horacio et al., 2012). The recent finding of oseltamivir binding pathway using GPU acceleration and SMD (Le et al., 2010) is an example that the combined improvement of theoretical algorithm and specialized hardware architecture has enabled us to increase the success rate and decrease the cost in rational drug discovery.

Author details

Ly Le
School of Biotechnology, Ho Chi Minh International University, Life Science Laboratory,
Institute for Computational Science and Technology at Ho Chi Minh City , Vietnam

Acknowledgement

The author wish to thank the Institute for Computational Science and Technology at Ho Chi Minh City and NAFOSTED (The National Foundation for Science and Technology Development) for partially support the research presented in this chapter.

6. References

Abed, Y.; Baz, M.; Boivin, G., Impact of neuraminidase mutations conferring influenza resistance to neuraminidase inhibitors in the N1 and N2 genetic backgrounds. *Antiviral Ther.* 2006, 11 (8), 971-976.

Andrew C. Kruse, Jianxin Hu, Albert C. Pan, Daniel H. Arlow, Daniel M. Rosenbaum, Erica Rosemond, Hillary F. Green, Tong Liu, Pil Seok Chae, Ron O. Dror, David E. Shaw, William I. Weis, Jürgen Wess, and Brian K. Kobilka, "Structure and Dynamics of the M3 Muscarinic Acetylcholine Receptor," *Nature*, vol. 482, no. 7386, 2012, pp. 552-556

Amaro, R. E.; Baron, R.; McCammon, J. A. An improved relaxed complex scheme for receptor flexibility in computer-aided drug design. *J. Comput.-Aided Mol. Des.* 2008, 22 (9), 693-705.

Butler, D., Swine flu goes global. *Nature.* 2009, (458), 1082-1083.

Berman HM, B. T., Bhat TN, Bluhm WF, Bourne PE, Burkhardt K, Feng Z, Gilliland GL, Iype L, Jain S, Fagan P, Marvin J, Padilla D, Ravichandran V, Schneider B, Thanki N, Weissig H, Westbrook JD, Zardecki C., The Protein Data Bank, Acta Crystallogr D Biol Crystallogr. 2002 Jun;58(Pt 6 No 1):899-907. Epub 2002 May 29.

Brooks BR, Bruccoleri RE, Olafson BD, States DJ, Swaminathan S, Karplus M: CHARMM - a program for macromolecular energy, minimization, and dynamics calculations. *J Comput Chem* 1983, 4:187-217.

Case DA, Cheatham TE, Darden T, Gohlke H, Luo R, Merz KM Jr, Onufriev A, Simmerling C, Wang B, Woods RJ: The AMBER biomolecular simulation programs. J Comput Chem 2005, 26:1668-1688

Cheng, L. S.; Amaro, R. E.; Xu, D.; Li, W. W.; Arzberger, P. W.; McCammon, J. A., Ensemble-Based Virtual Screening Reveals Potential Novel Antiviral Compounds for Avian Influenza Neuraminidase. *J. Med. Chem.* 2008, 51 (13), 3878-3894.

Christen M, Hünenberger PH, Bakowies D, Baron R, Bürgi R, Geerke DP, Heinz TN, Kastenholz MA, Kräutler V, Oostenbrink C, Peter C, Trzesniak D, van Gunsteren WF: The GROMOS software for biomolecular simulation: GROMOS05. *J Comput Chem* 2005, 26:1719-1751.

Collins, P. J.; Haire, L. F.; Lin, Y. P.; Liu, J.; Russell, R. J.; Walker, P. A.; Skehel, J. J.; Martin, S. R.; Hay, A. J.; Gamblin, S. J., Crystal structures of oseltamivir-resistant influenza virus neuraminidase mutants. *Nature* (London, U. K.) 2008, 453 (7199), 1258-1261.

De Jong, M. D.; Thanh, T. T.; Khanh, T. H.; Hien, V. M.; Smith, G. D.; Nguyen, V. C.; Cam, B. V.; Qui, P. T.; Ha, D. Q.; Guan, Y.; Peiris, J. S. M.; Phil, D.; Hien, T. T.; Farrar, J., Oseltamivir resistance during treatment of influenza A (H5N1) infection. *N. Engl. J. Med.* 2005, 353 (25), 2667-2672.

Ford Stephen, M.; Grabenstein John, D., Pandemics, avian influenza A (H5N1), and a strategy for pharmacists. *Pharmacotherapy* 2006, 26 (3), 312-22.

Jacob D Durrant and J Andrew McCammon, Molecular dynamics simulations and drug discovery, *BMC Biology* 2011, 9:71

Guo, L.; Garten, R. J.; Foust, A. S.; Sessions, W. M.; Okomo-Adhiambo, M.; Gubareva, L. V.; Klimov, A. I.; Xu, X., Rapid identification of oseltamivir-resistant influenza A(H1N1) viruses with H274Y mutation by RT-PCR/restriction fragment length polymorphism assay. *Antiviral Res.* 2009, 82 (1), 29-33.

Hardy DJ, Stone JE, Schulten K (2009) Multilevel summation of electrostatic potentials using graphics processing units. *J Paral Comp* 35: 164-177.

Hung T. Nguyen, Ly Le, Thanh N. Truong. Top-hits for H1N1pdm identified by virtual screening using ensemble-based docking.*PLoS Currents: Influenza*, 2009, RRN1030

Horacio Perez-Sanchez, Wolfgang Wenzel, Optimization Methods for Virtual Screening on Novel Computational Architectures, *Current Computer Aided-Drug Design,* Volume 7, Number 1, March 2011, ISSN: 1573-4099, pp.44-52

Holbeck, S. L., Update on NCI in vitro drug screen utilities. European journal of cancer (Oxford, England : 1990) 2004, 40 (6), 785-793.

Humphrey, W.; Dalke, A.; Schulten, K., VDM: visual molecular dynamics. *Journal of Molecular Graphics* 1996, 14 (1), 33-8, plates, 27-28.

Hess, B.; Kutzner, C.; van der Spoel, D.; Lindahl, R. GROMACS 4: Algorithms for highly efficient, load-balanced, and scalable molecular simulation. *J. Chem. Theory Comput.* 2008, 4 (3), 435-447.

Isralewitz B, Gao M, Schulten K (2001) Steered molecular dynamics and mechanical functions of proteins. *Curr Opin Struct Biol* 11: 224-230.

Irwin, J.; Shoichet, B., ZINC--a free database of commercially available compounds for virtual screening. Journal of chemical information and modeling 2005, 45 (1), 177-182.

Laver, G., Antiviral drugs for influenza: Tamiflu past, present and future. *Future Virol.* 2006, 1 (5), 577-586.

Le L.; Eric H. L., Thanh Truong; Klaus Schulten,. Molecular modeling of swine influenza A/H1N1, Spanish H1N1, and avian H5N1 flu N1 neuraminidases bound to Tamiflu and Relenza. *PLoS Currents: Influenza.* 2009, RRN1015.

Le L, Lee EH, Hardy DJ, Truong TN, Schulten K (2010) Molecular Dynamics Simulations Suggest that Electrostatic Funnel Directs Binding of Tamiflu to Influenza N1 Neuraminidases. *PLoS Comput Biol* 6(9): e1000939. doi:10.1371/journal.pcbi.1000939

Le, Q. M.; Kiso, M.; Someya, K.; Sakai, Y. T.; Nguyen, T. H.; Nguyen, K. H. L.; Pham, N. D.; Ngyen, H. H.; Yamada, S.; Muramoto, Y.; Horimoto, T.; Takada, A.; Goto, H.; Suzuki, T.; Suzuki, Y.; Kawaoka, Y., Avian flu: Isolation of drug-resistant H5N1 virus. Nature (London, U. K.) 2005, 437 (7062), 1108.

MacKerell AD, J., Bashford D, Bellott M, Dunbrack RL, Evanseck JD, Field MJ, Fischer S, Gao J, Guo H, Ha S, Joseph-McCarthy D, Kuchnir L, Kuczera K, Lau FTK, Mattos C, Michnick S, Ngo T, Nguyen DT, Prodhom B, Reiher WE, III, Roux B, Schlenkrich M, Smith JC, Stote R, Straub J, Watanabe M, Wiorkiewicz-Kuczera J, Yin D, Karplus M All-Atom Empirical Potential for Molecular Modeling and Dynamics Studies of Proteins. *Journal of Physical* Chemistry B 102: 3586-3616. 1998.

Malaisree M, Rungrotmongkol T, Nunthaboot N, Aruksakunwong O, Intharathep P, et al. (2008). Source of oseltamivir resistance in avian influenza H5N1 virus with the H274Y mutation. Amino Acid 37: 725-732.

Morris, G. M.; Goodsell, D. S.; Halliday, R. S.; Huey, R.; Hart, W. E.; Belew, R. K.; Olson, A. J. Automated docking using a Lamarckian genetic algorithm and an empirical binding free energy function. *J. Comp. Chem.* 1998, 19 (14), 1639-1662.

Phillips JC, Braun R, Wang W, Gumbart J, Tajkhorshid E, et al. (2005) Scalable molecular dynamics with NAMD. *J Comp Chem* 26: 1781-1802.

Rognan, D., Molecular dynamics simulations: A tool for drug design. *Perspectives in Drug Discovery and Design* 1998, 181-209.

Russell, R. J.; Haire, L. F.; Stevens, D. J.; Collins, P. J.; Lin, Y. P.; Blackburn, G. M.; Hay, A. J.; Gamblin, S. J.; Skehel, J. J., The structure of H5N1 avian influenza neuraminidase suggests new opportunities for drug design. *Nature* (London, U. K.) 2006, 443 (7107), 45-49.

S. Izvekov and G. A. Voth, "A Multiscale Coarse-Graining Method for Biomolecular Systems," J. Phys. Chem. B 109, 2469-2473 (2005).

Stewart J. J. P., Optimization of Parameters for Semiempirical Methods V: Modification of NDDO Approximations and Application to 70 Elements J. Mol. Modeling 13, 1173-1213 (2007).

Trott O., Olson A. J., AutoDock Vina: improving the speed and accuracy of docking with a new scoring function, efficient optimization and multithreading, Journal of Computational Chemistry 31 (2010) 455-461.

Wang, J., Wolf, R. M.; Caldwell, J. W.;Kollman, P. A.; Case, D. A. "Development and testing of a general AMBER force field". Journal of Computational Chemistry, 25, 2004, 1157-1174.

Wang Nick, X.; Zheng Jie, J., Computational studies of H5N1 influenza virus resistance to oseltamivir. Protein Sci 2009, 18 (4), 707-15.

Wishart, D. S.; Knox, C.; Guo, A. C.; Cheng, D.; Shrivastava, S.; Tzur, D.; Gautam, B.; Hassanali, M., DrugBank: a knowledgebase for drugs, drug actions and drug targets. *Nucl. Acids Res.* 2008, 36 (suppl_1), D901-906.

Zoete V., Cuendet M. A., Grosdidier A., Michielin O., SwissParam, a Fast Force Field Generation Tool For Small Organic Molecules, J. Comput. Chem, 2011, in press. PMID: 21541964, DOI: 10.1002/jcc.21816.

Structural Bioinformatics

On the Assessment of Structural Protein Models with ROSETTA-Design and HMMer: Value, Potential and Limitations

León P. Martínez-Castilla and Rogelio Rodríguez-Sotres

Additional information is available at the end of the chapter

1. Introduction

The prediction of the three-dimensional structure of a protein, starting with the amino acid sequence, is still an unsolved issue. However a number of important advancements have been made and some methods offer solutions to this problem, specially when the target sequence has homologues whose structure has been determined. In any case, it is important to evaluate the quality of the prediction, as none of the methods offers assurance of success. The ROSETTA-design-HHMer (Rd.HMM) protocol stands out among the current quality assessment methods, because it offers evidence of the biological appropriateness of the prediction. In addition, Rd.HMM can be used to guide the modeling process towards the improvement of the model's quality. This chapter deals with the principles behind this protocol and gives practical advice on how to use the Rd.HMM to evaluate the quality of a three-dimensional modeled structure of a protein, and how to use the information to improve the model. The limitations of the protocol are also discussed.

2. The folding problem is a NP-hard problem involving a degenerate informational code

As implied by the well-known Levinthal paradox (Levinthal, 1968), a full exploration of the entire conformational space theoretically available to a protein is out of the reach of current computational techniques. Equally unaccessible to nature is the sequence space available to polypeptide chains (Kono & Saven, 2001). Currently, the amount of available protein structures (the PDB) represents a fraction of the known protein amino acid sequences, and if the available sample is grouped in terms of different folds, the diversity in the PDB is even smaller. In addition, protein structure and function can tolerate a significant number of mutations. Both facts suggest an important degree of degeneracy between the information in polypeptide sequences and the associated code leading to their native structure (Bowie et al., 1990). In other words, the so-called folding code is degenerate.

However, even if the number of protein structural folds is smaller that the sequence space, the folding problem is still unsolved, because exploring the total number of conformations available to a protein or its energy landscape are NP-hard problems (Hart & Istrail 1997), and because the available methods to calculate the energy of a protein conformation imply a large systematic error (Faver et al., 2011).

The above facts set forth the intractability of solving the problem through an exhaustive search. Nevertheless, proteins in nature do reach a native structure in short times, and finding a native-like solution to the three-dimensional structure of a protein may not require a full examination of the conformational space, or its corresponding energy landscape. In fact, recent years have seen important progress in the search for solutions to the protein folding problem (Dill et al., 2008).

3. The problem of quality scoring for 3D models

In theory, the native three-dimensional structure of a protein must lie at an energy minimum, underneath all accessible intermediates with near-native fold. However, an accurate calculation of the energy for a protein conformation requires quantum chemical calculations. Properties such as electron-electron correlation, charge transfer, polarization, and bond break/formation, including proton exchange, involve quantum mechanical effects and cannot be correctly described using the equations of classical physics. The relevance of quantum mechanics for accurate energy calculations of protein-ligand complexes and protein conformations have been recently demonstrated (Raha and Merz, 2005). Numerical approximations to the electronic state of a multielectronic system have been developed for a variety of system up to date. But only a few simplified solutions, implying low-precision, can tackle an electronic macromolecular system, and even these demand a large amount of computational resources (He & Merz, 2010). The common simplifications, based on molecular mechanics, do carry a systematic error that precludes the accurate finding of the true native energy minimum (Faver et al., 2011).

Many methods have been proposed to model the three-dimensional structure of proteins starting from their amino acid sequence. Based on their use of experimental structural information, these methods can be classified into comparative modeling or *ab initio* methods.

Because rating the success of any method requires an impartial judge to be trustworthy, the scientific community implemented the contests for CRITICAL ASSESMENT OF THE STRUCTURE OF PROTEINS (CASP) (Kryshtafovych et al., 2009). In such contests, the judges are computer algorithms, which compare a 3D-structure solved by an experimental method (but yet unpublished) to a 3D-model predicted by a CASP contestant. The comparative modeling strategies have had a remarkable degree of success in the prediction of 3D-structures of soluble proteins, with the amino acid sequence as starting information.

Comparative modeling exploits the wealth of experimental structural information nowadays available for proteins (Rose et al., 2011), and relies on powerful sequence alignment algorithms (Wallace et al., 2005). In CASP contests, comparative modeling servers, such as I-TASSER (Roy et al., 2010), ROBETTA (Kim et al., 2004) and SAM-T08 (Karplus, 2009), have achieved a high success rate in their predictions for protein 3D-structures of low to intermediate difficulty (as defined by the CASP staff). Yet, one mayor limitation in these methods lies in the strategies used to match each amino acid in a target sequence to its corresponding best hosting spot in the 3D-structure of the template and, again, this is a NP-complete problem (Lathrop, 1994).

In *ab initio* methods, the laws of physics and chemistry and/or artificial intelligence are used to generate a prediction for a native-like folding solution of a protein with known amino acid sequence (Dill et al., 2008). While *ab initio* methods have been less successful than comparative modeling, these are the only choice if no suitable homologous 3D-template is available, for a given amino acid sequence (Kryshtafovych et al., 2009).

The above considerations are all fine when the question is to grade the methods and chose the one with highest success rate, but to date, no single method gives the correct answer every time. Yet, the final aim of such methods is to produce good native-like protein 3D-predictions, when experimental X-ray or NMR data are not available. How then is it possible to set apart models with wrong fold assignment, from those with a correct fold assignment, but with a mistraced sequence to 3D-fold alignment (Luthy et al., 1992)? Is it possible to identify cases where the fold assignment and the alignment are adequate, but the solution to the atom repacking of replaced amino acids is deficient? These questions lie behind the quality assessment of a protein 3D-structure prediction.

The quality assessment is of particular relevance in cases where a suitable 3D-template cannot be found, because the predicted 3D-model cannot be compared back the starting template. Again, this problem can be tackled with a number of strategies, and most of them have been implemented as computer software programs, and their validity tested at the CASP contests (Shi et al., 2009).

Quality assessment methods for the predicted 3D-structures of proteins can be classified according to their underlying principles:

i.   Physics-based methods use the regularities in chemical structures and the laws of physics and chemical bonding to find how much a 3D-structure deviates from the known canonical values. These methods may come in the form of force-fields and they report energies (Hu & Jiang, 2010), or may seek for abnormalities in geometrical and chemical features such as bonding lengths, bonding angles, dihedral torsion values, charge-charge distances and so on (Rodriguez et al. 1998).

ii. Statistics-based methods use the known 3D-structures to generate a set of probability distributions for a number of features of the experimentally solved structures. These distributions can be used as reference to judge the quality of a prediction. When these probability distributions are transformed into energies, using the Boltzmann law, the result is designated as a statistical potential. Although statistical potentials started as empirical constructs, their theoretical basis have been substantiated recently (Hamelryck et al., 2010). These constructs turned out be very useful since any experimental quantitative variable can be treated as an energy and used to generate a potential landscape for 3D-structures. Amongst these latter methods, ANOLEA (Melo & Feytmans, 1998) has a simple conception, and it can be calculated quickly and with a modest computer system, even for very large 3D-structures. Despite its simplicity, ANOLEA stands as one of the most reliable quality assessment indices (Chodanowski et al., 2008).

iii. Artificial intelligence programs such as neural networks, or support vector machines have shown limited success in predicting the 3D-structure of proteins, but their success in quality assessment has been acceptable. A number of these programs has appeared through the years and, again, these methods depend on experimental data to train or setup the program's intelligence (Wallner & Elofsson, 2003). Unfortunately, what features has the computer learned to judge is not always clear, and in some specific cases, the results may be unexpected.

iv. Finally, hybrid methods combine different strategies to test a 3D-structure quality. Amongst these methods, web metaservers, such as metaMQAP (Pawlowski etal., 2008), deserve a note, because they meld the scores from a number of servers into a weighted quality index of a 3D-structure.

While most methods mentioned above may be of value to assess the quality of a predicted protein 3D-structure, it is possible for a model to have acceptable geometrical features, resemble the fold of a structure in the PDB, and still represent a non-native 3D-conformation of the protein under consideration. We have designated this limitation as the appropriateness problem of a 3D-structure prediction. After a careful analysis of several related methods, in our opinion, only the recently published protocol ROSETTA-design-HMMer (Rd.HMM) (Martínez-Castilla & Rodríguez-Sotres 2010) offers robust and explicit evidence of the biological appropriateness of a protein 3D-structure.

4. The reverse folding problem

Due to the degeneracy of the amino acid sequence to three-dimensional fold translation code (Bowie et al., 1990), discussed above, proteins can tolerate amino acid changes in their sequence, as long as these changes do not fall in positions crucial to their folding stability, folding kinetics, macromolecular meaningful interactions, conformational transitions, ligand binding, or catalytic function. Therefore, two proteins sharing more than 40% sequence identity are likely to participate in the same or very similar cellular functions. Based on these considerations, sequence databases may be automatically annotated based on sequence homology between the new unannotated entries and already annotated ones.

As an additional consequence of the folding code degeneracy, the prediction of a 3D-fold starting with the amino acid sequence, i.e. the folding problem, is a far more complex problem than it is the reverse folding problem, which attempts to predict an amino acid sequence compatible with the atomic 3D-coordinates of a protein backbone. One of the first approaches to this problem was published by Eisemberg and co-workers (Luthy et al., 1992; Wilmanns & Eisenberg, 1995). According to their data, given a set of the atomic 3D-coordinates from the native 3D-structure of a protein, it is possible to reconstruct the amino acid sequence of the corresponding natural protein, with a good level of confidence.

A second attempt was published by the group of David Baker (Cheng et al., 2005), who expanded the search beyond the natural amino acid sequence of the protein, to explore part of the sequence space compatible with a given 3D-fold. These authors used the 3D-atomic coordinates from a protein backbone to complement the set of amino acid sequences from natural homologues, with a set of predicted artificial amino acid sequences. In the alignment from this set, they could distinguish the conservation due to structural constraints from the functional conservation. Their data indicated a clear tendency of functional sites to have sub-optimal free energies of stability and their computed sequence profiles diverged from the natural sequence profile. This method was offered as a web service to predict functional sites (Protinfo MFS, http://protinfo.compbio.washington.edu/mfs/, accesed on may 15, 2012).

In a later work, Chivian and Baker (Chivian & Baker, 2006) used a sophistication of the earlier approach to refine a sequence-to-structure alignment, as part of an homology modeling protocol. Their data showed an increase in the alignment's quality of a target amino acid sequence to a 3D-template. These authors integrated this alignment method in the ROBETTA 3D-structure prediction server (Kim et al., 2004). As mentioned in the preceding section, ROBETTA has been repeatedly among the top servers in recent CASP contests and, very likely, this alignment method is part of its success.

In the approaches discussed in this section, the authors applied strategies to account for the conformational flexibility of the backbone in their search, widening the range of amino acid choices for these segments. Therefore, the higher the backbone flexibility, the lower the conservation and the higher the likelihood of such site to be declared as functional. In addition, during the estimation a region's flexibility, part of the natural amino acid information must be retained, because the instability of any segment is intrinsically linked to the properties of the local side chains and their neighbors.

The alternative to this search is to accept the 3D-coordinates for the X-ray solved structure as valid equilibrium conformations, and ignore those segments where the excessive mobility prevented the assignment of atom positions. In NMR solved structures, there is usually more information on accessible conformations, and the approach may take this into account, or use the more populated conformation. In this last case, the conformational flexibility is lost, but the computed set of sequences will make a better sampling of the sequence space available to this particular equilibrium conformation.

From this considerations, any attempt to explore the sequence space available to a given fold clearly must accept some informational loss, but at this point, the sequence space compatible with a completely fixed backbone was in need of a deeper exploration.

In the Rd.HMM protocol (Martínez-Castilla & Rodríguez-Sotres 2010), ROSETTA-design (Rd) is used to redesign the 3D-structure of a protein by reassigning amino acids to every position in the structure, and with no restriction in the choice of amino acids or rotamers. To completely suppress the information present in the starting amino acid sequence, a preliminary redesign of the protein is made by imposing to the 3D-backbone a fixed new random sequence. To reduce any bias possibly introduced by this random sequence, this step is performed several times. When scored with the ROSETTA force-field for stability, the 3D-structures with randomized sequence have very high energies, because the artificial side chains will frequently fail to fit into the cavities left by the natural side chains, and neighboring contacts are likely to be unfavorable. In other words, these randomized sequence 3D-models are *in silico* constructs, meaningless in terms of chemistry or biology.

In the second step, Rd is used to redesign each 3D-structure with randomized sequence produced before, but this time with complete freedom of amino acid choice, and the reconstruction is done many times. Rd can be trusted to find amino acids combinations with high stability (Kuhlman et al., 2003; Jiang et al., 2008; Slovic et al., 2004; Butterfoss et al., 2006; see also next section) and each new redesign will harbor a new theoretically low-energy sequence of amino acids for the 3D-backbone under consideration, but most likely, a non-natural one, because the selection pressure in natural proteins is not limited to stability constraints (Cheng et al., 2005).

In the end, a set of amino acid sequences can be recovered from the corresponding set of 3D-redesigns, as large as requested, and representing a sample of theoretically possible, but naturally inexistent amino acid combinations, optimized only for 3D-fold stability. The theoretical stability of the redesigns are expected to exceed natural protein stability (Cheng et al., 2005; Butterfoss et al., 2006), but a folding pathway to the 3D-fold may not exist for such sequences, because ROSETTA-design has not been imprinted with any information related to the folding process. That is to say, no all redesigns are expected to fold correctly in experimental tests.

5. The merits of ROSETTA-design

ROSETTA-design (Rd) is a program developed by the group of David Baker (Kuhlman et al., 2003) with a remarkable success in the design of suitable amino acid sequences for a given-fold. The ROSETTA suite includes modules for protein structure refinement, *ab initio* protein folding predictions, antibody design, protein-ligand docking, protein-protein docking, and others. However the merits and limitations of those other protocols will not be discussed here.

Rd was created with one application in mind, namely "to find amino acid sequences able to fold into a given three-dimensional structure". To this aim, Baker's group developed three basic components: a modified force-field with a large penalty for atomic overlap, a rotamer database taken from the PDB and refined with quantum chemical calculations, and a Monte-Carlo search algorithm to replace the amino acid side-chains of the starting structure (Kuhlman et al., 2003).

The approach followed by Rd has proven very robust because it made possible to design the first artificial protein folding into a completely novel topology (Kuhlman et al., 2003). Rd has been also used with success to place a novel enzyme active site, of human design, into an unrelated protein (Jiang et al., 2008), and to convert a membrane protein into a soluble protein (Slovic et al., 2004), among other notable protein engineering applications (Butterfoss et al., 2006).

Monte-Carlo methods can be implemented in algorithms to various aims. Some are designed to provide an extensive sampling of a given landscape, but in other cases the algorithm is set to find a optimum (usually a minimum) in such landscape. The very well-known Metropolis algorithm (Metropolis et al., 1953) can be used for both purposes, but it has been theoretically proven to converge to the true optimum, if no time limit is set (Mengersen & Tweedie, 1966). In practice, Monte-Carlo methods may take too many steps and the search has to be stopped when the sampling is considered extensive enough, usually, well before the true optimum is determined (Cowles & Carlin, 1996).

Once again, due to the degeneracy in the folding code (see section 1), low-energy solutions for amino acid side chain replacements on a 3D-backbone have many local minima, and some may be within the reach of a short to moderate Monte-Carlo random-walk. Rd narrows down the list of amino acid rotamers to be tried at each α carbon, uses a computer-efficient code for energy calculations, an improved force-field, and has a curated database of rotamers, with improved geometries obtained through quantum mechanical calculations. In addition, Rd starts with a geometrical analysis of the structure and removes from the search amino acid sites where the local environment makes the choices' list too narrow or too undefined. The assignment at those sites becomes then trivial.

Finally, Rd can be fed with a list of amino acid choices for each residue in the 3D-backbone, ranging from not allowing changes, to the full set of 20 amino acids and all of their rotamers. Rd is, therefore, one of the most flexible programs for protein design (Butterfoss et al., 2006).

6. Hidden Markov models to deal with the reverse folding problem

A Markov model (MM) is a model of a stochastic process with the Markov property. The model has the Markov property if, along the random succession of states, the future state is determined by the present state only, with no influence of the previous states (Eddy, 2004). The change from one state to another is called a transition, and each state has an associated transition probability. The states are finite or countable, but the succession itself may be infinite.

A MM can be used to describe a number of natural phenomena. For example, in a chemical kinetic mechanism, the states are chemical intermediates and transition probabilities are rate equations (Shapiro & Zeilberger, 1982). When these states constitute symbol emitters and each state has a defined emission probability for each possible symbol, and a concatenation of states will broadcast a symbols' sequence, for instance, an amino acid sequence (Eddy et al., 1995).

A very simple sequence-generating MM may consist of two states (Fig. 1): Let the state S_1 be an emitter of any of the 20 amino acids abbreviations. Let the amino acid compositions of an infinite sequence of symbols produced by S_1 equal the composition of natural proteins. With a probability of 0.1, state S_1 may suffer a transition to a second emitter S_2. In turn, S_2 is able to emit a stop, or to transit back to S_1, with 0.9 probability. This two states will go forth and back to give an infinite number of sequences of short length, because, given the probabilities, sequences longer than a few tenths of amino acids will be very infrequent.

Since a MM is a stochastic device, it is unsuited to represent only one particular sequence, but instead, it can be a powerful tool to represent a subset of the sequence space, notably, a sequence alignment. Such MM represents the observed aligned sequences, usually a subset of all the possible sequences in the alignment, but the states of the model (each one encoding the probabilities of one or more alignment positions) cannot be observed. When such is the case, the MM is then said to be hidden (HMM). However, the Viterbi algorithm, the forward algorithm, and the Baum–Welch algorithm make it possible to compute the most likely parameters of the model's states, out of the observations available (Eddy, 2004; Eddy et al., 1995).

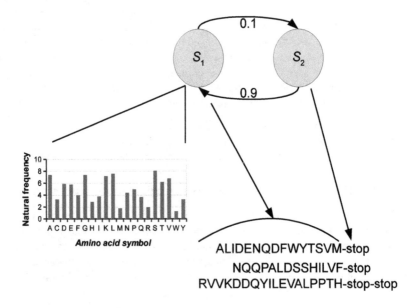

Figure 1. A simple Markov model to emit random amino acid sequences of variable length with an amino acid composition similar to that in natural proteins.

Because the HMM represents more sequences than those observed, it can be used to produce new sequences, but most importantly, for any available sequence in a database, its emission probability by the HMM can be calculated and compared to corresponding emission probability by a very general model, such as the one in figure 1. The ratio of these two probabilities can be used as an index or score, the higher the score, the higher the likelihood of the sequence being a member of the alignment. From this information, the expectancy of such an index value being due to chance can be estimated. Expectancies of one or above may indicate a meaningless score.

HMMer is a suite of programs developed by Sean Eddy (Eddy, 2004, Eddy et al., 1995) to create and use HMMs of amino acid and nucleic acid sequence alignments. HMMer has executables to estimate the parameters of a HMM from a sequence alignment and calibrate the model to allow a good estimation of scores and expectancies. Other executables will test a sequence database to extract those sequences with high score and low expectancy, aligning the new sequences to the model. Additional executables can create the starting HMM, use it to emit sequences with high probability of being members of the model, or update the model parameters using the newly discovered additional sequences.

One critical step in the HMM preparation is the starting alignment fed to HMMer (Eddy, 2004), because as mentioned in section 1, the optimal alignment of sequence sets is not a trivial problem (Lathrop, 1994). When a HMM gives poor results, it is frequently as a consequence of a defective alignment.

Another limitation of a HMM lies on its very definition, because a MM must be memoryless (Markov property). In the 3D-structure of proteins those amino acids brought into proximity during folding, must be of compatible nature from the sterical and chemical points of view. This property is stored in the sequence as sites with correlated variability, also known as mutual information. Its relevance has been recognized and exploited (Socolich et al., 2005), but HMM are unable to encode such information.

After the above discussion of HMMer features, we can consider its value in dealing with the large a set of amino acid sequences redesigned by the Rd protocol described in the preceding section:

1. Rd.HMM produces many sequences that can be trivially aligned, because every amino acid has biunivocal correspondence with a 3D-backbone site.
2. Using a HMM to represent the redesigned sequences will result in the statistical extension of the sample to sequences with a similar frequency profile. This extension is however inaccurate, because not all off the sequences possibly emitted by the HMM will actually be low-energy solutions to the 3D-backbone redesign (Hamelryck et al., 2010).
3. The HMM can be used to search those natural sequences having amino acid combinations suitable to the 3D-structure under analysis. The value of HMM in the analysis of relationships between biological sequences has been extensively documented (Eddy, 2004).
4. Due to (1), the search made in a database of natural sequences by means of the HMM will align each selected sequence in a structurally aware manner (Martínez-Castilla & Rodríguez-Sotres 2010). But given (2), such structurally aware alignment is somehow inaccurate, the lower the HMMer score, the less reliable this alignment becomes.

7. The unexpected sensitivity of Rd-HMMer

In theory, when a Rd.HMM is used to scan a general sequence database, such as the NCBI-nr (Jiang et al., 2008), a sequence is selected if it is considerably less likely to be generated at random, than to be emitted by the Rd.HMM. But the Rd-step leaves only information related to the 3D-fold, which is then fed into the HMM, thus any selected sequence should be able to fold into a 3D-structure very similar to the starting one. Sequences selected by HMMer should then belong to the same folding family.

One of the unexpected results of Rd.HMM is the sensitivity of this protocol, for instance, it is able to separate those sequences of the TIM-barrel fold that belong to the triose phosphate isomerase from those that belong to other TIM-barrels, such as the phosphoribosylpyrophosphate isomerase (PRAI) (Martínez-Castilla & Rodríguez-Sotres 2010).

Apparently, the Rd-step can imprint its artificial sequences with some details related to loop and turn shapes, as well as contact between secondary structure elements within the tertiary structure adopted by the original polypeptide chain. Then, only when two proteins with completely different activity retain an almost identical structure, a single Rd.HMM can score their corresponding sequences with a significant score. Such is the case of the novel engineered retroaldolases (RA-61, RA-22) and the corresponding templates used to host the newly designed amino acid catalyst, a β-1,4-*endo*-xylanse from *Nonomuraea flexuosa* and one indole-3-glycerol phosphate syntase from *Sulfolobus solfataricus* (Martínez-Castilla & Rodríguez-Sotres 2010; Jiang et al., 2008). This was also the case with the imidazoleglycerolphosphate synthase From *Thermotoga maritima* and the engineered imidazoleglycerol_evolvedcerolphosphate synthase (Martínez-Castilla & Rodríguez-Sotres 2010; Röthlisberger et al., 2008).

The remarkable sensitivity of the Rd.HMM protocol is reflected also in the change of the score reported for the 3D-structure of one protein resolved by NMR, as compared to its X-ray 3D-structure. An Rd.HMM produced with a X-ray 3D-structure will score its corresponding natural sequence with a value close to 0.6 times the length of its amino acid sequence. Instead a Rd.HMM from an NMR derived structure will report half of that score for its corresponding natural sequence (Martínez-Castilla & Rodríguez-Sotres 2010).

As an additional test of the Rd.HMM sensitivity, we compared the Rd.HMMs corresponding to subunit A from two prokaryotic glycyl-tRNA-synthases, one from *Thermus thermophilus* and another from *Thermotoga maritima*. These two X-ray resolved structures have a very similar core (Fig 2A), but the sequence similarity is below 15%. Despite the structural similarity, both proteins have extensive regions where the structure differs completely. Accordingly, the 1ATI:A Rd.HMM scored the *T. thermophilus* sequence (its corresponding natural one) with a value of 161.8 (score over sequence length 0.37) and a highly significant E-value (3.8×10^{-49}), but the *T. maritima* sequence received a negative score of -271.1 (score over sequence length -0.94) lacking statistical significance (E-value 2). In contrast, the 1J5W:A Rd.HMM scored the *T. thermophilus* sequence with a value of -200.0 (-

0.88) lacking significance (E-value 0.065), and the *T maritima* sequence (its corresponding natural one) received a positive score of 30.3 (0.11) and high statistical significance (*E*-value 8.4×10^{-17}). In these cases, the score was obtained lowering the software threshold, because in a standard search of the NCBI-nr the 1ATI:A Rd.HMM only identified the *T. thermophilus* glycyl-tRNA amino acid sequence and its homologues.

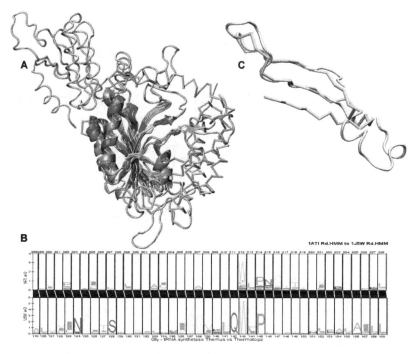

Figure 2. (A) Comparison of glycyl-tRNA synthetases from *Thermus thermophilus* (PDB 1ATI:A, yellow tube) and from *Thermotoga maritima* (PDB 1J5W:A, green trace). The core α/β region was superimposed using TOPOFIT (Ilyin et al., 2004) (shown as cartoons) and colored according to its sequence similarity from blue (identical) to white (dissimilar). The figure was prepared using VMD (Humphrey et al., 1996). (B) HMM logo of the profile to profile alignment (Schuster-Böckler & Bateman, 2005) of Rd.HMMs from glycyl-tRNA synthetases in (A). (C) The segments in (A) corresponding to the nodes in the alignment in (B)

In the previous example, the dissimilar regions have enough information to allow the discrimination between the structures. In addition, since the scores for the non-related sequence on each case were negative, the alignment produced by the Rd.HMM of both sequences is unreliable. Figure 2B shows the profile to profile comparison of HMM logos (Schuster-Böckler & Bateman, 2005) for the Rd.HMM derived from both glycyl-tRNA synthetases, which paired a significant subset of both Rd.HMMs. The corresponding segments were indeed structurally related (Fig. 2C).

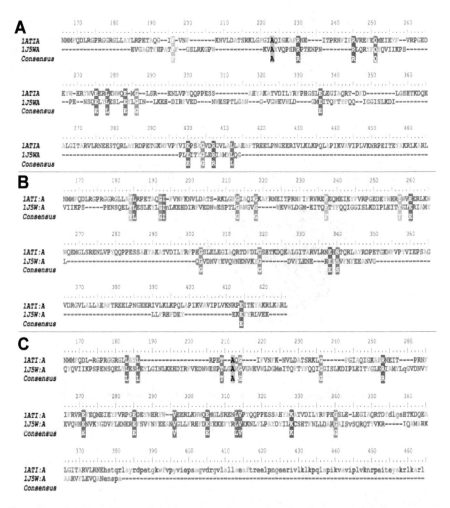

Figure 3. (A) TOPOFIT (Ilyin et al., 2004) sequence alignment based on the structural alignment in figure 2. Amino acids are aligned if their backbones are less than 3 Å apart. (B) Alignment guided by the Rd.HMM derived from 1ATI:A. (C) Alignment guided by the Rd.HMM derived from 1J5W:A. For clarity, only the section of the alignment including aminoacids 166 to 424 of 1ATI:A is shown.

Figure 3 (A to C) shows the lack of coincidence between the TOPOFIT structural alignment (Ilyin et al., 2004), and the two Rd.HMM based alignments for the core regions. A careful analysis of the alignments in figure 3 suggests a possible explanation for the notable specificity of 1ATI:A and 1J5W:A Rd.HMMs. While repacking the rotamers into the theoretical 3D-structures, Rosetta-design identifies sites of low or no variation, with higher informational content. Clearly these sites are distributed in a rather different way on the

1ATI:A, or 1J5W:A Rd.HMMs (Fig. 3 B and C), and only a fraction of these low-variance sites do coincide with structurally equivalent sites (Fig. 3A), making each Rd.HMM different enough.

A similar analysis of the lysozymes from lambda phage (or *E. coli*), T4 phage, chicken (*Gallus gallus*) and goose (*Anser anser anser*) led to very similar results.

A somehow artificial example comes from the Rosetta-designed non-natural proteins Top7 and M. This example is used to illustrate the interpretation of the Rd.HMM information in the next section.

8. The Rd-HMMer protocol: A practical guide

This section describes how to generate a Rd.HMM and interpret the results.

1.   Software requirements:
     •   Rosetta suite v. 2.3 or above. The examples given here apply to v. 2.3, but the porting to v. 3.1 is straightforward. Rd v. 2.1 is considerably faster, but exploration of the sequence space is better in Rd. v 3.1.
     •   HMMer v. 2 or above. The examples given here were done with v. 3, which is considerably faster, therefore recommended.
     •   VMD v. 1.8.7 or above. (Humphrey et al., 1996)
     •   SwissPDB viewer v. 4, or above (Kaplan &Littlejohn, 2001).
     •   Sequence databases. You may download the protein nr, SeqRef or UniProt-Sprot databases from the NCBI site (Sayers et al., 2010), or any other fulfilling your needs. As an alternative, you may prepare a small database using psi-blast at any server. It is recommended to include not only the sequences of proteins related to the structure of interest, but also other unrelated sequences, preferably selected at random.

VMD and SwissPDB viewer are not essential but are very useful for PDB file manipulation.

2.   Prepare your PDB file. Rd v. 2.3 requires your PDB file to have non-zero beta factors. Residues may be absent, as long as none of the corresponding backbone heavy atoms are present. Therefore atoms with types C, CA, N, C and O for a particular residue should be all present for each residue, or all absent. For an incomplete residue you may open your file with Swiss PDB viewer. This program will rebuild the missing atoms, which is recommended for models; but you can use the software to completely remove the residue, which is preferable for experimental data. A special case is the oxygen atom of the C-terminus (OXT), which is required by Rd. This atom can be rebuilt with SwissPDB viewer, but this is not done automatically. An alternative to Swiss PDB viewer is VMD using the PFSgen plugin. Although PDB manipulation in VMD requires more experience, its scripting language is more powerful.

If your structural PDB file comes from a modeling exercise, review the geometrical and sterical quality of your model. If required, refine it with molecular mechanics software. A more detailed description of this kind of problems in protein modeling and how to fix them can be found elsewhere (Chavelas Adame et al., 2011; Rosales-León et al., 2012).

3. Build many replicates of your PDB file with a random assignment of amino acid sequence. This can be done in two ways:

a. *With VMD.* Use the *atomselect* command to select the backbone atoms of all residues, one at a time, and change the residue name to any amino acid selected at random. In the C-terminal residue make sure to include the OXT atom in your selection. Then select all backbone atoms including the OXT and save the file. A script to do this with VMD can be requested to the corresponding author.

b. *With Rd.* Prepare several Rosetta input *resfile* with a tag *PICKAA X* (replace X for a random 1-letter amino acid code) for every position in the PDB file of interest. Then run Rd, once for each *resfile* you made, with the following command:

rosetta.gcc -s 1QYS.pdb-design -fixbb -chain A -resfile 1QYSaa.res-ndruns 1 -pdbout 1QYSAaa

Here, we assume 1QYS.pdb to be the starting PDB file, *A* to be the subunit of interest, *1QYSaa.res* is the *resfile*, and your result will be named *1QYSAaa_0001.pdb* (depending on the version, you will also need a paths.txt in your folder, or the path to the rosetta database should be indicated in the command line). In Rd v. 3.1, the *resfile* format and some command line options have changed (check Rosetta documentation for details).

This step can be repeated at will, to create many sequence-randomized PDB files, but in our experience, at least 10 are needed for a reliable HMM.

4. Rebuild each sequence-randomized PDB file with Rd. First you will need a *resfile* with the tag *ALLAA* (1QYSall.res), and a text file (pdb4rbld.lst) containing the names of all the sequence-randomized PDB file created in the previous step, one per line. Then, rebuild each input file 29 times using the command:

rosetta.gcc -design -fixbb -chain A-l pdb4rbld.lst -resfile 1QYSall.res -ndruns 29 -pdbout

You can generate many rebuilt PDBs per input file, but you need at least 100 sequences in the end to produce a representative HMM. In our experience, a better exploration of the sequence space results from many sequence-randomized input files and between 10 to 30 rebuilt PDBs for each input PDB file.

5. Extract the amino acid sequence for each rebuilt PDB file and save it in a text file (*1QYSA_a-O.fas*), in fasta format. This file represents an alignment, though a sequence alignment software is not necessary, due to the reasons commented at the end of section 5. Then use HMMer to prepare a hidden Markov model of your sequence alignment:

hmmbuild --informat afa 1QYSA_a-O.hmm 1QYSA_a-O.fas

If you are using HMMer v. 2.0, you need to calibrate your model with:

hmmcalibrate 1QYSA_a-O.hmm

6. Search a sequence database (*i.e.* NCBI-nr) with:

hmmsearch -E 100 -Z 10000000 1QYSA_a-O.hmm path2db/nr

Here a local copy of the nr is assumed to be in your system in fasta format. The -Z flag will scale the E-values to 10 million sequences. This is recommended to make E-values comparable, because E-values are linearly dependent on the size of the sequence database searched. The default E value is 10, but here it was set to 100 to lower the search threshold.

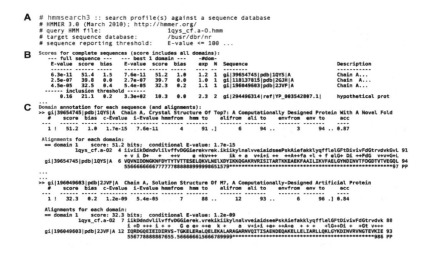

Figure 4. An HMMer search output result. The search was done using an Rd.HMM from Top7 (PDB id. 1QYS) and the NCBI-nr as database. (A) heading, (B) scores, (C) domain-parsed scores and alignments. The statistics at the end and some information was removed for brevity. The format is as in HMMer 3.0.

An extract of the results from a typical search is presented in figure 4. The HMMer search output will report three sections: (a) Heading, (b) scores for complete sequences, (c) domain parsing, alignments and statistics. As it can be seen, according to the information in the Rd.HMM from Top7, the Top7 amino acid sequence fits into the Top7 3D-atomic coordinates (1QYS). The most relevant sections are the scores and the alignment sections. Notice how this X-ray solved 3D-stucture reports an HMM score of 51.2, matching the sequence from amino acid 3 to 94, that gives a ratio of 0.56, close to the 0.6 average value for X-ray solved structures. The reason behind the relationship is not simple, but it holds for most X-ray solved structures (with a few exceptions) (Martínez-Castilla & Rodríguez-Sotres 2010). The second hit is the C-terminal fragment of Top7 solved by NMR, the score is 39.8 for a fragment of length 50 (ratio = 0.79). This last score is higher than the score for the complete sequence, because as shown in figure 4, the C-terminus has higher proportion of local coincidences to the HMM. In the alignment to the full sequence, the contribution of the N-terminus lowers the overall score. The alignment for the C-terminal fragment was omitted because it is identical to the 1QYS alignment from position 44 to 91 (Fig. 4C). The alignment shows a consensus for the hidden Markov model, as a reference, then the sequence found aligned separated by an intermediate mask. Uppercase letters indicate strong conservation, lower case letter conservative changes and plus sign a positive local score. The lower line, absent in HMMer 2 is the encoded posterior probability (d=0...9,*; * equals 9.5), where the approximate value of posterior probability for each site is given by equation (1).

$$pp = d \times 0.1 + 0.025 \qquad (1)$$

The final hit in the search in figure 4 is the M artificial protein. This protein was designed with Rosetta-design using the same Top7 folding. Its sequence is different, but it belongs to the same family of Rd proteins. The score is smaller than for Top7 (ratio of 32/(88-7), or 0.395), but still above 0.3 and with high statistical significance. Although Rd was used to design these proteins, the concordance reveals the robustness of the amino acid assignment made by Rd, and gives further support to the structurally aware nature of the Rd.HMM alignments.

The alignment is very useful to protein modeling, because it reveals the distribution of coincident regions between the 3D-atomic coordinates of the backbone and the amino acid sequence in the database. The following features are to be taken into account:

a. Frame shift. If the residue number in the 3D-structure has an offset relative to the amino acid numbering in the sequence, either from the beginning, or starting at some intermediate site; this is usually a sign of a wrong threading of the model and the template during the modeling step. In the example, there is a difference in amino acid numbering, but this is not a frame shift, as the first residue solved in the PDB is ASP-3, corresponding to node one in the HMM, then the first 3 HMM nodes did not match the Top7 sequence and were discarded by HMMer search making the first match to residue 6, at HMM node 4.

b. Insertion/deletions. An insertion in the sequence appears as a dot in the HMMer consensus, a deletion as dashes in the sequence found. Such changes are expected if the sequence is a homologue, and not the natural sequence that corresponds to the 3D-structures analyzed with Rd.HMM. They may occur also when the PDB file has some missing amino acids (this happens frequently, due to experimental limitations of X-ray crystalography). If so, you expect this insertions to match the missing amino acids. For *in silico* modeled structures this means a local threading error, or a local defect in the model.

c. Distribution of conserved sites. The higher the number of conserved sites, the better the model. However, some strained conformations have lower energy for glycine, proline and asparagine than for every other amino acid and these residues tend to appear as strongly conserved (Uppercase letters in the mask line, and in the Rd.HMM consensus). If the sequence conservation observed is dominated by these residues, you model may be wrong, even if your score has statistical significance.

9. Guiding the 3D-modeling of proteins with Rd-HMMer

There are many publications describing different approaches to the solution to the protein folding problem (Roy et al., 2010; Kim et al., 2004; Karplus, 2009; Melo & Feytmans, 1998) but most of them focus on the theory, or present a technical treatment. Fisher and Sali published a practical guide to the use of the popular modeling software MODELLER (Fiser & Sali 2003), where many useful hints are given. Recently, Chavelas-Adame and coworkers published a guide with emphasis on the use of open software [45]. The present account will not attempt to repeat the work, and only the most important conclusions are given here:

a. Many servers and software programs are available to aid the comparative modeling of proteins (Roy et al., 2010; Kim et al., 2004; Karplus, 2009; Melo & Feytmans, 1998; Rosales-León et al., 2012; Fiser & Sali 2003), some options are available for *ab initio* modeling (Kryshtafovych et al., 2009; Kim et al., 2004; Srinivasan et al., 2004; Xu & Zhang, 2012), and this list is far form complete. None of them achieves 100% success, and even the most successful can fail where other, usually less reliable, may succeed (Kryshtafovych et al., 2009; Melo & Feytmans, 1998).

b. A model is fundamentally wrong when the folding pattern in the model bears little or no relationship to the true native fold. Some models may offer a good approximation, but have wrong geometrical, sterical and/or chemical features at some locations, *i.e.* the bond lengths, angles, sidechain-sidechain contact distances and orientation may have important deviations from the expected values found in known chemical structures. This last kind are usually designated as unrefined models.

c. Unrefined models can be recognized with various energy scoring strategies (Luthy et al., 1992; Shi et al., 2009; Hu & Jiang, 2010; Melo & Feytmans, 1998); and can be corrected through the use of molecular mechanics software (Rosales-León et al., 2012; Fiser & Sali 2003), though this approach has limitations, as mentioned before (Faver et al., 2011; Hu & Jiang, 2010; Melo & Feytmans, 19985).

d. Wrong models instead may frequently be deceitful, because, due to their systematic error [5], a molecular mechanics force-field may report a low energy value, as long as the chemical and geometrical details are well refined. Rd.HMM offers a solution to this problem, because these models will produce an HMM search report with no hits, or will score sequences, other than the modeling target (Chavelas Adame et al., 2011; Rosales-León et al., 2012).

e. The analysis of the Rd.HMM search report may help in the identification of errors in the alignment between the target amino acid sequence and the template selected for comparative modeling. If you find a frame-shift or an unexpected insertion/deletion pair, you can use the HMM search alignment and realign the target sequence and the template. MODELLER is a very good choice for that aim (Fiser & Sali 2003). In addition, a wrongly threaded model can be recycled by replacing the consensus sequence with the PDB sequence in the model (which is the target sequence), and producing a target to target alignment, with the insertions and deletions suggested by HMMer. MODELLER can then be used to generate new models. This last procedure is only recommended if your HMMer score is positive and has good statistical significance, for otherwise, the structural inaccuracy of the Rd.HMMs becomes a serious issue.

f. Comparative modeling has been extended thanks to methods able to find templates with low sequence homology to the target (Wallace et al., 2005; Karplus, 2009). But sometimes the selected template is too distant. If the Rd.HMM of the candidate structures are obtained, these can be use to score the target sequence. The resulting scores, statistical significance and the alignment may guide your template selection. However, if the Rd.HMM of a template candidate gives a negative score, and still you decide to use it, do not trust the Rd.HMM alignment without further improvement using other tools, as it may be seriously flawed.

g. Finally, if you use the ROSETTA suite or the ROBETTA server to produce your models, these structures are expected to have a ROSETTA-like bias, *i.e.* their Rd.HMM scores will increase and a good model with this bias is expected to have a ratio of HMMer score to sequence length close to one. While in models produced with other software a Rd.HMM score ratio of 0.3 is acceptable, in a ROSETTA produced model this score is low and may reflect important flaws. Look at the alignment carefully, as recommended in the previous section.

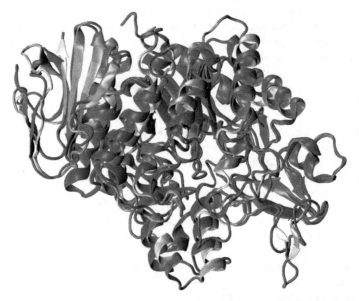

Figure 5. Comparison of the yeast α-glucosidase model produced included in the publication by Brindis et al (Brindis et al., 2011), with the X-ray solved structure of its homologue, the yeast isomaltase (Yamamoto et al., 2010). The isomaltase is shown as blue cartoons and the α-glucosidase cartoons are colored according to the amino acid rmsd from isomaltase, ranging from very low (blue) to intermediate (white) to high (red).

As an example of the advantages of Rd.HMM, we refer to two cases of recent success. Brindis and coworkers (Brindis et al., 2011) analyzed the effects of a natural product on α-glucosidase. This work reports a model for the budding yeast α-glucosidase used to analyze the molecular grounds for the (Z)-3-butylidenephthalide inhibitory action. In the preparation of the model, Rd.HMM allowed to detect a threading problem (insertion/deletion pair) in one β-strand in the core of the model. While the sheet was slid only a few Å from its position, the contact with neighboring strands completely distorted the chemical interaction network affecting the model stability. The correction of this problem and the use of molecular dynamics simulations led to a well refined and reliable model with a good Rd.HMM score. A few months later (when the paper was in press) the 3D-structure of a close homologue (isomaltase) was released (Yamamoto et al., 2010). The X-ray data corroborated the model quality, as the model core backbone has an rmsd of 1.81 Å form the experimental data. Figure 5 shows a superposition of both structures colored by backbone rmsd form blue (low) to white (medium) to red (high).

In a second example, the 3D-structure of two isoforms of plant inorganic pyrophophatases was obtained using a combined strategy of web servers, MODELLER and molecular dynamics simulations. The resulting models provided ground for the lack of quaternary structure in plant pyrophosphatases (Rosales-León et al., 2012). Although the sequences of several related isoforms were initially sent to the servers, only one isoform was correctly modeled, according to Rd.HMM, but the Rd.HMM of the good model gave an alignment for the sequence of a second isozyme. This alignment, and the correct model were then used to produce the second model. Though this last model was not directly based on experimental data, its quality was high, according to Rd.HMM (Rosales-León et al., 2012).

10. Rd-HMMer limitations

Since most Rd.HMM limitations have been mentioned. We only summarize them here:

a. Rd.HMM sensitivity makes it useful for medium to good quality models. Low quality models, may still be of use as starting points, but the Rd.HMM data will only indicate the low quality and will not allow to discriminate a wrong model from an unrefined one.
b. The structurally aware nature of the Rd.HMM alignments is to be trusted only for good quality models. As the Rd.HMM score drops, the sequence to structure correlation becomes weak.
c. Rd.HMM does not offer much information on how to modify the model to improve its appropriateness, other than the presence of insertion/deletions or sequence to structure frame-shifts.
d. A model may be badly refined and get a good Rd.HMM score, as long as Rosetta-design is able to process the backbone coordinates and repack the residues. Therefore, the Rd.HMM score is insufficient information. Information from other software, such as ANOLEA energy (Melo & Feytmans, 1998) or molecular mechanics energy (Hu & Jiang, 2010) is always required to test a model quality.
e. Finally, there is no formal proof for the perfect correspondence between a Rd.HMM high score and the prediction for the 3D-structure of a protein to be native-like. Therefore, from two predictions, of which only one represents the native fold, it might be possible to produce a high Rd.HMM score for the target sequence (a false positive). However, despite our best efforts we have only found the false negative case, *i.e.* a good prediction (or even a 3D-structure from experimental data) may give a low Rd.HMM score. To the best of our knowledge, among the quality assessment methods, this feature is unique to the Rd.HMM protocol.

11. Conclusions and perspectives

Although the Rd.HMM protocol is highly sensitive and its alignments become inaccurate when the HMM score decreases, it can be used to guide the comparative modeling of proteins, as the examples given in section 8 show. Even if the alignment employed is flawed, when the model is produced and analyzed with Rd.HMM, the flaw will become evident and the model can then be discarded, and additional modeling rounds may be tried.

An additional advantage of Rd.HMM alignments, as a guide to comparative modeling, comes form the fact that Rd.HMM models are independent of the functional constrains reflected in the conservation of active and binding sites. Since the Rd. step removes all conservation due to ligand binding and functional sites, other than that required to keep the structure stable, geometrical differences in the organization of two related, but not identical active sites will not affect the modeling process. In contrast, in the classic comparative modeling methods, the residue conservation at active and other functional sites is usually an important reference to perform the sequence to structure alignment. Then when a model in produced with the guidance of Rd.HMM, and a model with good quality and appropriateness is obtained, any coincidences in the active site geometry, would not come as a consequence of forcing the conserved residues in the target sequence to fall at the template's active site, but should be a consequence of meeting the structural requirements of the target.

From the above discussion, Rd.HMM is clearly a valuable tool, but has some limitations. We speculate that some of this limitations derive form the inability of HMMs to incorporate long range interactions, which can be detected as significant mutual information between distant positions in the sequence alignments. Currently we are working on the analysis of the mutual information in the Rosetta-designed sequence alignments using the statistical coupling analysis strategy (Socolich et al., 2005,Lockless et al., 1999). We hope this powerful statistical approach can extend the Rd.HMM and provide a richer tool.

Author details

León P. Martínez-Castilla and Rogelio Rodríguez-Sotres
Facultad de Química, Universidad Nacional Autónoma de México, México

Acknowledgement

Funding PAPIIT-DGAPA-UNAM IN210212, CONACyT CB2008-1-101186, PAIP-FQ-UNAM 4290-09, PAIP-FQ-UNAM 4290-07.

Abbreviations

NP-hard problem, as hard to solve as an NP-complete problem; NP-complete problem, no algorithm taking a polynomial-time exists for its solution; Rd, ROSETTA-design; MM,

Markov model; HMM, hidden Markov model; CASP, critical assessment of the structure of proteins; PDB, international protein data bank; TIM, triose phosphate isomerase.

12. References

Bowie, J., Reidhaar-Olson, J., Lim, W., & Sauer, R.(1990). Deciphering the message in protein sequences: tolerance to amino acid substitutions. *Science,* Vol. 247, No. 4948, (Mar 1990) pp. 1306-1310, ISSN 0036-8075 (print), 1095-9203 (electronic)

Brindis, F., Rodríguez, R., Bye, R., González-Andrade, M., & Mata, R.(2011). (Z)-3-butylidenephthalide from *Ligusticum porteri* , an α-glucosidase inhibitor. *J Nat Prod,* Vol. 74, No. 3, (Sep 2011) pp. 314-20, ISSN 0163-3864 (print) 1520-6025 (electronic)

Butterfoss, G. L. & Kuhlman, B.(2006). Computer-based design of novel protein structures. *Annu Rev Biophys Biomol Struct,* Vol. 35, (Jun 2006) pp. 49-65, ISSN 1056-8700

Chavelas Adame, E. A., Hernández-Domínguez, E. E., Gaytán-Mondrangón, S., Rosales León, L., Valencia-Turcotte, L., & Rodríguez-Sotres, R.(2011). A Hitchhiker's Guide to the modeling of the three-Dimensional structure of proteins. *International Color Biotechnology Journal,* Vol. 1, No. 1, (Nov 2011) pp. 26-35, ISSN 2226-0404 (electronic)

Cheng, G., Qian, B., Samudrala, R., & Baker, D.(2005). Improvement in protein functional site prediction by distinguishing structural and functional constraints on protein family evolution using computational design. *Nucleic Acids Research,* Vol. 33, No. 18, (Sep 2005) pp. 5861--7, ISSN 1362-4962 (print)

Chivian, D. & Baker, D.(2006). Homology modeling using parametric alignment ensemble generation with consensus and energy-based model selection. *Nucleic Acids Research,* Vol. 34, No. 17, (Sep 2006) pp. e112, ISSN 1362-4962

Chodanowski, P., Grosdidier, A., Feytmans, E., & Michielin, O.(2008). Local Alignment Refinement Using Structural Assessment. *PLoS ONE,* Vol. 3, No. 7, (Jul 2008) pp. e2645, ISSN 1932-6203 (electronic)

Cowles, M. K. & Carlin, B. P.(1996). Markov Chain Monte Carlo Convergence Diagnostics: A Comparative Review. *Journal of the American Statistical Association,* Vol. 91, No. 434, (Jun 1996) pp. 883-904, ISSN 0162-1459 (print), 1537-274X (electronic)

Dill, K. A., Ozkan, S. B., Shell, M. S., & Weikl, T. R.(2008). The protein folding problem. *Annu Rev Biophys,* Vol. 37, (Jun 2008) pp. 289-316, ISSN ISSN:1936-122X (print) 1936-1238 (electronic) 1936-122X (linking)

Eddy, S. R., Mitchison, G., & Durbin, R.(1995). Maximum discrimination hidden Markov models of sequence consensus. *J Comput Biol,* Vol. 2, No. 1, (Jan 1995) pp. 9--23, ISSN 1066-5277 (print); 1557-8666 (electronic)

Eddy, S. R.(2004). What is a hidden Markov model? *Nat Biotech,* Vol. 22, No. 10, (Oct 2004) pp. 1315--1316, ISSN 1087-0156

Faver, J. C., Benson, M. L., He, X., Roberts, B. P., Wang, B., Marshall, M. S., Sherrill, C. D., & Merz, Jr., K. M.(2011). The Energy Computation Paradox and *ab initio* Protein Folding. *PLoS ONE,* Vol. 6, No. 4, (Apr 2011) pp. e18868, ISSN e1932-6203

Fiser, A. & Sali, A.(2003). Modeller: generation and refinement of homology-based protein structure models. *Methods Enzymol,* Vol. 374, (Dec 2003) pp. 461-91, ISSN 978-0-12-182777-9

Hamelryck, T., Borg, M., Paluszewski, M., Paulsen, J., Frellsen, J., Andreetta, C., Boomsma, W., Bottaro, S., & Ferkinghoff-Borg, J.(2010). Potentials of Mean Force for Protein Structure Prediction Vindicated, Formalized and Generalized. *PLoS ONE*, Vol. 5, No. 11, (Nov 2010) pp. e13714, ISSN e1932-6203

Hart, W. E. & Istrail, S.(1997). Robust proofs of NP-hardness for protein folding: general lattices and energy potentials. *J Comput Biol*, Vol. 4, No. 1, (Jan 1997) pp. 1-22, ISSN 1066-5277 (print); 1557-8666 (electronic)

He, X. & Merz, K. M.(2010). Divide and Conquer Hartree-Fock Calculations on Proteins. *Journal of Chemical Theory and Computation*, Vol. 6, No. 2, (Jan 2010) pp. 405-411, ISSN 1549-9618 (print) 1549-9626 (electronic)

Hu, Z. & Jiang, J.(2010). Assessment of biomolecular force fields for molecular dynamics simulations in a protein crystal. *J Comput Chem*, Vol. 31, No. 2, (Jan 2010) pp. 371-80, ISSN 1096-987X

Humphrey, W., Dalke, A., & Schulten, K.(1996). VMD: visual molecular dynamics. *J Mol Graph*, Vol. 14, No. 1, (Feb 1996) pp. 33-38, ISSN 1093-3263

Ilyin, V. A., Abyzov, A., & Leslin, C. M.(2004). Structural alignment of proteins by a novel TOPOFIT method, as a superimposition of common volumes at a topomax point. *Protein Science: A Publication of the Protein Society*, Vol. 13, No. 7, (July 2004) pp. 1865-1874, ISSN 0961-8368

Jiang, L., Althoff, E. A., Clemente, F. R., Doyle, L., Röthlisberger, D., Zanghellini, A., Gallaher, J. L., Betker, J. L., Tanaka, F., Barbas, C. F., Hilvert, D., Houk, K. N., Stoddard, B. L., & Baker, D.(2008). *De novo* computational design of retro-aldol enzymes. *Science (New York, N.Y.)*, Vol. 319, No. 5868, (Mar 2008) pp. 1387-1391, ISSN 0036-8075 (print), 1095-9203 (electronic)

Kaplan, W. & Littlejohn, T. G.(2001). Swiss-PDB Viewer (Deep View). *Briefings in Bioinformatics*, Vol. 2, No. 2, (May 2001) pp. 195-197, ISSN 1477-4054 (print) 1467-5463 (electronic)

Karplus, K.(2009). SAM-T08, HMM-based protein structure prediction. *Nucleic Acids Res*, Vol. 37, No. Web Server issue, (July 2009) pp. W492-7, ISSN 1362-4962 (print)

Kim, D. E., Chivian, D., & Baker, D.(2004). Protein structure prediction and analysis using the Robetta server. *Nucleic Acids Res*, Vol. 32, No. Web Server issue, (Jul 2004) pp. W526-W531, ISSN 1362-4962 (print) 0305-1048 (electronic)

Kono, H. & Saven, J. G.(2001). Statistical theory for protein combinatorial libraries. packing interactions, backbone flexibility, and the sequence variability of a main-chain structure. *Journal of Molecular Biology*, Vol. 306, No. 3, (Feb 2001) pp. 607 - 628, ISSN 0022-2836

Kryshtafovych, A., Krysko, O., Daniluk, P., Dmytriv, Z., & Fidelis, K.(2009). Protein structure prediction center in CASP8. *Proteins*, Vol. 77, No. Suppl 9, (July 2009) pp. 5-9, ISSN 1097-0134

Kuhlman, B., Dantas, G., Ireton, G. C., Varani, G., Stoddard, B. L., & Baker, D.(2003). Design of a novel globular protein fold with atomic-level accuracy. *Science*, Vol. 302, No. 5649, (Nov 2003) pp. 1364--1368, ISSN 0036-8075 (print), 1095-9203 (electronic)

Lathrop, R. H.(1994). The protein threading problem with sequence amino acid interaction preferences is NP-complete. *Protein Engineering*, Vol. 7, No. 9, (Sep 1994) pp. 1059-1068, ISSN 1741-0134 (print) 1741-0126 (electronic)

Levinthal, C.(1968). Are there pathways for protein folding? *Journal de Chimie Physique et de Physicochimie Biologique*, Vol. 65, No. 1-4, (Jan 1968) pp. 44-45, ISSN 0021-7689

Lockless, S. W. & Ranganathan, R.(1999). Evolutionarily conserved pathways of energetic connectivity in protein families. *Science*, Vol. 286, No. 5438, (Oct 1999) pp. 295-299, ISSN 0036-8075 (print), 1095-9203 (electronic)

Luthy, R., Bowie, J. U., & Eisenberg, D.(1992). Assessment of protein models with three-dimensional profiles. *Nature*, Vol. 356, No. 6364, (Mar 1992) pp. 83--85, ISSN 0028-0836 (print)

Martínez-Castilla, L. P. & Rodríguez-Sotres, R.(2010). A score of the ability of a three-dimensional protein model to retrieve its own sequence as a quantitative measure of its quality and appropriateness. *PLoS One*, Vol. 5, No. 9, (Sep 2010) pp. e12483, ISSN e1932-6203

Melo, F. & Feytmans, E.(1998). Assessing protein structures with a non-local atomic interaction energy. *J Mol Biol*, Vol. 277, No. 5, (Apr 1998) pp. 1141-1152, ISSN 0022-2836

Mengersen, K. L. & Tweedie, R. L.(1966). Rates of convergence of the Hastings and Metropolis algorithms. *Annals of Statistics*, Vol. 24, No. 1, (Feb 1966) pp. 101-121, ISSN 0090-5364

Metropolis, N., Rosenbluth, A. W., Rosenbluth, M. N., Teller, A. H., & Teller, E.(1953). Equation of State Calculations by Fast Computing Machines. *The Journal of Chemical Physics*, Vol. 21, No. 6, (Jun 1953) pp. 1087-1092, ISSN 0021-9606 (print), 1089-7690 (electronic)

Pawlowski, M., Gajda, M. J., Matlak, R., & Bujnicki, J. M.(2008). MetaMQAP: a meta-server for the quality assessment of protein models. *BMC Bioinformatics*, Vol. 9, No. Sep, (Sep 2008) pp. 403, ISSN 1471-2105

Raha, K. & Merz, Jr, K. M.(2005). Large-scale validation of a quantum mechanics based scoring function: predicting the binding affinity and the binding mode of a diverse set of protein-ligand complexes. *J Med Chem*, Vol. 48, No. 14, (Jul 2005) pp. 4558-4575, ISSN 0022-2623 (print) 1520-4804 (electronic)

Rodriguez, R., Chinea, G., Lopez, N., Pons, T., & Vriend, G.(1998). Homology modeling, model and software evaluation: three related resources. *Bioinformatics*, Vol. 14, No. 6, (Jul 1998) pp. 523-528, ISSN 1460-2059 (print) 1367-4803 (electronic)

Rosales-León, L., Hernández-Domínguez, E. E., Gaytán-Mondragón, S., & Rodríguez-Sotres, R.(2012). Metal binding sites in plant soluble inorganic pyrophosphatases. An example of the use of ROSETTA design and hidden Markov models to guide the homology modeling of proteins. *Journal of the Mexican Chemical Society*, Vol. 56, No. 1, (Jan-Mar 2012) pp. 23-31, ISSN 1665-9686

Rose, P. W., Beran, B., Bi, C., Bluhm, W. F., Dimitropoulos, D., Goodsell, D. S., Prlic, A., Quesada, M., Quinn, G. B., Westbrook, J. D., Young, J., Yukich, B., Zardecki, C., Berman, H. M., & Bourne, P. E.(2011). The RCSB Protein Data Bank: redesigned web site and web services. *Nucleic Acids Res*, Vol. 39, No. Database issue, (Jan 2011) pp. D392-D401, ISSN 1362-4962 (print) 0305-1048 (electronic)

Röthlisberger, D., Khersonsky, O., Wollacott, A. M., Jiang, L., DeChancie, J., Betker, J., Gallaher, J. L., Althoff, E. A., Zanghellini, A., Dym, O., Albeck, S., Houk, K. N., Tawfik, D. S., & Baker, D.(2008). Kemp elimination catalysts by computational enzyme design.

Nature, Vol. 453, No. 7192, (May 2008) pp. 190-195, ISSN 0028-0836 (print) 1476-4687 (electronic)

Roy, A., Kucukural, A., & Zhang, Y.(2010). I-TASSER: a unified platform for automated protein structure and function prediction. *Nat Protoc,* Vol. 5, No. 4, (Mar 2010) pp. 725-738, ISSN 1754-2189 (print) 1750-2799 (electronic)

Sayers, E. W., Barrett, T., Benson, D. A., Bolton, E., Bryant, S. H., Canese, K., Chetvernin, V., Church, D. M., Dicuccio, M., Federhen, S., Feolo, M., Geer, L. Y., Helmberg, W., Kapustin, Y., Landsman, D., Lipman, D. J., Lu, Z., Madden, T. L., Madej, T., Maglott, D. R., Marchler-Bauer, A., Miller, V., Mizrachi, I., Ostell, J., Panchenko, A., Pruitt, K. D., Schuler, G. D., Sequeira, E., Sherry, S. T., Shumway, M., Sirotkin, K., Slotta, D., Souvorov, A., Starchenko, G., Tatusova, T. A., Wagner, L., Wang, Y., John Wilbur, W., Yaschenko, E., & Ye, J.(2010). Database resources of the National Center for Biotechnology Information. *Nucleic Acids Res,* Vol. 38, No. suppl 1, (Jan 2010) pp. D5-16, ISSN 1362-4962 (print) 0305-1048 (electronic)

Schuster-Böckler, B. & Bateman, A.(2005). Visualizing profile, profile alignment: pairwise HMM logos. *Bioinformatics,* Vol. 21, No. 12, (Jun 2005) pp. 2912-2913, ISSN 1367-4803 (print) 1460-2059 (electronic)

Shapiro, L. W. & Zeilberger, D.(1982). A Markov chain occurring in enzyme kinetics. *Journal of Mathematical Biology,* Vol. 15, No. 3, (Nov 1982) pp. 351-357, ISSN 0303-6812

Shi, S., Pei, J., Sadreyev, R. I., Kinch, L. N., Majumdar, I., Tong, J., Cheng, H., Kim, B.-H., & Grishin, N. V.(2009). Analysis of CASP8 targets, predictions and assessment methods. *Database (Oxford),* Vol. 2009, (Apr 2009) pp. bap003, ISSN 1758-0463

Slovic, A. M., Kono, H., Lear, J. D., Saven, J. G., & DeGrado, W. F.(2004). Computational design of water-soluble analogues of the potassium channel KcsA. *Proc Natl Acad Sci U S A,* Vol. 101, No. 7, (Feb 2004) pp. 1828-1833, ISSN 1091-6490

Socolich, M., Lockless, S. W., Russ, W. P., Lee, H., Gardner, K. H., & Ranganathan, R.(2005). Evolutionary information for specifying a protein fold. *Nature,* Vol. 437, No. 7058, (Sep 2005) pp. 512-8, ISSN 0028-0836 (print) 1476-4687 (electronic)

Srinivasan, R., Fleming, P. J., & Rose, G. D.(2004). Ab initio protein folding using LINUS. *Methods Enzymol,* Vol. 383, (Apr 2004) pp. 48-66, ISSN 978-0-12-391860-4

Wallace, I. M., Blackshields, G., & Higgins, D. G.(2005). Multiple sequence alignments. *Curr Opin Struct Biol,* Vol. 15, No. 3, (Jun 2005) pp. 261-266, ISSN 0959-440X

Wallner, B. & Elofsson, A.(2003). Can correct protein models be identified? *Protein Sci,* Vol. 12, No. 5, (May 2003) pp. 1073-1086, ISSN 1469-896X

Wilmanns, M. & Eisenberg, D.(1995). Inverse protein folding by the residue pair preference profile method: estimating the correctness of alignments of structurally compatible sequences. *Protein Eng,* Vol. 8, No. 7, (July 1995) pp. 627-39, ISSN 1741-0134 (print) 1741-0126 (electronic)

Xu, D., Zhang, J., Roy, A., & Zhang, Y.(2011). Automated protein structure modeling in CASP9 by I-TASSER pipeline combined with QUARK-based ab initio folding and FG-MD-based structure refinement. *Proteins,* Vol. 79, No. S10, (Aug 2011) pp. 147-160, ISSN 1097-0134

Yamamoto, K., Miyake, H., Kusunoki, M., & Osaki, S.(2010). Crystal structures of isomaltase from *Saccharomyces cerevisiae* and in complex with its competitive inhibitor maltose. *FEBS J,* Vol. 277, No. 20, (Oct 2010) pp. 4205-14, ISSN 1742-4658

Intelligent Data Analysis

Bacterial Promoter Features Description and Their Application on *E. coli in silico* Prediction and Recognition Approaches

Scheila de Avila e Silva and Sergio Echeverrigaray

Additional information is available at the end of the chapter

1. Introduction

The determination of when and how genes are "turned on and off" is a challenge in pos-genomic era. Differences between two species are closer to gene expression and regulation than to gene structures (Howard & Benson, 2002). The first and key step in gene expression is promoter recognition by RNA polymerase enzyme (RNAP). The promoter sequences can be defined as cis-acting elements located upstream of the transcription start site (TSS) of open reading frames (ORF). To make an analogy, genes represent the "computer memory" and promoters represent the "computer program" which acts on that memory. The study about promoters can assist in providing new models about the constitution of the computer program and how it operates (Howard & Benson, 2002).

The proper regulation of transcription is crucial for a single-cell prokaryote since its environment can change dramatically and instantly (Huffmann & Brennan, 2002). In face of this, the detailing of the principals and the organization of transcriptional process is helpful for understanding the complexity of biological systems involved, for instance, cellular responses to environmental changes or in the molecular bases of many diseases caused by microbes (Janga & Collado-Vides, 2007).

While several sequenced genomes have their protein-coding gene repertoire well described, the accurate identification and delineation of cis-regulatory elements remain elusive (Fauteux et al., 2008). At this moment, the challenges are to analyze the available sequences and to locate TSS, promoters and other regulatory sequences (Askary et al., 2009). The purpose of this review is to provide a brief survey of promoter sequences characteristics and the advances of computer algorithms for their analysis and prediction. This chapter is organized in two main sections. The established knowledge about biological features of the promoters will be described in the first section, focusing in their genetic role and sequence content constitution. This is an important topic for understanding the intrinsic difficulties in the *in silico* promoter prediction approaches. The second section is devoted to give a reasonably concise background of the most used methodologies for *E. coli* promoter prediction and recognition, presenting their applications, as well as their limitations.

2. The bacterial promoter sequences

A common feature of the transcriptional regulators is their ability to recognize specific DNA patterns in order to modulate gene expression (Jacques et al., 2006). The upstream regulatory region of the bacterial coding regions contains the promoter, that is, the DNA sequence which determines specific recognition by RNAP (Barrios et al., 1999). The following section presents a concerned description about the promoter sequences and their role as gene expression regulators.

2.1. Promoter sequences and gene expression specificity

In bacteria, RNAP holoenzyme consists of five subunits ($2\alpha,\beta,\beta',\omega$) and an additional sigma (σ) subunit factor (Figure 1). A collection of different σ subunits act as key regulators of bacterial gene expression. The σ factor led RNAP sequence-specific binding at promoter where melting of the DNA double strand occurs (Borukov & Nudler, 2003). The substitution of one σ factor by another can initiate the transcription of different groups of genes (Schultzaberger et al., 2006). The numbers of σ factors encoded in bacterial genomes is highly variable. It is possible that the number of σ factor genes is related to the diversity of lifestyles encountered by a bacterium (Janga & Collado-Vides, 2007).

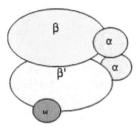

Figure 1. The RNAP enzyme (KEEG-modified[1]).
[1]Available on http://www.genome.jp/kegg/pathway/ko/ko03020.html).

The σ factors are labeled according to their molecular weight (e.g. σ^{24}, σ^{28}, σ^{32}, σ^{38}, σ^{54} and σ^{70}) and each one has been assigned to a global function role (Table 1). The σ^{70} is most commonly used σ factor in *E. coli*. It is the responsible for the bulk housekeeping transcriptional activity, for this reason it is responsible for the initiation of a large number of genes (Potvin & Sanschagrin, 2008; Schultzaberger et al., 2006).

Regardless of the σ factor, most of the promoters can be dissected into two functional sites, known as the -35 and -10 regions upstream of the TSS. Mutations in the consensus sequences of the promoters can affect the level of expression of the gene(s) they control, without altering the gene products themselves (Lewin, 2008). The canonical consensus and the number interspacing nucleotides recognized by the most important σ are presented on Table 1. Just for σ^{54}, the consensual region is located in the -12 and -24 nucleotides.

σ Factor	Gene	Cellular Uses	-35 consensus Region	Separation	-10 consensus Region	Reference
28	fliA	Flagellar genes	CTAAA	15 pb	GCCGATAA	Helmann & Chamberlin, 1987
32	rpoH	Heat shock Response	CCCTTGAA	13-15pb	CCCGATNT	Cowing et al., 1985
38	rpoS	Starvation Response	TTGACA	16-18pb	CTATACT	Typas et al., 2007
54	rpoN	Nitrogen Metabolism	CTGGNA	6pb	TTGCA	Barrios et al., 1999
70	rpoD	Housekeeping	TTGACA	16-18pb	TATAAT	Lisser & Margalit, 1993
24	rpoE	Heat shock Response	GGAACTT	15pb	GTCTAA	Rhodius et al.,2006

Table 1. *E. coli* σ factors and their promoter sequences binding sites (LEWIN, 2008).

A comprehensive study of the promoter content information was carried out by Schultzaberger et al. (2006). The authors have used the Claude Shannon's information theory and have built a promoter model by aligning and refining of 559 sequences upstream of TSS. The results for the promoter motifs showed, among others, two interesting results: *(i)* the difference of TSS prokaryotic information (0.39+-0.06 bits) in opposite to eukaryotic TSS (~3bits) and, *(ii)* the notorious high degree of conservation of the last nucleotide (T) in the -10 region. Another important discussion described in the paper is about the -10 extended region. According to Hook-Barnard et al. (2006), some promoters are functional without the -35 region and this missing information is compensated by four nucleotides upstream of the -10 element. Its consensus sequence is TRTG (according to IUPAC code, the letter R represents A or G). About this issue, the authors suggest that in prokaryotes the extended -10 may be an evolutionary predecessor to the modern bipartite promoter or vice versa. However, the second possibility does not explain the origin of bipartite promoter.

As it has been related so far, the promoter motifs are not strictly conserved within a set of promoters recognized by a given σ factor and also differ according to the σ factor which recognizes them. The structure of bacterial promoters limits the efficacy of prediction by a global analysis approach. A limited analysis of a putative promoter sequence by comparison with the σ^{70} promoter consensus motif can lead to an unacceptable rate of false negatives and incorrect assignments (de Avila e Silva et al., 2011).

2.2. Structural properties of promoter sequences

The motifs obtained from promoter sequences compilation are indicative of the existence of a nucleotide signal in them. Nonetheless, it also been demonstrated that primary DNA sequence is not the only source of information in the genome for the transcription regulatory process (Olivares-Zavaleta et al., 2006). According to many authors (e.g, Kanhere & Bansal, 2005a; Klaiman et al., 2009; Wang & Benham, 2006), not only regulatory sequences contain specific sequence elements that serve as target for interacting proteins, but also present different properties, such as: suitable geometrical arrangement of DNA (curvature), propensity to adopt a deformed conformation facilitating the protein binding (flexibility) and physical properties (e.g., stacking energy, stability, stress-induced duplex destabilization). Several studies have reported that eukaryotic and prokaryotic σ^{70}-dependent promoter sequences have lower stability, higher curvature and lesser flexibility than coding sequences (Gabrielian & Bolshoy, 1999; Kanhere & Bansal, 2005a).

DNA stability is a sequence-dependent property based on the sum of the interactions between the dinucleotides of a given sequence. It is possible to calculate the DNA duplex stability and to predict the melting behavior if the contribution of each nearest-neighbor interaction is known (SantaLucia & Hicks, 2004). A eukaryotic and prokaryotic promoter stability analysis was carried out by Kanhere & Bansal (2005a). The authors reported that promoters from three bacteria which have different genome composition (A+T composition: *E. coli* 0.49, *B. subtilis* 0.56 and *C. glutamicum* 0.46) show low stability peak around the -10 region. It is also reported that the average stability of upstream region is lower than the average stability of downstream region.

Intrinsic DNA curvature and bendability were shown to be important as physical basis in many biological processes, in particular in those which have interaction of DNA with DNA-binding site proteins, such as transcription initiation and termination, DNA origins of replication and nucleosome positioning (Gabrielian & Bolshoy, 1999; Jáuregui et al., 2003; Nickerson & Achberger, 1995; Thiyagarajan et al., 2006). Specifically, bending is related with twists and short bends of approximately 3 base-pairs, while curvature refers to loops and arcs involving around 9 base-pairs (Holloway et al., 2007). DNA curvature in prokaryotes is usually present upstream of the promoter but sometimes within the promoter sequence (Jáuregui et al., 2003; Kozobay-Avraham et al., 2006). The distribution of curved DNA in promoter regions is evolutionarily preserved, since orthologous groups of genes with highly curved upstream regions were identified (Kozobay-Avraham et al., 2006). As related by Pandey & Krishnamachari (2006), sequences derived from non-coding regions had similar overall base composition but different curvature values from promoter regions, indicating that the differences in curvature values are not just the consequence of base composition but also the organization of bases in sequences.

Another DNA feature that can distinguish promoter sequences is stress-induced DNA duplex destabilization (SIDD). According to Wang & Benham (2006), SIDD is not directly related to primary sequence alone, nor equivalent to stability of DNA double helix. In this complex process, the differences between the energy cost of strand separation for the specific base pairs involved and the energy benefit from fractional relaxation of the superhelical stress provides the energies that govern SIDD. Promoters are strongly associated with regions of low SIDD energy. Certain non-coding regions containing promoters or terminators are unstable, while transcripted regions remain stably duplexed under the stress imposed by negative superhelicity. The change of the level of superhelicity on a promoter region can shows a variety of effects on the expression of the genes it encodes (Wang & Benham, 2006).

As related so far, the promoters present organizational properties which, in different scales, may play a significant role in the transcription process. Recent studies have reported promising results using DNA structural or biophysical properties as predictors of promoter regions, either alone or associated with the sequence composition. A concerned description of these approaches and their results will be presented in the next section.

3. *In silico* promoter prediction

In silico promoters prediction and recognition is an active research topic in molecular biology and a challenge in bioinformatics. The correct classification of a given DNA sequence as promoter or non promoter improves genome annotation and allows generating hypotheses in the context of the bacterial transcription initiation process and gene function (de Avila e Silva et al., 2011; Jacques et al., 2006).

Experimental methods applied to the identification of promoters by molecular methods can be laborious, time-consuming and expensive. Consequently, it is important to develop algorithms that can rapidly and accurately evaluate the presence of promoters (Jacques et al., 2006; Li & Lin, 2006). A variety of *in silico* techniques have been used to identify TSS and to characterize σ factor-DNA interactions. Despite the wide range of research carried out in promoter prediction, these techniques are still not fully developed, particularly for genome scale applications. Currently, many programs for promoters and TSS prediction are available. However, their results are not completely satisfactory due to their rate of false positive predictions (Askary et al., 2008; Li & Lin, 2006). An overview about how to evaluate a classification performance of a given approach and the results of some published papers especially devoted to improve promoter prediction will be described in the following sections.

3.1. Performance measures for the evaluation of promoter classification programs

A classification model (or classifier) is a mapping from instances of predicted classes (Fawcett, 2006). The promoter prediction problem is a kind of binary classification, as the input sequence can be classified in only one class of two non-overlapping classes (Sokolova & Lapalme, 2009). The result of a classifier during testing is based on the counting of the correct and incorrect classifications from each class (Bradley, 1997). In this way, the four possible outcomes of a classification model evaluate this correctness (Bradley, 1997; Fawcett, 2006; Sokolova & Lapalme, 2009):

i.   TP: promoter sequences classified as promoter (true positive);
ii. TN: non-promoter sequences recognized as non-promoters (true negative);
iii. FP: non-promoter sequences classified as promoter (false positive);
iv. FN: promoters classified as non-promoter sequences (false negative).

This information is then normally displayed in a two-by-two confusion matrix (Table 2). A confusion matrix is a form of contingency table showing the differences between the true and predicted classes for a set of labeled examples (Bradley, 1997).

Data Class	Classified as promoter	Classified non-promoter
Promoter	True positive (TP)	False negative (FN)
Non-promoter	False positive (FP)	True negative (TN)

Table 2. Confusion matrix for classification results

Although the confusion matrix shows the whole information about the classifier's performance, it is the basis for many common metrics (Bradley, 1997; Fawcett, 2006). The often used performance measures are accuracy, sensitivity, specificity, precision and receiver operating characteristics ROC graphs. Their formulas are presented in equations 1 to 4. The accuracy measure gives an overall effectiveness of a classifier. Alternative measures are sensitivity (proportion of observed promoter sequences that are predicted as such) and specificity (probability of a classifier identifies non-promoter sequences). Additionally, the precision is related to the class agreement of identified promoters given by the classifier (Sokolova & Lapalme, 2009). A reliable performance of a promoter prediction program is the harmonic average of the sensitivity and specificity. A ROC graph is a technique for visualizing, organizing and selecting classifiers based on their performance (Figure 2). ROC graph allows visualizing and selecting classifiers based on their performance. It is presented as two-dimensional graphs in which TP rate is plotted on the Y

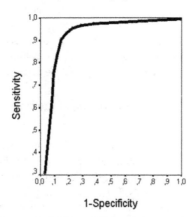

1-Specificity

Figure 2. An example of ROC curve obtained from NN simulations results of *E. coli* promoter prediction and recognition (de Avila e Silva et al., 2011b)

axis and FP rate is plotted on the X axis. A common method associated with the ROC graph is to calculate the area under the ROC curve, abbreviated AUC. The AUC of a classifier is equivalent to the probability that the classifier will rank a randomly chosen positive instance higher than a randomly chosen negative instance. Further information about the ROC curve can be found in Fawcett (2006).

$$Accuracy = \frac{TP + TN}{TN + TP + FN + FP} \tag{1}$$

$$Specificity = \frac{TN}{TN + FP} \tag{2}$$

$$Sensibility \ or \ recall = \frac{TP}{TP + FN} \tag{3}$$

$$Precision = \frac{TP}{TP + FP} \tag{4}$$

3.2. Position-weight matrices

Consensus sequences have been used to predict promoters by simple pattern matching. These strategies for promoter identification are usually based on a prior knowledge of some characterized sequences (Jacques et al., 2006). The first alignments of E. coli promoters were carried out by Hawley & McClure (1983), Galas et al. (1985), Lisser & Margalit (1993). From those compilations, the promoter consensual motifs were established.

A more sophisticated approach based on alignment is the Position-Weight Matrix (PWM). In this two-dimensional array, the rows represent one of the nucleotides A, T, C or G and the columns represent the analyzed motif. This accepted method yields results by aligning examples of referenced sequences, which allow estimating the base preference at each position of a matrix (Song et al., 2007). A weight is assigned to each base at each position in the promoter sequence and the final score of a candidate sequence decreases according to given differences of the reference matrix. Detailed information about the first implementations and the mathematical background can be found in Stormo (2000).

Huerta & Collado-Vides (2003) use a two stage PWM code-named Cover. This approach searches for conserved motifs using multiple sequence alignment methods and generates weight matrices for σ^{70}-dependent promoter sequences. Aiming to select the best matrices, the authors added some criteria, such as the spacers between -10 and -35 hexamers, the distance from -10 region and the start codon, the distance from -10 region and the TSS, and statistical analysis and the matrix score. Despite the 86% of predictive capacity of this approach, the accuracy obtained was 53%. This value indicates that this approach presents a high number of false positives.

Li & Lin (2006) have proposed a variation from PWMs called Position Correlation Scoring Matrix (PCSM). This approach considers the position-specific weight matrices at ten specific positions for the promoter. A PCSM for promoter and another for non-promoter training sequences sets have been computed. For classifying a new test sequence, the resulted scores from promoter and negative PCSM were used. Based on those scores, the sequence was identified as promoter only if the score was higher for positive PCSM. The results achieved in this paper present sensitivity of 91% and specificity of 81%. In order to predict promoters in the whole genome, the PCSM was applied and all the 683 experimentally identified σ^{70}-dependent promoter sequences were successfully predicted. Besides that, 1567 predictions were considered as probable promoters.

To predict σ^{28} promoter-dependent sequences of ten gamma-proteobacteria species, Song et al. (2007) carried out an alternative approach based on PWM named as Position Specific Score Matrix (PSSM). The species chosen were *E. coli, Bacillus subtilis, Campylobacter jejuni, Helicobacter pylori, Streptomyces coelicolor, Corynebacterium glutamicum, Vibrio cholera, Shewanella oneidensis, Xanthomonas oryzae* and *Xanthomonas campestris*. This approach involved two steps: *(i)* a simple pattern-matching with the short *E. coli* σ^{28} promoter consensus sequence (TAAAG-N$_{14}$-GCCGATAA) for predicting σ^{28} promoters upstream of mobility and chemotaxis genes in test species; *(ii)* these predicted promoters were used to generate a preliminary PSSM for each species. The total length of DNA analyzed for each bacteria was between 4×10^5 bp and 7×10^5 bp. The cut-off values chosen were set to control the false positive rate at 1 every 5×10^5 bp of sequence analyzed using random DNA sequence of 5×10^7 pb. Although the performance measures were not present by the authors, this paper is devoted to predict other promoter sequences than those recognized by σ^{70} and it shows interesting results about the σ^{28} consensual promoter sequences.

PWM models are commonly used because they are a simple predictive approach. Moreover, they are a convenient way to account for the fact that some positions are more conserved, than others (Stormo, 2000). However, in a large number of sequences the consensus can be insufficiently conserved, that is, they present insertions, deletions, variable spacing between elements or they are difficult to define. In such cases, this approach yield many false predictions (Kalate *et al.*, 2003). Another limitation is the assumption that the occurrence of a given nucleotide at a position is independent of the occurrence of nucleotides at other positions (Stormo, 2000). Additionally, the use of this approach is highly influenced by the cut-off value chosen, since low cut-off values encourage a high false positive rate, while high cut-off values encourage a high false-negative rate (Song et al., 2007).

3.3. Machine Learning

Machine Learning (ML) concerns the development of computer algorithms which allow the machine to learn from examples. The classification (or pattern recognition) is an important application of ML techniques in bioinformatics due to their capability of capturing hidden knowledge from data. This is possible to achieve even if the underlying relationships are unknown or hard to describe. Additionally, they can recognize complex patterns in an automatic way or distinguish exemplars based on these patterns (Cen *et al.*, 2010; Sivarao *et al.*, 2010).

ML approaches usually split the data set into training and test groups. They learn from examples (training data), and the set of examples, which were not exposed to the classifier in the training process, are used to test the classification model. Among all ML techniques, Support Vector Machines (SVM) and Artificial Neural Network (ANN) applications have produced promising results in the promoter prediction problem. For this reason, the purpose of this section is to provide an explanation about the basic ideas of these two ML approaches.

3.3.1. Support vector machines

SVM has been applied to identify important biological elements including protein, promoters and TSS, among others. This technique is used in bioinformatics as not only it can represent complex nonlinear functions but it also has flexibility in modeling diverse sources of data. This approach, introduced by Vapnik and his collaborators in 1992, is usually implemented as binary classifiers and it yields results by two key concepts: the separation of the data set into two classes by a hyperplane, and the application of supervised learning algorithms denoted as kernel machines (Ben-Hur et al., 2008; Kapetanovic et al., 2004; Polat & Günes, 2007). In a simple way (Figure 3), SVM classifies the data by: *(i)* drawing a straight line which separates the positive examples in one side and negative examples in the other side and, *(ii)* computing the similarity of two points with the kernel function (Ben-Hur et al., 2008). The kernel function is crucial for SVM, since the knowledge captured from the data set is obtained if a suitable kernel is defined (Ben-Hur et al., 2008). Further information and mathematical background of SVM can be found in Abe (2010), Ben-Hur et al. (2008), and Zhang (2010).

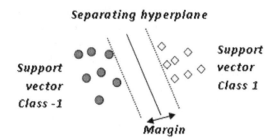

Figure 3. Representation of the basic idea of the SVM classification

Some published paper devoted to promoter prediction using SVM. L. Gordon et al. (2003) carried out SVM with alignment kernel in two different data sets: promoters and coding regions, and promoters and non-promoter intergenic regions. The average error achieved was 16.5% and 18.6%, respectively for the data sets used. This method is preferable in cases which present a sufficient number of known promoter regions, but might not know anything about their composition (L. Gordon et al., 2003). This tool is available online in http://nostradamus.cs.rhul.ac.uk/~leo/sak_demo/. Another SVM carried out by J. J. Gordon et al. (2006) made a joint prediction of *E. coli* TSS and promoter region. Their approach was based on an ensemble SVM with a variant of string kernel. This classifier combines a PWM and a model based on the distribution of distances from TSS to gene start. They have achieved results close to those previously described in the literature (average error rate of 11.6%). The authors report that their results open up the application of SVM on the prediction and recognition of special categories of regulatory motifs. Moreover, the authors also claim that this model can be broad to other bacterial species which present similar consensus sequences and TSS location.

By using a combination of feature selection and *least square support vector machine (LSSVM)*, Polat and Günes (2007) have proposed an approach named FS_LSSVM based in two steps. In the first step, the feature selection process was carried out aiming to reduce the dimensionality of *E. coli* promoter sequences with the use of C4.5 decision tree rules. As a result, the data set, which originally presented 57 attributes, was reduced to 4 attributes. After this process, the second step made the prediction of promoter sequences with the application of the LSSVM algorithm. The success rate (capability of recognizing promoter sequences) of this approach was of 100%. In face of this result, the authors claim that FS_LSSVM has the highest success rate and can be helpful in the promoter prediction and recognition issue. Nonetheless, this approach was carried out in a small data set (53 promoters and 53 non-promoters sequences) which does not represent the available entire set of *E. coli* σ^{70}-dependent promoter sequences (600 sequences experimental identified, approximately). In a small data set, the lack of conservation that characterizes bacterial promoter sequences cannot be detected, explaining the high efficiency reported.

The SVM algorithms present many advantages in their use when compared with other methods. First of all, SVM produces a unique solution since it is basically a linear problem. Second, SVM is able to deal with very large amounts of dissimilar information. Third, the discriminant function is characterized by only a comparatively small subset of the entire training data set, thus making the computations noticeably faster (Kapetanovic et al., 2004). On the other hand, a problem of SVM is its slow training, as it is trained by solving a quadratic programming problem with the number of variables equal to the number of training data (Abe, 2010).

3.3.2. Artificial Neural Networks

The artificial neural networks (ANN) are powerful computational tools inspired (they are not a faithful models of biological neural or cognitive phenomena) on the structure and behavior of biological neurons (Hilal et al., 2008; Wu, 1996). As in the human brain, the basic unit of ANN is called artificial neuron (Figure 4b), and it can be considered as a processing unit which performs a weighted sum of inputs (Hilal et al., 2008). In a simplest form, ANN can be viewed as a graphical model consisting of networks with interconnected units. The connection from a unit *j* to unit *i* usually has a weight denoted by W_{ij}. The weights represent information being used by the net to solve a problem (Wu, 1996).

Bacterial Promoter Features Description and Their Application on E. coli in silico Prediction and Recognition Approaches

251

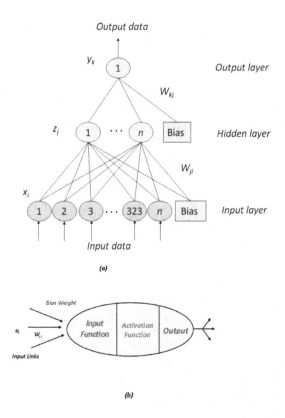

Figure 4. In (a) an example of MLP architecture and in (b) an artificial neural representation

The way by which the neurons are interconnected defines the ANN architecture. There are many kinds of architecture, but this review describes only the multilayer perceptron (MLP) architecture. The reasons for this choice are the capability of MLP capture and discover high-order correlations and/or relationships in input data and its wide applicability on promoter prediction (Hilal et al., 2008; Wu, 1996). Three-layer ANN (Figure 4a) is known as universal classifier as it is able to classify any labeled data correctly if there are no identical data in different classes (Baldi & Brunak, 2001).

The MLP presents three kinds of layers: input layer, output layer, and hidden layers (Figure 4a). The input layer contains the neurons which receive the information from external sources and passes this information to the hidden layer for network processing. The use of hidden neurons makes the learning process harder to visualize, since the search has to be conducted in a much larger space of possible functions in order to decide how input features should be represented by the hidden neurons. The output layer contains neurons that receives processed information and sends output signals out of the system. In all layers there is a bias input which provides a threshold for the activation of neurons (Hilal et al., 2008). The neurons in a given layer are fully connected by weights with the neurons on the adjacent layer. Each layer is comprised of a determined number of neurons. The number of input neurons corresponds to the number of input variables into the ANN, and the number of output neurons is the same as the number of desired output variables. The number of neurons in the hidden layer(s) depends on the application of the network (Hilal et al., 2008).

MLPs have been applied successfully to solve many problems by training them in a supervised way with a highly popular algorithm known as back-propagation (Wu, 1996). This algorithm is the most widely used to adjust the connection weights. During the training of multilayer neural networks classifiers, the weights are usually corrected so that the sum of squares error between the network outputs and the desired output are minimized (Abe, 2010).

The first NN promoter prediction, as presented by Demeler and Zhou (1991), had simple architecture and the results showed high accuracy and false positive rate. More complex architectures were applied by Mahadevan and Ghosh (1994), who used a combination of two ANN to identify *E. coli* promoters of all spacing classes (15 to 21 bases). The first ANN was used to predict the consensus motifs, while the second was designed to predict the entire sequence containing varying spacer lengths. Since the second NN used the information of the entire sequence, there were possible dependencies between the bases in various positions. This procedure presents as result a poor prediction (recall). To predict and find relevant signals related to TSS, Pedersen and Engelbrecht (1995) devised two ANN with different windows on the input data. An interesting result obtained from the sequence content information analysis suggests that important regions for promoter recognition include more positions on the DNA than usually assumed (-10 and -35 region). In spite of the high false positive rate, the interesting idea of both papers was to measure the relative information and the dependencies between bases in various positions. A comprehensive summary of the first ANNs application on promoter prediction can be obtained from Wu (1997).

Neural Networks Promoter Prediction (NNPP) is - up to now - one of the few online available tools (http://www.fruitfly.org/seq_tools/promoter.html). NNPP was originally developed to predict core promoter regions in *Drosophila melanogaster* (Reese, 2001). However, this tool was also trained to predict *E. coli* promoter sequences. NNPP is based on a neural network where the prediction for each promoter sequence element is combined in time-delay neural networks for a complete promoter site prediction (Reese, 2001). An improved version of NNPP was obtained by addition of the distance between the TSS and TLS (Burden et al., 2005). Despite the improved sensitivity (86%), the NNPP approach gives a large number of false positives (precision 54%).

DNA promoter information, other than nucleotide composition, was used as ANN input data by several authors. Rani *et al.* (2007) propose a global feature extraction scheme which extracts an average signal from the entire promoter sequence of 80 bp length. The resulting signal was composed by a combination of promoter dinucleotides. After this procedure,

MLP training was carried out with the promoter signal as positive examples and four different negative data sets: *(i)* genes, *(ii)* genes and non-promoter intergenic sequences, *(iii)* 60% AT reach random sequences and *(iv)* 50% AT reach random sequences. The specificity values for each data set were 79%, 88%, 98% and 99%, respectively. For the sensitivity, the results achieved were 80%, 63%, 93% and 95%. After the ANN results simulations, the authors spliced the promoter data in two linearly separable groups: a major data set and a minor data set. The first group was composed by sequences which were correctly classified by ANN, and the misclassified sequences were grouped in the minor data set. Although it was possible to separate the sequences in two groups, both set of promoter sequences showed a similar signal in the dinucleotide space. The authors claim that the feature extraction and classification methods are generic enough to be applied to the more complex problem of eukaryotic promoter recognition. Although highly efficient, this approach is limited to the AT-rich sigma sequences like σ^{70}, as showed by the promoter sequence description obtained from de Avila e Silva et al. (2011).

By using an ANN architecture fed by difference in DNA stability values between upstream and downstream regions in vicinity of known TSS, Askary *et al.* (2009) presented an approach named N4 devoted to *E. coli* TSS prediction. In this paper, the ANN input sequence slides a 414-nucleotides window with sliding size of one nucleotide. Each window was applied in the form of 413 nearest neighbors (or dinucleotides). The results obtained show sensitivity and precision of 94%. The initial state of this ANN was the Kanhere and Bansal's algorithm (described in the section 3.4) which was improved by the training process. In fact, the authors transpose the idea of the Kanhere and Bansal's algorithm into the ANN architecture. An interesting result presented in this paper, was the analysis of how the promoter information was used by N4 to learn. They show that N4 learn from the -10 and -35 motifs, and the +160 position. A single alteration at the +160 position makes N4 to recognize a non-promoter sequence as promoter. This position is downstream of TLS which indicates that this approach probably uses the position of ORF for the accurate prediction of TSS.

Rani and Bapi (2007) used *n*-gram as feature for a neural network classifier for promoter prediction in *Escherichia coli* and *Drosophila melanogaster*. An *n*-gram is defined as a selection of *n* contiguous characters from a given character stream. The authors show that the number of *n*-grams which presents the best results for *E. coli* was n=3 against a negative examples set consisting of gene and non-promoter intergenic segments. The performance measures presented were: sensitivity of 67.75%, specificity of 86.10% and precision of 80.0%. According to the authors, these results reinforces the idea that 3-grams usage a pattern which can distinguishing a promoter of other sequences, since higher order *n*-grams features was not powerful enough to discriminate promoter and non-promoter. In addition to this result, the authors apply challenge the 3-grams on promoter identification in the whole genome. The identification of 19 NCBI annotated promoters was 100% positive and encouraging them to propose this methodology as a potential promoter annotation tool.

An ANN-based approach was used by de Avila e Silva et al. (2011) for promoter prediction according to the σ factor which recognizes the sequence. This bioinformatics tool, denoted as BacPP, was developed by weighting rules extracted from ANNs trained with promoter sequences known to respond to a specific σ factor. The information obtained from the rules was weighted to optimize promoter prediction and classification of the sequences according to σ factor which recognize them. The accuracy results for *E. coli* were 86.9%, 92.8%, 91.5%, 89.3%, 97.0% and 83.6% for σ^{24}, σ^{28}, σ^{32}, σ^{38}, σ^{54} and σ^{70} dependent promoter sequences, respectively. As related by the authors, the sensitivity and specificity results showed similar values, indicating that this tool present a reduction of false positive rate. In contrast to tools previously reported in the literature, BacPP is not only able to identify bacterial promoters in background genome sequence, but it is also designed to provide pragmatic classification according to σ factor. By separating the promoter sequences according their σ factor which recognize them, the authors have demonstrated that the current boundaries of prediction and classification of promoters can be dissolved. Moreover, when applied to a set of promoters from diverse *enterobacteria*, the accuracy of BacPP was 76%, indicating that this tool can be reliably extended beyond the E. coli model.

In spite of the ANN capability capture imprecise and incomplete patterns, such as individual promoter motifs including mismatches (Cotik et al., 2005), this ML approach can present some intrinsic difficulties. Many decisions related to the choice of ANN structure and parameters are often completely subjective. The final ANN solution may be influenced by a number of factors (e.g., starting weights, number of cases, number of training cycles, etc.). Besides, the overtraining needs to be avoided, since it results in ANN which memorizes the data, instead of to do a generalization of them (Kapetanovic et al., 2004).

3.4. Other approaches

The symbolic representation of DNA nucleotides given by the letters A,T,G,C lead to many studies which aiming at understanding its structure through distributions, complexities, redundancy and statistical regularities (Krishnamachari et al., 2004). All this kind of information have a theoretical potential to be a distinguish feature of promoter sequences. Some papers are devoted to applied this features either alone or in combination with other approaches for improve promoter prediction results.

Kanhere and Bansal (2005b) developed their own promoter recognition approach based on differences of DNA stability between promoter and coding regions. That tool was improved by Rangannan e Bansal (2007) and achieves sensitivity of 98% and a just precision of 55%. The authors claim that this stability-based approach can be used to annotate entire genome sequences for promoter regions. According to the authors, the low precision can be reduced if it was combined with other sequence based methods. Additionally, they argue that this method can be used to investigate characteristic properties of specific subclasses of promoters, as well as other functional elements which no exhibit obvious consensus sequences.

Jacques et al. (2006) describe a novel approach based on matrices representing the genomic distribution of hexanucleotides pairs. The principal strategy was based on the observation that the promoters are over-represented in intergenic regions relative to the whole genome.

This approach was carried out for ten prokaryotic genomes and the analysis of characterized promoter sequences generates a sensibility of the matrices generated. These results present different sensibility values according to the analyzed bacteria. The lowest value was 29.4% for *C. glutamicum* and the highest value was 90.9% for *Bradyrhizobium japonicum*. For the other genomes (*E. coli, B. subtilis, S. coelicolor, H. pylori, C. jejuni, Staphylococcus aureus, Mycobacterium tuberculosis* and *Mycoplasma pneumonia*), the sensibility achieved was around 45%. According to the authors, these results suggest that transcription factor DNA binding sites from various bacterial species have a genomic distribution significantly different from that of non-regulatory sequences. Besides the lower sensitivity values for some species, this paper presents the potential of genomic distribution as indicator of DNA motif function. This algorithm took advantage of a yet unexploited concept, can be used in a wide variety of organisms, required almost no previous knowledge of promoter sequences to be effective and can be combined with other methodologies. Additionally, the authors claim that this approach can be designed to predict precise promoter sequences using any annotated prokaryotic genome.

The SIDD values were used by Wang and Benham (2006) for demonstrating that this information can be useful when applied to promoter prediction. They define a promoter as extending from positions -80 to +20 with respect to the TSS and they define strong SIDD as any value below 6 kcal/mole. SIDD values correctly predicted 74.6% of the real promoters with a false positive rate of 18%. When the SIDD values were combined with -10 motifs scores in a linear classification function, they predict promoter regions with better than 90% accuracy. The authors attribute their success to the fact that about 80% of documented promoters contain a strong SIDD site. The authors also observed a bimodal distribution of SIDD properties, which can reflect the complexity of transcriptional regulation, suggesting that SIDD may be needed to initiate transcription from some promoters, but not others.

4. Conclusions

A brief survey of currently *E. coli* promoter information and their recognition and prediction approaches was presented. In order to improve the *in silico* promoter prediction, an appreciation of the biological mechanistic of promoter sequences is necessary. In this way, the comprehensive analyses of bacterial promoter sequences revealed the fact that the sequence dependent properties are important and can be exploited in developing *in silico* tool for promoter prediction.

The currently available approaches described in this paper make efforts to reduce the number of false predictions. Recent bioinformatics applications are increasingly appreciating the DNA structural features and incorporating this kind of information for detecting promoter tools. Some works shows the advantage of the use of the feature selection or extraction process as an important part of pattern recognition, since this procedure can decrease the computation cost and increase the performance of the classification (Polat and Günes, 2009). One of the goals of promoter recognition is to locate promoter regions in the genome sequence. Predicting promoters on a genome-wide scale is problematic due to the higher number of false positive predictions caused by the large amount of DNA analyzed. It is important for consideration the fact that a given classification method is not universally better than other, since each method has a class of target functions for which it is best suited (Bradley, 1997).

Author details

Scheila de Avila e Silva and Sergio Echeverrigaray
University of Caxias do Sul, Brazil

Acknowledgement

The authors would like to express their gratitude to the University of Caxias do Sul by the financial support applied in the research project.

5. References

Abe, S. (2010). *Support vector machines for pattern classification*, Springer, ISBN 978-184-9960-97-7, London.

Askary, A.; Masoudi-Nejad, A.; Sharafi, R.; Mizbani, A.; Parizi, S. N.; Purmasjedi, M. (2009). N4: A precise and highly sensitive promoter predictor using neural network fed by nearest neighbors. *Genes & Genetic Systems*, Vol.84, No.6, pp. 425-430.

Baldi, P.; Brunak, S. (2001). *Bioinformatics: the machine learning approach*, (2. Ed), ISBN 0-262-02506-X, MIT Press, Cambridge.

Barrios, H.; Valderrama, B.; Morett, E. (1999). Compilation and analysis of σ54-dependent promoter sequences. *Nucleic Acids Research*, Vol.27, No.22, pp. 4305–4313.

Ben-Hur, A.; Ong, C. S.; Sonnenburg, S. Schölkopf, B., Rätsch, G. (2008). Support Vector Machines and Kernels for Computational Biology. *PLOS Computational Biology*, Vol. 4, No. 10, e1000173.

Borukov, S.; Nudler, E. (2003). RNA polymerase holoenzyme: structure, function and biological implications. *Current Opinion in Microbiology*, Vol.6, No.2, (April, 2003), pp. 93–100.

Boser, B. E., Guyon, I., and Vapnik, V. (1992). A training algorithm for optimal margin classifiers. In Computational Learing Theory, pages 144–152.

Bradley, A. P. (1997). The use of area under the ROC curve in the evaluation of Machine Learning algorithms. *Pattern Recognition*, Vol.30, No.7, pp. 1145–1159.

Burden, S.; Lin, Y.-X.; Zhang, R. (2005). Improving promoter prediction for the NNPP2.2 algorithm: a case study using Escherichia coli DNA sequences. *Bioinformatics*, Vol.21, No.5, pp. 601-607.

Cen, L.; Dong, M.; Yu, H. L. Z.L.;Chan, P. (2010). Machine learning methods in the application of speech emotion recognition, In: *Application of Machine Learning*, Y. Zhang (Ed.), pp.1-20, InTech, ISBN 978-953-307-035-3, India.

Cotik, V.; Zaliz, R. R.; Zwir, I. (2005). A hybrid promoter analysis methodology for prokaryotic genomes. *Fuzzy Sets and Systems*, Vol.152, No.1, (May, 2005), pp.83-102.

Cowing, D.W.; Bardwell, J.C.A.; Craig, E.A.; Woolford, C.; Hendrix, R.W.; Gross, C. (1985) Consensus sequence for *Escherichia coli* heat-shock gene promoters. *Proc. Natl. Acad. Sci*, Vol.80, pp. 2679–2683.

de Avila e Silva, S.; Echeverrigaray, S.; Gerhardt, G. J. L. (2011a). BacPP: Bacterial promoter prediction—A tool for accurate sigma-factor specific assignment in enterobacteria. *Journal of Theoretical Biology*, Vol.287, pp. 92-99.

de Avila e Silva, S.; Gerhardt, G. J. L.; Echeverrigaray, S. (2011b). Rules extraction from neural networks applied to the prediction and recognition of prokaryotic promoters. *Genetics and Molecular Biology*, Vol.34, No.2, pp. 353-360.

Demeler, B.; Zhou, G. (1991). Neural network optimization for *E. coli* promoter prediction. *Nucleic Acids Research*, Vol.19, No.,pp.1593-1599.

Fauteux, F.; Blanchette, M.; Strömvik, M. V. (2008). Seeder: discriminative seeding DNA motif discovery. *Bioinformatics*, Vol. 24, No. 20, pp 2303–2307.

Fawcett, T. (2006). An introduction to ROC analysis. *Pattern Recognition Letters*, Vol.27, pp. 861–874.

Gabrielian, A.; Bolshoy, A. (1999). Sequence complexity and DNA curvature. *Computers and Chemistry*, Vol.23, pp. 263–274.

Galas, D. J.; Eggert, M.; Waterman, M. S. (1985). Rigorous pattern-recognition methods for DNA sequences: Analysis of promoter sequences from *Escherichia coli*. *Journal of Molecular Biology*, Vol.186, No.1, (November, 1985), pp. 117–128.

Gordon, J. J.; Towsey, M. W.; Hogan, J. M.; Mathews, S. A.; Timms, P. (2006). Improved prediction of bacterial transcription start sites. *Bioinformatics*, Vol. 22, No.2, pp. 142-148.

Gordon, L.; Chervonenkis, A.; Gammerman, A. J.; Shahmuradov, I. A.; Solovyev, V. V. (2003). Sequence alignment for recognition of promoter regions. *Bioinformatics*, Vol.19, No.15, pp. 1964-1971.

Hawley, D. K.; McClure, W. R. (1983). Compilation and analysis of Escherichia coli promoter DNA sequences. *Nucleic Acids Research*, Vol.11, No.8, (April, 1983), pp. 2237–2255.

Helmann, J.D.; Chamberlin, M.J. (1987). DNA sequence analysis suggests that expression of flagellar and chemotaxis genes in *Escherichia coli and Salmonella typhimurium* is controlled by an alternative sigma factor. *Proc. Natl. Acad. Sci. USA,* Vol. 84, pp. 6422–6424.

Hilal, N.; Ogunbiyi, O. O.; Al-Abri, M. (2008). Neural network modeling for separation of bentonite in tubular ceramic membranes. *Desalination,* Vol. 228, pp. 175-182.

Hook-Barnard, I., Johnson, X.B., Hinton, D.M. *Escherichia coli* RNA polymerase enzyme of σ70- dependent promoter requiring a -35 DNA element and an extended -10 TGn motif, Journal of Bacteriology 188 (2006) 8352-8359.

Holloway, D.T.; Kon, M.; DeLisi, C. (2007). Machine learning for regulatory analysis and transcription factor target prediction in yeast. *Systems and Synthetic Biology,* Vol. 1, No. 1, pp. 25–47.

Howard, D.; Benson, K. (2002). Evolutionary computation method for pattern recognition of
   cis-acting sites. *BioSystems*, Vol.72, pp.19-27.

Huerta, A.M.; Collado-Vides, J. (2003) Sigma^{70} promoters in *Escherichia coli*: specific
   transcription in dense regions of overlapping promoter-like signals, *Journal of Molecular
   Biology*, Vol.333, pp. 261–278

Huffmann, J. L.; Brennan, R. G. (2002). Prokaryotic transcription regulators: more than just
   the helix-turn-helix motif. *Current Opinion in Structural Biology*, Vol.12, pp.98-106.

Jacques, P-E.; Rodrigue, S.; Gaudreau, L.; Goulet, J.; Brzezinski, R. (2006). Detection of
   prokaryotic promoters from the genomic distribution of hexanucleotides pairs. *BMC
   Bioinformatics*, Vol. 7:423.

Janga, S.C.; Collado-Vides, J. (2007). Structure and evolution of gene regulatory networks in
   microbial genomes. *Research Microbiology* Vol.158, pp. 787–794.

Jáuregui, R.; Abreu-Goodger, C.; Moreno-Hagelsieb, G., Collado-Vides, J.; Merino, E. (2003)
   Conservation of DNA curvature signals in regulatory regions of prokaryotic genes.
   Nucleic Acids Research, Vol. 31, No. 23, pp. 6770-6777.

Kalate, R. N., Tambe, S. S., Kulkarni, B. D., Artificial neural networks for prediction of
   mycobaterial promoter sequences, Computational Biology and Chemistry 27 (2003) 555-
   564.

Kanhere, A., Bansal, M. (2005a). Structural properties of promoters: similarities and
   differences between prokaryotes and eukaryotes. *Nucleic Acids Research*, Vol. 33, pp.
   3165-3175.

Kanhere, A., Bansal, M. (2005b). A novel method for prokaryotic promoter prediction based
   on DNA stability. *BMC Bioinformatics*, Vol.6, pp. 1471-2105.

Kapetanovic, M., Rosenfeld, S., Izmirlian, G. (2004). Overview of commonly used
   bioinformatics methods and their applications. Ann N Y Acad Sci 1020 10–21.

Klaiman, N. T.; Hosid, S.; Bolshoy, A.; (2009). Conservation of DNA curvature signals in
   regulatory regions of prokaryotic genes. *Computational Biology and Chemistry*, Vol. 33,
   pp. 275-282.

Kozobay-Avraham, L.; Hosid, S.; Volkovich, Z.; Bolshoy, A. (2006). Involvement of DNA
   curvature in intergenic regions. *Nucleic Acids Research*, Vol.34, No.8, pp. 2316-2327.

Krishnamachari, A.; Mondal, M.V.; Karmeshu (2004). Study of DNA binding sites using the
   Renyi parametric entropy measure. *Journal of Theoretical Biology*, Vol. 227, pp. 429–436

Lewin, B., 2008. *Genes IX*. Jones & Bartlett Publishers, ISBN 13:978-0-7637-4063-4, Sudbury.

Li, Q-Z., Lin H. (2006). The recognition and prediction of σ^{70} promoters in Escherichia coli K-
   12. *Journal of Theoretical Biology*, Vol.242, pp. 135–141.

Lisser, S.; Margalit, H. (1993). Compilation of E. coli mRNA promoter sequences, *Nucleic
   Acids Research*, Vol.21, No.7, pp. 1507–1516.

Mahadevan, I.; Ghosh, I. (1994). Analysis of *E. coli* promoter structures using neural
   networks. *Nucleic Acids Research*, Vol.22, pp. 2158-2165.

Nickerson, C.A.;Achberger, E.C. (1995). Role of curved DNA in binding of *Escherichia coli*
   RNA polymerase to promoters. *Journal of Bacteriology*, Vol.157, pp.5756-5761.

Olivares-Zavaleta, N.; Jáuregui, R.; Merino, E. (2006). Genome analysis of *Escherichi coli* promoters evidences that DNA static curvature plays a more important role in gene transcription than has previously been antecipated. *Genomics*, Vol. 87, pp. 329-337.

Pandey, S. P.; Krishnamachari, A. (2006). Computational analysis of plant RNA Pol-II promoters. *Biosystems*, Vol.83, pp. 38-50.

Pedersen, A. G. & Engelbrecht, J. Investigations of Escherichia coli promoter sequences with artificial neural networks: new signals discovered upstream of the transcriptional startpoint, Proc Int Conf Intell Syst Mol Biol 3 (1995) 292-299

Polat, K.; Günes, S. (2007). A novel approach to estimation of *E. coli* promoter gene sequences: Combining feature selection and least square support vector machine (FS_LSSVN). *Applied Mathematics and Computation*, Vol. 190, pp. 1574-1582.

Potvin, E.; Sanschagrin, F.; Levesque, R. C. (2008). Sigma factors in *Pseudomonas aeruginosa*, *Federation of European Microbiological Societies*, Vol.32, pp. 38–55.

Rangannan, V.; Bansal, M. (2007).Identification and annotation of promoter regions in microbial genome sequences on the basis of DNA stability. *Journal of Biosciences*, Vol.32, No.5, pp. 851-862.

Rani, T.S.; Bhavani, S.D.; Bapi, R.S. (2007) Analysis of *E. coli* promoter recognition problem in dinucleotide feature space. *Bioinformatics*, Vol.23, No.5, pp. 582-588.

Reese, M.G. (2001) Application of a time-delay neural network to promoter annotation in the *Drosophila melanogaster* genome. *Computers and Chemistry*, Vol.26, pp. 51-56.

Rhodius, V. A., W. C. Suh, G. Nonaka, J. West, and C. A. Gross. (2006). Conserved and variable functions of the σ^E stress response in related genomes. PLoS Biol. 4:0043-0059.

Santalucia, J. Jr.; Hicks, D. (2004). The thermodynamics of DNA Structural Motifs. *Annual Review of Biophysics and Biomolecular Structure*, Vol. 33, pp. 415-440.

Shultzaberger, R.K.; Chen, Z.; Lewis, K.A.; Schneider, T.D.; (2007). Anatomy of *Escherichia coli* σ^{70} promoters. *Nucleic Acids Research*, Vol.35, No.3, pp. 771–788.

Sivarao, P. B.; El-Tayeb, N. S. M.; Vengkatesh, V.C. (2010). Neural network multilayer perceptron modelling for surface quality prediction in laser machining, In: *Application of Machine Learning*, Y. Zhang (Ed.), pp.1-20, InTech, ISBN 978-953-307-035-3, India

Sokolova, M.; Lapalme, G. (2009). A systematic analysis of performance measures for classification tasks. *Information Processing and Management*, Vol.427, pp. 427-437.

Song, W.; Maiste, P.J.; Naiman, D.Q.; Ward, M.J. (2007). Sigma 28 promoter prediction in members of the Gammaproteobacteria. *Federation of European Microbiological Societies*, Vol.271, pp. 222-229.

Stormo, G.D. (2000). DNA binding sites: Representation and discovery. *Bioinformatics*, Vol.16, No.1, pp. 16-23.

Thiyagarajan, S.; Rajan, S.; Gautham, N. (2006). Effect of DNA structural flexibility on promoter strength - molecular dynamics studies of *E. coli* promoter sequences. *Biochemical and Biophysical Research Communications*, Vol.341, pp. 557–566.

Typas, A.; Becker, G; Hengge, R. (2007). The molecular basis of selective promoter activation by the σ^S subunit of RNA polymerase. *Molecular Microbiology,* Vol.63, No.5, pp. 1296–1306

Wang, H.; Benham, C. J. (2006). Promoter prediction and annotation of microbial genomes based on DNA sequences and structural responses to superhelical stress. *BMC Bioinformatics,* Vol. 7:248.

WU, Cathy H. (1996). Artificial neural networks for molecular sequence analysis. *Computers & Chemistry,* Vol. 21, No. 4, pp. 237-256.

Zhang, Y. (2010). *New Advances in Machine Learning,* InTech, ISBN 978-953-307-034-6, India.

Chapter 11

Novel microRNA Cloning Using Bioinformatics

Yoshiaki Mizuguchi, Takuya Mishima, Eiji Uchida and Toshihiro Takizawa

Additional information is available at the end of the chapter

1. Introduction

MicroRNAs (miRNAs) participate in several biological processes, including development, differentiation, apoptosis, and proliferation (**1, 2**) through imperfect pairing with target messenger RNAs (mRNAs) of protein-coding genes and transcriptional or post-transcriptional regulation of their expression (**3, 4**). Approaches to miRNA detection, such as parallel sequencing technologies may replace conventional sequencing (**5**). The GS 454 technology can produce a similar number of longer (100–150-nucleotides (nt)) sequence reads in a single analysis run, with the advantage that this method can derive the complete sequence of the mature miRNA. Moreover, recent studies on miRNA profiling performed with cloning techniques suggest that sequencing methods are suitable for the detection of novel miRNAs, modifications, and precise compositions, and that cloning frequencies calculated by clone count analysis strongly correlate with the concentrations measured by Northern blotting, and are reproducible. The achievement of comprehensive profiling of miRNA in human diseases requires exhaustive qualitative and quantitative analyses. Here we show the techniques and the some of the results of the miRNA transcriptomes in the liver using sequencing. This serves as a critical step in clarifying the functional significance of specific miRNAs as they relate to liver diseases.

2. Techiniques of MicroRNA cloning and bioinformatics for MiRNAome

2.1. MicroRNA cloning

The method for microRNA cloning and sequencing that we moderated from the original ones are shown in Fig1. We cloned small RNA by a modification of the published miRNA cloning protocol of Lagos-Quintana et al. (**6**). In brief, total RNA samples were extracted using ISOGEN (Nippon Gene, Tokyo, Japan), separated in a denaturing polyacrylamide gel, and the 18–24 nt fraction was recovered. Next, 5'- and 3'-adapters were ligated to the RNAs Ligation of small RNAs with DNA_RNA chimera linkers at both termini [3' linker oligonucleotide (5′/5 Phos/rCrUrGrUAGGCACCATCAATdi-deoxyC-3 ′) and the 5′ linker oligonucleotide (5′-ATCGTrArGrGrCrArCrCrUrGrArArA-3′)] and RT-PCR was carried out.

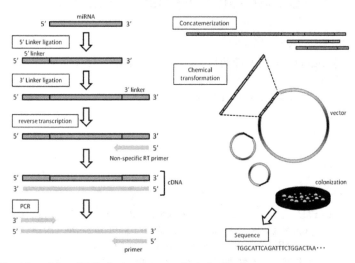

Figure 1. Overview of the miRNA cloning. See paper body for details.

Amplification of the cDNA fragments was obtained by two consecutive rounds of PCR. Specific restriction enzyme digestion of the adaptors allowed for concatemerization of the cDNA into larger fragments. These fragments were then cloned into a vector to create a cDNA library. Concatemerization increases the length of informative sequences obtainable from each clone. we concatenated more than 20 cDNAs into a single fragment using a BanI restriction enzyme (New England Biolabs, Ipswich, MA, USA), a DNA ligation kit ver. 2.1 (Takara Bio, Shiga, Japan), and a Geneclean III kit (Qbiogene, Irvine, CA, USA) prior to TA cloning. The concatenated products were then inserted into plasmids and sequenced (Fig1).

The sequences were compared to human DNA to determine the genomic origin of the small RNA. It was important to avoid contamination from other samples and molecular-weight makers during electrophoresis. Such contaminants considerably diminished the accuracy and efficiency of miRNA cloning. We avoided contamination by performing the cloning procedure separately for each sample, by using a special gel with a small plastic rod that divided the sample and marker lanes, and by using separate vats for each gel for ethidium bromide staining. We made small RNA libraries by excising a portion of a polyacrylamide gel containing species 18–24 nt in length to avoid contaminating our purified RNAs with piRNAs **(7)**.

2.2. Bioinformatics analysis of the sequence data

We performed a homology search for all cloned small RNAs and a secondary structural analysis for all novel miRNA candidates.

2.2.1. Comparing the cloned sequences with those of known RNAs

The vector sequence, the 5'and 3' linkers, and their coupled sequences (CTGTAGGCACCTGAAA) were removed. Those extracted sequences composed of 16–30 nt were defined as valid small RNAs and were subjected to followings. The small RNA sequences were analyzed for homology with known RNAs, including miRNA, piwi-interacting (pi) RNA, rRNA, tRNA, small nuclear (sn) RNA, small nucleolar (sno) RNA, and mRNA, and human genomic DNA sequences. The databases used were: miRNA (mature- and pre-), Sanger Database.; piRNA, the NCBI Entrez Nucleotide database; rRNA, the European ribosomal RNA database; tRNA, the Genomic tRNA database; sn/snoRNA, RNAdb and NONCODE; mRNA, NCBI Reference Sequence; and human genomic sequences, the UCSC Genome Bioinformatics Site. In our searches, we defined the cloned sequencing results that had higher than 90% homology as valid if they met our criteria for sequence error, erroneous PCR amplification, and 3'- and 5'-end variations. Clones with 100% homology with human genomic DNA but did not match known RNAs when compared to the above databases were termed novel miRNA candidates and were subjected to further analysis. The result is shown in table1.

Reads (%)	HCC	ANL	Sum
Total	314,359	268,708	583,067
miRNA	256,64 (81.6)	208,038 (77.4)	464,687 (79.7)
piRNA	2,983 (0.9)	1,440 (0.5)	4,423 (0.8)
rRNA	5,474 (1.7)	10,161 (3.8)	15,635 (2.7)
tRNA	1,703 (0.5)	621 (0.2)	2,324 (0.4)
snRNA	700 (0.2)	343 (0.1)	1,043 (0.2)
snoRNA	654 (0.2)	747 (0.3)	1,401 (0.2)
mRNA	6,053 (1.9)	7,279 (2.7)	13,332 (2.3)
Genome	2,799 (0.9)	3,149 (1.2)	5,948 (1.0)
Others	15,588 (5.0)	34,686 (12.9)	71,174 (12.2)

Table 1. Annotation of the sequenced small RNAs

2.2.2. Secondary structure analysis of Novel microRNAs

The two-dimensional precursor miRNA (pre-miRNA) configurations of our novel miRNA candidates were predicted according to the method described previously (8) with some modifications. Briefly, 196-nt of genomic sequence was added to the candidate sequences (88-nt at each end). Each candidate sequence was divided into 110-nt windows and subjected to two-dimensional analysis along its entire length, using the RNAfold software (Vienna RNA Secondary Structure Package (9)). The configurations that had the lowest free energy and that had a high conservation (described below) and met the following criteria were termed novel miRNAs: (a) contained a stem-loop configuration; (b) cloned mature miRNA sequence portion consisted of more than 16-nt in its double-stranded region; (c) the loop contained fewer than 20-nt; (d) the internal loop contained fewer than 10-nt; and (e) the bulge contained fewer than 5-nt. Furthermore, novel sequences with overlapping positions in the genome were grouped together. Novel antisense miRNAs are defined with above criteria (a)-(e) but without conservation score if they are coded in same chromosomal region.

2.2.3. Determination of hairpin conservation of Novel MicroRNAs

We classified all the candidate miRNAs using the PhastCon database at the University of California at Santa Cruz.(10, 11) This database has scores for each nucleotide in the human genome relative to its degree of conservation when compared to nucleotides in the armadillo, bush baby, cat, chicken, chimpanzee, cow, dog, elephant, frog, fugu, guinea pig, hedgehog, horse, lizard, medaka, mouse, opossum, platypus, rabbit, rat, rhesus monkey, shrew, stickleback, tenrec, tetraodon, tree shrew, and zebrafish. The algorithm is based on a phylogenetic hidden Markov model that uses best-in-genome pairwise alignment for each species (based on BLASTZ), followed by multiple alignment of the twenty eight genomes. A hairpin was defined as conserved if the average PhastCon conservation score over the 28 species for any 15-nt sequence in the hairpin stem was at least 0.8 .(12)

3. Other techniques for MicroRNAome

3.1. Real-time PCR analysis of known miRNAs

Real-time PCR was performed on an ABI7300 (Applied Biosystems, Foster City, CA, USA) using various mirVana qRTPCR primer sets (Ambion, Austin, TX, USA) and a SYBR ExScript RT-PCR kit (Takara Bio), or with TaqMan miRNAs assays (Applied Biosystems), a High capacity cDNA archive kit (Applied Biosystems), and Absolute QPCR ROX mix (Abgene, Rochester, NY, USA), according to the manufacturers' instructions. As an endogenous control, 5SrRNA or U6 snRNA was used.

3.2. Ago2-immunoprecipitation and PCR analysis of novel miRNAs

After bioinformatic analysis of the sequence data, we further validated novel miRNAs by using a combination of Ago2-immunoprecipitation (13) followed by PCR-based miRNA detection (14). Briefly, 50 ml Dynabeads protein G slurry (Invitrogen) was immobilized with

20 mg human P4 anti-mouse Ago2 monoclonal antibody (clone 2D4, Wako Pure Chemical Industries, Osaka, Japan). One hundred fifty micrograms of human tissue P4 were homogenized in 1.5 ml of a cell lysis solution (provided in miRNAs isolation kit, Wako) using a Polytron PT1200C homogenizer (Kinematica AG, Lucerne, Switzerland) for 10 s at 4 8C, and then 1.5 ml of the cell lysis solution was added into the homogenized solution. Following incubation for 15 min on ice, lysate was centrifuged at 20 000 g for 20 min at 4 8C and filtered through a 0.8 mmSupor Acrodisc syringe filter (Pall Corporation, Ann Arbor, MI, USA). One milliliter of the filtered lysate was incubated with 25 ml of the anti-Ago2-Dynabead protein G for incubation for 60 min at 4 8C. After immunoprecipitation, Ago2-

associated RNAs were isolated from the immunoprecipitate according to the manufacture's protocol (Wako). We confirmed that the immunoprecipitate contained human P5 Ago2 protein of w100 kDa in size by western blot (data not shown). Non-immune human IgG (Sigma) was used as a control for Ago2-immunoprecipitation. Preparation of the cDNA library using the Ago2-associated RNAs and semi-quantitative PCR analysis of the above-mentioned novel miRNA candidates were performed, as reported previously **(14)**. A small RNA-specific primer and a universal reverse primer RTQ-UNIr **(14)**, were used for amplification of each of the small RNAs. The PCR products were analyzed on a 12% polyacrylamide gel. The primers for the human GAPDH were used for negative control.

3.3. PCR analysis of novel miRNAs (Alternative method of 3.2)

After bioinformatic analysis of the sequence data, we further validated novel miRNAs by PCRbased miRNA detection **(14)**. Briefly, small RNAs were isolated using the mirVana™ miRNA isolation kit (Ambion). Small RNA samples were polyadenylated with Poly(A) Tailing Kit (Ambion) and were purified with Acid-Phenol:Chloroform and with filter cartridge provided in the mirVana Probe & Marker Kit (Ambion). To generate a small RNA cDNA library, tailed RNA were reverse transcripted using RTQ primer**(14)** and the samples were purified using the QIAquick

spin PCR purification kit (QIAGEN). A small RNA-specific primer and a universal reverse primer RTQ-UNIr **(14)**, were used for amplification of each of the small RNAs. The PCR products were analyzed on a 12% polyacrylamide gel. The primers for the human GAPDH were used for negative control.

3.4. Real-time PCR-based miRNA expression profiling

Total miRNA (350 ng) was reverse-transcribed using Megaplex RT Primers (Applied Biosystems). The resulting cDNAs were pre-amplified using Megaplex PreAmp Primers (Applied Biosystems) and the pre-amplified products applied to a TaqMan Human MicroRNA Array Panel (A and B, v2.0).

3.5. siRNA, Pre-miR and anti-miR transfections

Cultured cells were transfected with precursor hsa-miR-200c and hsa-miR-141 (ID: PM11714; PM10860); Anti-miR™ 200c and 141 inhibitors (ID: MH11714; MH10860) (Ambion, Austin, TX) for 8 hours in serum free medium. Serum supplemented medium was added and gene and protein expression measured at the indicated time points.

4. Study designs

Sequencing using 454 sequencing and conventional cloning from 22 pair of HCC and adjacent normal liver (ANL) and 3 HCC cell lines identified reliable reads of more than 300000 miRNAs from HCC and more than 270000 from ANL for registered human miRNAs.

5. Detected novel microRNAs using cloning

Eleven novel opposite miRNAs (defined as miRNAs cloned from the other arm of precursors from which known miRNAs have been cloned) were identified from the annotated miRNAs (Figure 2A).Based on above criteria, a scan of all the novel miRNA candidates identified 245 novel precursors, representing putative 210 novel mature miRNAs (Figure 2B).

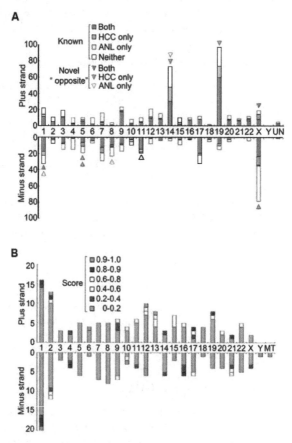

A: Chromosomal locations of our cloned mature miRNAs which correspond to previously identified pre-miRNAs. The bar graphs indicate the location of mature miRNAs (both our cloned miRNAs and previously identified miRNAs) based on known pre-miRNA sequences. Many of our cloned sequences were found in these regions. Arrowheads indicate novel "opposite" miRNAs cloned in our experiments. These sequences represent mature miRNAs which originate on the opposite DNA strand of the known precursor miRNA.

B: The 222 novel mature miRNAs identified in our study were checked for species conservation using the PhastCon database and their corresponding hairpin conservation scores charted in this figure.

Figure 2. Qualitative analysis of miRNAs in the human liver.

Accession Number	Most frequent sequence	Strand	Chr.	Precursor			
				Start	End	PhastCon score	dG (kcal/mol)
AB372573	TGCAATGGTTGTCCTGAGA	+	1	30294032	30294114	0.00	-28.6
AB372574	GTGGGGGAGAGGCTGTCA	+	1	150066781	150066870	0.00	-50.7
AB372575	TTGCACAACTCTCACATTC	+	1	152498870	152498979	0.39	-38.2
AB372576	CCCCTCACTTCTCCGTCATATC	+	1	153367241	153367332	0.05	-28.8
AB372577	CCCCAGATTCCACACC	+	1	154326362	154326427	0.85	-28.9

Table 2. Summary of the novel miRNAs
Summary of predicted novel miRNAs. The predicted novel miRNAs with their PhastCon scores are listed. And the most frequent cloned sequences, genome locations, clone counts, and conservation scores calculated with PhastCon are listed. The stem-loop is a 110-nt sequence derived by computational prediction. The precursor structures are listed in Table 3.

```
AB372573
UUGGA    U-       CAG     CCCC   AUUGA        CUUGUU
     CUC  GACAGCC  UGUA    UGG    GGGGGG
     GAG  CUGUUGG  ACGU    ACC    CCCCCU         A
A----    UC       UA-     ----   A-----       ACUGUU

AB372574
---      ACA-             UG  -   UG      ---         G
   CCAGGC    GGCCUUUCCU  CC UUCC  GGCCU    UCCUGG  G
   GGUCCG    UCGGAGAGGG  GG GAGG  CCGGG    AGGACU  C
CUA       ACUG              -- U   UG     UCG        U

AB372575
A        CAGUGUAU  AG  U       -       U    UAAC--      CCA    UA
GGGGGGA          GCA  AG AAUGUG GAGUU GUGC      UCUAG    GCU
CCUCCUU          UGU  UC UUACAC CUCAA CACG      AGGUC   UGA  A
G        UUU-----  CU  -       U       -    UUAAAU      AG-    UU

AB372576
CCAAACCCUGA    GAG       GUAG      C     U  -    C-  CUGUA
        GCU   CCUAGA   AUGAC GAGG AG GAGGG   GG
        CGA   GGGUCU   UACUG CUCU UC CUCCC   CC         G
A----------       ---       A---      C    - A    CU  UUUUA

AB372577
UGG       AGA     A    -     -- C    G
   UCCCC   UUCC CACC CAGU  GG GCCA C
   AGGGG   AGGG GUGG GUCG  CU UGGU U
GG-       G--     A    C     AG U    C
```

Table 3. Samples of the Secondary structures of predicted novel miRNAs. The predicted novel miRNAs with their particular ID numbers are listed. The mature miRNAs are depicted in blue in the drawing of the precursor.

We cloned 210 novel microRNA candidates. Samples of the novel microRNAs that were detected from our study and its bioinformatics data are tabulated in Table 2 and 3. And those novel miRNAs have been deposited with DDBJ under consecutive accession codes from AB372573 to AB372814.

6. Future direction

We have been demonstrated the usefulness and accuracy of sequencing in genetic research of the liver. One of the main problems with applying sequencing to the miRNA transcription research is that sequencing is a time-consuming procedure. And an important consideration for the discovery of miRNA by sequencing is the difficultly in identifying miRNAs that are expressed at low levels, at highly specific stages or in rare cell types. Moreover, a serious problem is that some miRNAs are difficult to profile precisely due to their physical properties or post-transcriptional modifications, such as RNA editing. In principle, these limitations can be overcome by extensive sequencing of small RNA libraries from a broad range of samples. For differential display, the sequencing-based method has the theoretical advantage in that it has the capability to discover and detect novel miRNAs. Based on our sequence variability results, especially with regard to RNA modifications, the accuracy of the sequence-based method is expected to be superior to that of the hybridization-based method. For the prediction of novel miRNAs, methods that rely on phylogenetic 1 genes. To overcome this problem, we made use of a computational approach for structural conservation criteria using the thermodynamic stability and intrinsic structural features of miRNAs. In clinics, pathologists often meet difficult situations in which they cannot clearly tell whether the tissue specimens they are observing are malignant or benign. Thus, in our opinion, using some miRNAs as a tumor marker would help clinicians to clearly determine whether that tissue is cancerous. miRNA sequences followed by bioinformatics have greater power than individual miRNAs or other clinic-pathological variables for the detection of high risk patients' groups with poor prognoses. There is currently little data available as to how we can use each miRNA to predict high risk groups; however, additional future miRNA work and data accumulation will elucidate such criteria. And further investigation is warranted to clarify the mechanism of aberrant expression of miRNAs in cancer and its participation in carcinogenesis. Nevertheless, these findings show that sequence-based miRNA profiling has potential for the confirmation of precise miRNA dynamics in a specific disease. In addition, it will increase our understanding of the mechanisms and factors involved in human liver cancer.

Author details

Yoshiaki Mizuguchi and Eiji Uchida
Nippon Medical School, Department of Surgery for Organ Function and Biological Regulation, Japan

Takuya Mishima and Toshihiro Takizawa
Nippon Medical School, Department of Molecular Anatomy and Medicine, Japan

7. References

[1] Bartel DP (2004) MicroRNAs: genomics, biogenesis, mechanism, and function. Cell 116: 281–297.

[2] Harfe BD (2005) MicroRNAs in vertebrate development. Curr Opin Genet Dev 15: 410–415.

[3] Bartel DP, Chen CZ (2004) Micromanagers of gene expression: the potentially widespread influence of metazoan microRNAs. Nat Rev Genet 5: 396–400.

[4] Rajewsky N (2006) microRNA target predictions in animals. Nat Genet 38 Suppl: S8–13.

[5] Meyers BC, Souret FF, Lu C, Green PJ (2006) Sweating the small stuff: microRNA discovery in plants. Curr Opin Biotechnol 17: 139–146.

[6] Lagos-Quintana M, Rauhut R, Yalcin A, Meyer J, Lendeckel W, et al. (2002) Identification of tissue-specific microRNAs from mouse. Curr Biol 12: 735–739.

[7] Kim, VN. (2006) Small RNAs just got bigger: Piwi-interacting RNAs (piRNAs) in mammalian testes. *Genes Dev.* 20: 1993-1997.

[8] Mineno J, Okamoto S, Ando T, Sato M, Chono H, et al. (2006) The expression profile of microRNAs in mouse embryos. Nucleic Acids Res 34: 1765–1771.

[9] Hofacker IL (2003) Vienna RNA secondary structure server. Nucleic Acids Res 31: 3429–3431.

[10] Schwartz S, Kent WJ, Smit A, Zhang Z, Baertsch R, et al. (2003) Human-mouse alignments with BLASTZ. Genome Res 13: 103–107.

[11] Siepel A, Haussler D (2004) Combining phylogenetic and hidden Markov models in biosequence analysis. J Comput Biol 11: 413–428.

[12] Berezikov E, Guryev V, van de Belt J, Wienholds E, Plasterk RH, et al. (2005) Phylogenetic shadowing and computational identification of human microRNA genes. Cell 120: 21–24.

[13] Azuma-Mukai A, Oguri H, Mituyama T, Qian ZR, Asai K, Siomi H, Siomi MC Characterization of endogenous human Argonautes and their miRNA partners in RNA silencing. (2008) Proc Natl Acad Sci U S A 105: 7964-7969.

[14] Ro S, Park C, Jin J, Sanders KM, Yan W (2006) A PCR-based method for detection and quantification of small RNAs. Biochem Biophys Res Comm 351:756-763.

Websites for database used in this manuscript

NCBI Entrez Nucleotide database, http://www.ncbi.nlm.nih.gov/entrez/query.fcgi?db=Nucleotide; European ribosomal RNA database, http://psb.ugent.be/rRNA/; Genomic tRNA database , http://lowelab.ucsc.edu/GtRNAdb/; RNAdb, http://research.imb.uq.edu.au/randb/;

NONCODE, http://www.bioinfo.org.cn/NONCODE/; NCBI Reference Sequence,
ftp://ftp.ncbi.nih.gov/refseq/; UCSC Genome Bioinformatics Site, http://genome.ucsc.edu;
OncoDb HCC, http://oncodb.hcc.ibms.sinica.edu.tw/index.ht

Chapter 12

Computational Approaches for Designing Efficient and Specific siRNAs

Suman Ghosal, Shaoli Das and Jayprokas Chakrabarti

Additional information is available at the end of the chapter

1. Introduction

Small RNA mediated RNA interference (RNAi) is a widely adopted mechanism towards immunity in plants and invertebrates. Two types of small RNAs- small interfering RNA (siRNA) and microRNA (miRNA), play key role in RNA interference either through cleaving or through translational repression of the target mRNA by guiding RNA induced silencing complex (RISC) to its target site. siRNA is a small RNA (19-23 nucleotides) which is complementary to part of their target mRNA [1]. siRNAs are very efficient in target gene knockdown that makes synthetic siRNA's perfect choice for use in experiments for silencing genes to examine their function. In addition, siRNA have good potential in drug development for therapeutic purpose [2]. Exogenous synthetic siRNAs are designed to target a part of the coding region in the target mRNA [3]. But, as evident from experiments, all siRNAs are not equally efficient in target gene silencing. The potency of siRNAs is largely dependent upon the selection of the region it targets. A displacement of 5-6 nucleotide position hugely alters the efficiency of siRNA. The reason behind this alteration of efficiency is the alteration in local sequence and structural features of the target region. These variations in sequence and structural features correlate with target accessibility, RISC loading or stimulation of immune response. A lot of study has been done in the field of rational siRNA designing to find appropriate parameters that facilitate designing of effective siRNAs [4]. Several commercial suppliers and non-profit educational institutes contribute to the research for searching appropriate siRNA selection parameters for improving potency of designed siRNAs. Progresses have been made in targeting success rate compared to the early days- from as low as 0-10% targeting success rate, today siRNAs have reached average 50% targeting success rate. Still there are many scopes to improve siRNA designing. For efficient designing, the siRNA selection parameters must be arranged and weighted in such a way that ensures optimal result while selecting the siRNA target site. There are some previously suggested guidelines about parameter weight assignment like rational or weighted methods. These guidelines were made in the early days of siRNA selection research with small number of data, when experimentally knockdown validated siRNA dataset was scarce. But with increasing amount of knockdown validated siRNA datasets, new parameter optimization methods must come out to ensure selection of potent siRNAs in a bigger scenario. Today, high throughput siRNA screening experiments have become a common technique to investigate thousands of gene functions at a time to study some specific pathway. These experiments use siRNA libraries targeting transcripts in a genome wide range. But the success of these experiments relies on the knockdown success rate of the siRNAs in the library. After two decades of research, still many of these large scale screening experiments fail because of a large number of non-functional siRNAs present in the libraries used in these experiments. So, still there are needs for improvement in the siRNA selection algorithm and efficient parameter optimization.

Another main challenge in computational siRNA designing lies in the specificity issue of siRNAs. Exogenous siRNAs often induce off-target effects that arise from near perfect or imperfect sequence complementarity with other mRNAs resulting in false positive phenotype during RNAi-based study of gene functions. The type of gene regulation resulting from imperfect sequence complementarity resembles target regulation by endogenous miRNAs- hence this type of off-targeting is called miRNA-like off-targeting. Minimization of miRNA-like off-targets involves choosing a siRNA with a seed region sequence that has fewer targets in the 3′ UTR of other mRNAs. The siRNA seed region is a 6 or 7 nucleotide sequence (the 2-8th nucleotide position) from 5′ end of siRNA guide strand and finding complementary sequence with this 6 or 7 nucleotide seed in the 3′ UTRs of unintended transcripts results in a huge number of potential targets. A majority of these predicted targets are not practically relevant, as in practice, a large number of these predicted off-targets may not be silenced at all. Like miRNA targets, siRNA targets are also dependent on target accessibility and other sequence features around the target site. So, a more rational approach is needed when predicting the siRNA off-targets resulting from partial sequence complementarity. This chapter focuses on current siRNA designing parameters and the approaches towards minimizing the off-target effects as provided by the in-silico siRNA designing solutions and then discuss a bit about a customized off-target reducing algorithm that will be useful to avoid particular genes from being off-targeted.

2. Guidelines for selecting potent siRNAs

As discussed earlier, potency of siRNAs varies greatly with selection of target region. The parameters responsible for effectiveness of siRNAs being target accessibility, uniqueness of target region, absence of SNP sites etc. Other parameters worth considering while selecting the target site is the consideration of alternatively spliced isoforms of the target gene [5].

A parameter which greatly influences siRNA potency is RISC loading of the intended antisense strand [6]. Only one strand of the siRNA duplex enters into RISC and guides the complex to the target mRNA for its silencing. So, the choice of strand that enters into RISC complex plays the vital role in the whole silencing process. Generally RISC complex chooses the siRNA strand which has weaker 5′ end binding energy. So this thermodynamic property should be ensured while selecting siRNAs. Also there are a number of sequence compositions that are said to be important for recognition of the intended strand by RISC and some parameters for enhancing the stability of siRNA duplex are also worth considering while selecting siRNAs. These rules can be divided into three categories 1) Selection of target region, 2) Structural and Thermodynamic Consideration and 3) Sequence Characteristics.

2.1. Selection of target region

Selection of the target region for siRNA should satisfy some constraints to ensure effective silencing. Target site should be analyzed for its position within the mRNA, presence of polymorphic site or other considerations like homology with other mRNAs or its alternatively spliced isoforms.

2.1.1. Selection of target starting site

Generally siRNAs are targeted to a part of the coding region of an mRNA. The target site should be deep inside the open reading frame (ORF) of the target mRNA for efficient silencing. Generally it is advised to start from 50-100 nucleotides downstream of the AUG start codon. Besides targeting the coding region, some siRNAs may also be designed to target the 3′ un-translated region (UTR) of an mRNA. This type of targeting is especially done in case of experiments conducted for restoration of original phenotype. In such cases it is advised to start targeting regions at least 15-20 nucleotides downstream of the stop codon.

2.1.2. Consideration for alternative splicing

In eukaryotic organisms frequent alternative splicing results in diversification of mRNAs. To account for the alternative splicing, it is necessary to evaluate a common target region where siRNAs can be designed to knockdown a specific mRNA isoform or multiple mRNA isoforms from a target gene.

2.1.3. Absence of homology with other mRNAs

Cellular mRNAs with 15/16 or more consecutive base match with the siRNA, are likely to be silenced and degraded by the siRNA. So target sites with 15 or more consecutive base homology with any other mRNA should be avoided.

2.1.4. Avoiding target sites having polymorphic locus

Target regions having single nucleotide polymorphic (SNP) sites should be avoided.

2.2. Structural and thermodynamic consideration

siRNA potency largely depends upon structural constraints of the target region. Heavily structured sites are less likely to be bound by siRNAs as these sites are not accessible by siRNAs. The relative binding energy of the 5' and 3' ends of the siRNA with the target site play a vital role in the choice of strand to be incorporated into RISC complex and thus is one of the most important parameter to be considered during siRNA design.

2.2.1. Presence of Secondary structure

It has been suggested that presence of local secondary structures (stem loops) in the target site restricts its accessibility to RISC and hence reduces the efficiency of the siRNA. So it is necessary to filter out those potential inaccessible target sites with strong secondary structures. The prediction of local secondary structure can be made by numerous RNA secondary structure prediction tools or packages like Mfold [7] or Vienna RNA package [8] - that mainly predict minimum free energy secondary structure of a RNA sequence.

2.2.2. Thermodynamic property for efficient RISC loading

In a siRNA duplex, antisense strand with relatively low energy in 5' end is favourable for its loading into RISC complex. So, there should be difference in binding energy between the 5' end of the sense and antisense strand.

2.3. Sequence characteristics

Years of research for finding appropriate designing parameters identified some sequence parameters enriched within efficient siRNAs. These sequence characteristics often contribute to efficient RISC loading or siRNA sequence specificity or stability issues.

2.3.1. Position specific nucleotide composition

Sequence analysis of effective siRNAs revealed many position specific nucleotide compositions for enhancing potency of the siRNA. Some of these preferences are listed below in table 1-

2.3.2. Sequence feature for efficient RISC entry

siRNA guide strands with low energy at 5' end are favored for entering the RISC complex. So, presence of at least three (A/U)s in the seven nucleotides at the 3' end of the sense strand is preferable.

2.3.3. siRNA duplex stability

Target sites with low GC content (generally less than 55%) has a greater potential for being functional siRNA site, as too high GC content can impede the loading of siRNAs into RISC complex. Also, too low GC content is not favourable because too low GC content can destabilize the siRNA duplex and reduce their affinity to target mRNA binding. Analysis of effective siRNAs showed G/C content between 35% and 60% is most favorable.

Position specific nucleotides
Presence of A base at position 19 of the sense strand.
Presence of U base at position 10 of the sense strand.
Presence of A base at position 3 of the sense strand.
A base other than G or C at position 19 of the sense strand.
A base other than G at position 13 of the sense strand.
Presence of A base at the 2nd nucleotide position of the sense strand.
Presence of C base at the 4th nucleotide position of the sense strand.
Absence of C base at the 6th nucleotide position of the sense strand.
Absence of U base at the 7th nucleotide position of the sense strand.
Presence of C base at the 9th nucleotide position of the sense strand.
Presence of A base at the 17th nucleotide position of the sense strand.
Absence of C base at the 18th nucleotide position of the sense strand.
No occurrences of four or more identical nucleotides in a row.
No occurrences of G/C stretch of length 7 or longer.

Table 1. Position specific nucleotide composition prefered in functional siRNAs

3. Choice of appropriate parameters

All the parameters discussed above are not equally important for selection of efficient siRNAs. By far, many research groups have conducted studies for evaluation of effective parameter sets for siRNA selection. Gong et al. studied 276 known siRNA selection parameters on a sufficiently large set of 3277 experimentally validated siRNAs targeting 1518 genes to identify common parameters that effectively distinguishes functional siRNAs from non functional ones [9]. They were able to identify 34 features associated with improved siRNA efficacy among which 27 features were associated with greater than 70% efficacy. They examined combination of siRNA features to find their cooperative effects on potent siRNA selection and used a disjunctive rule merging (DRM) algorithm to generate a bunch of non-redundant rules set to efficiently predict functional siRNAs and lower the false positive predictions. Table 2 list 17 features set associated with greater than 90% efficacy and used for optimal features combination.

siRNA selection parameter
F1 2nd nucleotide = A
F2 4th nucleotide = C
F3 6th nucleotide ≠ C
F4 7th nucleotide ≠ U
F5 9th nucleotide = C
F6 17th nucleotide = A
F7 18th nucleotide ≠ C
F8 19th nucleotide = (A/U)
F9 At least three (A/U)s in the seven nucleotides at the 3' end
F10 No occurrences of four or more identical nucleotides in a row
F11 No occurrences of G/C stretches of length 7 or longer
F12 G/C content is between 35 and 60%
F13 Tm is between 20 and 60°C
F14 Binding energy of N16–N19 > -9 KCal/Mol
F15 Binding energy of N16–N19 – binding energy of N1–N4 is between 0 and 1 KCal/Mol
F16 Local folding potential (mean) ≥ -22.72 KCal/Mol
F17 Target site is on CDS

Table 2. Feature sets predicted to be associated with greater siRNA efficacy as described by Gong et al.

4. Prediction of siRNA potency

Computational prediction of siRNA potency relies on assessment of appropriate designing parameters combined with their optimal weight distribution. Since the early era of siRNA designing researches, many studies are made for finding optimal weights for siRNA selection parameters. Raynolds et al. proposed a method for rational siRNA designing with appropriate parameter weights, by empirical study of 180 experimentally validated efficient siRNAs [10]. The designed siRNAs were given a score based on weighted summation of these parameters and a score threshold was used to identify efficient siRNAs. Table 3 lists the parameters used in the study with their weight distributions.

siRNA selection parameter	Parameter weight
GC content 30% to 52%	Satisfying this criteria earns 1 point
Occurence of 3 or more A/U base pair at position 15-19 of sense strand	Each A/U base pair in this region earns 1 point
Low internal stability at target site (melting temperature T_m>-20°c)	Satisfying this criteria earns 1 point
Presence of A at position 19 of the sense strand	Satisfying this criteria earns 1 point
Presence of A at position 3 of the sense strand	Satisfying this criteria earns 1 point
Presence of U at position 10 of the sense strand	Satisfying this criteria earns 1 point
Absense of G or C at position 19 of the sense strand	Failure to satisfy this criteria decreases 1 point
Absense of G at position 13 of the sense strand	Failure to satisfy this criteria decreases 1 point
Threshold for efficient siRNAs	score>=6

Table 3. Parameters used in Raynold's algorithm with their weights

Since then many siRNA designing algorithm worked on different weight distribution schemes for improved prediction of siRNA potency and some even used machine learning algorithms.

4.1. Use of machine learning algorithms for classification of functional siRNAs

After many years of research about the guidelines for selection of effective siRNAs, we are a few steps ahead in the process of improving the targeting success rate. But for better targeting success, the siRNA selection parameters provided in various guidelines needs to be optimized. Still there is no reliable guideline for optimization of weights of siRNA selection parameter. Machine learning algorithms like Support vector machine or artificial neural network can serve excellent purpose, when trained with sufficient volume of biologically validated siRNA data sets [11]. Some online siRNA designing tools (like BioPredsi and Genescript siRNA target finder) use machine learning algorithms for classification of effective siRNAs from non-effective ones.

4.1.1. Use of artificial neural network for siRNA classification

Artificial neural networks (ANNs), as they aim to mimic the working of biological networks through a connectionist approach to computation, provide a powerful method of identifying highly complex traits in data sets. ANNs are generally very efficient classifiers in case of complex patterns in the given data set as they can adaptively change their weighting parameters during the learning process. ANNs have been broadly applied in the biological sciences. The prediction quality and generalization capabilities of an ANN of fixed size depend on a sufficiently large training set of directly comparable data points.

Biopredsi siRNA designing algorithm from Novartis lab used Stuttgart Neural Net Simulator to train algorithms on a data set of 2182 randomly selected siRNAs targeted to 34 mRNA species [11]. It reliably predicted activity of 249 siRNAs of an independent test set (Pearson coefficient $r = 0.66$) and siRNAs targeting endogenous genes at mRNA and protein levels.

4.1.2. Support Vector machine based classification

Support Vector Machine (SVM) is a non-probabilistic binary linear classifier. Given a set of training examples, each marked as belonging to one of two categories, an SVM training algorithm builds a model that assigns new examples one of the two categories. An SVM is called the maximum margin classifier that optimizes the margin between the example points belonging to two classes so that their gap is maximized.

A newly developed siRNA designing tool enables improved selection of potent siRNAs by application of a Support Vector machine based optimization of a set of eight siRNA selection parameters. The support vector machine is trained with the feature set of 200 highly efficient and 200 poorly efficient siRNA candidates, collected from siRecords, a database of validated siRNAs [12]. The support vector machine is trained using a Gaussian kernel and Sequential Minimal Optimization (SMO) algorithm [13]. It has been tested with huge number of experimentally validated data samples from four different sources and gave sufficiently good result.

5. Experimentally validated siRNA datasets

The effectiveness of the siRNA designing rules should be tested on biologically validated siRNA datasets. On the early days of RNAi research, these biologically validated datasets were scarce. But now, with emerging high throughput technologies, large amount of validated siRNA data is being generated. Some databases are created by manual curation of literature describing validation of siRNA mediated silencing. siRecords [12] is one such database where siRNAs are marked with their respective silencing efficacy (low, medium, high and very high). MIT siRNA database [14] consists of siRNAs designed by Qiagen with validated knockdown efficiency and marked with mRNA knockdown level.

6. Improving specificity of siRNAs

The specificity of siRNAs is a big issue in siRNA mediated gene silencing experiments. Exogenous siRNAs are reported to have off-target effects arising from either silencing unintended targets or toxic effects arising from their recognition by innate immune system [15].

The recognition of siRNAs by innate immune system can result from interferon response triggered by double stranded siRNA duplex or sequence dependent stimulation of toll like receptors. Avoiding some sequence motifs and a constraint related to the siRNA duplex length can effectively reduce immune response stimulation [16].

siRNAs silence unintended transcripts in mainly two ways: transcripts with near perfect complementarity are cleaved while transcripts with imperfect complementarity are translationally repressed. mRNAs other than intended targets which exhibit near perfect sequence complementarity with the siRNA are likely to be degraded by the siRNA. This kind of off-targets can be avoided by choosing targets sites that do not have a large number of consecutive base homology with any other mRNA.

siRNAs down regulate a set of transcripts with 3′ UTR complementarity to the 5′ portion of the corresponding siRNA guide strand. These 5′ ends of the guide strand resemble the seed region of endogenous microRNA and are responsible for target recognition. Such off-targets are regulated by translational repression like miRNA target regulation. This kind of off-target cannot be fully avoided but can be reduced by computational design.

6.1. Stimulation of innate immune response

siRNAs can induce potential unwanted effects by activating innate immune system. Exogenous siRNAs are prone to be recognized by Toll-like receptors (TLRs), mainly TLR7, TLR8 and TLR9. TLR7 and TLR8 recognize synthetic siRNAs in a sequence dependent manner [16]. There seems to be preferential recognition of GU-rich sequences. AU rich sequences can also be immune stimulatory. Selecting siRNA sequences lacking GU rich regions can provide siRNAs with low immune stimulatory activity. Also presence of the motif "GUCCUUCAA" the 4-base motif "UGGC" in the siRNA is known to be immune stimulatory [17]. So, this motif should be avoided in the time of designing of siRNAs. The length of the siRNA is also an important factor for stimulation of immune response- the minimum length of siRNA to be recognized by innate immune system is in the range of 19 nucleotides.

6.2. Near perfect complementarity with other mRNAs

mRNAs other than intended targets which exhibit near perfect sequence complementarity with the siRNA are likely to be degraded by the siRNA. This kind of off-targets can be avoided by choosing targets sites that do not have many consecutive base homologies with any other mRNA. Actually siRNAs can potentially silence transcripts with more than 11 base complementarity including base matches corresponding its 9th-11th nucleotides. But as finding unique 11 base target site is impossible, the siRNA designing algorithms try to find unique target sites that do not have 15 or more consecutive base homology with other transcripts.

6.3. miRNA-like off-target effect

siRNAs down regulate a set of transcripts with 3′ UTR complementarity to the 5′ portion of the corresponding siRNA guide strand. These 5′ ends of the guide strand resemble the seed region of endogenous miRNA which is responsible for target recognition. Such off-targets are regulated by translational repression like miRNA target regulation. That is why this kind of off-target effect is called miRNA-like off-target effect [18, 19]. This kind of off-target cannot be fully avoided but can be reduced by computational design. Consideration for minimization of such off-target effect involves imposing a threshold for number of off-target genes. All of the present day online siRNA designing techniques consider only the quantitative approach for minimizing miRNA-like off-target effect by restricting the number of off-targets [20]. To go beyond mere quantitative approach and look for the functional correlation between the on-target and the genes off-targeted by the siRNA will certainly prove to be beneficial in minimizing miRNA-like off-target effect. A newly developed siRNA designing tool is aimed for such off-target minimization considering functional correlation of the off-target and the direct target (explained in section 9).

7. Prediction of siRNA off-targets

Prediction of miRNA-like off-targets involves finding the seed complementarity of the siRNA with the 3'UTR of a non-target mRNA. But considering only seed region complementarity identifies a large number of off-targets that could not be actually targeted. So, a more rational approach is needed for prediction of siRNA off-targets that needs understanding the miRNA target recognition procedure. Parameters like local AU content near the seed region or accessibility of the target site within the 3'UTR of the predicted off-target play roles in siRNA off-target detection also [21]. To have a more reliable prediction of off-targets, some siRNA designing solutions consider the stability factor of the duplex formed by siRNA guide strand seed region and mRNA 3' UTR target as the off-targets forming duplex with lower stability are less likely to be actually silenced by the siRNA [22]. These tools examine thermodynamic property of the siRNA seed-mRNA duplex and carefully choose siRNAs with seed sequences that are predicted to form less thermodynamically stable duplex with the target mRNA. Some siRNA designing solutions consider conservation of such target regions among closely related species to determine the candidate mRNAs most likely to be silenced by miRNA-like mechanism [23]. Table 4 gives the mechanism adopted by different online siRNA designing solutions for minimizing off-targets.

In a detailed investigation of all possible seed sequence and their frequency of complimenting the 3' UTRs of human mRNAs, it is shown that the seeds can be classified into low, medium and high frequency classes according to the number 3' UTR sites targeted by them [24]. The low frequency seeds have targets around 350, while the medium and high frequency seeds have targets around 2500 and more than 4800 respectively. So, it is obvious that siRNAs having a seed region that falls into the low frequency group will have fewer off-targets. But then in many cases, presence of such seed sequences can decrease the potency of the siRNA because they often contain stretches of identical nucleotides or other features unfavorable for a potent siRNA. So, there is a tradeoff between potency and specificity of a siRNA which have to be dealt with in their computational designing. Seed complement frequency (SCF) is the frequency of the complement of the hexamer/heptamer seed region within 3' UTR of an mRNA [24]. It is a major parameter which greatly enhances specificity of siRNA off-target prediction, but at the cost of decreasing sensitivity. Some microRNA target site features as uncovered by combining computational and experimental approaches, also apply to the siRNA off-target prediction problem. A study reported potential silencing of transcripts having consecutive 11 or more bases complementarity with miRNA or siRNAs including siRNA bases 9-12. These transcripts are more likely to be cleaved by the siRNA. Some other off-target prediction parameters include secondary structure analysis for target accessibility prediction and A/U base richness near target site [25]. For reliable off-target prediction, an optimized combination of all the above mentioned parameters is needed.

siRNA designing tool	Approaches towards minimization of miRNA-like off-target effects
BIOPREDsi [http://www.biopredsi.org/].	siRNA seed region match in combination with 10 or more bases of additional homology to unintended target genes is used for pediction of off-targets. siRNAs predicted to have a large number of off-targets are rejected.
siRNA Target Finder [https://www.genscript.com/ssl-bin/app/rnai].	Depending on their proprietary off-target prediction database, a threshold of seed match for a specific species is applied which is computed by a probability model which has general biological significance. siRNAs predicted to have a large number of off-targets are rejected.
siDESIGN Center [http://www.dharmacon.com/sidesign].	Chooses siRNAs that has a seed sequence with lower seed compliment frequency.
siDirect [http://sidirect2.rnai.jp].	siDirect selects siRNAs with lower melting temperature (Tm value) at the seed region, which contains 7 nucleotides at positions 2-8 from 5′ end of the guide strand as the capability of siRNA to induce this seed-dependent off-target effect is highly correlated with the thermodynamic stability of the duplex formed between the seed region of the siRNA guide strand and its target mRNA.
siDRM [http://sidrm.biolead.org/]	For each candidate siRNA, *siDRM* checks and reports if its seed region (position 2–8) has full homology to the 3′ UTR region of another transcript, and this homology region is followed by four consecutive mismatches. siRNAs predicted to have a large number of off-targets are rejected.
Whitehead WI siRNA Selection Program [http://jura.wi.mit.edu/bioc/siRNAext/].	Predicts off-targets based on the seed region complementarity as well as conservation of the target site among related species (human, mouse, rat, dog and chicken). siRNAs predicted to have a large number of off-targets are rejected.

Table 4. Off-target minimization techniques of different siRNA designing tools.

8. Discussion about selected siRNA designing tools

Several siRNA sequence selection algorithms have been developed in the past decade that relies on intrinsic sequence, stability and target accessibility features of functional siRNAs. Different siRNA selection algorithms follow different set of rules derived from some well-known siRNA design parameters as discussed above. In general, these algorithms rely on features like- low GC content, absence of siRNA self-alignment, absence of internal repeat, thermodynamic conditions favouring efficient RISC entry, absence of homology to other mRNAs and some position specific nucleotide compositions. Few of them also consider silencing of alternatively spliced isoforms of the given gene. Different algorithms use different techniques for combination of parameters and their weight distribution- ranging from empirical observation to sophisticated machine learning. In spite of a large number of online siRNA design solutions, few of them consider miRNA-like off-targeting potential of synthetic siRNAs. Consideration for minimization of such off-target effect involves imposing a threshold for number of off-target genes. Table 5 lists some of the online siRNA designing solutions with their designing parameters.

siRNA selection tool	Thermodynamic deference between sense and antisense strand 5′ end	Target accessibility	Alternative splicing	Off-target(near complementary)	miRNA-like off-target
Ambion siRNA Target Finder [http://www.ambion.com/techlib/misc/siRNA_finder.html].	Considered	Not Considered	Not Considered	Considered	Not Considered
AsiDesigner [http://sysbio.kribb.re.kr:8080/AsiDesigner/menuDesigncr.jsf]	Considered	Considered	Considered	Considered	Not considered
BIOPREDsi [http://www.biopredsi.org/].	Considered	Not Considered	Not Considered	Considered	Considered
siRNA Target Finder [https://www.genscript.com/ssl-bin/app/rnai].	Considered	Considered	Not Considered	Considered	Considered
BLOCK-iT RNAi Designer [https://rnaidesigner.invitrogen.com/rnaiexpress].	Considered	Considered	Not Considered	Considered	Not Considered
IDT RNAi Design [http://www.idtdna.com/Scitools/Applications/RNAi/RNAi.aspx].	Considered	Considered	Not Considered	Considered	Not Considered
MicroSynth siRNA design [http://www.microsynth.ch/499.0.html].	Considered	Not Considered	Not Considered	Considered	Not Considered

siRNA selection tool	Thermodynamic deference between sense and antisense strand 5′ end	Target accessibility	Alternative splicing	Off-target(near complementary)	miRNA-like off-target
Promega siRNA Target Designer [http://www.promega.com/siRNADesigner/program/].	Considered	Considered	Not Considered	Considered	Not Considered
siDESIGN Center [http://www.dharmacon.com/sidesign].	Considered	Not Considered	Considered	Considered	Considered
siDRM [http://sidrm.biolead.org/]	Considered	Considered	Not Considered	Considered	Considered
siDirect [http://sidirect2.rnai.jp]	Considered	Considered	Not Considered	Considered	Considered
Imgenex siRNA tool [http://www.imgenex.com/sirna_tool.php].	Considered	Considered	Not Considered	Considered	Not Considered
siSearch [http://sonnhammer.cgb.ki.se/siSearch/siSearch_1.7.html].	Considered	Considered	Not Considered	Considered	Not Considered
Whitehead WI siRNA Selection Program [http://jura.wi.mit.edu/bioc/siRNAext/].	Considered	Considered	Not Considered	Considered	Considered

Table 5. A comparison of siRNA designing parameters in different siRNA designing tools

9. Importance of functional off-target filtering

Considering only quantity of the off-targets and not the functions of individual off-targets can lead to inefficient handling of the miRNA-like off-target issue. Often in siRNA screening experiments, it has been reported that the desired output is affected because of silencing of unintended off-targets those sometimes are themselves member of the upstream pathway components of the direct target gene [26]. In such cases it can be useful to avoid specifically some off-targets that can cause more harmful or undesirable effects. It should be considered that during silencing process siRNA should not silence any mRNA from the same pathway the target mRNA is part of. In case of investigation of a gene function, if any gene from the same pathway is silenced rather than target gene then it will be difficult to investigate the actual phenotype of silencing the gene under investigation. For e.g. in a siRNA screening experiment designed for novel members of the transforming growth factor (TGF)-b pathway in a human keratinocyte cell line, dominant off-target effect was observed due to unintended silencing of two known upstream pathway components, the TGF-b receptors 1 and 2 (TGFBR1 and TGFBR2). Such off-target silencing activity poses threats of confusing and misleading results. Also the siRNAs suggested by the online siRNA selection tools often are predicted to have off-targets that belong to the same pathway or somehow related to the direct target.

Das et al reported designing of a siRNA designing tool using a simple approach towards minimizing miRNA-like off-target effect through user feedback. Here, the user can actually choose from the list of potential off-target genes, the off-targets he/she wants to filter out, by considering the effect of silencing of those off-target genes. This tool statistically evaluates present day siRNA design rules such as- low GC content, absence of long stretches of identical nucleotides, thermodynamic conditions favouring efficient RISC entry, absence of homology to other mRNAs, absence of immune stimulatory motifs in the RISC entering strand of the siRNA duplex and some position specific nucleotide compositions, in a database of validated siRNAs [12] used in experiments to examine the threshold parameters. A support vector machine, trained with the optimal features set, is used for classifying potential and effective siRNAs. Moreover, with other parameters, it predicts the potential miRNA-like off-target genes for each candidate siRNA, sets a threshold for the number of off-targets to minimize miRNA-like off-target effect and presents the list of predicted off-target genes. A feedback mechanism allows the user to choose specific genes that needs to be filtered out from the list of predicted off-target genes recursively until his/her needs are met. This technique gives a more rational approach towards handling the miRNA-like off- target issue.

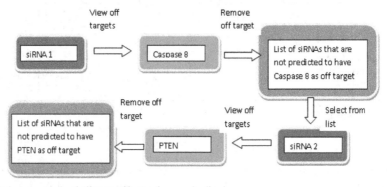

Figure 1. An example of off-target filtering by user feedback

10. Conclusion

As many guidelines are available for selection of efficient siRNAs and they promise to improve efficacy in silencing, much progress has been made in designing siRNAs with improved targeting success rate. Now the main challenge in in-silico siRNA design is reducing the unintended effects arising from inadvertent targets. While the off-targets with near perfect sequence complementarity with the given siRNA is taken care of much efficiently by targeting against a unique region of the target mRNA, which can be found by homology searching with other mRNAs of the organism, miRNA-like off-targets remain to be addressed with efficiency. The few online siRNA designing solutions those consider for reducing such off-targets rely on reducing the number of off-targets. Even then a compromise has to be made between potency and specificity as siRNA sequences that could give higher specificity often comes with lower potency. Now approaching this specificity issue arising from miRNA-like off-targets of a siRNA from a different point of view, like the functional off-target filtering discussed in previous section, may prove to be beneficial and may emerge as a new paradigm for designing efficient siRNAs with customized specificity.

Author details

Suman Ghosal, Shaoli Das and Jayprokas Chakrabarti
Indian Association for the Cultivation of Science, Kolkata, India

Acknowledgement

We thank Sanga Mitra and Smarajit Das of Indian Association for the Cultivation of Science for their valuable suggestions.

11. References

[1] Grosshans H. & Filipowicz W. (2008). The expanding world of small RNAs. *Nature,* Vol. 451, (April 2008), pp. (414)

[2] De Fougerolles A., Vornlocher H.P., Maraganore J., Lieberman J. (2007). Interfering with disease: a progress report on siRNA-based therapeutics. *Nature Reviews Drug Discovery,* Vol. 6, (June 2007), pp. (443)

[3] Elbashir S.M., Harborth J., Lendeckel W., Yalcin A., Weber K., Tuschl T. (2001). Duplexes of 21-nucleotide RNAs mediate RNA interference in cultured mammalian cells. *Nature,* Vol. 411, (May 2001), pp. (494)

[4] Pei Y. & Tuschl T. (2006). On the art of identifying effective and specific siRNAs. *Nature Methods,* Vol. 3, (September 2006), pp. (670)

[5] Park Y.K., Park S.M., Choi Y.C., Lee D., Won M., Kim Y.J. (2008). AsiDesigner: exon-based siRNA design server considering alternative splicing. *Nucleic Acids Research,* Vol. 36, (September 2008), pp. (97)

[6] Khvorova A., Reynolds A., Jayasena S.D. (2003). Functional siRNAs and miRNAs Exhibit Strand Bias. *Cell,* Vol. 115, (November 2003), pp. (505)

[7] Zuker M. (2003). Mfold web server for nucleic acid folding and hybridization prediction. *Nucleic Acids Res.* Vol. 31, (July 2003), pp. (3406)

[8] Hofacker I.L. (2003). Vienna RNA secondary structure server. *Nucleic Acids Research,* Vol. 31, (July 2003), pp. (3429)

[9] Gong W., Ren Y., Xu Q., Wang Y., Lin D., Zhou H., Li T. (2006). Integrated siRNA design based on surveying of features associated with high RNAi effectiveness. BMC Bioinformatics. Vol. 7, (November, 2006), pp. (516)

[10] Reynolds A., Leake D., Boese Q., Scaringe S., Marshall W.S., Khorova A. (2004). Rational siRNA design for RNA interference. *Nature Biotechnology,* Vol. 22, (September 2004), pp. (326)

[11] Huesken D., Lange J., Mickanin C., Weiler J., Asselbergs F., Warner J., Meloon B., Engel S., Rosenberg A., Cohen D., Labow M., Reinhardt M., Natt F., Hall J. (2005). Design of a genome-wide siRNA library using an artificial neural network. *Nature Biotechnology,* Vol. 23, (July 2005), pp. (995)

[12] Ren Y., Gong W., Xu Q., Zheng X., Lin D., Wang Y., Li T. (2006). siRecords: an extensive database of mammalian siRNAs with efficacy ratings. *Bioinformatics*, Vol. 22, (January 2006), pp. (1027)

[13] Platt J. C. (1999) Fast training of support vector machines using sequential minimal optimization, Advances in kernel methods. *MIT Press Cambridge*, pp. (185)

[14] MIT siRNA database [http://web.mit.edu/sirna/sirnas-human.html].

[15] Jackson A.L. & Linsley P.S. (2010). Recognizing and avoiding siRNA off-target effects for target identification and therapeutic application. *Nature Review Drug Discovery*, Vol. 9, (January 2010), pp. (57)

[16] Judge D., Sood V., Shaw J.R., Fang D., McClintock K., MacLachlan I. (2005). Sequence-dependent stimulation of the mammalian innate immune response by synthetic siRNA. *Nature Biotechnology*, Vol. 23, (March 2005), pp. (457)

[17] Fedorov Y., Anderson E.M., Birmingham A., Reynolds A., Karpilow J., Robinson K., Leake D., Marshall W.S., Khvorova A. (2006). Off-target effects by siRNA can induce toxic phenotype. *RNA*, Vol. 12, (March 2006), pp. (1188)

[18] Birmingham A., Anderson E.M., Reynolds A., Ilsley-Tyree D., Leake D., Fedorov Y., Baskerville S., Maksimova E., Robinson K., Karpilow J., Marshall W.S., Khvorova A. (2006). 3' UTR seed matches, but not overall identity, are associated with RNAi off-targets. *Nature Methods*, Vol. 3, (March 2006), pp. (199)

[19] Burchard J., Jackson A.L., Malkov V., Needham R.H.V., Tan Y., Bartz S.R., Dai H., Sachs A.B., Linsley P.S. (2009). MicroRNA-like off-target transcript regulation by siRNAs is species specific. *RNA*, Vol. 15, (February 2009), pp. (308)

[20] Wang L. & Forest Y.M. (2004). A Web-based design center for vector-based siRNA and siRNA cassette. *Bioinformatics*, Vol. 20, (September 2004), pp. (1818)

[21] Nielsen C.B., Shomron N., Sandberg R., Hornstein E., Kitzman J., Burge C.B. (2007). Determinants of targeting by endogenous and exogenous microRNAs and siRNAs. *RNA*, Vol. 13, (November 2007), pp. (1894)

[22] Ui-Tei K., Naito Y., Nishi K., Juni A., Saigo K. (2008). Thermodynamic stability and Watson–Crick base pairing in the seed duplex are major determinants of the efficiency of the siRNA-based off-target effect. *Nucleic Acids Research*, Vol. 36, (November 2008), pp. (7100)

[23] Yuan B., Latek R., Hossbach M., Tuschl T., Lewitter F. (2004). siRNA Selection Server: an automated siRNA oligonucleotide prediction server. *Nucleic Acids Research*, Vol. 32, (July 2004), pp. (130)

[24] Anderson E. M., Birmingham A., Baskerville S., Reynolds A., Maksimova E., Leake D., Fedorov Y., Karpilow J. & Khvorova A. (2008). Experimental validation of the importance of seed complement frequency to siRNA specificity. *RNA*, Vol. 14, (May 2008), pp. (853)

[25] Kiryu H., Terai G., Imamura O., Yoneyama H., Suzuki K., Asai K. (2011). A detailed investigation of accessibilities around target sites of siRNAs and miRNAs. *Bioinformatics*, Vol. 27, (July 2011), pp. (1788)

[26] Schultz N., Marenstein D.R., De Angelis D.A., Wang W.Q., Nelander S., Jacobsen A., Marks D.S., Massagué J., Sander C. (2011). Off-target effects dominate a large-scale RNAi screen for modulators of the TGF-β pathway and reveal microRNA regulation of TGFBR2. *Silence*, Vol. 2, (March 2011)

Chapter 13

Research on Pattern Matching with Wildcards and Length Constraints: Methods and Completeness

Haiping Wang, Taining Xiang and Xuegang Hu

Additional information is available at the end of the chapter

1. Introduction

The practical importance of the string matching problem should be obvious to everyone. For typical word-processing applications, immense amounts of work have been done on this subject. However, with the developments in bioinformatics (Cole et al., 2005), information retrieval (Califf et al., 2003), pattern mining (Xie et al., 2010; Ji et al., 2007; He et al., 2007), etc, sequential Pattern Matching with Wildcards and Length constraints (PMWL) has attracted more and more attention. It is not difficult to think up realistic cases where PMWL plays an important role. In Dan Gusfield's book (Gusfield, 1997), they give an example about *transcription factor* to illustrate the concept of wildcard. A *transcription factor* is a protein that binds to specific locations in DNA and regulates the transcription of the DNA into RNA. In this way, production of the protein that the DNA codes for is regulated. Many transcription factors are found and can be separated into families characterized by specific substrings containing wildcards. They use *Zinc Finger*, a common transcription factor as an example. It has the following signature:

CYS¢¢CYS¢¢¢¢¢¢¢¢¢¢¢¢HIS¢¢HIS

Where CYS is the amino acid cysteine and HIS is the amino acid histidine. They also give a conclusion that if the number of wildcards is bounded by a fixed constant, the problem can be solved in linear time.

Another respective example is about *promoter*. In bioinformatics, *promoter* will help researchers to quickly locate the starting position of the intron from hundreds of millions of the sequence of *ACGT*. Among these promoters, *TATA* box is a common one (Manber & Baeza-Yates, 1991). It has very loose sequence specificity, so many *TATA* sequences are not

TATA box. As a result, indirect positioning by pairs of sites is needed. The commonly used one is *CAATCT* sequence. The DNA sequence *TATA* is a common promoter that often occurs after the sequence *CAATCT* within 30-50 wildcards. Therefore, matching patterns with wildcards becomes especially crucial in exploring valuable information from DNA sequences.

There are many applications that involve pattern matching with wildcards and various researches have provided many solutions to different forms of this problem. Fischer and Paterson were the first to generalized pattern matching with wildcards (Fischer & Paterson, 1974): given a pattern P and a text T, either of which may contain wildcards, denoted by ¢, the goal is to locate all P's occurrences in T. ¢ can match any letter in a given alphabet, such as a¢¢c¢t. Unlike previous work, Chen, et al. proposed a PMWL problem integrating two problems(Chen et al., 2006): one is complex local constraints which means the user can specify a different range of wildcards between each two consecutive letters of P, for example, a¢[0,3]c¢[1,3]t. Another one is global length constraints. The user can constrain the length of each matching substring of T in which P occurs. Therefore, flexible constraints of wildcards conduct flexible jump of the matching positions. The definition of PMWL problem is an extension of Fischer and Paterson's definition and the introduction of complex local constraints increase the flexibility. On one hand, this definition of pattern is more suitable for areas such as bioinformatics; on the other hand, the size of the matching candidate positions is in the exponential increment which greatly increases the complexity of the problem solving.

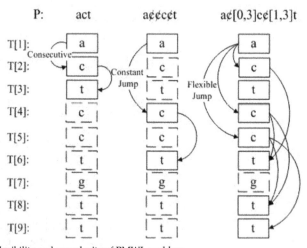

Figure 1. The flexibility and complexity of PMWL problem

From a view of practical point, they also proposed two issues: with and without the *one-off* condition (Chen et al., 2006; Min et al., 2009). In their problem definition, users have more flexibility to search on sequences and the *one-off* condition has both theoretical and practical significance. *One-off* condition means that every letter in T can be used once at most. In practical applications, with and without the *one-off* condition has practical meaning in specific areas. For example, in sequential pattern analysis in data mining, P can be treated as a candidate shopping pattern, the user is interested in how frequently P occurs in one document, it makes sense to count each occurrence for once, what is more, the *one-off* condition also makes the problem solving possible. However, under the *one-off* condition, how to allocate limited text resource to each matching occurrences, in order to obtaining the maximum number of occurrences, belongs to optimization problem. In the allocation of resources, the matching of different letters in the pattern possess a strong correlation, which conducts the selection of matching positions in the combination of explosive growth. Since it is difficult to develop a complete matching strategy in this problem, almost existed algorithms for PMWL are using greedy matching strategies, which is the root reason why matching algorithm is not complete. This article will focus on SAIL algorithm (Chen et al., 2006) which is a representative algorithm for PMWL problem and will also describe RSAIL (Wang et al., 2010), SBO (Wu et al., 2011), BPBM (Guo et al., 2011) algorithm which are all designed to solve PMWL problem in different conditions. The each of above algorithms has its own characteristics in the data structures and matching strategies, which will be analyzed in this paper.

What is more, since the theoretic and practical importance of the definition of PMWL, we need to research the nature of this problem. To our best knowledge, there are still no efficient methods on this problem, because as for completeness of the problem, we still do not know whether it could be solved in polynomial time. In this article, we will research the completeness of PMWL under certain condition. In the traditional matching problem, description of pattern and text information is the key to the algorithm design, however, flexibility and complexity of the PMWL problem all depends on the pattern features, so this article will focus on pattern information, especially the pattern features including the size of alphabet, the length of pattern, the *gap* of wildcards in the pattern, etc. We will also investigate the relationship between pattern features and completeness, and use the approximate ratio judgment. Further more, since the definition itself is produced in realistic background, we need to consider the situation in real biological background and improve the solution of the problem. Based on the above, we choose this topic as a research object in this book.

This capture is organized as follows: In section 2 we will give the development, definition and application of PMWL problem; Section 3 will show the representative algorithms, we will introduce their structure, strategy, complexity and completeness; Section 4 will analyze the PMWL problem completeness based on pattern features. We will give our conclusions in section 5.

2. Pattern matching with wildcards and length constraints

The sequential pattern matching problem is to given a Text T and a pattern P as input, and output all the occurrences of P in T. After Fischer and Paterson's work, there are a variety of non-standard definitions of the pattern matching problem: the approximate matching (He et al., 2007), the swapped matching (Amir et al., 2000), the Parameterized matching (Amir et al., 2009), etc. They all belong to *Non-standard Stringology* problem (Muthukrishnan, 1994). Many of them are still open problems.

2.1. The development of PMWL problem

After years of development, these *Non-standard Stringology* problems always focus on a problem: that is, how to conduct the traditional pattern matching definition to be more flexible to adapt the development of application. The *don't cares* problem always focus on how to combine the wildcards and the pattern. After Fischer and Paterson's work, Cole et al. considered a slightly different problem (Cole et al., 2004), where instead of fixing the number of ¢s between two consecutive letters in P and T, they fixed the total number of ¢s in P. The disadvantage of these problem definitions is that the number of ¢s is a constant but not a range. This limits flexibilities for the user's queries. To alleviate the problem of a fixed number of ¢s, Kucherov et al. (Kucherov et al., 1995) proposed a solution to allow an unbounded number of ¢s between two consecutive letters in a given pattern. Given a set of such patterns, their objective is to find whether any of these patterns matches some substring of the text that does not contain any ¢.Obviously, allowing an unbounded number of ¢s still does not offer the users enough flexibilities to control their queries. Manber et al. (Manber & Baeza-Yates, 1991) proposed an algorithm for string matching with a sequence of wildcards. They considered the following problem: given two pattern strings P and Q, each of which consists of letters, and an integer g, all occurrences of the form $P¢_{0-g}Q$ in the text are returned. The number of ¢s between P and Q is in the range of $[0, g]$, and the text does not contain any ¢. This problem was so-called exact string matching with variable-length *don't cares*. Chen et al. sum up all these definitions into three conditions (Chen et al., 2006): firstly, there is a wildcard between two consecutive letters in P, for example A¢[0,1]T¢[0,2]G¢[1,3]C; secondly, every letter in T can only be used once for matching; thirdly, there is a global constraint to limit the matching occurrence length. We call the problem satisfying above definition PMWL problem, which has been used in approximate matching, pattern mining, information retrieval, etc.

2.2. The potential applications of the PMWL problem

1. Text Indexing: There is a large amount of hypertext information on the Internet. How to effectively obtain information that meet users' needs is becoming more and more urgent. Text indexing is a method to solve this problem. How to determine the position of user-specified pattern (may contain wildcards) is a challenge task.

2. Data stream is becoming more and more crucial in many new database applications such as data warehouse and sensor network. Mining dependence or association in large amounts of data flow has practical value and during which the sequential pattern matching with wildcards is the first and the most important step. In addition, in data mining, sequential pattern mining also search frequent patterns as in transaction sequence, a typical instance is the similar consuming pattern of many consumers, for example, buying a desktop, a laser printer, a digital camera and an LCD screen monitor in turn, between each of them exists a certain time interval. Mining such typical user mode, which is obviously a pattern matching with wildcards, will has a great influence on the market.

3. Network Security: Pattern matching methods in network security and intrusion detection need high performance. A complete IDS (Intrusion Detection System) based on Snort rules needs to optimize hundreds of rules and many of them need to do pattern matching efficiently for the entire data partition of a package. Efficient pattern matching and mining with wildcards constraints give the system administrator a more flexible and accurate solution to locate the suspicious users.

2.3. Problem statement for PMWL

Definition 1 Let Σ be an alphabet, $T = t_0 t_1 ... t_{n-1} \in \Sigma^*$ is called a **text** of Σ where $n = |T|$ is the length of T. A **pattern** is a tuple $P = (p, g)$ where $p = p_0 p_1 ... p_{m-1}$ is a sequence of characters, which belong to the alphabet Σ , and $g = g_0 g_1 ... g_{m-2}$ is a sequence of wildcards. And $m = |P|$ is the length of P. The interval of wildcards between p_i and p_{i+1} is denoted by $g_i = g(N_i, M_i)$ where $0 \le i \le m - 1$, called the **local constraints**. N_i and M_i is the upper and lower limit of wildcard. Such as $P = a\xcent[1,3]g$, where 1, 3 is respectively the lower and upper limit of local constraints. $\xcent[1,3]$ means the wildcards between a and g is referring to a string which length is 1~3. Given interval [*minLen, maxLen*], set *globalLength* = $t[a_{m-1}]$ - $t[a_0]$ +1, if *globalLength* $\in$ [*minLen, maxLen*], then it is called **global constraint** (Chen et al., 2006).

Definition 2 Given a pattern $P = (p, g)$, $p = p_0 p_1 ... p_{m-1}$, $g_i = g(N_i, M_i)$. The *max* $\{M_i - N_i\}$ where $0 \le i \le m - 1$ is called the *gap* of local constraints, named **Gap** for short. For example, $P = a\xcent[0,2]g\xcent[1,4]g$, then *gap* = *max*{2 - 0, 4 - 1} = 3.

PMWL problem can be defined by the above definition:

Definition 3 PMWL problem (Pattern Matching with Wildcards and Length constraints)

Pattern Matching with Wildcards and Length constraints meets the following conditions:

1. ¢s can occur between each two consecutive letters in pattern and are independent to each other;
2. ¢s between two consecutive letters can match a string which length is limited by *local constraints*, and the total length of pattern is limited by *global constraint*;
3. *One-off* condition is taken into consideration that every letter in T can only be used once for matching $p_j (0 \le j \le m - 1)$ and as soon as there exists one occurrence of P in T when T is being scanned from left to right it will be returned.

Definition 4 Given a text T and a pattern P, if there is a sequence of matching positions $A = (a_1, a_2, ..., a_{m-1})$, where $t[a_i] = p[i]$ for every $0 \le i < m - 1$, we say **A** is a matching **occurrence** of P. A set of occurrences $A_1, A_2, ..., A_t$ constitute an occurrence set U where t is the number of occurrences, and also named **matching number** in our paper.

Definition 5 Let t be the matching number of A, if there is no occurrence set A' with the matching number t', and $t' > t$, then A is called a **complete occurrence set**. If there is another occurrence set U, with the matching number $t_u = t$, the U is equivalent to A. Specially, if A is complete, and so is U. So the complete occurrence set is not always unique.

3. Algorithms for PMWL

The results of traditional matching algorithm are complete, so the focus of research is to improve the matching efficiency. As a kind of searching problem, the key to solving matching problem is how to use and extract information getting from text and pattern. KMP, BM algorithm uses automata to describe the pattern characteristics, and deposit information obtained from scanning during matching process into automata. Algorithm visits the automata, when the jump distance needs to be calculated, thus to avoid obtaining the pattern information repeatedly and to ensure the jump in matching process does not affect the final result. The basic idea the suffix tree is to use the tree structure to describe the text information, and to avoid scanning the same text repeatedly when matching a set of patterns. We believe that data structure and search strategy are crucial for traditional algorithms to access to information of text and pattern. Reasonable data structure is better to explore the potential of the computer, such as bit parallel technology, and can also be a more reasonable representation of the sequence information, such as automata. In addition, there exist the sliding window, indexes and other data structures. Reasonable matching strategy makes better use of sequence information. These strategies can approximately be divided into prefix searching, suffix searching and factor searching (Navarro & Raffinot, 2001).

	Characteristics	Representative algorithms	Methods	Remarks
prefix searching	Forward search to find the longest common prefix of text and pattern strings in searching window	KMP Shift-And	Deterministic automata Bit parallel, non-deterministic automata	Most of them are sliding window technique, the scope of algorithm application depends on the alphabet size and the pattern length
suffix searching	Backward search to find the longest common suffix of text and pattern strings, can skip some text characters, the difficulty is how to safely move the window	BM Horspool	Pre-calculation of the three functions used to determine the safe jumping distance Improve the function of the BM, can have a greater jump distance, especially suitable for larger alphabet	
factor searching	Backward search to determine whether the suffix of text in searching window is a substring of pattern string	BDM BNDM BOM	Suffix automaton Bit parallel Factor Oracle automaton, suitable for longer pattern	

Table 1. Analysis of the traditional pattern matching algorithms

As different extension of traditional matching problem, PMWL problem, approximate matching, and swap matching all belong to the *Non-standard Stringology* problem. Problems in this field mostly belong to the optimization problem, and most of them have not yet been completely solved, such as PMWL and approximate matching problems with wildcards etc. What PMWL and traditional matching problem have in common are:

1. From the view of algorithm itself, the data structures and matching strategies are as the key of algorithm design.
2. From the view of describing the object, how to effectively describe the patterns and text information is the key to solve the problem.

What PMWL and traditional matching problem have in difference are:

1. For PMWL, there is no complete solving yet, so algorithm evaluation criteria include both time efficiency and solution quality; but traditional matching algorithm is only concerned with matching time.
2. The flexibility and complexity of the PMWL problem definition are reflected in the pattern, therefore, compared with traditional matching, PMWL pay more attention to the description of the pattern information. Pattern characteristics are extremely associated with the solution of PMWL problem.

Next, we will give the representative algorithms for solving PMWL problem, and detailed description of their design ideas from the perspective of data structure and matching strategy.

3.1. The SAIL Algorithm

Description of SAIL Algorithm (Chen et al., 2006):

Input: A text $T = t_0t_1...t_{n-1}$, a pattern $P = p_0p_1...p_{m-1}$, local constraints $g_i = g(N_i, M_i)$, global constraints [*minLen*, *maxLen*].

Output: Occurrences of P in T satisfying the constraints.

The Steps of the algorithm:

1. *Location*: ① Search position i where $t[i] = p[m-1]$, and locate position k where $t[k] = p[0]$ by considering the global constraint. ② Cut out a substring in T from $t[k]$ to $t[i]$ named T'. ③ Build the table with the row and column according to T' and P.
2. *Forward*: Scan the table forward, and mark all the positions satisfying the local and global constraints. They are the potential matching positions.
3. *Backward*: Scan the table backward, and select the *left-most* position in the marked cells every row that compose an occurrence. Then mark them used.

Generally, SAIL starts from the beginning of T to search position i where $t[i] = p[m-1]$. After that, SAIL conducts two phases, the *Forward* phase and the *Backward* phase. In the *Forward* phase, SAIL determines whether there is a potential matching occurrence by using a search table. Afterwards, if a potential matching occurrence can be determined, *Backward* phase is triggered out to output an optimal occurrence by using the *left-most* strategy.

A running example for SAIL:

In this subsection, we show how SAIL works with a running example where P, T and constraints are given as follows.

0	1	2	3	4	5	6	7	8	9
T t	t	a	a	g	g	c	c	c	c

P a¢[0,1]g¢[0,1]c¢[0,1]c, $minLen = 6$, $maxLen = 7$

Table 2. A running example for SAIL

Step 1. Scan the $P[m-1]$, that is the letter 'c', in T from left to right. The first matching position is 6, and then SAIL enters the *Location* phase. Use the global constraint [6, 7] to locate $P[0]$'s position, that is the letter 'a'. We get the scanning range is [6-6, 7-6]. However there are no matching in [0, 1]. Then SAIL move on.

Step 2. The second matching position is 7, and we can locate $P[0]$ in position 2. Then we get the substring "aaggcc" from T. In this way global constraint is satisfied.

Step 3. Build a 4x6 table. The row stand for character in P, and the column is the substring. Then set the position pos[3][5], pos[0][0] and pos[0][1] to 1.

Step 4. Enter *Forward* and set all the positions to 1 in the table, which satisfy the local constraints.

Positions in *Text*						
Positions in *Table*						
a						
g						
c						
c						

Table 3. The constructed search table pos[j][i-start] when $P[m-1]$ is 7

Step 5. Enter *Backward* and select the left-most one from the marked positions in each row, and they are highlighted. In this way, we will get an occurrence {2, 4, 6, 7} and mark the four positions used.

Step 6. Go on to execute *Location* and get the third matching position is 8, then we can build the table below. Notice the positions of 6, 7 have been used. Under the *one-off* condition, all used positions (marked as * in Table) of T are never considered for further matching again. If the *one-off* condition is not considered, SAIL will get another two occurrences {2, 4, 6, 8} and {3, 5, 7, 9}. Then the *Forward* phase returns false, and SAIL go back to *Location*.

Step 7. In position 9, the *Forward* also returns false. Finally, SAIL output only one occurrence {2, 4, 6, 7}.

Positions in *Text*						
Positions in *Table*						
		*		*	*	
a						
g						
c						
c						

Table 4. The constructed search table pos[*j*][*i*-start] when *P*[*m*-1] is 8

The time complexity and completeness analysis:

O(SAIL) = O(*n* + *klmg*) where *n* is the length of *T*, *k* is the frequency of *P*'s last letter occurring in *T*, *l* is the user-specified maximum length for each matching substring, *m* is the length of *P*, and g is the maximum *gap* of wildcards in *P*.

Two important issues, *Online searching* and *Optimization*, are taken into consideration to design SAIL. As for optimization, under the *one-off* condition, SAIL determines which occurrence is an optimal one if multiple occurrences end at a *P*[*m*-1]'s position by applying the *left-most* strategy. As a heuristic algorithm, SAIL utilizes a kind of greedy strategy to select a set of occurrences; consequently, SAIL may obtain locally optimal solution which lead to losing occurrences in offline searching.

Form the above example, we can know that a complete occurrence set for text *T* is {{2, 4, 6, 8}, {3, 5, 7, 9}}, but SAIL's output is {{2, 4, 6, 7}}.

We believe that the SAIL's data structure is based on the sliding window, the *Location* also uses the *left-most* strategy, so it is possible to lose occurrences, for instance:

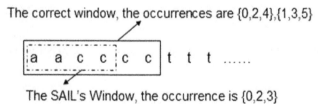

Figure 2. A sliding window in SAIL

Obviously, in the above example, SAIL loses occurrences in offline condition because of the selection of character *c*'s matching position. For further observation, it is not difficult to find that character *c* appears in the pattern twice. If pattern is a¢[0,1]g¢[0,1]c, SAIL will get a complete occurrence set, that is, {{2, 4, 6},{3, 5, 7}}. Further experiments show that, the recurring appearances of pattern characters influence the quality of matching occurrences obtained by the algorithm. In next part, we will analyze the completeness of PMWL based on pattern features.

3.2. The RSAIL Algorithm

Description of RSAIL Algorithm (Wang et al., 2010):

Definition 6 Given a pattern P, if there are letters $p[i] = p[j]$ where $0 \leq i \leq m\text{-}1, 0 \leq j \leq m\text{-}1$, P is called a **pattern with Recurring characters,** and **R pattern** in short, such as a¢[0,1]c¢[0,1]c¢[0,1]t.

Definition 7 Given a pattern P, if all the letters in P are different, P is called a **pattern with No-Recurring characters** and **NR Pattern** for brevity, such as a¢[0,1]c¢[0,1]g¢[0,1]t.

Definition 8 Given a pattern P, if there is a position i such that $p[i] = p[i+1] = \ldots\ldots = p[m\text{-}1]$ where $1 \leq i < m\text{-}1$, P is called a pattern with recurring tail characters and **RT pattern** in short. Such as a¢[0,1]c¢[0,1]c. As we can see, the RT pattern is a special form of the R pattern.

From the above discussion, in the research of Chen et al., since they only concern about the on-line situation, their proof of SAIL's completeness is incomplete, which is only suitable for the on-line situation. What is more, it ignores the interaction between different occurrences.

We find that SAIL satisfies the completeness under a certain restriction, i.e. the pattern with no-recurring character (NR pattern), such as a¢[0, 1]t¢[0, 1]g¢[0, 1]c¢[0, 1]. The concept of NR pattern has practical significance, for example, in text mining, where the text is a sequence of words, the NR pattern reflects the semantic relation between words.

We utilize the symmetry to scan the text and the pattern. Then convert an RT pattern into an R pattern.

1. According to the characteristic of P, if it is not an RT pattern, we directly call SAIL; otherwise go to (2);
2. Reverse T and P, respectively get T', P';
3. Call SAIL, and obtain the occurrences of P' in T';
4. Obtain the occurrences of P in T by coordinate transformation of the obtained solution.

Obviously, since the time of the identification of pattern's characteristics is linear, O (RSAIL) = O (SAIL).

Experiments and Analysis:

We will give a set of experiments to illustrate two problems:

1. Analysis of the complete extent of the SAIL algorithm;
2. The comparison of the complete extent of RSAIL and SAIL algorithm;

Considering there is no algorithm can obtain the completeness occurrences of PMWL problem in polynomial time, we have developed a text generator (Xie et al., 2010) to generate experimental text, by which way we can know the completeness occurrences in order to analyze the complete extent of algorithm. In addition, the patterns used in these experiments are all RT patterns.

	Experiment1	Experiment 2	Experiment 3	Experiment 4
Size of alphabet Σ	4	4	4	7
Length of pattern m	3	4	5	5
gap	0~30	0~30	0~30	0~30

Table 5. The parameters in the experiments.

The experimental results and analysis:

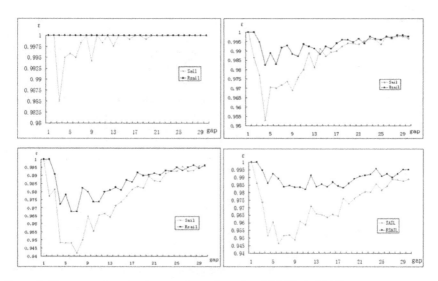

Figure 3. The approximate ratio experimental results of RSAIL and SAIL

From the above images, SAIL itself is already a near-complete algorithm, in the above graphs, the average approximation ratio of SAIL is higher than 0.94;For the RT patterns, the completeness of RSAIL is better than SAIL in different Σ, m and gap. Thus, not only a revised algorithm is obtained, the SAIL's deficiency on handling RT patterns is also proved from another aspect.

3.3. The BPBM Algorithm

Description of BPBM Algorithm (Guo et al., 2011):

Like the SAIL algorithm, the BPBM algorithm also focuses on pattern matching in online sequential text with both flexible *gap* constraints by user's specification and the *one-off* condition. BPBM is based on bit-parallel technology to simulate the matching process and adopt two nondeterministic finite state automatons (NFAs). One is a search mechanism to identify all pattern *P*'s suffix, and another one is a security window transition mechanism which accelerates the scanning process by dropping useless sequences in text.

BPBM has following characteristics:

1.   BPBM also uses the *left-most* strategy to obtain the maximal occurrence of pattern in text, and return all these matching position sequences. This algorithm combines bit-parallel technology with nondeterministic finite state automatons. It also simplifies the calculation of shift distance of the security window transition, which gets good results. BPBM inherits the advantage of BM algorithm to skip some of characters in text, which conducts the algorithm with a sub linear average time complexity. Therefore, the time complexity of BPBM is lower compared to SAIL.

2.   Compared with Gaps-Shift-And algorithm and Gaps-BNDM algorithm, since they are all based on bit-parallel technology, their time performances are equal, however, because BPBM improves the formula of ε-transition in matching process, BPBM is fit for all patterns. In addition, BPBM returns a concrete set of matching position sequence, which makes it more applicable.

3.   Compared with SAIL, SAIL applies two-dimensional table as data structure, but BPBM is base on bit-parallel technology. Since the difference in data structure, BPBM has a better time performance. The similarity between these two algorithms is they all utilize the *left-most* strategy, therefore, they are all heuristic algorithm with greedy strategy. In addition, the matching occurrences of these two algorithms are same and both incomplete.

3.4. The SBO Algorithm

Description of BPBM Algorithm (Wu et al., 2011):

Wu et al. propose a new nonlinear structure called *Nettree* to deal with pattern matching with flexible constraints of wildcards. A *Nettree* is a kind of directed acyclic graph (DAG) with edge labels. They apply a heuristic algorithm to select better occurrence (SBO). In this algorithm, they use two strategies: Strategy of Greedy Search Parent, SGSP and Strategy of *right-most* Parent, SRMP to two occurrences of the same leaf, and select the better one as occurrence. The core idea of SGSP is finding an approximately optimal parent (AOP) of current node in each step; while the core idea of SRMP is finding the right-most parent node of current node in each step.

In *off-line* conditions, owing to its heuristic strategy, SBO can obtain more occurrences than SAIL and BPBM in most cases, but it is still incompleteness. However, the time complexity of SBO algorithm is $O(gap*n*(n+m^2))$ which is nonlinear of length of text. Further more, experiments show that, in general, SBO indeed consumes more time than SAIL. In SBO, the improvement of solution's quality is relying on using heuristic strategies repeatedly, and this also consumes a lot of time. Therefore, we need consider the balance between completeness and time efficiency of algorithm. What is more, SAIL originally is not designed for *off-line* condition, as an *on-line* algorithm, it only has current information, so when applying it to *off-line* matching it will definitely be imperfect. But SBO uses global information to search occurrences, it also uses heuristic strategies to search on solution space. With the improvement of occurrences' quality, there are two problems: more information need more place to store, so the space complexity of SBO is $O(gap^*m^*n)$, the next one is more information means more calculations thus consuming more time.

3.5. Other algorithms

In many literatures, similar problems are defined and various algorithms are put out to solve certain problems. Morgante, et al. (Morgante, et al., 2004) described a structured model, which can be considered as 'compound patterns' made of a list of simple motifs and a list of intervals that specify at what distances adjacent motifs should occur. They gave a detailed description of the biological background of the problem definition. For example, many retrotransposons belonging to the Ty1-copia group contain a match of MT¢[115,136]MTNTAYGG¢[121,151]GTNGAYGAY, which consists of three patterns and two intervals. As the paper pointed out, structured motifs are called classes of Characters and Bounded Gaps (CBG) expressions in Navarro and Raffinot, but use of these expressions is quite different: the underlying motivation for CBG expressions is searching in database like PROSITE and a sequence of this kind is usually not very long, while structured motifs can be very long since gaps may span many letters. As we can see, the concept of CBG and structured motifs are all have practical meaning. Because of the different application background, they design different algorithms to solve their problems. From the application point, this paper also considered a problem of q-approximation match which means just finding partial motifs in the sequence. In this paper, they proposed a two-step procedure which is used in many algorithms for PMWL: firstly, finding the occurrences of all the component patterns; secondly, combining the occurrences that satisfy the distance constraints into a structured motif. For step two, they gave a detailed algorithm to build a directed acyclic graph according to the positions of the component patterns and interval constraints. Then they discussed how to output all the occurrences in detail. In (Rahman et al., 2006), the definition of their problem likes SAIL, but they don't consider global constraints and the *one-off* searching. In addition, just like paper (Chen et al., 2006), the local constraints exist between two substrings, while in SAIL, exist between any two consecutive letters. Certainly, a single character is a substring, but in this paper, all these substrings are used to build an AC automaton. It is not efficient to build a Trie structure over a set of single letters. This paper also used a two-step procedure: firstly using AC automaton to get occurrences of each sub-patterns in orders and combine them. They built an implicit graph, in which vertices are partitioned into several sets in order according to the corresponding sub-pattern and edges between two consecutive sets means two positions in these two consecutive sets fit corresponding local constraints. To output all P in T, we have to enumerate all possible paths in the implicit directed graph which length is the number of sub-patterns in the pattern. Morgante, et al. (Morgante, et al., 2004) applied a revised depth first searching algorithm. Philip Bille et al. (Bille et al., 2010) defined a concept named variable length *gap* (VLG) which is a pattern formed by a sequence of strings and variable length gaps. Obviously, this definition is almost the same with above works. Unlike Rahman's work, although this paper also applies AC automaton, it maintains a sorted list containing the ranges defined by previously reported relevant occurrences, and naturally it uses the *left-most* strategy to count an occurrence as soon as it appears. Haapasalo et al. (Haapasalo et al., 2011) extended the usual dictionary matching problem to the case in which patterns may include single wildcards, or wildcard strings of variable length with fixed or unlimited upper bound. And their algorithm is designed for *on-line* matching: the text is scanned only once, and the matches for all patterns are reported at the point of occurrence. Firstly, they constructed an AC PMA (pattern matching automaton) with output tuples identifying the keywords of the patterns to be matched. The idea in their algorithm is that they recognize keywords by the PMA and check whether or not a newly found keyword forms a continuation of a pattern prefix found thus far.

3.6. Discussion

Because of the complexity of the PMWL problem definition, we believe that the matching occurrence of PMWL problem is with high degrees of freedom. In traditional matching problem with fixed-length wildcard, the positions of each match in the same set of the matching occurrence are relatively fixed to each other. Therefore, to determine the position of any one character, a set of matching occurrences have been identified. We believe that matching of each character in above problem has a strong correlation. For instance, in pattern a¢g¢¢c, $p[2] - p[1] = 1$, $p[3] - p[2] = 2$. However, for pattern in PWML, matching positions of adjacent characters are bounded by local constraints, which means matching of each character has a weak correlation, and to determine the positions of all characters, a set of matching occurrences could have been identified, that is, freedom degree of matching increases. This is an important factor leads to the complexity of the PMWL problem, which greatly increases the difficulties of searching process in matching algorithms. In order to get a complete solution, a lot of backtracking operation are required, making it difficult to be completed in polynomial time, therefore, almost all PMWL algorithms use greedy strategies in matching process. This is destined to incomplete results. However, on the other hand, although the above algorithms are not complete, we find that when length of pattern is shorter than 6, the approximation ratio of these algorithms are more than 0.9. Consequently, the next work can be considered form two aspects: 1, based on SAIL algorithm etc, improving the time efficiency, like BPBM; 2, designing algorithm for PMWL under certain conditions, such as RSAIL's work for RT pattern. We believe that the pattern features, data structures and matching strategies will continue to be the center for PMWL algorithm design.

	SAIL	RSAIL	BPBM	SBO
Matching strategy	*left-most* (greedy strategy)	*left-most, right-most* (greedy strategy)	*left-most* (greedy strategy)	*SGSP,SRMP* (greedy strategy)
Data structure	Sliding window	Sliding window	Bit-parallel	Nettree
Time consumption	All polynomial time and SBO > RSAIL = SAIL > BPBM			
Completeness	All incompleteness, in general SBO > RSAIL > SAIL = BPBM			

Table 6. The strategy, structure, time consumption and completeness of PMWL methods

4. Analysis of PMWL based on pattern features

In the traditional matching problems, how to search pattern in text much faster as well as the correlation between pattern and text are paid more attention. But the characteristics of the pattern itself are paid little direct attention, because traditional matching problems can always have complete occurrences. The main characteristic of PMWL is with flexible wildcards, which leads to a large number of candidate matching positions. And the conflict between these occurrences will cause the final output incompleteness. However, our research shows that the direct cause which impacts PMWL incompleteness is not wildcards; it is the pattern characteristics directly conduct PMWL incompleteness. This is much different from traditional matching problems.

4.1. The impact of the alphabet, the length of pattern and the gap on completeness

In the traditional pattern matching research, the length of pattern and the size of alphabet are key elements influencing time complexity when analyzing traditional matching problems. Taking into account PMWL problem definition, upper and lower limits of the length constraints probably affect problem solving. Especially, instead of upper and lower limits themselves, the distance between the upper and lower limits, that is gap, are taken into consideration. Therefore, the parameters related to the algorithm completeness may be the size of alphabet, the length of pattern and distance between the upper and lower limits, denoted as Σ, m, and gap respectively. In this article, the approximate degree of completeness of the algorithm will be measured by approximation ratio ε. Consequently, we try to build following model:

$$\varepsilon = F (\Sigma, m, gap) \tag{1}$$

Taking into account that the size of Σ is determined in a specific area, for example, in bioinformatics, DNA sequences can be defined on $\Sigma = \{a, c, g, t\}$, the above formula can be simplified as $\varepsilon = F (m, gap)$. In experiment project, input text is a biology DNA sequence, so $\Sigma = \{a, c, g, t\}$. Then the remaining parameter values are as follows: $gap \in [1, 30]$, $m \in [3, 9]$, consequently, there are $30*7 = 210$ groups of experiments. The aim is to find approximation ratio ε.

Firstly, pattern P is generated randomly by pattern generator according to Σ, m, and gap. For example, when $m = 5$, $\Sigma = \{a, c, g, t\}$, $gap = 2$, a¢[0,2]c¢[0,2]c¢[0,2]t¢[0,2]g is a qualified pattern. For simplicity, in generated patterns, each two consecutive characters have the same length constraints i.e. gap. Then, what needs to be done is calculating approximate ratio ε for each pattern. Since $\varepsilon = N(U_{ALG}) / N(U_{opt})$, we need to know $N(U_{opt})$. However, it is not desirable to directly solve this from a text T, since there is no any known algorithm to obtain the completeness solution. If we use a simple brute-force, the exponential time will be need. Therefore, we have developed a text generator, which can generate text T according to P and $N(U_{ALG})$. In addition, SAIL algorithm is currently regarded as the most representative algorithm for PMWL problem, since SAIL firstly adopts the *left-most* strategy which is applied in different situations and technologies such as BPBM(Guo et al., 2011) algorithm and the mining algorithm MAIL(Xie et al., 2010). Based on the above analysis, we have SAIL as a research object, that is, $N(U_{ALG}) = N(U_{SAIL})$.

In summary, the concrete steps of the experiment are as follows:

1. For given Σ, m and gap, 100 patterns p_i are generated randomly, where $i = 1, 2,.., 100$;
2. For pattern p_i, given $N(U_{opt}) = 100$, text length n = 2000, generate text T_i;
3. For T_i, call SAIL algorithm to get $N(U_{SAIL})$;
4. Calculating $\varepsilon_i = N(U_{ALG}) / N(U_{opt})$;
5. Calculating $\varepsilon = \sum_{i=0}^{100} \varepsilon_i / 100$.

	Experiment1	Experiment 2
Σ	4	7
m	3~9	3~9
gap	1~29	1~29

Table 7. Parameters in experiments for $\varepsilon = F\,(gap)$

The experimental results：

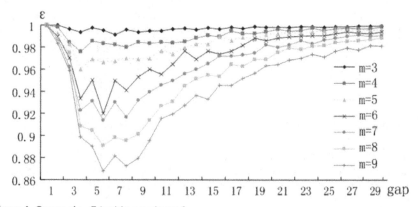

Figure 4. Curves of $\varepsilon = F\,(gap)$ in experiment 1

By the *figure* 4, as m increases, ε is gradually decreasing. As the *gap* increases, the trend of ε is decreasing first and then increases, especially when $gap = 1$ and $\varepsilon = 1$, since the *left-most* strategy can obtain a complete occurrence set. With the increase of gap, ε begin to decline because when the *gap* is becoming greater, the probability of matching occurrences overlap is becoming greater and the algorithm is becoming more easily to lose occurrences; when *gap* is sufficient, although matching occurrences are still overlap, greater *gap* reserve enough space for matching, making the remaining occurrences which have not yet been still have enough resources. Moreover, it is worth noting that the minimum of these curves can be reached when *gap* is about 7, and have nothing to do with the pattern length.

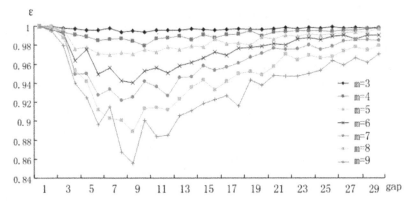

Figure 5. Curves of $\varepsilon = F\,(gap)$ in experiment 2

In *figure* 5, the trend of curves is the same as in *figure* 4. The difference between them is curves in *figure* 5 reach the minimum when *gap* is about 9~11. It can be found that the impact of Σ, m, and *gap* on the curves is that the change of *gap* determines the trend of the curve, m affects the magnitude of this change, and Σ makes the curve do translational move.

	A	B	C	D	E
	1.79E-07	-1.31E-05	3.27E-04	-2.98E-03	1.0032
	4.97E-07	-3.74E-05	9.59E-04	-8.81E-03	1.0072
	9.95E-07	-7.37E-05	1.85E-03	-1.65E-02	1.0142
	1.98E-06	-1.44E-04	3.51E-03	-3.05E-02	1.0276
	2.45E-06	-1.79E-04	4.44E-03	-3.94E-02	1.038
	3.20E-06	-2.36E-04	5.94E-03	-5.40E-02	1.061
	3.55E-06	-2.64E-04	6.68E-03	-6.16E-02	1.0672
0	3.84E-06	-2.87E-04	7.33E-03	-6.82E-02	1.0688
1	4.11E-06	-3.10E-04	8.01E-03	-7.61E-02	1.0796
2	4.58E-06	-3.39E-04	8.61E-03	-8.13E-02	1.0809
3	4.79E-06	-3.53E-04	8.98E-03	-8.57E-02	1.0805
4	5.44E-06	-3.97E-04	9.99E-03	-9.47E-02	1.0922

Table 8. Parameters in mathematic model

After a series of experiments, we speculate that $\varepsilon = A^*gap^4 + B^*gap^3 + C^*gap^2 + D^*gap + E$, where A, B, C, D and E are parameters and for different m there are different parameters. We try to use this model to illustrate the relation between gap and approximation ratio ε.

Use this parameter table, some of illustrations for $m = 3, 4......14$ are listed below, where horizontal axis is the gap, vertical axis is the ε.

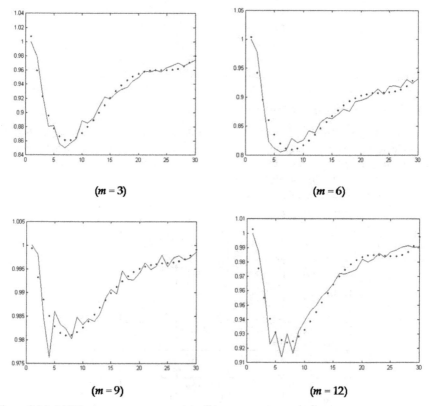

$(m = 3)$ $(m = 6)$

$(m = 9)$ $(m = 12)$

Figure 6. Model fitting

We believe this model can be used to predict the completeness of solutions given a certain pattern. For example, given $m = 10$, $\Sigma = \{a, c, g, t\}$, $gap = 5$, this model shows the prediction of approximation ratio ε of SAIL algorithm is about 0.878. Therefore, this model can be used in pattern mining showed as below.

PMWL pattern mining evaluation mechanism

Input: Given T, Σ, m, gap, support sup

Output: pattern P

As we know, mining algorithm strategy is to learn from the strategy of matching algorithm, so PMWL pattern mining problem is naturally based on PMWL matching problem. For example, in mining algorithm MAIL (Xie et al., 2010), although a graph structure is utilized which conducts it different from SAIL; it is still based on the *left-most* strategy. As a result, they have the same degree of completeness. Therefore, our model can propose an evaluation mechanism for mining.

4.2. The impact of pattern *rep* on completeness

In next part, we will put forward another important concept, named *rep*, and analyze its impact on completeness. We first give an example to illustrate the reason why this concept is needed. Given $m = 4$, $\Sigma = \{a, c, g, t\}$, $gap = 2$, the corresponding patterns maybe $P_1 = a¢[0,2]c¢[0,2]g¢[0,2]t$ or $P_2 = a¢[0,2]c¢[0,2]c¢[0,2]t$. They have the same Σ, m and gap. However, when applying SAIL or BPBM, the completeness of solutions is not the same, since for P_1 algorithms can obtain complete solutions while for P_2 can not.

Considering two examples below:

	0	1	2	3	4	5	6
T	b	c	b	b	b	c	c
P			b¢[1,2] b¢[1,2]c				

Table 9. Example 1 for *rep* concept

A complete occurrence set of this example is {{0, 3, 5}, {2, 4, 6}}, the number of matching occurrences is 2. It is not difficult to find that, in SAIL algorithm, for *position* 5, the selection of position 2 as $p[1]$'s occurrence by the *left-most* strategy will consume the position for the next matching occurrence. We can guess that, the recurring 'b' character in this pattern affect the quality of matching occurrences.

	0	1	2	3	4	5
T	a	a	c	c	c	c
P	a¢[0,1] c¢[0,1]c					

Table 10. Example 1 for *rep* concept

In this example, A complete occurrence set is {{0, 2, 4}, {1, 3, 5}}, the number of matching occurrences is 2. If we use SAIL algorithm and first obtain {0, 2, 3}, then we will only get this occurrence and lose {0, 2, 4}, {1, 3, 5}. Obviously, the recurring 'b' character in this pattern affects the completeness.

From above examples, the matching of recurring character in the pattern may determine the completeness of the algorithm. As a result, we consider this repeatability as an element to influence the completeness.

In order to quantify the repeatability, the concept of repeatability, *rep*, is proposed in this paper.

Definition 9 Given a pattern $P = p_0p_1...p_{m-1}$, let $f_{ij} = (p_i, p_j)$ be all binary combinations of characters in pattern P

Let $f_{ij} = \begin{cases} 0, p_i \neq p_j \\ 1, p_i = p_j \end{cases}$, and $rep = \sum_{i=0}^{m-1}\sum_{j=0}^{m-1} f_{ij}$, where $0 \leq i, j \leq m-1$, and $i \neq j$. then *rep* is the

repeatability of characters in pattern. It shows the number of pairs of the same characters in pattern.

Definition 10 Given occurrences A and S, if $a[i] = s[k]$ where $0 \leq i \leq m-1$, $0 \leq k \leq m-1$, we say A conflicts with S. For example, T = aacccc, P = a¢[0,1]c¢[0,1]c, {0,2,3} conflicts with {0,2,4} and {1,3,5}. And "c" is the conflict letter.

For simplicity, global length constraint is deliberately ignored in our proof, and it does not affect the conclusion.

LEMMA 1 Given two occurrences A, S, if A and S come from the same occurrence set, then $a[i] \neq s[k]$ where $0 \leq i \leq m-1$, $0 \leq k \leq m-1$.

Proof: Assume $a[i] = s[k]$, then A conflicts with S, so they can not belong to the same set. The contradiction is achieved. Lemma 1 is proved.

LEMMA 2 Given two occurrences A and S where $S \in U_{SAIL}$. If there is a conflict between A and S, and let $a[t]$ and $s[i]$ be the conflict positions. According to the definition 10, under the *one-off* condition, A should be discarded. Moreover, if $i = t$, then $s[i] = a[i]$; if $i \neq t$, $s[i] < a[i]$ where $0 \leq i \leq m-1$. For instance, $S = \{0, 2, 3\}$, $A = \{1, 2, 4\}$, for $s[1] = a[1]$, the conflict position is 1, and the other positions satisfy $s[0] < a[0]$, $s[2] < a[2]$.

Proof: Assume $s[i] > a[i]$, then $a[i]$ is in the left of $s[i]$ in T. In accordance with the *left-most* strategy of SAIL, the *left-most* one prior to others is selected, which is $a[i]$. Due to the issue, $S \in U_{SAIL}$, so $s[i]$ should be selected. The contradiction is achieved. Thus, $s[i] \leq a[i]$. If $i = t$, $s[i] = a[t] = a[i]$, and if $i \neq t$, $s[i] = a[t] \neq a[i]$. It is obvious to concluded that $s[i] < a[i]$.

LEMMA 3 Given a text T, a pattern P and an occurrence S. Let U_{SAIL} be the occurrence set of SAIL. If $S \notin U_{SAIL}$, S conflicts with at least one occurrence in U_{SAIL}.

Proof: Assume S does not conflict with any occurrence in U_{SAIL}. Then it indicates that the reason why SAIL lose S can only be the length constraint. According to the definition 4, all the occurrences satisfy the length constraint. The contradiction is achieved. So the lemma is proved.

LEMMA 4 Let U_{SAIL} be the occurrence set of SAIL, and U_{opt} be the optimal one. Let N_{SAIL} (N_{opt}) be the matching number in U_{SAIL} (U_{opt}).

(1) If U_{SAIL} is the completeness set, $N_{SAIL} = N_{opt}$ is satisfied.

(2) Otherwise, $N_{SAIL} < N_{opt}$ is obtained and there is a conflict between U_{SAIL} and U_{opt}.

(3) If the condition holds $N_{opt} = 1$, $N_{SAIL} = N_{opt}$ is obtained.

(4) If there is no conflict, $N_{SAIL} = N_{opt}$ is achieved.

Proof: It is obvious to conclude (1) is obviously true. According to the definition 5, if $N_{SAIL} < N_{opt}$, there is an occurrence S satisfying $S \in U_{opt}$ and $S \notin U_{SAIL}$. Due to LEMMA 3, S conflicts with at least one occurrence in U_{SAIL}. That is U_{opt} is conflict with U_{SAIL}. So (2) is proved. With regard to (3), let S be the unique occurrence of U_{opt}. Assume $N_{SAIL} < N_{opt}$, then $N_{SAIL} = 0$. That is SAIL has no occurrence. In accordance with LEMMA 3, S conflicts with at least one occurrence of SAIL. But U_{SAIL} is empty, so there is no conflict. Thus the contradiction is achieved. And (3) is proved. With regard to (4), it is obvious $N_{SAIL} \leq N_{opt}$. We assume $N_{SAIL} < N_{opt}$, then there is an occurrence S satisfying $S \in U_{opt}$ and $S \notin U_{SAIL}$. Due to LEMMA 3, S conflicts with at least one occurrence in U_{SAIL}. That is U_{opt} and U_{SAIL} have a conflict. The contradiction is achieved. So (4) is proved.

LEMMA 5 Given two occurrence sets U_1, U_2, if U_1 conflict with U_2, there are two sub-sets u_1, u_2 with a conflict where $u_1 \subseteq U_1$, $u_2 \subseteq U_2$.

Proof: Assume there is no sub-sets with a conflict. All the matching positions of U_1 and U_2 have no conflict. According to definition 10, U_1 and U_2 have no conflict and satisfy the *one-off* condition. The contradiction is achieved. Lemma 5 is proved.

LEMMA 6 Given two occurrence sets U_1, U_2, U_2 is U_{opt}. If there is a conflict between U_1 and U_2, and $N(U_1) < N(U_2)$, there are two subsets u_1, u_2 where $u_1 \subseteq U_1$, $u_2 \subseteq U_2$, u_1 is conflict with u_2 and $N(u_1) < N(u_2)$.

Proof: In accordance with LEMMA 5, there are subsets u_1, u_2 where $u_1 \subseteq U_1, u_2 \subseteq U_2$ with conflict. Let $U_1 = u_{11} \cup u_{12} \cup \ldots\ldots \cup u_{1n}$, $U_2 = u_{21} \cup u_{22} \cup \ldots\ldots \cup u_{2m}$, and u_{1i}, u_{2j} are arbitrary subsets where $u_{1i} \subseteq U_1$, $u_{2j} \subseteq U_2$, $1 \leq i \leq n$, $1 \leq j \leq m$. We discuss in three conditions: ① u_{1i}, u_{2j} have no conflict and do not satisfy $N(u_{1i}) < N(u_{2j})$, then U_1, U_2 have no conflict and $N(U_1) = N(U_2)$, the contradiction is achieved. ② u_{1i}, u_{2j} have a conflict and do not satisfy $N(u_{1i}) < N(u_{2j})$, then U_1, U_2 have no conflict, the contradiction is achieved. ③ u_{1i}, u_{2j} have no conflict and satisfy $N(u_{1i}) < N(u_{2j})$, then $N(U_1) = N(U_2)$, the contradiction is achieved. So u_{1i}, u_{2j} have a conflict and satisfy $N(u_{1i}) < N(u_{2j})$. Lemma 6 is proved.

THEOREM 1 Given a text T, a pattern P, if SAIL is incomplete, P must be R pattern.

Proof: Let U_{SAIL} be the occurrence set of SAIL, U_{opt} is the completeness set, N_{SAIL} is the matching number of SAIL, and N_{opt} is the complete matching number. Consider the SAIL is incompleteness, according to LEMMA 4, $N_{SAIL} < N_{opt}$, and U_{SAIL} conflicts with U_{opt}. Due to LEMMA 6, we get two subsets u_1, u_2 with conflict, which are satisfying $N(u_1) < N(u_2)$ where $u_1 \subseteq U_{SAIL}$, $u_2 \subseteq U_{opt}$. Without loss of generality, let $N(u_1) = 1$, $N(u_2) = 2$. Set $u_1 = \{S\}$, $u_2 = \{A, B\}$, that is $S \in U_{SAIL}$, $A \in U_{opt}$, $B \in U_{opt}$. Let:

$T = t[0]$, $t[1]\ldots t[i]\ldots t[n-1]$, $t[i]$ is stand for the *ith* letter in T where $i = 0,1,2\ldots\ldots n-1$

$P = p[0], p[1]... p[i]... p[m-1], p[i]$ is stand for the *ith* letter in P where $i = 0,1,2......m-1$

$A = a[0], a[1]... a[u]... a[m-1], a[i]$ is stand for the *ith* character maching position of occurrence A where $i = 0,1,2...m-1$

$B = b[0], b[1]... b[w]... b[m-1]$, another occurrece.

$S = s[0], s[1]... s[i]... s[k]... s[m-1]$, another occurrece.

Let $a[u], b[w]$ be the positions in A, B, which conflict with $s[i], s[k]$ in S *separately*. We assume other positions in A and B do not conflict with the occurrences in U_{SAIL}. $\therefore a[u] = s[i], b[w] = s[k]$ $\therefore t[a[u]] = t[s[i]], t[b[w]] = t[s[k]]$ $\because$ According to the definition 4, $t[a[u]] = p[u], t[s[i]] = p[i], t[b[w]] = p[w], t[s[k]] = p[k]$ $\therefore p[u] = p[i], p[w] = p[k]$

It would be discussed in the following two cases:

① $u \neq i$ or $w \neq k$

② $u = i$ and $w = k$

For ①, when if $u \neq i$, $\because p[u] = p[i]$ $\therefore$ There are two of the same letters from different positions in P. $\therefore$ According to definition 6, P is an R pattern. For the case of $w \neq k$, similarly, it can be proved.

Then we will prove the other condition is impossible, and conclude P is R pattern.

For ②, we obtain $a[u] = s[i] = s[u], b[w] = s[k] = s[w]$. There is $u \neq w$. $\because$ Assume $u = w$, then $u = i = w = k$ $\therefore a[u] = s[i] = s[k] = b[w]$. Consider A, B belong to the same occurrence set, which contradicts with LEMMA 1 $\therefore u \neq w$. Without loss of generality, let $u < w$, according to LEMMA 2 $\because$ SAIL adopts the *left-most* strategy, and $S \in U_{SAIL}, A, B \notin U_{SAIL}$ $\therefore s[u] < b[u], s[w] < a[w]$ $\because a[u] = s[u], b[w] = s[w]$

$$\therefore a[u] < b[u], b[w] < a[w] \tag{1}$$

And $\because u < w$, we can obtain $b[u] < b[w]$

$A = ...a[u].............a[w]...$

$B = ...b[u]...b[w].........$

The occurrence $\{b_0, b_1,..., b_u,...,a_w,..., a_{m-1}\}$ can be considerd as $\{\{b_0, b_1,...,b_u\}, \{b_u,...,a_w\}, \{a_w,..., a_{m-1}\}\}$.

According to the definition 4, $\{a_0, a_1,...,a_u,...,a_w,...,a_{m-1}\}$ and $\{b_0, b_1,...,b_u,...,b_w,...,b_{m-1}\}$ satisfy the local constraints. So $\{a_w,..., a_{m-1}\}$ and $\{b_0, b_1,...,b_u\}$ satisfy the local constraints.

Due to $\{b_u,...,a_w\}$, we can get $\{ b_u, b_{u+1}..., a_{w-1}, a_w \}$.

From the equation (1), $a[u] < b[u], b[w] < a[w]$, and according to the definition 4:

$$b[i] < b[i+1], a[i] < a[i+1] \text{ where } u \leq i \leq w-1 \tag{2}$$

There is a t satisfying:

$$b[t+1] < a[t+1] \text{ and } a[t] < b[t] \text{ where } u \leq t \leq w\text{-}1 \tag{3}$$

$A = ...a[u]......a[t]..............a[t+1].........a[w]...$

$B = ...b[u] ......b[t]......b[t+1]......b[w].........$

Assume there is no t satisfying the condition, consider $b[t] \neq a[t]$ where $u \leq t \leq w$. Then due to any t there is $a[t+1] < b[t+1]$ or $a[t] > b[t]$ where $u \leq t \leq w\text{-}1$. Consider $a[u] < b[u]$, there is $a[u+1] < b[u+1]$. Due to $a[u+k] < b[u+k]$, we can obtain $a[u+k+1] < b[u+k+1]$ where $0 \leq k \leq w\text{-}u\text{-}1$. Then we can induce $a[i] < b[i]$ where $u \leq i \leq w$. It contradicts $b[w] < a[w]$, so the assume is incorrect Due to equation (2) and (3), $a[t] < b[t] < b[t+1] < a[t+1]$ where $u \leq t \leq w\text{-}1$.

$$b[t+1] - b[t] < a[t+1] - b[t] < a[t+1] - a[t] \tag{4}$$

That is $a[t]$ and b$[t\text{-}1]$ satisfy the local constraints. In this way, $\{ b_u, b_{u+1}..., a_{w\text{-}1}, a_w \}$can be considered as $\{\{ b_u, b_{u+1}...,b_{t\text{-}1}\},\{b_t, a_{t+1}\},\{ a_{t+2} ..., a_{w\text{-}1}, a_w \}\}$. In accordance with definition 4, $\{ b_u, b_{u+1}...,b_{t\text{-}1}\},\{ a_{t+2} ..., a_{w\text{-}1}, a_w \}$ satisfy the local constraints. $\therefore \{ b_u, b_{u+1}..., a_{w\text{-}1}, a_w \}$ satisfy the local constraints. $\therefore$ From the above analysis, $\{b_0, b_1,...,b_u,...,a_w,..., a_{m\text{-}1}\}$ satisfy the local constraints.

However, according to the theorem, the other positions in A,B do not conflict with U_{SAIL} except for $a[u]$, $b[w]$. That is, $\{b_0, b_1,...,b_u,a_w,...,a_{m\text{-}1}\}$ satisfies the *one-off* condition. $\therefore \{b_0, b_1,...,b_u, a_w,..., a_{m\text{-}1}\}$ is another occurrence, and does not conflict with any occurrences in U_{SAIL}. But U_{SAIL} does not include this occurrence. It contradicts with LEMMA 3. Thus, condition ② is impossible. And from the analysis of ①, under the condition of the theorem, P must be R pattern. The theorem 1 is proved.

THEOREM 2 Given a text T, a pattern P, if P is NR pattern, then SAIL is complete.

Proof: It is the inverse negation of THEOREM 1. Apparently, THEOREM 2 is true.

THEOREM 3 Given a text T, a pattern P, if P is R pattern, then SAIL is incomplete.

Proof: It can be concluded from the analysis and example in section 2.

THEOREM 4 If the pattern fulfills *gap* = 0, SAIL is complete.

Proof: If *gap* = 0, the wildcard is a constant. For example a¢[1,1]c¢[2,2]c is converted into a¢c¢¢c. There won't be any conflict or exist seizing between occurrences. SAIL will perform complete.

Experiment design[1]: $\sum$= 4, m = {5,7,9}, *gap* = [0,3], *rep* = {0,1,2,3,4,6,7,10,11,15, 21,28,35}. In each set of experiments, 20 patterns are randomly generated; the final result is the average.

Analysis of experimental results: with increment of *rep*, the curve of approximation ratio gradually decreases, followed by a slight increase. The reason for decline is that *rep* lead to more nested occurrences, resulting in a greater degree of the possibility of losing occurrences; the reason for the increscent is that larger *rep* can cause more extreme pattern. For instance, when $\sum$ = 4, m = 7, *rep* = 21, patterns like P_1 =

---

[1] When $\sum$ and m are determined, *rep* can only be some certain values, because *rep* has correlation with $\sum$ and m

a¢[0,3]a¢[0,3]a¢[0,3]a¢[0,3]a¢[0,3]a¢[0,3]a which is difficult to find a special text containing nested occurrences of such pattern, will be produced. For P_1, the text like "aaaaaaaaaaaaaa" contains nested occurrences of this pattern. Obviously, this extreme text is very rare. Therefore, under the premise of nested occurrences are not easily to be formed, the approximation ratio will be increased slightly.

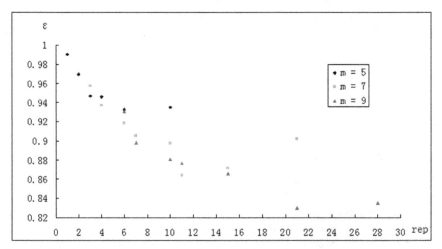

Figure 7. The relation between *rep* and approximation ratio ε

Next we will analyze the relationship between the repeatability *rep* and alphabet size Σ, pattern length *m*. Original problem: a pattern which length is *m*, and alphabet size is Σ, what is the expectation of repeatability E(*rep*)?

This description is equivalent to the model of 'taking ball from the bag' in the combination mathematics:

There is a bag of balls, and $|\Sigma|$ kinds of colors, taking *m* balls from the bag with replacement, then in fetched balls, how many pairs of the same color?

m Σ	3	4	5	6	......	m
3	3/3	6/3	10/3	15/3	......	$C_m^2 / 3$
4	3/4	6/4	10/4	15/4	......	$C_m^2 / 4$
5	3/5	6/5	10/5	15/5	......	$C_m^2 / 5$
6	3/6	6/6	10/6	15/6	......	$C_m^2 / 6$
......	......	......	......	......	......	......
Σ	3/|Σ|	6/|Σ|	10/|Σ|	15/|Σ|	......	$C_m^2/|\Sigma|$

Table 11. The relationship between Σ, *m* and *rep*

Finally, we can deduce:

$$E(rep) = \frac{C_m^2}{|\Sigma|} \qquad (2)$$

5. Conclusions

As an extension of traditional matching problem, the PMWL problem has aroused more and more attention because of its unique flexibility and complexity. Based on problem definition and drawing on research idea in traditional matching problem, this article introduces SAIL, RSAIL, SBO and BPBM which are representative algorithms for PMWL in three important respects: the data structures, the matching strategies and the characteristics of pattern. The article also analyzes the pros and cons of the above algorithms from the point of quality of the solution and time complexity, and gives experimental matching results by using real DNA data. Among them, the SAIL algorithm is the first to propose the method of solving PMWL problem, it uses the sliding window structure and the representative *left-most* matching strategy. This paper finds that in short patterns, the approximation ratio of SAIL is higher than 0.9, while in longer patterns, the occurrences obtained by SAIL are of poor quality; the quality of occurrences obtained by SBO is best, but its time consumption has a non-linear relationship with the length of text; BPBM utilizes bit parallel technology to improve the efficiency of matching greatly, but also is impact by the machine word; for pattern with repeated letters in tail, RSAIL uses symmetry to improve the quality of occurrences under certain conditions, thus providing a solving idea to PMWL problem, but in longer patterns and wilder gaps, the efficiency is not obvious.

Afterwards, this article focus on relationship between approximation ratio ε and alphabet size Σ, pattern length m, wildcards span *gap* and repeatability *rep*. Firstly, this article proposes the model $\varepsilon = F (\Sigma, m, gap)$, describing the functional relationship between pattern characteristics and approximation ratio approximately; secondly, this article proves PMWL's completeness under the conditions of $rep = 0$; finally, the relationship between the pattern features are also analyzed and$m$ in addition, relationship that $E(rep) = \frac{C_m^2}{|\Sigma|}$ is proposed.

In future work, the formal description of the PMWL problem will be considered, in order to explain the complexity of the problem better, thus helping algorithm design and analysis for problem complexity.

Author details

Haiping Wang, Taining Xiang and Xuegang Hu
Hefei University of Technology, China

6. References

Amir, A., Aumann, Y., Landau, G., Lewenstein, M. & Lewenstein, N. (2000). Pattern matching with swaps, *Journal of Algorithms*, 37(2): 247-266

Amir, A. & Navarro, G. (2009). Parameterized matching on non-linear structures, *Information processing letters*, 109(15): 864-867

Baeza-Yates, R. & Gonnet, G. (1992). A new approach to text searching, *Communications of the ACM*, 35(10): 74–82

Bille, P., Gørtz, I. L., Vildhøj, H. & Wind, D. (2010). String matching with variable length gaps, *Proceedings of 17th SPIRE*, pp. 385–394

Brudno, M., Steinkamp, R. & Morgenstern, B. (2004). The CHAOS/DIALIGN WWW server for multiple alignment of genomic sequences, *Nucleic Acids Research*, 32: 41–44

Califf, M. E. & Mooney, R. J. (2003). Bottom-up relational learning of pattern matching rules for information extraction, *Journal of Machine Learning Research*, 4(6): 177-210

Chen, G., Wu, X. D., Zhu, X.Q., Arslan, A. N. & He, Y. (2006). Efficient string matching with wildcards and length constraints, *Knowledge and Information Systems*, 10(4): 399–419

Cole, J.R., Chai, B., Marsh, T. L., Farris, R. J., Wang, Q., Kulam, S. A., Chandra, D. M., McGarrell, D. M., Schmidt, T. M., Garrity, G. M. & Tiedje, J. M. (2005). The ribosomal database project(RDP-11): Sequences and tools for high-throughput rRNA analysis, *Nucleic Acids Research*, 33(1): 294-296

Cole, R., Gottlieb, L. A. & Lewenstein, M. (2004). Dictionary matching and indexing with errors and don't cares, *Proceedings of the 36th ACM Symposium on the Theory of Computing*, ACM Press, New York, NY, USA, pp. 91–100

Fischer, M. J. & Paterson, M. S. (1974). String matching and other products, *In Karp RM(ed) Complexity of computation, Massachusetts Institute of Technology*, Cambridge, MA, USA, vol 7, pp. 113-125

Gusfield, D. (1997). Algorithms on strings, trees and sequences: computer science and computational biology, chapter 6, Cambridge University Press

Guo, D., Hong, X. L., Hu, X. G., Gao, J., Liu, Y. L., Wu, G. Q. & Wu, X. D. (2011). A Bit-Parallel Algorithm for Sequential Pattern Matching with Wildcards, *Cybernetics and Systems*, 42(6): 382-401

He, D., Wu, X. D. & Zhu, X. Q. (2007). SAIL-APPROX: An efficient on-line algorithm for approximate pattern matching with wildcards and length constraints, *IEEE International Conference on Bioinformatics and Biomedicine (BIBM'07)*, IEEE Computer Society, pp. 151–158

He, Y., Wu, X. D., Zhu, X. Q. & Arslan, A. N. (2007). Mining Frequent Patterns with Wildcards from Biological Sequences [C], *IEEE International Conference on Information Reuse and Integration*, Las Vegas, IL, pp. 329-334

Ji, X. N., Bailey, J. & Dong, G. Z. (2007). Mining minimal distinguishing subsequence patterns with gap constraints, *Knowledge and Information Systems*, 11(3): 259-286

Kucherov, G. & Rusinowitch, M. (1995). Matching a set of strings with variable length don't cares, *Proceedings of the 6th Symposium on Combinatorial Pattern Matching*, Springer, Berlin Heidelberg New York, pp. 230–247

Manber, U. & Baeza-Yates, R. (1991). An algorithm for string matching with a sequence of don't cares, *Information Processing Letters*, 37(3): 133–136

Min, F., Wu, X. D. & Lu, Z. Y. (2009). Pattern matching with independent wildcard gaps, *Eighth IEEE International Conference on Dependable, Autonomic and Secure Computing(DASC-2009)*, Chengdu, China, pp. 194-199

Morgante, M., Policriti, A., Vitacolonna, N. & Zuccolo, A. (2004). Structured motifs search, *Proceedings of the 8th annual international conference on Computational molecular biology*, In print

Muth, R. & Manber, U. (1996). Approximate multiple string search, *Combinatorial Pattern Matching, Springer*, pp. 75–86

Muthukrishnan, S. & Krishna, P. (1994). Non-standard stringology: algorithms and complexity [C], *Proceedings of the twenty-sixth annual ACM symposium on Theory of computing New York*, NY, USA, pp. 770-779

"National center for biotechnology information website", [online], available: http://www.ncbi.nlm.nih.gov/

Navarro, G. & Raffinot, M. (2001). Flexible pattern matching in strings: practical on-line search algorithms for texts and biological sequences, Cambridge University Press

Rahman, M. S., Iliopoulos, C., Lee, I., Mohamed, M. & Smyth, W. F. (2006). Finding Patterns with Variable Length Gaps or Don't Cares, *Computing and Combinatorics, 12th Annual International Conference*, COCOON 2006, Taipei, Taiwan, August 15-18, Proceedings. Vol. 4112

Sagot, M. F. & Viari, A. (1996). A Double Combinatorial Approach to Discovering Patterns in Biological Sequence, *Proceedings of the 7th Symposium on Combinatorial Pattern Matching*, Springer, pp. 186-208

Wang, H. P., Xie, F., Hu, X. G., Li, P. P. & Wu, X. D. (2010). Pattern Matching with Flexible Wildcards and Recurring Characters, *Proceedings of 2010 IEEE International Conference on Granular Computing*, pp. 782-786

Wu, Y. X., Wu, X. D., Jiang, H. & Min, F. (2011). A Heuristic Algorithm for MPMGOOC, *Chinese Journal of Computers*, 34(8): 1452-1462

Xie, F., Wu, X. D., Hu, X. G., Gao, J., Guo, D., Fei, Y. L. & Ertian, H. (2010). Sequential Pattern Mining with Wildcards [C], *22nd IEEE International Conference on Tools with Artificial Intelligence (ICTAI)*, pp. 241-247

Zhang, M. H., Kao, B., Cheung, D. W. & Yip, K. Y. (2005). Mining periodic patterns with gap requirement from sequences, *Proceedings of ACM SIGMOD*, Baltimore Maryland, pp. 623–633

Chapter 14

Ensemble Clustering for Biological Datasets

Harun Pirim and Şadi Evren Şeker

Additional information is available at the end of the chapter

1. Introduction

Recent technologies and tools generated excessive data in bioinformatics domain. For example, microarrays measure expression levels of ten thousands of genes simultaneously in a single chip. Measurements involve relative expression values of each gene through an image processing task.

Biological data requires both low and high level analysis to reveal significant information that will shed light into biological facts such as disease prediction, annotation of a gene function and guide new experiments. In that sense, researchers are seeking for the effect of a treatment or time course change befalling. For example, they may design a microarray experiment treating a biological organism with a chemical substance and observe gene expression values comparing with expression value before treatment. This treatment or change make researchers focus on groups of genes, other biological molecules that have significant relationships with each other under similar conditions. For instance, gene class labels are usually unknown, since there is a little information available about the data. Hence, data analysis using an unsupervised learning technique is required. Clustering is an unsupervised learning technique used in diverse domains including bioinformatics. Clustering assigns objects into the same cluster, based on a cluster definition. A cluster definition or criterion is the similarity between the objects. The idea is that one needs to find the most important cliques among many from the data. Therefore, clustering is widely used to obtain biologically meaningful partitions. However, there is no best clustering approach for the problem on hand and clustering algorithms are biased towards certain criteria. In other words, a particular clustering approach has its own objective and assumptions about the data.

Diversity of clustering algorithms can benefit from merging partitions generated individually. Ensemble clustering provides a framework to merge individual partitions from different clustering algorithms. Ensemble clustering may generate more accurate clusters than individual clustering approaches. Here, an ensemble clustering framework is implemented as described in [10] to aggregate results from K-means, hiearchical clustering and C-means algorithms. We employ C-means instead of spectral clustering in [10]. We also use different data sets. Two different biological datasets are used for each algorithm. A comparison of the results is presented. In order to evaluate the performance of the ensemble clustering approach, one internal and one external cluster validation indices are used. Silhouette (S) [31] is the internal validation index and C-rand [23] is the external one. The chapter reviews some clustering algorithms, ensemble clustering methods, includes implementation, and conclusion sections.

2. Clustering algorithms

Clustering biological data is very important for identification of co-expressed genes, which facilitates functional annotation and the elucidation of biological pathways. Accurate predictions can serve as a guide for targeting further experiments and generating additional hypotheses. Furthermore, accurate predictions can facilitate identification of disease markers and targets for drug design [4]; clustering can also be used to determine whether certain patterns exist near viral integration sites[16].

Current algorithms used in gene clustering have some drawbacks. For example, K-means algorithm is sensitive to noise that is inherent in gene expression data. In addition, the solution (i.e. the final clustering) that the K-means algorithm finds may not be a global optimum since it relies on randomly chosen initial objects. However, K-means-based methods are prevalent in the literature such as [12, 17, 33]. K-means works upon randomly chosen centroid points that represent the clusters. The objects are assigned to the closest clusters based on distance calculation regarding centroid points. For example, the dataset illustrated in Figure 1 is assigned two centroids.

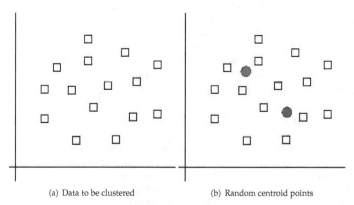

(a) Data to be clustered   (b) Random centroid points

Figure 1. The dataset and two centroid points

The distance between any object from the dataset to both of the centroid points are calculated and the objects are assigned to the closest cluster represented by the closest centroid point as seen in Figure 2. Then new centroid points of clusters are calculated and objects are assigned to the closest clusters regarding the distance to new centroid points. Recalculation of centroid points and assignment of objects to new clusters goes on till centroids points remain the same as in Figure 3.

Another method, Self-organizing Map (SOM), is one of the machine-learning techniques widely used in gene clustering. A recent study is [14]. SOM requires a grid structured input that makes it ineffective.

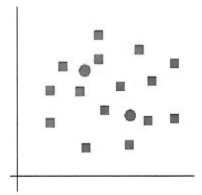

Figure 2. Initial clusters

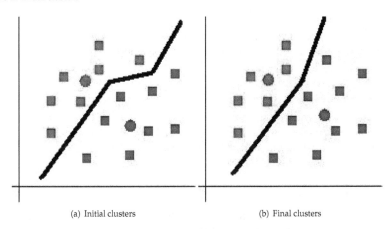

(a) Initial clusters   (b) Final clusters

Figure 3. Iteration of K-means

Hierarchical clustering (HC) algorithms are also widely used and area of two types: agglomerative and divisive. In agglomerative approach objects are all in different clusters and they are merged till they are all in the same cluster as seen in Figure 4.   Two important drawbacks of the HC algorithms are that they are not robust and they have high computational complexity. HC algorithms are "greedy" which often means that the final solution is suboptimal due to locally optimal choices being made in initial steps, which turn out to be poor choices with respect to the global solution. A recent study is [26].

Graph-theoretical clustering techniques exist in which the genomic data are represented by nodes and edges of a graph.   Network methods have been applied to identify and characterize various biological interactions [13]. Identification of clusters using networks is

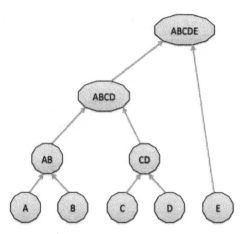

Figure 4. Agglomerative approach

often intractable, that is finding an optimal partition of a graph is an NP-hard problem [1]. NP-hard is a class of problems that are at least as hard as NP-complete problems. NP-complete is a class of problems that are in NP and reducible to an NP-complete problem in polynomial time. Some examples of graph theory-based clustering approaches are: [30] and [24].

Model-based clustering approaches are the ones using probability distributions to predict the distribution of gene expression data. However, gene expression data does not have a unique distribution. Some examples are given in [19] and [34].

Sub-space clustering (biclustering) methods, which employ the reasoning that one gene may belong to multiple pathways or no pathways are also used in the literature as in [28]. There are also optimization-based algorithms as in [15], spectral algorithms as in [25], fuzzy algorithms as in [32], meta-heuristics as in [18] used for clustering genomic data.

3. Ensemble clustering

Combining diverse partitions from different clustering algorithms may result in high quality and robust clusters, since ensemble approaches such as bagging and boosting used in classification problems have proven to be effective [22]. The fact that the objects have various features makes it difficult to find an optimal clustering of similar objects. In other words, objects may be classified based on different features such as size, color, and age. In that sense, ensemble clustering is a promising heuristic combining results based on different features.

Figure 5 represents a clustering ensemble framework. CAs are clustering algorithms, Ps are partitions generated by them, N is number of clustering algorithms and partitions F_C is the consensus function and CP is the consensus partition.

Ensemble clustering requires the following tasks [2]:

1. selection of base clustering algorithms
2. definition of a consensus function

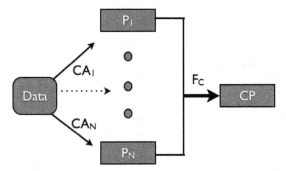

Figure 5. Ensemble clustering framework

3. merging of individual partitions by the chosen consensus function

[2] apply an ensemble approach for clustering scale-free graphs. They use metrics based on the neighborhood which uses the adjacency list of each node and considers the nodes as having several common neighbors, the clustering coefficient, and the shortest path betweenness of nodes in the network. The scale-free graph used in the study is from a budding yeast PPI network that contained 15147 interactions between 4741 proteins. It is reported that ensemble clustering can provide improvements in cluster quality for scale-free graphs based upon the preliminary results. [3] propose an ensemble clustering framework to extract functional modules that are relevant biologically in protein-protein interaction (PPI) networks. Their method attempts to handle the noisy false positive interactions and specific topological interactions present in the network. The method uses graph clustering algorithms, repeated bisections, direct k-way partitioning, and multilevel k-way partitioning, to obtain the base partitions. The method utilizes two topological distance matrices. One of the distance matrices is based on the clustering coefficient [36], and the other distance matrix is generated using the betweenness measure [29]. The proposed study demonstrates a soft ensemble method such that proteins are allowed to be assigned to more than one cluster. Empirical evaluation of the different ensemble methods in the study shows the superior performance of the proposed ensemble framework.

Fuzzy clustering algorithms are widely used with well-understood properties and benefits in various applications. Nevertheless, there has been very little analysis of using fuzzy clustering algorithms in regards to generating the base partitions in cluster ensembles. [35] compares hard and fuzzy C-means [7] algorithms in the well-known evidence-accumulation framework of cluster ensembles. In the study, it is observed that the fuzzy C-means approach requires much fewer base partitions for the cluster ensemble to converge, and is more tolerant of outliers in the data.

[5] propose a fuzzy ensemble clustering approach to address the issue of unclear boundaries between the clusters from the biological and biomedical gene expression data analysis. The approach takes into account their inherent fuzziness. The goal of the study is improving the accuracy and robustness of clustering results. After applying random projections to obtain lower dimensional gene expression data, the method applies the fuzzy K-means algorithm on the low dimensional data to generate multiple fuzzy base clusters. Then, the fuzzy clusters are combined using a similarity matrix where the elements of the matrix are generated by the

fuzzy t-norms algorithm, and finally, the fuzzy K-means algorithm is applied to the rows of the similarity matrix to obtain the consensus clustering. It is demonstrated that the proposed ensemble approach is competitive with the other ensemble methods.

High throughput data may be generated by microarray experiments. If the dataset is very large, it is possible to generate an ensemble of clustering solutions, or partition the data so that clustering may be performed on tractable-sized disjoint subsets [20]. The data can then be distributed at different sites, for which a distributed clustering solution with a final merging of partitions is a natural fit. [20] introduce two new approaches to combining partitions represented by sets of cluster centers. It is stated that these approaches provide a final partition of data that is comparable to the best existing approaches and that the approaches can be 100,000 times faster while using much less memory. The new algorithms are compared with the best existing cluster ensemble approaches that cluster all of the data at once, and a clustering algorithm designed for very large datasets. Fuzzy and hard K-means based clustering algorithms are used for the comparison. It is demonstrated that the centroid-based ensemble merging algorithms presented in the study generated partitions which are as good as the best label vector method, or the method of clustering all the data at once. The proposed algorithms are also more efficient in terms of speed.

[11] propose evidence accumulation clustering based on dual rooted prim tree cuts (EAC-DC). The proposed algorithm computes the co-association matrix based on a forward algorithm that repeatedly adds edges to Prim's minimum spanning tree (MST) to identify clusters until a satisfying criterion is met. A consensus cluster is then generated from the co-association matrix using spectral partitioning. Here, a MST is a fully connected sub-graph with no cycles and a dual-rooted tree is obtained by finding the union of two sub-trees. They test their approach using the Iris dataset [8], the Wisconsin breast cancer dataset [27] (both obtained from [9]) and synthetic datasets, and presented a comparison of their results with other existing ensemble clustering methods.

[22] use a cluster ensemble in gene expression analysis. In the proposed ensemble framework, the partitions generated by each individual clustering algorithm are converted into a distance matrix. The distance matrices are then combined to construct a weighted graph. A graph partitioning approach is then used to generate the final set of clusters. It is reported that the ensemble approach yields better results than the best individual approach on both synthetic and yeast gene expression datasets.

[10] merge multiple partitions using evidence accumulation. Each partition generated by a clustering algorithm is used as a new piece of knowledge, to help uncover the relationships between objects. For this chapter, we adopt their ensemble approach. The core idea behind the ensemble approach here is constructing the co-association matrix by employing a voting mechanism for the partitions generated using individual clustering algorithms. A co-association matrix C is constructed based upon the formulation below, where n_{ij} is the number of times the object pair (i, j) is assigned to the same cluster among the N different partitions:

$$C(i, j) = \frac{n_{ij}}{N}$$

After constructing the co-association matrix, [10] use single linkage hierarchical clustering to obtain the new cluster tree (dendrogram) and then use a cut-off value corresponding to the maximum life time (difference between merge points where branching starts) on the tree.

They also employ the same ensemble framework using K-means partitions with different parameters. They test their algorithms on ten different datasets, comparing the results with other ensemble clustering methods. They report that their ensemble approach can identify the clusters with arbitrary shapes and sizes, and perform better than the other combination methods.

4. Implementation

We employ the ensemble approach described in [10]. Different set of base clustering algorithms are chosen and implemented on protein and lymphoma datasets.

Protein dataset consists of 698 objects (corresponding to protein folds) with 125 attributes. The protein dataset contains 698 proteins from 125 samples. The real clusters correspond to the four classes of protein−folds: α, β, α/β and $\alpha+\beta$ protein classes. DLBCL−B is 2−channel custom cDNA microarray dataset. This is a B cell lymphoma dataset with predefined three subtypes [21].

The ensemble clustering algorithm uses an array of vectors data structure for each of the file, in order to use the dynamic memory allocation and starts with initializing the file content in the vectors. The algorithm also processes the vectors and generates two temporary matrices with the dimension of maximum vector length. The ensemble clustering algorithm steps are as follows:

Algorithm 1 Ensemble Clustering Algorithm

Require: partitions
Ensure: distance matrix

  for $i = 0$ *to* $max(V[n])$ **do**
    for $j = 0$ *to* $max(V[n])$ **do**
      for $k = 0$ *to* n **do**
        if $V[k].elementAt(i) = V[k].elementAt(j))$ **then**
          $C[i][j] = C[i][j] + 1/n$
        end if
        $D[i][j] = 1 - C[i][j]$
      end for
    end for
  end for

Here, n is the number of files, $V[n]$ are the vectors holding the content of each file. $max(V[n])$ is the length of the longest vector, $C[i][j]$ is the co-association matrix and $D[i][j]$ is the distance matrix. The algorithm iterates through the two dimensional matrix via i and j loop variables inside a nested loop at lines 1 and 2 and for each member of the matrix, all the vectors are processed inside the loop via k loop variable at line 3. The condition of equality for the selected vector with the selected loop variables i and j, causes an increase on the co-association matrix elements at lines 4 and 5. Finally the distance matrix is calculated at line 7. After obtaining the distance matrix, hierarchial clustering with complete linkage is used to generate the dengrogram. The dendrogram is cut at a certain level to obtain consensus partition.

Ensemble approach is coded as a java application which is available upon request. The software allows addition of many partitions to generate the distance matrix of the corresponding ensemble. Files including the partitions can be added by clicking on the "Add File" button as seen in Figure 6. Distance matrix of the ensemble is generated by "Calculate" button.

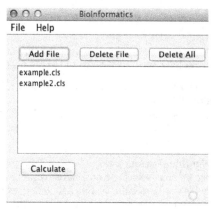

Figure 6. File input interface

The output is displayed on a separate screen as demonstrated on Figure 7. The output with csv format can be written into a file by clicking on the "Output CSV" button.

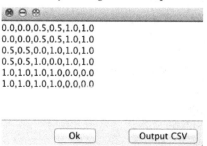

Figure 7. Example clusters

Considering two different partitions of a dataset with six objects which are (1, 1, 2, 1, 3, 3) and (2, 2, 2, 1, 3, 3), the algorithm's output is the distance matrix:

$$\begin{pmatrix} 0 & 0 & 0.5 & 0.5 & 1 & 1 \\ 0 & 0 & 0.5 & 0.5 & 1 & 1 \\ 0.5 & 0.5 & 0 & 1 & 1 & 1 \\ 0.5 & 0.5 & 1 & 0 & 1 & 1 \\ 1 & 1 & 1 & 1 & 0 & 0 \\ 1 & 1 & 1 & 1 & 0 & 0 \end{pmatrix}$$

The distance matrix is used in hierarchical clustering with complete linkage and the following dendrogram is generated. The dendrogram is cut at a level to give three clusters. The corresponding partition is (1, 1, 1, 2, 3, 3) which is the same as second partition (2, 2, 2, 1, 3, 3).

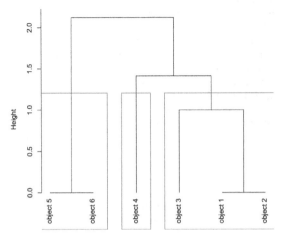

Figure 8. Example clusters

We employ hierarchical clustering, K-means and C-means to obtain base partitions. K-means and hierarchical clustering algorithm are implemented using R base package, C-means is implemented using R e1071 package. Silhouette and C-rand indices are utilized to evaluate the performance of individual and ensemble algorithms. Silhouette and C-rand values are calculated using R clusterSim and flexclust packages respectively. Silhouette is an internal measure of compactness and separation of clusters [6]. The silhouette index values are between -1 and 1 representing worst and best values. C-rand is an external measure of agreement between two partitions. C-rand has maximum value of 1 and it can take negative values. The silhouette and C-rand values found by the base and ensemble algorithms are given in Table 1. Ensemble approach improves clustering result both for the protein and DLBCL-B datasets. Ensemble approach finds better C-rand value, 0.157 than values by K-means and C-means, 0.127 for the protein dataset. Ensemble approach also finds the best C-rand value, 0.135 compared to values generated by individual clustering algorithms, 0.021, 0.063, 0.098. However, the ensemble approach makes S values worse in most cases.

Dataset	Method	Num. of clusters	S value	C value
Protein	HC	4	0.344	0.199
	K-means	4	0.379	0.127
	C-means	4	0.379	0.127
	Ensemble	4	0.078	0.157
DLBCL-B	HC	3	-0.034	0.021
	K-means	3	-0.015	0.063
	C-means	2	-0.005	0.098
	Ensemble	3	-0.017	0.135

Table 1. Index values for base and ensemble algorithms

5. Conclusion

Clustering groups of objects such that similar ones are placed in the same cluster, and in its application to biological datasets are very important in that it can help identification of natural groups of biological entities that might give insight about biomarkers. In this chapter, we review some clustering algorithms applied to biological data. Ensemble clustering approaches for biological data are also reviewed. Implementation of K-means, C-means and HC algorithms and merging of the algorithms using an ensemble frame work are presented using two different datasets. The datasets are protein and DLBCL-B. Two different cluster validation indices, adjusted rand and silhouette, are used for comparing the partitions from individual algorithms and ensemble clustering. Investigating Table 1, we conclude that merging individual partitions improves C-rand values meaning that ensemble approach finds partitions similar to the real partitions. Ensemble approach is coded as a Java application and available upon request.

Acknowledgement

Authors thank Dilip Gautam for his contribution to this chapter. The work of Şadi Evren Şeker was supported by Scientific Research Projects Coordination Unit of Istanbul University, project number YADOP-16728.

Author details

Harun Pirim
King Fahd University of Petroleum and Minerals

Şadi Evren Şeker
Istanbul University, Turkey

6. References

[1] Arora, S., Rao, S. & Vazirani, U. [2009]. Expander flows, geometric embeddings and graph partitioning, *Journal of the ACM* 56(2): 1–37.
URL: *http://doi.acm.org/10.1145/1502793.1502794*

[2] Asur, S., Parthasarathy, S. & Ucar, D. [2006]. An Ensemble Approach for Clustering Scale-Free Graphs, *KDD-2006 Workshop on Link Analysis, 12th ACM SIGKDD International Conference on Knowledge Discovery and Data Mining*.

[3] Asur, S., Ucar, D. & Parthasarathy, S. [2007]. An ensemble framework for clustering protein–protein interaction networks, *Bioinformatics* 23(13): 29–40.
URL: *http://dx.doi.org/10.1093/bioinformatics/btm212*

[4] Asyali, M. H., Colak, D., Demirkaya, O. & Inan, M. S. [2006]. Gene expression profile classification: A review, *Current Bioinformatics* pp. 55–73.
URL: *http://dx.doi.org/10.2174/157489306775330615*

[5] Avogadri, R. & Valentini, G. [2009]. Fuzzy ensemble clustering based on random projections for dna microarray data analysis, *Artificial Intelligence in Medicine* 45(2-3): 173–183. URL: *http://dx.doi.org/10.1016/j.artmed.2008.07.014*

[6] Bandyopadhyay, S., Mukhopadhyay, A. & Maulik, U. [2007]. An improved algorithm for clustering gene expression data, *Bioinformatics* 23(21): 2859–2865.

[7] Bezdek, J. C. [1981]. *Pattern Recognition with Fuzzy Objective Function Algorithms*, Kluwer Academic Publishers, Norwell, MA, USA.

[8] Fisher, R. A. [1936]. The use of multiple measurements in taxonomic problems, *Annals Eugen.* 7: 179–188.

[9] Frank, A. & Asuncion, A. [2010]. UCI machine learning repository.
URL: *http://archive.ics.uci.edu/ml*

[10] Fred, A. L. N. & Jain, A. K. [2005]. Combining multiple clusterings using evidence accumulation, *IEEE Transaction on Pattern Analysis and Machine Intelligence* 27: 835–850.

[11] Galluccio, L., Michel, J.J., O., Comon, P., Hero, A. O. & Kliger, M. [2009]. Combining multiple partitions created with a graph-based construction for data clustering, *Proceedings of IEEE International Workshop on Machine Learning for Signal Processing*, Grenoble, France, pp. –.

[12] Geraci, F., Leoncini, M., Montangero, M., Pellegrini, M. & Renda, M. E. [2009]. K-boost: a scalable algorithm for high-quality clustering of microarray gene expression data, *Journal of Computational Biology* 16(6): 859–873.

[13] Ghazalpour, A., Doss, S., Zhang, B., Wang, S., Plaisier, C., Castellanos, R., Brozell, A., Schadt, E. E., Drake, T. A., Lusis, A. J. & Horvath, S. [2006]. Integrating genetic and network analysis to characterize genes related to mouse weight, *PLoS Genetics* 2(8).
URL: *http://dx.plos.org/10.1371*

[14] Ghouila, A., Yahia, S. B., Malouche, D., Jmel, H., Laouini, D., Guerfali, F. Z. & Abdelhak, S. [2009]. Application of multi-som clustering approach to macrophage gene expression analysis, *Infection, Genetics and Evolution* 9(3): 328–336.

[15] Glover, F. W. & Kochenberger, G. [2006]. New optimization models for data mining, *International Journal of Information Technology and Decision Making* 5(4): 605–609.

[16] Gumus, E., Kursun, O., Sertbas, A. & Ustek, D. [2012]. Application of canonical correlation analysis for identifying viral integration preferences, *Bioinformatics* 28(5): 651–655.

[17] Gungor, Z. & Unler, A. [2008]. K-harmonic means data clustering with tabu-search method, *Applied Mathematical Modelling* 32(6): 1115–1125.

[18] He, Y. & Hui, S. C. [2009]. Exploring ant-based algorithms for gene expression data analysis, *Artificial Intelligence in Medicine* 47(2): 105–119.

[19] Heath, J. W., Fu, M. C. & Jank, W. [2009]. New global optimization algorithms for model-based clustering, *Computational Statistics and Data Analysis* 53(12): 3999–4017.

[20] Hore, P., Hall, L. O. & Goldgof, D. B. [2009]. A scalable framework for cluster ensembles, *Pattern Recognition* 42(5): 676–688.
URL: *http://dx.doi.org/10.1016/j.patcog.2008.09.027*

[21] Hoshida, Y., Brunet, J. P., Tamayo, P., Golub, T. R. & Mesirov, J. P. [2007]. Subclass mapping: Identifying common subtypes in independent disease data sets, *PLoS ONE* 2(11): 1195.
URL: *http://dx.plos.org/10.1371*

[22] Hu, X. & Yoo, I. [2004]. Cluster ensemble and its applications in gene expression analysis, *Proc. 2nd conference on Asia-Pacific bioinformatics (APBC'04)*, Australian Computer Society, Inc., Darlinghurst, Australia, Australia, pp. 297–302.

[23] Hubert, L. & Arabie, P. [1985]. Comparing partitions, *Journal of Classification* 2: 193–218. 10.1007/BF01908075. URL: *http://dx.doi.org/10.1007/BF01908075*

[24] Huttenhower, C., Flamholz, A. I., Landis, J. N., Sahi, S., Myers, C. L., Olszewski, K. L., Hibbs, M. A., Siemers, N. O., Troyanskaya, O. G. & Coller, H. A. [2007]. Nearest neighbor

networks: clustering expression data based on gene neighborhoods, *BMC Bioinformatics* 8(250): 1–13.

[25] Kim, J. & Choi, S. [2006].   Semidefinite spectral clustering, *Pattern Recognition* 39: 2025–2035.

[26] Langfelder, P., Zhang, B. & Horvath, S. [2008].   Defining clusters from a hierarchical cluster tree: the dynamic tree cut package for r, *Bioinformatics Applications Note* 24(5): 719–720.

[27] Mangasarian, O. L. & Wolberg, W. H. [1990]. Cancer diagnosis via linear programming, 23(5): 1–18.

[28] Mitra, S., Das, R., Banka, H. & Mukhopadhyay, S. [2009].   Gene interaction - an evolutionary biclustering approach, *Information Fusion* 10: 242–249.

[29] Newman, M. E. J. & Girvan, M. [2004]. Finding and evaluating community structure in networks, *Physical Review E* 69(026113): 1–15.

[30] Phan, V., George, E. O., Tran, Q. T. & Goodwin, S. [2009]. Analyzing microarray data with transitive directed acyclic graphs, *Journal of Bioinformatics and Computational Biology* 7(1): 135–156.

[31] Rousseeuw, P. [1987]. Silhouettes: A graphical aid to the interpretation and validation of cluster analysis, *Journal of Computational and Applied Mathematics* 20(1): 53–65.
URL: *http://dx.doi.org/10.1016/0377-0427(87)90125-7*

[32] Saha, S. & Bandyopadhyay, S. [2009].   A new point symmetry based fuzzy genetic clustering technique for automatic evolution of clusters, *Information Sciences* 179(19): 3230–3246.

[33] Tseng, G. C. [2007]. Penalized and weighted k-means for clustering with scattered objects and prior information in high-throughput biological data, *Bioinformatics* 23(17): 2247–2255.

[34] Wang, S. & Zhu, J. [2008]. Variable selection for model-based high-dimensional clustering and its application to microarray data, *Biometrics* 64(2): 440–448.

[35] Wang, T. [2009].   Comparing hard and fuzzy c-means for evidence-accumulation clustering, *Proceedings of the 18th international conference on Fuzzy Systems*, FUZZ-IEEE'09, IEEE Press, Piscataway, NJ, USA, pp. 468–473.
URL: *http://dl.acm.org/citation.cfm?id=1717561.1717643*

[36] Watts, D. J. & Strogatz, S. H. [1998].   Collective dynamics of 'small-world' networks, *Nature* 393(6684): 440–442.
URL: *http://dx.doi.org/10.1038/30918*

Permissions

The contributors of this book come from diverse backgrounds, making this book a truly international effort. This book will bring forth new frontiers with its revolutionizing research information and detailed analysis of the nascent developments around the world.

We would like to thank Dr. Horacio Pérez-Sánchez, for lending his expertise to make the book truly unique. He has played a crucial role in the development of this book. Without his invaluable contribution this book wouldn't have been possible. He has made vital efforts to compile up to date information on the varied aspects of this subject to make this book a valuable addition to the collection of many professionals and students.

This book was conceptualized with the vision of imparting up-to-date information and advanced data in this field. To ensure the same, a matchless editorial board was set up. Every individual on the board went through rigorous rounds of assessment to prove their worth. After which they invested a large part of their time researching and compiling the most relevant data for our readers. Conferences and sessions were held from time to time between the editorial board and the contributing authors to present the data in the most comprehensible form. The editorial team has worked tirelessly to provide valuable and valid information to help people across the globe.

Every chapter published in this book has been scrutinized by our experts. Their significance has been extensively debated. The topics covered herein carry significant findings which will fuel the growth of the discipline. They may even be implemented as practical applications or may be referred to as a beginning point for another development. Chapters in this book were first published by InTech; hereby published with permission under the Creative Commons Attribution License or equivalent.

The editorial board has been involved in producing this book since its inception. They have spent rigorous hours researching and exploring the diverse topics which have resulted in the successful publishing of this book. They have passed on their knowledge of decades through this book. To expedite this challenging task, the publisher supported the team at every step. A small team of assistant editors was also appointed to further simplify the editing procedure and attain best results for the readers.

Our editorial team has been hand-picked from every corner of the world. Their multi-ethnicity adds dynamic inputs to the discussions which result in innovative outcomes. These outcomes are then further discussed with the researchers and contributors who give their valuable feedback and opinion regarding the same. The feedback is then collaborated with the researches and they are edited in a comprehensive manner to aid the understanding of the subject.

Apart from the editorial board, the designing team has also invested a significant amount of their time in understanding the subject and creating the most relevant covers. They scrutinized every image to scout for the most suitable representation of the subject and create an appropriate cover for the book.

The publishing team has been involved in this book since its early stages. They were actively engaged in every process, be it collecting the data, connecting with the contributors or procuring relevant information. The team has been an ardent support to the editorial, designing and production team. Their endless efforts to recruit the best for this project, has resulted in the accomplishment of this book. They are a veteran in the field of academics and their pool of knowledge is as vast as their experience in printing. Their expertise and guidance has proved useful at every step. Their uncompromising quality standards have made this book an exceptional effort. Their encouragement from time to time has been an inspiration for everyone.

The publisher and the editorial board hope that this book will prove to be a valuable piece of knowledge for researchers, students, practitioners and scholars across the globe.

List of Contributors

Mohd Fakharul Zaman Raja Yahya and Umi Marshida Abdul Hamid
School of Biology, Faculty of Applied Sciences, MARA University of Technology Shah Alam, Shah Alam Selangor, Malaysia

Shubhalaxmi Kher
Electrical Engineering, Arkansas State University, USA

Jianling Peng
Samuel Roberts Noble Foundation, USA

Eve Syrkin Wurtele
Department of Genetics, Development and Cell Biology, Iowa State University, USA

Julie Dickerson
Electrical and Computer Engineering, Iowa State University, USA

Felipe García-Vallejo
Physiological Sciences Department, Scientific Director of the Laboratory of Molecular Biology and Pathogenesis, School of Basic Sciences, Health Sciences Faculty, Universidad del Valle, Cali, Colombia

Martha Cecilia Domínguez
Laboratory of Molecular Biology and Pathogenesis, School of Basic Sciences, Health Sciences Faculty,
Universidad del Valle, Cali, Colombia

Matthew Ezewudo, Promita Bose, Kajari Mondal, Viren Patel, Dhanya Ramachandran and Michael E. Zwick
Department of Human Genetics, Emory University School of Medicine, Atlanta, GA, 30322, USA

Imre Pechan
Evopro Informatics and Automation Ltd, Budapest, Hungary

Béla Fehér
Department of Measurement and Information Systems, Budapest University of Technology and Economics, Budapest, Hungary

Hugo Saldanha, Edward Ribeiro, Carlos Borges, Aletéia Araújo, Ricardo Gallon, Maristela Holanda and Maria Emília Walter
University of Brasília, Brazil

Roberto Togawa
Embrapa/Genetic Resources and Biotechnology, Brazil

João Carlos Setubal
University of São Paulo, Brazil

María J. R. Yunta
Universidad Complutense, Madrid, Spain

Ly Le
School of Biotechnology, Ho Chi Minh International University, Life Science Laboratory, Institute for Computational Science and Technology at Ho Chi Minh City, Vietnam

León P. Martínez-Castilla and Rogelio Rodríguez-Sotres
Facultad de Química, Universidad Nacional Autónoma de México, México

Scheila de Avila e Silva and Sergio Echeverrigaray
University of Caxias do Sul, Brazil

Yoshiaki Mizuguchi and Eiji Uchida
Nippon Medical School, Department of Surgery for Organ Function and Biological Regulation, Japan

Takuya Mishima and Toshihiro Takizawa
Nippon Medical School, Department of Molecular Anatomy and Medicine, Japan

Suman Ghosal, Shaoli Das and Jayprokas Chakrabarti
Indian Association for the Cultivation of Science, Kolkata, India

Haiping Wang, Taining Xiang and Xuegang Hu
Hefei University of Technology, China

Harun Pirim
King Fahd University of Petroleum and Minerals

Sadi Evren Seker
Istanbul University, Turkey

Printed in the USA
CPSIA information can be obtained
at www.ICGtesting.com
JSHW011504221024
72173JS00005B/1202